AF906155

Accounting for the Public Interest

# Advances in Business Ethics Research

A Journal of Business Ethics Book Series


*Series Editors*

**Deborah C. Poff,** *Brandon University*
**Alex C. Michalos,** *Brandon University*

*Editorial Board*

**Stephen Brammer,** *University of Bath*
**E. Holly Buttner,** *University of North Carolina at Greensboro*
**Nobuyuki Chikudate,** *Asia University*
**Michelle Greenwood,** *Monash University*
**Simon Shun-Man Ho,** *University of Macau*
**Kit-Chun Joanna Lam,** *The University of Hong Kong*
**Thomas Maak,** *ESADE Business School*
**Gedeon J. Rossouw,** *University of Pretoria*
**Scott Vitell,** *University of Mississippi*



For further volumes:
http://www.springer.com/series/8805

Steven Mintz
Editor

# Accounting for the Public Interest

## Perspectives on Accountability, Professionalism and Role in Society

Springer

*Editor*
Steven Mintz
Acounting and Law
California Polytechnic State University
San Luis Obispo, CA, USA

ISBN 978-94-007-7081-2 ISBN 978-94-007-7082-9 (eBook)
DOI 10.1007/978-94-007-7082-9
Springer Dordrecht Heidelberg New York London

Library of Congress Control Number: 2013949241

© Springer Science+Business Media Dordrecht 2014
This work is subject to copyright. All rights are reserved by the Publisher, whether the whole or part of the material is concerned, specifically the rights of translation, reprinting, reuse of illustrations, recitation, broadcasting, reproduction on microfilms or in any other physical way, and transmission or information storage and retrieval, electronic adaptation, computer software, or by similar or dissimilar methodology now known or hereafter developed. Exempted from this legal reservation are brief excerpts in connection with reviews or scholarly analysis or material supplied specifically for the purpose of being entered and executed on a computer system, for exclusive use by the purchaser of the work. Duplication of this publication or parts thereof is permitted only under the provisions of the Copyright Law of the Publisher's location, in its current version, and permission for use must always be obtained from Springer. Permissions for use may be obtained through RightsLink at the Copyright Clearance Center. Violations are liable to prosecution under the respective Copyright Law.
The use of general descriptive names, registered names, trademarks, service marks, etc. in this publication does not imply, even in the absence of a specific statement, that such names are exempt from the relevant protective laws and regulations and therefore free for general use.
While the advice and information in this book are believed to be true and accurate at the date of publication, neither the authors nor the editors nor the publisher can accept any legal responsibility for any errors or omissions that may be made. The publisher makes no warranty, express or implied, with respect to the material contained herein.

Printed on acid-free paper

Springer is part of Springer Science+Business Media (www.springer.com)

# Contents

# Reviewers

| | |
|---|---|
| Mohammad Abdolmohammadi | Bentley University |
| Dennis Bline | Bryant University |
| Leonard J. Brooks | University of Toronto |
| Anthony H. Catanach Jr. | Villanova University |
| Doug Cerf | California Polytechnic State University, San Luis Obispo |
| Charles Cullinan | Bryant University |
| Mary Curtis | University of North Texas |
| Andrew J. Felo | Nova Southeastern University |
| Andy Garcia | Bowling Green State University |
| Amy Hageman | Kansas State University |
| Theresa A. Hammond | San Francisco State University |
| Duane Helleloid | University of North Dakota |
| Karen L. Hooks | Florida Atlantic University |
| Cynthia Jeffrey | Iowa State University |
| Marianne Jennings | Arizona State University |
| Joanne C. Jones | York University |
| Julia Karcher | University of Louisville |
| Cheryl Lehman | Hofstra University |
| Theresa Libby | University of Waterloo |
| Lois S. Mahoney | Eastern Michigan |
| Dawn W. Massey | Fairfield University |
| Janet Mobus | Pacific Lutheran University |
| Mary Ellen Oliverio | Pace University |
| Barbara Porco | Fordham University |
| Robin Radtke | Clemson University |
| Diane H. Roberts | University of San Francisco |
| Deborah Seifert | Illinois State University |
| Brian P. Shapiro | University of St. Thomas (St. Paul) |

| | |
|---|---|
| Michael K. Shaub | Texas A&M University |
| David E. Stout | Youngstown State University |
| Linda Thorne | York University |
| John Thornton | Azusa Pacific University |
| Joan Van Hise | Fairfield University |

# Introduction

Accounting, accountability and ethics are national and global concerns and are framed in the context of the role of professions within society. The chapters in this book explore the role of accounting as a social practice and community of professionals charged with protecting the public interest.

Professional accountants are engaged in internal management decisions, auditing, financial reporting, and tax planning. The authors examine what does it mean to be an accounting professional and what obligations exist as a result of the importance of accounting to society.

Accountants as professionals working in the public arena are explicitly charged to serve the public good. Demand for transparency in corporate reporting is evolving in response to creditor and investor concerns about corporate social and environmental accounting as part of the publicly available corporate report with assurance or attestation by the professional accountant.

Perceptions of whistle-blowing and facilitation payments by corporations are examples of two areas where the public interest is at stake. The Foreign Corrupt Practices Act and Dodd-Frank Financial Reform Act in the US, and bribery laws in the UK and Australia, deal with these issues in the context of professional responsibilities. In addition to financial statement fraud, these practices present challenges to the way in which books and records are kept and whether the internal controls help to expose such practices.

The chapters summarized below are the thoughts of scholars who have devoted a great deal of time to analyzing the role of accounting to society. I am deeply indebted to them for their contribution to this book and furtherance of the dialogue that must continue to evolve as professionalism in accounting meets the challenge of reporting on matters that threaten the public interest.

Reviewers generously gave their time and diligence to critically assess the value of the contributions to this book. Without their efforts it would not have been possible to produce thought-provoking pieces that I hope will stimulate continued discourse on how accounting professionals can better meet their public interest obligation.

Steven Mintz
California Polytechnic State University, San Luis Obispo

# Summary of Contributions

## Professionalism in Accounting: Myth or Reality?

*Call of Duty: A Framework for Auditors' Ethical Decisions* by Michael K. Shaub and Robert L. Braun

Examination of the role of duty and virtue in audit professionalism and ethical decision making within the context of the public interest obligation for truth telling, dissenting and confronting, and independence.

*Professionalizing the Tax Accounting Profession: Fulfilling Public-Interest Reporting Responsibilities* by Martin Stuebs and Brett Wilkinson

Application of the fraud triangle in examining the shift in the tax profession from a public interest ideal to the pursuit of business self-interests as evidenced by marketing and tax shelter practices.

*The Bloom Is Off the Rose: Deprofessionalization in Public Accounting* by Timothy J. Fogarty

Critical analysis of how increased commercialization has affected professionalism in accounting, the community of practice, self-regulation, and the public interest.

## An Ethic of Accountability, Societal Responsibilities, and Accounting for the Public Interest

*Taking Pluralism Seriously Within an Ethic of Accountability* by Jesse Dillard and Judy Brown

Critical analysis of agnostic pluralism as a framework to evaluate accounting systems and accounting for economic assets in a democratic process that recognizes the need for participation of multiple interests.

*Social and Economic Implications of Increasing Income Inequality: Accountability Concerns* by Sue Ravenscroft and Christine A. Denison

Discussion of the responsibilities of the accounting profession to disclose the role corporations play in distributing societal resources and its effects on the public interest.

*Professionalism, the Public Interest, and Social Accounting* by Gordon Boyce

Critical analysis of the contribution that social accounting might make to understand the relationship between accounting and the public interest.

## Defining the Public Interest in Accounting

*Alternative Perspectives on Accounting in the Public Interest* by C. Richard Baker

Exploration of different social science approaches to accounting research and the implications for defining the public interest obligation of accounting professionals.

*The IFAC Framework: International Accounting and the Public Interest* by Paul F. Williams

Critical review of the IFAC framework for regulating the global accounting profession in the context of underlying market and client considerations and the profession's historical function of accountability to society.

## Corporate Social Responsibility and Environmental Reporting

*Developing Corporate Reporting in the Public Interest: The Question of Mandatory CSR Reporting and the Potential for Its Integration with Financial Reporting* by Cynthia Jeffrey and Jon D. Perkins

Discussion of the need for mandatory corporate social reporting, perceived benefits from disclosure, and increased comparability of international financial reports in light of the role of the Global Reporting Initiative (GRI), regulation, and assurance of CSR reporting.

*Environmental Disclosure as Legitimation: Is It in the Public Interest?* by Dennis M. Patten

Exploration of the use of voluntary environmental disclosure as a tool of legitimacy given the public interest dimension of accounting and need for enhanced transparency and accountability in financial reports.

## Virtue and Public Interest Considerations of Bribery and Whistle-Blowing

*Facilitation Payments in International Business Transactions: Law, Accounting, and the Public Interest* by Cindy Davids

Examination of facilitation payments and legal acceptability, governance, compliance, and public interest considerations in the context of ant-bribery guidelines (OECD) and bribery laws in the US (FCPA), UK, and Australia including record-keeping requirements.

*Whistle-Blowing in the Classroom: The Influence of Students' Perceptions of Whistleblowers* by Richard A. Bernardi, Evan S. Goetjen, and Jennifer M. Brax

Empirical study of the perceptions of students on cheating based on the intent to blow the whistle and prior whistle-blowing experience using Falk's model for ethical behavior that relies on virtue ethics to assess the likelihood of blowing the whistle on cheating.

# Contributors

**C. Richard Baker** School of Business, Adelphi University, Garden City, NY, USA

Department of Accounting, Rouen Business School, Rouen, France

**Richard A. Bernardi** Gabelli School of Business, Roger Williams University, Bristol, RI, USA

**Gordon Boyce** Department of Accounting, La Trobe University, Melbourne, Australia

**Robert L. Braun** Department of Accounting and Finance, College of Business, Southeastern Louisiana University, Hammond, LA, USA

**Jennifer M. Brax** Gabelli School of Business, Roger Williams University, Bristol, RI, USA

**Judy Brown** School of Accounting and Commercial Law, Victoria University Wellington, Wellington, New Zealand

**Cindy Davids** School of Law, Deakin University, Melbourne, Australia

**Christine A. Denison** Department of Accounting, Iowa State University, Ames, IA, USA

**Jesse Dillard** School of Management, Queens University Belfast, Belfast, UK

Victoria University Wellington, Wellington, New Zealand

**Timothy J. Fogarty** Department of Accounting, Weatherhead School of Management, Case Western Reserve University, Cleveland, OH, USA

**Evan S. Goetjen** Gabelli School of Business, Roger Williams University, Bristol, RI, USA

**Cynthia Jeffrey** Department of Accounting, Iowa State University, Ames, IA, USA

**Dennis M. Patten** Department of Accounting, Illinois State University, Normal, IL, USA

**Jon D. Perkins** Department of Accounting, Iowa State University, Ames, IA, USA

**Sue Ravenscroft** Department of Accounting, Iowa State University, Ames, IA, USA

**Michael K. Shaub** Department of Accounting, Mays Business School, Texas A&M University, College Station, TX, USA

**Martin Stuebs** Hankamer School of Business, Baylor University, Waco, TX, USA

**Brett Wilkinson** Hankamer School of Business, Baylor University, Waco, TX, USA

**Paul F. Williams** People College of Management, North Carolina State University, Raleigh, NC, USA

# Part I
# Professionalism in Accounting: Myth or Reality?

# Chapter 1
# Call of Duty: A Framework for Auditors' Ethical Decisions

**Michael K. Shaub and Robert L. Braun**

## 1.1 Introduction

Although over a decade has passed since Enron, WorldCom, and the Sarbanes-Oxley Act thrust auditing into the spotlight and forced the accounting profession to re-examine its responsibilities, it is still unclear how the profession's views of its obligations have changed. The establishment of the Public Company Accounting Oversight Board (PCAOB) to regulate the U.S. auditing profession resulted, at least in part, from a perception that auditors were largely pursuing self-interest rather than fulfilling their professional responsibilities in the public interest. But while the establishment of the PCAOB meant the end of self-regulation, there is little evidence that the auditing profession has made any structural adjustments to reinforce professionalism.

What exactly does it mean to be a professional? What is the auditor required to do in order to fulfill the responsibilities of a professional? We believe the answers lie within the concept of duty. The purpose of this chapter is to build a proactive case for the auditing profession to assume its responsibility—its duty—to serve the public interest. In doing so, we will contrast a duty-focused approach to the current emphasis on consequentialist calculation reinforced in codes of conduct and authoritative standards. Subsequent sections explore duty's central role in defining professions and discuss how shifting toward the duty perspective is crucial for the auditor to fulfill the obligations of the profession. The chapter concludes with recommendations for the profession.

---

M.K. Shaub (✉)
Department of Accounting, Mays Business School,
Texas A&M University, College Station, TX 77843, USA
e-mail: mshaub@mays.tamu.edu

R.L. Braun
Department of Accounting and Finance, College of Business,
Southeastern Louisiana University, Hammond, LA 70402, USA
e-mail: bbraun@selu.edu

S. Mintz (ed.), *Accounting for the Public Interest: Perspectives on Accountability, Professionalism and Role in Society*, Advances in Business Ethics Research 4,
DOI 10.1007/978-94-007-7082-9_1, © Springer Science+Business Media Dordrecht 2014

## 1.2 Characteristics of a Profession

Accountants have long regarded themselves as professionals, and virtually every code of conduct governing associations of accountants presumes that they are. Although no universally accepted standard exists establishing the essential qualities of professions, three characteristics are salient throughout the literature, beginning with Carr-Saunders and Wilson's (1933) pioneering work. These attributes are (1) development of intellectual skill or knowledge, (2) adherence to shared values reflected in a code of conduct, and (3) responsibility to serve in the public interest.[1]

These attributes are common to other professions. For example, the American Medical Association (2011) Code of Medical Ethics includes principles to, among other things:

1. "…continue to study, apply, and advance scientific knowledge [and] maintain a commitment to medical education … ."
2. View the principles as "… standards of conduct which define the essentials of honorable behavior for the physician… ."
3. "… be honest in all professional interactions… .", and
4. "… recognize a responsibility to participate in activities contributing to the improvement of the community and the betterment of public health."

Likewise, the American Bar Association (2011) Model Rules of Professional Conduct require that attorneys be competent and "cultivate knowledge of the law beyond its use for clients… ." In addition, "[t]he profession has a responsibility to assure that its regulations are conceived in the public interest and not in furtherance of parochial or self-interested concerns of the bar."

Of the three attributes, the duty to serve in the public interest seems to pose the greatest controversy and challenge. The idea that skills are important is not controversial. Indeed, even the simplest definition of the term professional as, "one who is engaged in an activity as a main paid occupation" suggests a level of skill and proficiency that is worthy of compensation. But, if the discussion began and ended with skill, athletes would be professionals of the highest order—an assertion that flies in the face of our understanding of professionalism.

Most would agree that the notion of professionalism extends beyond skill to include values. Generally, accountancy has been willing to be subject to a code of conduct that reflects its values. For example, the Anderson Committee (AICPA 1986) that produced the AICPA's restructured Code of Professional Conduct in 1988 argued for a principles-based code centered on fundamental values (Shaub 1988). While the Code retains rules that are minimum standards that must be met and interpretations and rulings to explain the application of the rules, it is driven by principles that are aspirational. As such, it represents an attempt to embody the collective conscience

[1] Elsewhere in this volume, Fogarty (2014) provides a complementary analysis of attributes of a profession. The five attributes employed in his chapter correlate highly with the items presented here.

of the profession in recognition of its moral dimension (Frankel 1989). We cede discussion of the extent to which auditors embody the intellectual skill and shared values to Fogarty's (2014) contribution to this monograph (i.e., his discussion of specialized knowledge and community of practice) choosing, instead, to focus on public interest and autonomy.

The public interest attribute presents the greatest challenge to the profession. The assertion of a duty to serve in the public interest is not controversial, per se. The International Federation of Accountants' Code of Ethics for Professional Accountants (IFAC 2010, 100.01) asserts that, "A distinguishing mark of the accountancy profession is its acceptance of the responsibility to act in the public interest." The Code of Professional Conduct of the American Institute of Certified Public Accountants (AICPA) contains similar language and also states its public interest principle as follows, "Members should accept the obligation to act in a way that will serve the public interest, honor the public trust, and demonstrate commitment to professionalism." (AICPA 2012a, ET 53) Indeed, it is arguable that auditing is unique among professions in that the public is the primary beneficiary of the work of the auditor, not necessarily the contracting client. That is, while the public interest outcome is a product of the doctor/patient or lawyer/client relationship, the public interest outcome is the very reason that the audit is required. Does the profession fully embrace its duty to serve the public? Or, is the profession too willing to "moralize without examining its morals" as Terrell and Wildman (1992, 403) observed regarding the legal profession?

While the accounting profession has stated its commitment to the principle of putting the public interest first, ethics rules that shield client information as confidential and that allow the provision of adjunct services to audit clients undermine this claim. In addition, individuals outside the profession have argued that auditor independence is impossible (Bazerman et al. 1997) or that government employees could more faithfully execute audits in the public interest (Westra 1986). These concerns invite consideration of a fourth attribute commonly associated with professions—autonomy.

Autonomy, in the sense that the community grants power to train, license, and regulate to the profession itself, is commonly included in the analysis of professions (Greenwood 1957). We do not include it with skill, values, and duty to the public interest, however, because it is contingent upon, rather than equal to, the others. The erosion of autonomy in the accounting profession post-Sarbanes-Oxley emphasizes this point—especially with regard to the public interest characteristic. The decision to rescind a portion of the auditing profession's autonomy did not result from the view that auditors lack specialized knowledge. In fact, the complexity of the manipulative devices used by Enron and others enhanced public appreciation of the need for significant audit skills. Nor did the provisions focus on reexamination of the values of the profession, though the extent to which auditors embraced those values was questioned. Regulations to limit autonomy resulted from the perception that auditors were not placing public interest at the forefront of their professional responsibilities, "their inability to respond effectively to market expectations" in the words of IFAC (2003, 10). In order to prevent further erosion of autonomy, auditors need to renew their commitment to serve the public interest. Auditors can answer the "call of duty" by enhancing their understanding of the concept of duty and implementing the concept in decision-making.

## 1.3 Balancing Ethical Decision-Making

The skill, values, and duty referred to earlier as being the standards for a professional provide a framework for balanced ethical decision-making. Balance is implicit in IFAC guidance in which fundamental principles linked to duty and virtue are identified (IFAC 2010, 100.04), and used in a process whereby "…a professional accountant should determine the appropriate course of action that is consistent with the fundamental principles identified. A professional accountant should also weigh the consequences of each possible course of action." (IFAC 2010, 100.17) While consequences are to be considered, the guidance is clear that they are not to be the first or only considerations.

Balanced ethical decisions require not only the technical skill to know what to do, but the moral courage to do it. This involves identifying duties and consequences related to an ethical decision (Hunt and Vitell 1986, 1993, 2006) and acting in a virtuous manner. Rest's four-component model identifies four processes involved in producing a moral act (1979, 1983, 1984, 1985, 1986, 1994; Bebeau and Thoma 1999; Rest et al. 1999; Bebeau 2002) The four processes are (1) sensing that the situation involves the well-being of others,[2] (2) reasoning as to what ought to be done,[3] (3) deciding to take a moral action (as opposed to a self-interested action),[4] and (4) acting in a manner consistent with moral conviction.[5] The model emphasizes the importance of feed-back and feed-forward loops among the four processes in which failure in any one of the processes can result in moral failure (Dellaportas et al. 2011).

Duties, virtue, and consequence evaluation are three perspectives from which moral agents approach the execution of the four processes. Figure 1.1 demonstrates how each of the three perspectives might be invoked in the four-component process.

---

[2] Without sensitivity as to the role of duty in a decision context and an understanding of how to incorporate duty into reasoning processes, the auditor cannot reach an appropriate ethical judgment.

[3] Auditors are made intellectually aware of their duty as professionals to protect the public interest through accounting education and professional socialization (Frankel 1989).

[4] According to Thorne (1998, 298), "… *moral virtue* is the positive attribute of character which describes an individual's direct concern for the interests of others despite personal risks (Pincoffs 1986), and *ethical motivation* describes an individual's willingness to place the interests of others ahead of his or her own (Rest 1994)." This is the stage at which the auditor assumes the moral duty to protect the public interest.

[5] Aristotle (1925, 1103a–1103b) recognizes the importance of ethical behavior in building virtue: "we become just by doing just acts, temperate by doing temperate acts, brave by doing brave acts." The virtuous person fulfills duties by acting.

In order to act morally, I need to engage in four different processes, at some level. First, I need to sense that an issue has a moral component. If I were unable to sense the moral component, my decision might not be immoral, but the process would be amoral. Second, I need to apply a reasoning process that takes morality into account. Third, I need to make a moral choice that places values and principles ahead of self-interest. Finally, I need to have the courage to act in accordance with the moral decision. The table below relates those four components of moral action to the major classifications of ethical perspectives. The ethical perspectives are discussed more fully thereafter.

| Process | Duty | Virtue | Consequentialism |
|---|---|---|---|
| **Sensing**—This is how I identify the dilemma and frame the issue. | I identify dilemmas in which my roles are in conflict. I view the ethical choice in terms of the responsibilities that I have to the stakeholders. | I identify dilemmas in which my values are in conflict. I view the ethical choice in terms of the kind of person that I want to be and what my choice says about who I am. | I identify dilemmas based on the conflict between desired and potential outcomes. I view the ethical choice in terms of the outcomes that I might produce. |
| **Reasoning**—This is how I engage ethical judgment. These are the factors I consider. | In making ethical judgments, my focus is on the responsibilities that I have (and everyone has) going into the situation and what duties I have within the situation. My focus is on my duties rather than my inclinations. | I consider my own character traits and motivations within the situation and the motivations of others in making ethical judgments. I consider the purpose (or reason for being) of the item under consideration. I attempt to discern the essential nature of my role. | My focus is on the future. What will happen as a result of each of the alternatives? Which alternative produces the most good (or least bad)? I try to quantify all of the consequences associated with each alternative in making ethical judgments. |
| **Deciding**—This is how I arrive at my ethical intention. This is the decision rule that I use. | My ethical intention is to act according to a law that I give myself as a rational human being. My choice should be universalizable. I should wish that everyone would make the same choice. I should treat people as a worthy end rather than a means to an end. Principle: The best decision is the one that uses a process that respects the basic rights of the individuals involved. | My ethical intention is to choose the action that reflects the most honorable virtues and that is consistent with the essential purpose of the items involved. Principle: The best decision is the one that is consistent with important virtues. | My ethical intention is to choose the alternative that produces the greatest good. Principle: The best decision is the one that produces consequences that are best for...<br>• Society (utilitarian).<br>• Me (egoism). |
| **Acting**—This is what I hope to achieve through my ethical behavior. | My behavior is right based upon the rational process by which anyone would objectively determine it to be right, not necessarily based upon the outcome. It is consistent with my responsibilities in any situation. | My behavior should contribute to the development of my character and make the world a "better" place. | My behavior should produce the most good. |

**Fig. 1.1** Producing a moral action—a framework

The figure illustrates the fundamental differences in the perspectives. A consequentialist perspective focuses on the outcomes while a duty perspective focuses on the rational processes that can be universally applied. According to the duty perspective, morality stems from autonomous choice that can be applied categorically rather than hypothetically based upon outcome. The virtue perspective is contrasted to the others through its inward focus, examining the extent to which alternatives are consistent with the character and values of the decision maker. Although an individual tends to adopt a particular perspective that influences his or her approach, viewing moral issues from other perspectives could lead to more balanced moral behavior. This may be especially important for auditors who tend to default to consequentialist perspectives. Balancing decision-making by considering duty and virtue can help the auditor to meet public interest obligations. The International Education Standards Board of the IFAC (2003) emphasizes this point by including education related to consequences, virtue, and duties. While consequence-based utilitarian theories dominate business school education (Shaub and Fisher 2008), the principles of the profession are oriented toward duty and virtue. Figure 1.1 provides the opportunity to engage each of the major perspectives throughout the process of producing moral action.

Duties may arise from a number of sources: responsibilities to the company or to shareholders, professional codes of conduct (AICPA, IFAC, IMA, IIA, etc.), family responsibilities, and personal and moral convictions. One of the explicit duties of the professional is to make the public interest primary, consistent with the IFAC definition of the profession above. "The coverage of values and attitudes in education programs for professional accountants should lead to a commitment to … the public interest and sensitivity to social responsibilities." (IFAC 2004) This public interest focus is identical in the exposure draft revising this international education standard (IFAC 2011) and is also one of the six principles driving the AICPA Code of Professional Conduct (AICPA 2012a).

Even people who generally ignore duties consider consequences at some level when making ethical decisions. Some people consider only consequences to themselves, qualifying as psychological egoists; or, if they consider that approach the only ethical behavior, they are ethical egoists (Rachels 1986). Many people consider the consequences to others as well, following decision processes that resemble utilitarianism[6] in their efforts to maximize the excess of good over bad consequences for all. But it is very difficult for people to be objective in these calculations, as they tend to overweigh the importance of costs and benefits to themselves or to causes or organizations that especially matter to them.

The call for balanced ethical decision-making holds that it is not enough for auditors to do a complex calculation of consequences, even one that is utilitarian and does not favor the benefits or costs of one person over another (Freeman 1984). In fact, the ICAEW (2008, 13) indicates that "[t]he role of audit is not to assess and balance different stakeholder expectations and determine that they have been met …" Auditors must seriously consider the duties that may restrain behaviors that would maximize personal benefit, or even total benefit to all. The primary reason that this is true is that the job assigned to the auditor by society is not to maximize benefits, but to minimize harm (Shaub 1996; Fogarty 2014). As a result, the auditor must be involved in behaviors that might otherwise be avoided, notably suspicious or skeptical behaviors, that Deutsch (1962) defines as behaviors to prevent harm.

Thus, the assertion of balanced ethical decision-making is that there may be times when auditors should engage in behaviors that do not maximize beneficial consequences, and that maximizing beneficial consequences does not relieve auditors of their duties. One reason for the moral hazard of ignoring duties is that duties

[6] Utilitarianism is a form of consequentialism. Utilitarianism is the dominant theory in classical economics.

are more effective than consequences at restraining unethical behavior. Only when there is no overriding duty would consequences become relevant.

In addition to duty, virtue—as described in Fig. 1.1—serves an important role in balanced ethical decision-making. MacIntyre (1984) indicates that virtues reflect the ideals of a community. Sommers (1993) argues that exposure to Aristotle's arguments for the importance of the virtues is effective in undermining a simple default to relativism, to believing that what is morally right depends on the person. In a world without reference to virtues, values can simply be another word for preferences.

Auditors' virtue is particularly important in the situations of uncertainty that lead to auditor-client disagreements (Mintz 1995; Jones et al. 2003). Libby and Thorne (2007) develop a measure of auditors' virtue consistent with MacIntyre's (1984) idea that the virtues should reflect the auditing community's ideals. Their chartered accountants' top five ranked non-instrumental (character) virtues are integrity, truthfulness, independence, objectivity, and dependability. The top five ranked instrumental (action) virtues are diligence, alertness, carefulness, resourcefulness, and being consultative. The commitment to virtuous behavior potentially energizes auditors' willingness to assume their duties.

While consequentialist calculation dominates the accountant's technical training, duty and virtue are the basis for the principles of the profession. Principles are the ideals toward which accountants are called to strive. The language of duty and virtue dominate the expression of principles in the AICPA's Code of Professional Conduct. Duty-based calls to observe responsibilities, obligations, and public interest appear throughout the principles, as do virtue-based calls to integrity, objectivity, and independence. These calls are not conditional upon the consequences that might result in the circumstances.

Auditors should always be cautious about the net benefits of making decisions that may look morally questionable later, especially when there is no obvious virtue involved in the decision. Even if there is no moral duty that is evident, people will focus on the CPA's calculations later as evidence of moral bankruptcy. The KPMG tax shelter case detailed by Stuebs and Wilkinson (2014) in this monograph and Arthur Andersen's shredding of Enron documents provide stunning examples.

Court decisions in the Enron and KPMG tax shelter cases sent a message that jurors see harm prevention as an accountant's duty.[7] In both cases, the accountants apparently believed that the chosen alternative would maximize benefit to the client and firm. In both cases harm prevention to those outside of the circle of influence over the decision was apparently disregarded. Jurors are more likely to punish behavior that violates norms, even if it does not explicitly violate rules or standards, unless extra steps are taken to prevent harm (Prentice and Koehler 2003; Kadous and Mercer 2011). Clearly, the accountants involved with Enron and those aggressively marketing tax shelters did not take these extra steps to prevent harm. Nor did they balance egoistic consequence-based reasoning with consideration of duties and virtues.

[7] Although this chapter focuses on auditors rather than tax accountants, the close professional association between the two groups makes it relevant. For a more detained discussion of professionalism in tax accounting, see Stuebs and Wilkinson's (2014) chapter in this monograph.

The KPMG partner's cold calculation that the benefits of client revenue would exceed the cost of fines and penalties, if detected (Bryan-Low 2003), served not only as proof of ethical failure but also as the basis for moral outrage. It was not the fact that the calculation was executed in such a woefully inept manner; it was the fact that a calculation contemplating an illegal act was made in the first place that motivated the $456 million settlement with the Securities and Exchange Commission (SEC) (Stuebs 2010).

Similarly, Arthur Andersen's decision to shred documents ahead of an expected Department of Justice investigation of their involvement with Enron is an example of a decision dominated by calculation rather than virtue. Although not presented as an explicit calculation, it was the image of auditors stuffing the shredders that sealed the firm's fate. The massive shredding operation began three days after an Andersen conference call in which high-level executives discussed the SEC's investigation of Enron (Department of Justice 2002). The idea that the auditors must have calculated that the evidence in the documents would be more costly than the penalties for destroying those documents could have motivated the indictment. In both the tax shelter and Enron cases, the accountant had an overriding duty to the public interest that made consequentialist calculation irrelevant and inappropriate. In both cases, the absence of virtues that the public expects of auditors fueled outrage.

Ironically, auditors unconvinced by an argument for virtue might be persuaded by the dire consequences associated with the absence of virtue. It was the calculating nature of the partners at KPMG—the complete absence of virtue—that served as the basis for the large penalties. Similarly, it was the perception of the act of shredding documents as a cowardly effort to avoid responsibility that left an indelible stain on Arthur Andersen. While a consequentialist argument for virtue or duty is antithetical to the tenets of Nichomachean ethics and the duty perspective, it may be what it takes to convince auditors inclined toward calculation of the merit of a more balanced approach to ethical decision-making.

Shifting toward a more balanced approach in which duty to serve the public interest informs decision-making as described in Fig. 1.1 would require heightened awareness of three obligations that are inherent to the audit profession and then framing decisions, making decisions, and acting in a manner consistent with these obligations. We propose that three fundamental obligations of the auditor are:

1. Truth-telling
2. Dissenting and confronting
3. Honestly self-assessing independence and professionalism

Though a case can be made that auditors have other important obligations, these three important duties that are linked to the definition of auditing[8] help reinforce auditing's role as a profession. We assert that a tendency toward consequentialist

[8] Auditing is a systematic process of objectively obtaining and evaluating evidence regarding assertions about economic actions and events to ascertain the degree of correspondence between those assertions and established criteria and communicating the results to interested users (American Accounting Association 1973, 2).

calculation has contributed to laxity in fulfilling these obligations. A more balanced approach in which duty and virtue play more significant roles would help auditors re-orient themselves toward the public interest. The discussion that follows expands the case for each of the obligations identified above through analysis of professional standards and extant research.

### *1.3.1 Truth-Telling*

The first obligation of the audit professional is the duty to tell the truth (Libby and Thorne 2007). Though this would seem to be an obvious and simple obligation, institutional and economic forces are often aligned against the kind of transparency and full disclosure that this duty and virtue would require. That is, while aspirational principles of the Code of Professional Conduct call for truth-telling, the complexity of the environment in which auditors operate and the rules that govern how they are to operate in this complex environment suggest that optimizing or even satisficing behavior could be the norm. Integrity, objectivity, and transparency could be the casualties of this satisficing behavior (Shaub and Fisher 2008).

Integrity, a word deriving from the Latin root *integer* meaning intact or whole, can be applied to buildings of sound construction, data that is uncorrupted, territory that is undivided, and honor that is intact. Integrity implies reliability, that something is consistent with what it purports to be. And, according to the AICPA Code of Professional Conduct:

> Integrity requires a member to be, among other things, ***honest and candid*** within the constraints of client confidentiality. Service and the public trust should not be subordinated to personal gain and advantage. Integrity can accommodate the inadvertent error and the ***honest*** difference of opinion; it cannot accommodate ***deceit*** or subordination of principle. (AICPA 2012a, ET 54.02, emphasis added)

Though this duty is required of all CPAs, it is especially important for the auditor in order to protect the public. As is clear from rule 301 of the AICPA Code of Professional Conduct, client confidentiality does not restrain an auditor from revealing violations of accounting principles or auditing standards—first to the client and then to those relying on the misstatements through appropriate disclosures, including regulators.

According to the AICPA Code, "The principle of objectivity imposes the obligation to be impartial, ***intellectually honest***, and free of conflicts of interest (AICPA 2012a, ET 55.01, emphasis added)." And the AICPA Code establishes a duty of transparency (Shaub and Fisher 2008) on all CPAs in stating:

> Members employed by others to prepare financial statements or to perform auditing, tax, or consulting services are charged with the same responsibility for objectivity as members in public practice and must be ***scrupulous in their application of generally accepted accounting principles and candid in all their dealings with members in public practice***. (AICPA 2012a, ET 55.04, emphasis added)

The terms honest, candid, and intellectually honest appear in the Principles section of the AICPA's Code of Professional Conduct and are aspirational. For auditors who believe that duty extends only to rule observance, the duty to tell the truth may be obscured by rules emphasizing confidentiality (i.e., AICPA Code of Conduct Rule 301) and materiality. The duties that undergird a profession go beyond simple compliance with legal rules, and they often involve acting consistently with principles of behavior by possessing certain virtues, such as truthfulness (Libby and Thorne 2007). A simple default to rules ignores the inherent duty to maximize full disclosure and focuses on materiality.

#### 1.3.1.1 Is "Not Materially Misstating" the Same as Truth-Telling?

An amount or disclosure is material if it would make a difference to a reasonably informed user of financial statements. The focus on the user of the financial statements should orient auditors toward a public interest perspective in its application. Ironically, the opposite appears to be true. Focusing instead on a calculation of what would be misleading, auditors reorient the focus of materiality toward consequentialism (Shaub 2005).

Most auditors would agree that materiality is a fundamental concept in audit planning. In fact, U.S. auditing standards have generally held that audit planning is fundamentally based on the auditor's evaluation of audit risk and materiality. Both auditing and accounting standards in the U.S. have incorporated materiality. The audit opinion uses "material" in both the scope and the opinion paragraphs, and each new U.S. accounting standard issued by the Financial Accounting Standards Board contains the following proviso: "The provisions of this statement need not be applied to *immaterial* items."

Rather than being morally governed by a duty to search for truth, auditors are guided by a consequentialist calculation. For instance, Houghton and Fogarty (1991) found in one study that auditors waived 75 % of all detected errors. The practical implication of a reliance on materiality alone is the tendency to think that there is no "truth." Financial statements contain numerous estimates, leading to serial materiality issues. And the more complex the company is, the greater the number of estimates that are necessary to produce the financial statements. This habit of imprecision creates the tendency for clients to believe that the amount of an audit adjustment, and even the audit adjustment itself, is negotiable. Gibbins et al. (2001) report that the practice of partners negotiating with clients regarding audit differences is more the rule than the exception. Hatfield et al. (2010) find that the magnitude of the difference and feelings of reciprocity based on prior negotiations influence proposed auditor adjustments in negotiations. Is it possible that along with audit adjustments, there is a perception that duty and public interest are negotiable?

The Giant Stores and Enron cases are two examples where public interest arguably did not even make it to the negotiating table. In the famous fraud at Giant Stores, management stopped arguing over the auditor's proposed adjustments once the earnings number reached their target (Knapp 2004). And Andersen passed on a

1997 adjustment that represented 48 % of Enron's earnings; according to the majority of quantitative materiality guidelines in the professional literature, this amount really was quantitatively "immaterial" (Brody et al. 2003), revealing a vulnerability to abuse in the U.S. auditing standards.

Even some quantitatively immaterial amounts may be qualitatively material. They are important not so much for their amount as for their nature. In Staff Accounting Bulletin No. 99, The SEC identifies a number of examples of potential adjustments that fit this description (SEC 1999). These and other examples have been incorporated into the U.S. auditing standards in AU 312.60 (AICPA 2012b) in response to the SEC's concern that auditors were allowing their clients too much freedom in determining what was material. Nelson et al. (2005) recommended that standard setters should mandate adjustment if a misstatement is material either in a single period or cumulatively—guidance that the SEC adopted in SAB No. 108. Previously, many firms allowed their clients to treat items as immaterial if they were considered immaterial on either a single period or a cumulative basis.

Auditors have rationalized fraudulent financial reporting on the basis of cumulative immateriality in audits of Sunbeam, Waste Management, Enron, Xerox, and others. Although the soundness of the assumptions invoked in those arguments is highly questionable, we assert that the tendency to invoke the materiality argument at all on detected misstatements is at odds with the auditor's duty to tell the truth. Consistent with this view, Hall (1988) calls materiality.

> . . . an understanding of what is important … . An auditor's sense of materiality lies at the heart of his professional judgment. … A well-developed concept of materiality is particularly important because the concept is subject to abuse. Many acts have been justified, many sins excused, on the basis of their alleged immateriality. (Hall 1988, 78–79)

Materiality is a construct that is invoked to relieve auditors of the need to audit the financial statements down to the penny. It is not intended to relieve auditors of the duty to hold clients accountable to the truth.

#### 1.3.1.2 Consequentialism in Professional Standards—Effects on Truth-Telling

Although fundamental duties lie at the heart of the auditing profession, institutional and regulatory forces seem to orient practitioners toward consequentialism. Emphasis on enforceable rules of conduct such as materiality rather than unenforceable principles might suggest to auditors that it is appropriate to locate moral worth in consequential calculations rather than fundamental duties. Rather than relying on the accounting profession's historic commitment to a series of professional duties, the profession has adopted a consequentialist approach to many ethical issues. Consequentialist calculations make sense in evaluating audit risk or in determining whether an indirect investment impairs an auditor's independence. Accounting for contingencies is also consequentialist; for example, evaluations such as "probable" and "reasonably estimable" are required to record a loss contingency and also to evaluate material weaknesses in internal control (AICPA 2012b, AU 325.06).

These approaches are perfectly sensible and provide a reasonable approach to managing audit risk. As such, we are not calling for a review of this guidance. Our point is that the orientation toward consequentialist calculation coupled with the dominance of utilitarianism in economic theory as taught in business schools (Shaub and Fisher 2008; Kidwell et al. 2012) trains the auditor to think in these terms, perhaps to the exclusion of duty or virtue. Pure reliance on calculations can lead auditors to rely on rules that may, in retrospect, make no sense. For example, the ability to avoid consolidating certain off-balance-sheet financing entities if there was as little as three percent outside ownership was certainly a contributing factor in Enron's ability to mask its deteriorating financial condition from the market and, perhaps, from Arthur Andersen (Feng et al. 2009). In fact, the initial uproar was because Enron had funded part of that three percent for some of its entities, not that the rule itself short-circuited fair presentation.

#### 1.3.1.3 Why Consequentialism Is Problematic for Truth-Telling in the Profession

So, why is an emphasis on consequentialist calculations problematic for the auditing profession? Accurate consequentialist calculations are intended to maximize benefit, but the auditor's duty is to minimize harm (Shaub 1996). Minimizing harm to financial statement users by providing an audit opinion is the primary reason auditors have a license. Yet auditors in the United States have found over the last several decades that the surest route to increased profitability was to maximize benefits for their clients and, to the extent that their goals are integrally tied to their clients' goals (Shaub 2004), maximize benefits for themselves. This is not a utilitarian calculation of "the greatest good for the greatest number," but something that more nearly approaches ethical egoism. Thus, without the explicit acceptance of a duty to the public interest or the constraint of virtuous behavior, the auditor is focused on self-interest and its related calculations.

This will reflect itself disproportionately in failures in areas of the audit that require extensive judgment, such as accounting estimates. The public portions of PCAOB inspection reports show that audits of accounting estimates are widely problematic, reflecting insufficient professional skepticism about management's representations based on materiality judgments by the auditor. In its *2012 Transparency Report*, Deloitte lists estimates of long-lived and intangible assets, loan losses, liabilities, and investments among the problem areas identified by inspections (Deloitte 2012, 24). These types of estimates affect a variety of firms across many industries and any movement toward international accounting and auditing standards would only heighten concern about the adequacy of professional skepticism in these areas.

Another reason that relying on consequentialist calculations is problematic is that there is significant evidence that accountants are poor consequence calculators, particularly long-term consequence calculators. This may be the result of overconfidence, a trait that research shows is common in the general population

(Fischhoff et al. 1977) and in auditors. For auditors, this overconfidence extends to evaluations of subordinates, and it is greater the more sophisticated the subordinate (Kennedy and Peecher 1997) and the more complex the task (Han et al. 2007). Many materiality decisions, particularly those that could lead to litigation, and virtually all negotiations with the client would be considered complex tasks.

The price to the profession of overreliance on consequentialist calculations and poor execution of those calculations came in the form of outside regulation by the PCAOB. Arthur Andersen partners in Houston and Chicago made bad calculations that, in effect, brought the firm's practice to an end. CPAs involved in scandals at ESM Government Securities, which temporarily shut down all the state banks in Ohio, and KPMG's tax shelter controversy, mentioned earlier, represent only two of many anecdotal examples of CPAs as bad consequence calculators.

So while materiality may continue to be important to the allocation of audit effort, the focus it puts on consequentialist calculations can potentially undermine auditors' commitment to truth-telling. Materiality assessments warrant close evaluation by those responsible for assuring that audits meet accounting firm quality standards. Relying on potentially self-interested calculations rather than a commitment to truth-telling to make ethical decisions undermines auditors' claim to being a profession acting in the public interest.

In the language of the framework presented in Fig. 1.1, auditors framing the truth-telling dilemma within a consequentialist context would focus on outcomes and calculations rather than responsibilities and virtues. Decision-making would focus on financial statement users as parts of a wealth maximizing problem rather than respecting them as ends in and of themselves. Truth-telling becomes an option associated with an expected value rather than a responsibility that is essential to the purpose of auditing. Although professional guidance, the audit context, and human nature provide training and incentives to default to consequentialist approaches to truth-telling, the framework offers guidance to overcome the resulting tendencies.

### *1.3.2 Dissent and Confrontation*

The second obligation of an audit professional is to do what Sonnenfeld (2002, 111) sees as critical to the role of corporate directors—to see "dissent as an obligation." The auditor's duty is not just to detect material misstatement, but to be part of the process that helps prevent it by ensuring that audit clients have adequate internal controls and by reporting significant deficiencies to the company's board. For public companies the auditor must also identify and report on material internal control weaknesses to the public. And if it is directors' responsibility to dissent as overseers who have a common mission with management, it is even more the responsibility of the external auditor, as an outside monitor, to provide this check to management's potentially self-interested motivations. In fact, the two should work together in this process.

> Audit firms and audit partners should not fear removal from their role if they challenge management strongly. Management and Audit Committees also have a responsibility for ensuring that the corporate culture and environment is one which encourages open dialogue with their auditors at all levels. (Auditing Practices Board 2010, 3)

Mautz and Sharaf (1961, 14) liken the auditor's role to that of an editor: to criticize, examine, and judge management's assertions. The PCAOB's (2012, 2) recent guidance on skepticism further emphasizes the point, "The engagement partner is responsible for, among other things, setting an appropriate tone that emphasizes the need to maintain a questioning mind throughout the audit and to exercise professional skepticism in gathering and evaluating evidence, so that, for example, engagement team members have the confidence to challenge management representations."

One of an auditor's most challenging duties in ensuring the accuracy of financial statements is client confrontation. But, auditors who see themselves as "trusted business advisors" may be less likely to assume this role, instead focusing on maximizing the client management's return. Arthur Andersen actually used this as a catch phrase within the firm, and went so far as to trademark the phrase in 1990 (trademarkia.com 2012). The AICPA's Vision 2025 Report indicates that this view of client service is not only accepted within the profession, but seen as a strategic initiative: "CPAs must continue to evolve as strategic partners of clients, business and employers, applying multidisciplinary and integrated problem solving to expand traditional services and enhance nontraditional offerings and the perception of trusted advisor (AICPA 2012c)." The problem with this is that society has not assigned auditors this role, and that the Sarbanes-Oxley Act imposed specific provisions to minimize the profession's expansion of this role because of its threat to auditors' independence.

Carey and Doherty (1966), in their classic treatise on ethics in the accounting profession, describe independence this way:

> A CPA should be independent in the sense that he should not be dominated by his client. He should not accept uncritically the client's own statements of his financial affairs. He should give candid advice, even though it may be unpalatable. At the risk of losing the engagement, the CPA should insist on a course of action which he thinks is right, though the intensity of his insistence may vary with the importance of the matter under consideration. (1966, 130–131)

The Public Oversight Board's Panel on Audit Effectiveness (2000, xiv) addressed the issue of dissent and confrontation directly by invoking virtues that are essential for auditors:

> ...auditors must possess the discipline, fortitude and ability to stand up to management or to an audit committee or board of directors. They need to be able to say, "No, that's not right!"

While the consequences of standing up to management or the board may be negative with respect to the auditor's self-interest, failing to do so is at odds with the virtues of the profession and its duty to the public interest.

It is difficult to determine the extent to which auditors provide candid, unpalatable advice to their clients. It is difficult to measure auditors' discipline, fortitude and ability to stand up to management. However, the advent of PCAOB reports in the past decade has provided initial evidence that exercising professional skepticism continues to be a challenge for auditors of public companies.

Dissent and confrontation are often associated with negative personal outcomes. Viewed only as a calculation, only the most unbiased and circumspect process is likely to serve the public interest. The framework in Fig. 1.1 provides a tool for auditors committed to balanced ethical behavior to frame the issue as a duty—seeing it as an obligation that is essential to the role of the auditor. An auditor aware of the essential obligation of dissent is more likely to exhibit the behavior than one who plugs the variables into an expected value calculation.

### *1.3.3 Honest Self-Assessment of Independence and Professionalism*

The third obligation of an audit professional discussed here is to regularly perform an honest self-assessment of independence and professionalism. The U.S. Supreme Court established the connection between this obligation and duty explicitly in its ruling in *U.S. vs. Arthur Young and Co.* (1984):

> By certifying the public reports that collectively depict a corporation's financial status, the independent auditor assumes a public responsibility transcending any employment relationship with the client. The independent public accountant performing this special function owes ultimate allegiance to the corporation's creditors and stockholders, as well as to the investing public. This "public watchdog" function demands that the accountant maintain total independence from the client at all times and requires complete fidelity to the public trust.

As mentioned earlier, the duty of objectivity requires not just freedom from conflicts of interest, but an ability to be "intellectually honest (AICPA 2012b, ET 55.01)." This impartiality does not come naturally; people are naturally self-interested. In the words of Carey and Doherty, "A professional attitude must be learned. It is not a natural gift. It is natural to be selfish—to place personal gain ahead of service (1966, 5)." Being intellectually honest requires a commitment to adopting the perspective of a professional, as well as instituting objective processes that will help auditors to assess when slippage may have occurred. As the American Accounting Association's Committee on Basic Auditing Concepts states, "… independence is the *sine qua non* attribute of an auditor (AAA 1973, 13)."

Auditors must be aware of threats to their professionalism (IFAC 2010, 100.10), particularly to their independence (AICPA 2012a, ET 100.13–100.19). They must also be aware of the potential to move from rational trust to emotional trust in their relationships with their clients. Auditors, over time, have the potential to become deeply interdependent with, and even deeply dependent on, their clients professionally (Shaub 2004).

The International Federation of Accountants (2010) recognizes five primary threats to auditor independence against which accounting firms need to establish adequate safeguards; the AICPA has expanded that list to seven (AICPA 2012a, ET 100.13–100.19). Self-review threats arise from auditors providing assurance on their own work. When auditors promote a client's position or opinion, they are subject to advocacy threats to independence. Adverse interest threats generally arise from pending or threatened litigation with the client. Familiarity or trust threats exist when a close relationship makes the auditor too sympathetic to the client's interests. Undue influence threats arise from attempted coercion by the client, whether through threats, pressure, or gifts. Financial self-interest threats can include direct and material indirect interests in the client, loans, joint ventures, and even overreliance on the client as a revenue source. Finally, management participation threats are the result of assuming various management roles (AICPA 2012a, ET 100.13–100.19).

Familiarity or trust threats are perhaps the subtlest, and yet the most potentially damaging, threats to auditor independence. Trust involves the willingness to risk harm. A "close" relationship may short-circuit likelihood calculations about the client's trustworthiness, reducing the auditor's independence, and thus professional skepticism (McAllister 1995; Shaub 2004). And these calculations of the client's trustworthiness (Kee and Knox 1970) impact other auditor calculations, including evaluations of the three components of audit risk and materiality judgments.

Within the context of the framework in Fig. 1.1, the interdependence or dependence that results from threats such as familiarity and self-interest can entangle consequences to client and auditor, making objective calculations unlikely, at best. When auditors understand that independence is essential to the nature of the audit function and that strict independence is the only condition that is universalizable, the auditor has a chance to act out of duty to serve the public interest rather than inclination toward self-interest.

In summary, we conclude that protecting the public interest requires that the auditor recognize three fundamental duties—truth-telling, dissenting from and confronting client assertions when necessary, and honestly self-assessing independence and professionalism. Recognizing and assuming these duties allows the auditor to make balanced ethical decisions rather than simply relying on calculations. But to do this will require auditors to act virtuously. The next section provides practical recommendations for how auditors can assume these duties.

## 1.4 Recommendations for the Profession

This final section of the chapter suggests ways that the audit profession can answer its call of duty and preserve its professionalism. The obligations identified here are integrally linked to the concept of duty. Without a commitment to balanced ethical decision-making, the accounting profession is unlikely to be willing to recognize the explicit obligations laid out here. If consequences are all that matters, then duties can be ignored. If the obligations are less than suggested here, they ought to be consistent with the historic idea of a profession.

If there is a single evident duty, it is to maximize truth-telling, consistent with the definition of auditing. The auditor's role is to compare economic results with reported financial results for agreement. In order to get to that truth, dissent from management opinions is often necessary. Confrontation may be required to ensure accurate information presentation. But in order for auditors to fairly assess their susceptibility to being misled by clients and therefore be insufficiently skeptical, they must regularly assess their interdependence with, and emotional or financial attachment to, clients.

Effective adoption of these obligations will require a multi-pronged approach by accounting firms involving training, evaluative tools, peer review, oversight, and an openness to outside evaluation (AICPA 2012a, ET 100.20–100.26). Accounting firms and corporations alike have increased ethics training since the passage of the Sarbanes-Oxley Act. Training sessions explicitly addressing these obligations, if supported by an accounting firm's senior management, provide the opportunity to train young auditors in professional skepticism, whereas mixed messages from superiors may actually train the professional skepticism out of them (Shaub and Lawrence 2002).

All accounting firms have evaluative processes in place to make decisions about client acceptance and continuation. Professional skepticism is both a state of mind in a particular circumstance (Shaub and Lawrence 1996) and a trait that can potentially be measured (Hurtt 2010; Quadackers et al. 2009). Measures of their auditors' professional skepticism and of the firm's independence would strengthen this evaluation process. Much as their audit clients have devoted significant resources (and additional audit fees) to internal control documentation to respond to the requirements of section 404 of the Sarbanes-Oxley Act, so auditors and their firms should develop the types of evaluative measures that will reinforce their independence and help them maintain the exclusive right to provide audits in the United States.

We are not just recommending sophisticated disclosure and tracking mechanisms to insure independence. We are referring to comprehensive evaluations of clients along the lines of the earlier mentioned IFAC or AICPA threats to independence, with formal annual evaluations that tie to client continuance decisions, staff assignments and rotation, and brainstorming during planning. We believe that these should also be part of internal firm review, peer review, and PCAOB review processes. The Center for Audit Quality, in cooperation with governance organizations, recently developed a tool that allows audit committees to perform an annual evaluation of their auditors' performance on a series of characteristics, including independence, objectivity, and professional skepticism (Center for Audit Quality 2012). If auditors are going to be routinely reviewed by audit committees on these characteristics, there seems little to gain from avoiding self-evaluation.

Peer review and firm review continue to be important ways of improving practice (AICPA 2012a, ET 100.24). For large CPA firms with at least 100 public clients, the PCAOB provides an annual inspection of compliance with laws, rules, and professional standards in connection with audits. Those firms with fewer public clients must have inspections every 3 years. While the AICPA peer review system has been criticized because none of the large international firms has received anything but a "pass" rating from one of the other large firms, there is at least a glimmer of evidence that this trend might be changing. In the summer of 2012, Ernst & Young gave Deloitte a "Pass with Deficiency" rating for evidence of inadequate application of redesigned firm standards intended to be more principles based. However, barring a change of heart by the American accounting profession to have the AICPA appoint practice inspectors similar to the Canadian inspection model, more attention should be turned in peer review and firm review engagements to evaluating evidence of objectivity, independence, and professional skepticism, in addition to the standard focus on the technical evaluation of audit documentation quality.

At the very least, firms can develop a score related to the threats to their objectivity annually on each engagement. While objectivity is a state of mind that cannot be observed, factors such as the individual auditor's length of time serving on the same client or percentage of the year's chargeable hours spent on a client are measures that potentially impact objectivity over time. Non-disqualifying relationships that are below independence thresholds, but which require disclosure to the firm, could also affect an auditor's objectivity score.

To some this may seem overkill. But Deloitte documents the importance of this approach in its *2012 Transparency Report*, listing among the areas needing improvement based on the nonpublic portion of multiple years of PCAOB inspections the following:

> Adequacy of certain firm policies, such as those relating to responding to risks identified in the engagement risk classification process, *consideration of materiality and evaluations of unadjusted audit differences, materiality guidance for multilocation audits, accounting consultation, independence considerations* related to business relationships, and the archiving of working papers.
>
> Certain general observations concerning audit performance, including *professional skepticism*, supervision and review procedures, education and training, partner evaluations, processes for monitoring audit performance (including internal inspections, root causes, and *independence*), and the consistency and completeness of certain remediation activities.
>
> Procedures related to the *preapproval of nonaudit services* and the ability of U.S. engagement partners to assess a non-U.S. member firm's qualifications and knowledge of U.S. accounting principles and auditing standards. (Deloitte 2012, 25, emphasis added)

It would be easy to criticize Deloitte for the list of issues that need addressing, including the independence and professional skepticism issues that are emphasized in this chapter. However, the transparency of their disclosure process in the report is an excellent example of an accounting firm modeling for their clients the commitment to full disclosure. This same type of transparency is what is needed in the capital markets, and it is the auditor's obligation to ensure that full disclosure is a priority for audit clients.

Shaub (2004) has suggested the use of independence partners to serve as evaluators of the firm's independence from their clients on an annual basis. Much as the engagement quality review partner provides an outside perspective on the quality of the audit, the independence partner has the potential to head off developing independence problems before they impair auditors' objectivity. Unlike the review partner, this partner's work would primarily be done during the planning stage of the audit. In fact, this partner would be part of the team evaluating whether to accept an audit client in the first place. This is consistent with the AICPA's recommendation in ET 100.26.16-17 (AICPA 2012a), which suggests the following safeguards:

16. The involvement of another professional accountant who (1) reviews the work that is done for an attest client or (2) otherwise advises the attest engagement team (This individual could be someone from outside the firm or someone from within the firm who is not otherwise associated with the attest engagement.)
17. Consultation on engagement issues with an interested third party, such as a committee of independent directors, a professional regulatory body, or another professional accountant.

Finally, CPA firms may want to consider forming ethics and independence "boards of directors" with a majority of outside "directors." These outsiders would be individuals with no other ties to the accounting firm other than serving on this board. Where self-interest is so strongly enmeshed in client service, it is important for accounting firms to receive unbiased outside advice to ensure their objectivity. Most auditors have no trouble recommending this type of corporate governance structure to their clients. And while CPA firms may not need this type of board to provide them with financial advice on running the accounting firm, it only makes sense to have someone objective look at those areas of practice in which it is most difficult for auditors to maintain perspective. Practitioners with regulatory experience (e.g., with the SEC or the PCAOB) serving on these boards could provide a different outlook that will challenge the audit firm management's view of its own objectivity.

## 1.5 Conclusion

Historically, when the accounting profession has been unwilling to regulate itself and assume its obligations, government has stepped in with regulations that decrease autonomy. The profession's unwillingness to fully acknowledge and embrace its duty to serve the public interest and to adhere to critical virtues continues to lead to increasing regulation, and to regulators' explicit interference in and constraints on the marketplace for audit services. Because the PCAOB is dissatisfied with the extent to which auditors are fulfilling their duties, current regulatory discussions are designed to maximize truth-telling through an expanded audit report (PCAOB 2011a) and to ensure adequate client confrontation, even if it requires mandatory rotation of audit firms (PCAOB 2011b). And a failure by the AICPA to make peer review rigorous enough to provide for accounting firms' honest self-assessment has led directly to what many accounting firms consider an increasingly intrusive and punitive PCAOB inspection process (Johnson 2009). As Edmund Burke observed two centuries ago, "Men are qualified for civil liberty in exact proportion to their disposition to put moral chains upon their own appetites." (Burke 1791).

Having experienced a decade of growth in esteem for the auditing profession, it would be natural to relax, rather than strengthen, systems that focus on duties and core values. The tendency would be to leverage the brand by seeking expanded market permissions and increased visibility of its value proposition (AICPA 2012c). Doing so could be justified by consequentialist calculations of maximized benefit. Advice to balance consideration of consequences with serious consideration of the duties and virtues inherent in the role of an auditor may be exactly what auditors need in this time of growth, however. Focusing on responsibilities to tell the truth, dissent, confront, and look closely in the mirror is what clients need to hear from auditors and what auditors need to hear from each other. To continue in their roles as professionals, auditors must freely choose to accept these obligations and recommit to values in order to be trusted to protect the public interest. It remains to be seen whether the auditing profession is capable of putting aside self-interest sufficiently to do it.

## References

American Accounting Association. 1973. *Studies in accounting research #6: A statement of basic auditing concepts, committee on basic auditing concepts*. Sarasota: American Accounting Association.

American Bar Association. 2011. *Model rules of professional conduct*. Available at http://www.americanbar.org/groups/professional_responsibility/publications/model_rules_of_professional_conduct/model_rules_of_professional_conduct_preamble_scope.html. Downloaded 18 Sept 2011.

American Institute of Certified Public Accountants. 1986. *Restructuring professional standards to achieve professional excellence in a changing environment*. New York: AICPA.

American Institute of Certified Public Accountants. 2012a. *Code of professional conduct*. New York: AICPA.

American Institute of Certified Public Accountants. 2012b. *Codification of statements on auditing standards*. New York: AICPA.

American Institute of Certified Public Accountants. 2012c. *CPA vision 2025*. New York: AICPA.

American Medical Association. 2011. *Principles of medical ethics, AMA code of medical ethics*. Available at http://www.ama-assn.org/ama/pub/physician-resources/medical-ethics/code-medical-ethics/principles-medical-ethics.page. Downloaded 18 Sept 2011.

Aristotle. 1925. *Nichomacean ethics*. Trans. D. Ross. New York: Oxford University Press. Book II Chapter 3. 1103a–1103b.

Auditing Practices Board. 2010. *Auditor scepticism: Raising the bar* (August). London: Financial Reporting Council. http://www.frc.org.uk/getattachment/2a1e0146-a92c-4b7e-bf33-305b3b10fcd2/Discussion-Paper-Auditor-Scepticism-Raising-the-Ba.aspx. Downloaded 7 Dec 2012.

Bazerman, M.H., K.P. Morgan, and G.F. Loewenstein. 1997. The impossibility of auditor independence. *Sloan Management Review* 38(4): 89–94.

Bebeau, M.J. 2002. The defining issues test and the four component model: Contributions to professional education. *Journal of Moral Education* 31(3): 271–295.

Bebeau, M.J., and S.J. Thoma. 1999. Intermediate concepts and the connection to moral education. *Educational Psychology Review* 11(4): 343–360.

Brody, R.G., D.J. Lowe, and K. Pany. 2003. Could $51 million be immaterial when Enron reports income of $105 million? *Accounting Horizons* 17(2): 153–160.

Bryan-Low, C. 2003. KPMG didn't register strategy. *The Wall Street Journal,* November 17: C1–C9.

Burke, E. 1791. *Letter to a member of the National Assembly*. Retrieved February 20, 2013 from *Quote it Completely: A World Reference Guide to More than 5,500 Memorable Quotations from Law and Literature*, ed. Eugene C. Gerhart at http://books.google.com

Carey, J., and W. Doherty. 1966. *Ethical standards of the accounting profession*. New York: American Institute of Certified Public Accountants.

Carr-Saunders, A.M., and P.A. Wilson. 1933. *The professions*. Ann Arbor: Clarendon.

Center for Audit Quality. 2012. *Audit committee annual evaluation of the external auditor* (October) New York: Center for Audit Quality. http://www.thecaq.org/resources/pdfs/AuditorAssessment.pdf. Downloaded 7 Dec 2012.

Dellaportas, S., B. Jackling, P. Leung, and B.J. Cooper. 2011. Developing an ethics education framework for accounting. *Journal of Business Ethics Education* 8: 63–82.

Deloitte. 2010. *Sustainability reporting: The emerging challenge*. New York: Deloitte Touche Tohmatsu.

Deloitte. 2012. *Committed to quality: Deloitte LLP 2012 transparency report* (July). New York: Deloitte LLP. http://www.deloitte.com/assets/Dcom-UnitedStates/Local%20Assets/Documents/AERS/us_aers_transparency_report_committed_to_quality_080312.pdf. Downloaded 16 Aug 2012.

Department of Justice. 2002. *Deputy attorney general transcript news conference Arthur Andersen indictment* (March 14, 2002), DOJ Conference Center. http://www.justice.gov/archive/dag/speeches/2002/031402newsconferncearthurandersen.htm. Downloaded 17 Aug. 2012.

Deutsch, M. 1962. Cooperation and trust: Some notes. In *Nebraska symposium on motivation*, ed. M.R. Jones. Lincoln: University of Nebraska Press.

Feng, M., J. Gramlich, and S. Gupta. 2009. Special purpose vehicles: Empirical evidence on determinants and earnings management. *The Accounting Review* 84(6): 1833–1876.

Fischhoff, B., P. Slovic, and S. Lichtenstein. 1977. Knowing with certainty: The appropriateness of extreme confidence. *Journal of Experimental Psychology. Human Perception and Performance* 3: 552–564.

Fogarty, T. 2014. The bloom is off the rose: Deprofessionalization in public accounting. In *Accounting for the public interest: Perspectives on accountability, professionalism and role in society*, ed. S. Mintz. 51–72. Heidelberg: Springer.

Frankel, M. 1989. Professional codes: Why? How? And with what impact? *Journal of Business Ethics* 8: 109–115.

Freeman, R.E. 1984. *Strategic management: A stakeholder approach*. Boston: Pitman.

Gibbins, M.S., S. Salterio, and A. Webb. 2001. Evidence about auditor-client management negotiation concerning clients' financial reporting. *Journal of Accounting Research* 76(December): 535–563.

Greenwood, E. 1957. Attributes of a profession. *Social Work* 2: 44–55.

Hall, W. 1988. What does it take to be an auditor? *Journal of Accountancy* 165(1): 72–80.

Han, J., K. Jamal, and H.-T. Tan. 2007. *Are auditors overconfident in predicting the knowledge of other auditors?* Working paper, University of Hong Kong, University of Alberta, and Nanyang Technological University. Available at http://papers.ssrn.com/sol3/papers.cfm?abstract_id=977362

Hatfield, R.C., R.W. Houston, C.M. Stefaniak, and S. Usrey. 2010. The effect of magnitude of audit difference and prior client concessions on negotiation of proposed adjustments. *The Accounting Review* 85(5): 1647–1668.

Houghton, C., and J. Fogarty. 1991. Inherent risk. *Auditing: A Journal of Practice and Theory* 10(1): 1–21.

Hunt, S.D., and S.J. Vitell. 1986. A general theory of marketing ethics. *Journal of Macromarketing* 6: 5–16.

Hunt, S.D., and S.J. Vitell. 1993. The general theory of marketing ethics: A retrospective and revision. In *Ethics in marketing*, ed. N.C. Smith and J.A. Quelch, 775–784. Homewood: Irwin.

Hunt, S.D., and S.J. Vitell. 2006. The general theory of marketing ethics: A revision and three questions. *Journal of Macromarketing* 26(2): 143–153.

Hurtt, R.K. 2010. Development of a scale to measure professional skepticism. *Auditing: A Journal of Practice and Theory* 29(1): 149–171.

Institute of Chartered Accountants in England and Wales (ICAEW). 2008. *Stakeholder expectations of audit*. London: Institute of Chartered Accountants in England and Wales.

International Federation of Accountants (IFAC). 2003. *Rebuilding public confidence in financial reporting: An international perspective*. New York: International Federation of Accountants.

International Federation of Accountants (IFAC). 2004. *International education standard IES 4: Professional values, ethics, and attitudes*. New York: International Federation of Accountants (IFAC).

International Federation of Accountants (IFAC). 2010. *IFAC code of ethics for professional accountants*. New York: International Federation of Accountants (IFAC).

International Federation of Accountants (IFAC). 2011. *Proposed revised international education standard IES 4: Professional values, ethics, and attitudes*. New York: International Federation of Accountants (IFAC).

Johnson, S. 2009. *Deloitte to PCAOB: Don't second-guess us*. CFO.com (April 21). Available at http://www.cfo.com/printable/article.cfm/13524221. Downloaded 24 Jan 2012.

Jones, J., D. Massey, and L. Thorne. 2003. Auditors' Ethical reasoning: Insights from past research and implications for the future. *Journal of Accounting Literature* 23: 42–103.

Kadous, K., and M. Mercer. 2011. *Jury verdicts against auditors under precise and imprecise accounting standards*. Unpublished working paper, Emory University and DePaul University.

Kee, H., and R. Knox. 1970. Conceptual and methodological considerations in the study of trust and suspicion. *Journal of Conflict Resolution* 14: 357–366.

Kennedy, J., and M.E. Peecher. 1997. Judging auditors' technical knowledge. *Journal of Accounting Research* 35(2): 279–293.

Kidwell, L.A., D.G. Fisher, R.L. Braun, and D.L. Swanson. 2012. Learning objectives for ethics education. *Accounting Education: An International Journal* 21(1): 1–22.

Knapp, M.C. 2004. *Contemporary auditing: Real issues and cases*, 5th ed. Mason: Thomson South-Western.

Libby, T., and L. Thorne. 2007. The development of a measure of auditors' virtue. *Journal of Business Ethics* 71: 89–99.

MacIntyre, A. 1984. *After virtue*. Notre Dame: University of Notre Dame Press.

Mautz, R.K., and H.A. Sharaf. 1961. *The philosophy of auditing*. Sarasota: American Accounting Association.

McAllister, D.J. 1995. Affect- and cognition-based trust as foundations for interpersonal cooperation in organizations. *Academy of Management Journal* 38: 24–59.

Mintz, S. 1995. Virtue ethics and accounting education. *Issues in Accounting Education* 10(2): 247–267.

Nelson, M., S. Smith, and Z. Palmrose. 2005. The effect of quantitative materiality approach on auditors' adjustment decisions. *The Accounting Review* 80/3(July): 897–920.

Pincoffs, E. L. 1986. *Quandaries and virtues: Against reductionism in ethics*. Lawrence: University of Kansas Press.

Prentice, R., and J. Koehler. 2003. A normality bias in legal decision making. *Cornell Law Review* 88: 583–650.

Public Company Accounting Oversight Board. 2011a. *Concept release no. 2011–003: Concept release on possible revisions to PCAOB standards related to reports on audited financial statements and related amendments to PCAOB Standards* (June 21). Available at http://pcaobus.org/Rules/Rulemaking/Docket034/Concept_Release.pdf. Downloaded 24 Jan 2012.

Public Company Accounting Oversight Board. 2011b. *Concept release no. 2011–006: Concept release on auditor Independence and audit firm rotation* (August 16). Available at http://pcaobus.org/Rules/Rulemaking/Docket037/Release_2011-006.pdf. Downloaded 24 Jan 2012.

Public Company Accounting Oversight Board. 2012. *Staff audit practice alert no. 10: Maintaining and applying professional skepticism in audits* (December 4). Available at http://pcaobus.org/Standards/QandA/12-04-2012_SAPA_10.pdf. Downloaded 10 Dec 2012.

Public Oversight Board Panel on Audit Effectiveness. 2000. *Report and recommendations*. Stamford: Public Oversight Board.

Quadackers, L., T. Groot, and A. Wright. 2009. *Auditors' skeptical characteristics and their relationship to skeptical judgments and decisions*. Working paper, Vrije Universiteit, Amsterdam. Available at http://ssrn.com/abstract=1478105 or doi:10.2139/ssrn.1478105

Rachels, J. 1986. *The elements of moral philosophy*. New York: Random House.

Rest, J.R. 1979. *Development in judging moral issues*. Minneapolis: University of Minnesota Press.
Rest, J. R. 1983. Morality, In *Manual of child psychology: Vol. 3, Cognitive development*, vol. eds. J. Flavell and E. Markman, gen. ed. P. Mussen, 556–629. New York: Wiley.
Rest, J.R. 1984. The major components of morality. In *Morality, moral behavior and moral development*, ed. W. Kurtines and J. Gerwitz, 24–38. New York: Wiley.
Rest, J.R. 1985. An interdisciplinary approach to moral education. In *Moral education: Theory and application*, ed. M.W. Berkowitz and F. Oser, 9–25. Hillsdale: Lawrence Erlbaum.
Rest, J.R. 1986. *Moral development: Advances in research and theory*. New York: Praeger Press.
Rest, J.R. 1994. Background: Theory and research. In *Moral development in the professions*, ed. J. Rest and D. Narvaez, 1–26. Hillsdale: Lawrence Erlbaum.
Rest, J.R., D. Narvaez, M.J. Bebeau, and S.J. Thoma. 1999. *Postconventional moral thinking: A neo-Kohlbergian approach*. Mahwah: Lawrence Erlbaum.
Securities and Exchange Commission. 1999. *SEC staff accounting bulletin no. 99: Materiality*. Available online at http://www.sec.gov
Shaub, M.K. 1988. Restructuring the code of professional ethics: A review of the Anderson committee report and its implications. *Accounting Horizons* 2(December): 89–97.
Shaub, M.K. 1996. Trust and suspicion: The effects of situational and dispositional factors on auditors' trust of clients. *Behavioral Research in Accounting* 8: 154–174.
Shaub, M.K. 2004. Trust as a threat to independence: Emotional trust, auditor-client interdependence, and their impact on professional skepticism. *Research on Professional Responsibility and Ethics in Accounting* 9: 169–188.
Shaub, M.K. 2005. Materialism and materiality. *International Journal of Accounting, Auditing and Performance Evaluation* 2(4): 347–355.
Shaub, M.K., and D.G. Fisher. 2008. Beyond agency theory: Common values for accounting ethics education. In *Advancing business ethics education*, ed. D. Swanson and D. Fisher, 305–328. Charlotte: Information Age.
Shaub, M.K., and J.E. Lawrence. 1996. Ethics, experience, and professional skepticism: A situational analysis. *Behavioral Research in Accounting* 8(Suppl): 124–157.
Shaub, M.K., and J.E. Lawrence. 2002. A taxonomy of auditors' professional skepticism. *Research on Accounting Ethics* 8: 167–194.
Sommers, C.H. 1993. Teaching the virtues. *The Public Interest* 111: 3–13.
Sonnenfeld, J. 2002. What makes great boards great. *Harvard Business Review* 80: 106–113.
Stuebs, M. 2010. Moral confrontation: An essential companion to moral imagination. *Research on Professional Responsibility and Ethics in Accounting* 14: 57–78.
Stuebs, M., and B. Wilkinson. 2014. Professionalizing the tax accounting profession: Fulfilling public-interest reporting responsibilities. In *Accounting for the public interest: Perspectives on accountability, professionalism and role in society*, ed. S. Mintz. 27–49. Heidelberg: Springer.
Terrell, T.P., and J.H. Wildman. 1992. Rethinking professionalism. *Emory Law Journal* 41: 403–405.
Thorne, L. 1998. The role of virtue in auditors' ethical decision making: An integration of cognitive-developmental and virtue-ethics perspectives. *Research on Accounting Ethics* 4: 291–308.
Trademarkia.com. 2012. *"Trusted Business Advisor" trademark record*. Available at http://www.trademarkia.com/trusted-business-advisor-74034893.html. Downloaded 15 Aug 2012.
*U.S. v. Arthur Young & Co*. 1984. 465 U.S. 805, pp. 817–818.
Westra, L.S. 1986. Whose "loyal agent? Towards an ethic of accounting. *Journal of Business Ethics* 5(2): 119–128.

# Chapter 2
# Professionalizing the Tax Accounting Profession: Fulfilling Public-Interest Reporting Responsibilities

**Martin Stuebs and Brett Wilkinson**

## 2.1 Introduction

In the next chapter, Tim Fogarty provides compelling evidence that accounting is in the process of deprofessionalizing; that is, accounting is losing its claim to professional status. One of the reasons for this deprofessionalization is that the accounting profession has lost its focus on public interest responsibilities. The focus on public interest responsibilities means placing societal interest ahead of self-interest when these interests are in conflict. Accounting has an inherent public interest role and both practitioners and accounting academics should be concerned about the erosion of this role. Although the public interest role is often associated with the auditing profession, it is equally important in the tax profession. Tax accountants walk a fine line between promoting the interests of their clients as part of their tax advocacy role and protecting the integrity of the tax system as part of their role as tax professionals. Recently, however, the former has dominated almost exclusively.

In this chapter, we present suggestions for forwarding and improving the professional status of tax accounting. Ultimately, this requires changing current values that have permeated the profession. This is not an easy process. Fogarty (2014) concludes that we need to understand how values become embedded in social practices. Our goal is to understand this process and, based on such an understanding, to make suggestions for change. To achieve our goal, we draw on the sociology literature. This literature provides a foundation for understanding how structures (like professions) arise and how they change over time. Specifically, we use the Barley and Tolbert (1997) model that provides a helpful pattern for understanding why structures tend to persist through time and how they can change. We use this

M. Stuebs (✉) • B. Wilkinson
Hankamer School of Business, Baylor University, Waco, TX 76798-8002, USA
e-mail: Marty_Stuebs@baylor.edu; Brett_Wilkinson@baylor.edu

S. Mintz (ed.), *Accounting for the Public Interest: Perspectives on Accountability, Professionalism and Role in Society*, Advances in Business Ethics Research 4,
DOI 10.1007/978-94-007-7082-9_2, © Springer Science+Business Media Dordrecht 2014

model to understand both the current status of our profession and to identify ways for reversing the current trajectory.

The remainder of the chapter is organized as follows. First, we outline an ideal state of the tax profession. Suggestions for change are only meaningful if there is a clear goal toward which we are working. Second, we examine the distance between the ideal state (the goal) and the current state of the profession. We use the fraud triangle as means of understanding this distance. Third, we examine the Barley and Tolbert (1997) model from the sociology literature as a mechanism for understanding structural change. Essentially, the model helps us understand how we might move from the current structure toward the ideal structure. Finally, we conclude by proposing a path to change based on the Barley and Tolbert model.

## 2.2 The Normative Professional Ideal (The Goal)

### *2.2.1 A General Reporting Model*

The tax profession is a specialized example of a more general reporting environment. Figure 2.1 presents an ideal general reporting model. Three parties are involved: the reporter, reportee, and report user(s).

The reporter issues a report based on an assessment of reportee performance. The report serves two general purposes. First it accurately measures and substantively reflects reportee performance. Second, it communicates information about

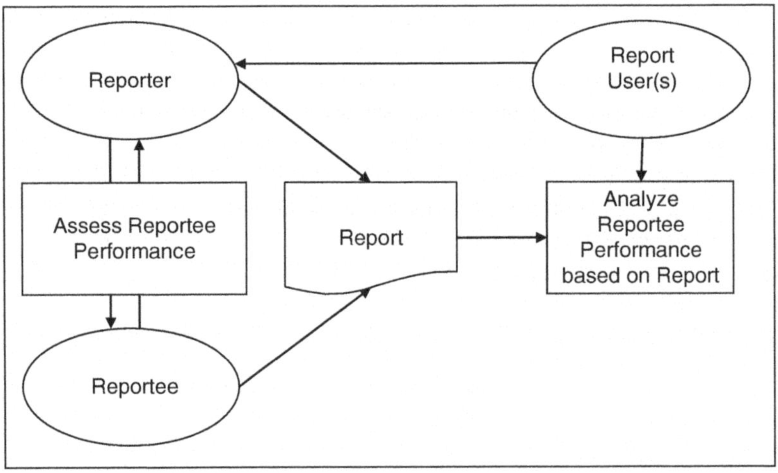


**Fig. 2.1** A general reporting system

the reportee's performance to users who rely on this information for analysis and decision making. Because reporters control both what and how information is reported in the system's reports, they play a critically important public interest role. In essence, reporters have a dual obligation: they must balance the needs of the reportee (who wants to present its operations in the best possible light) against the public interest (protecting the users of the report). Reporters fulfill and satisfy these dual public interest responsibilities and build trust in a healthy, functioning reporting system by reporting truthful, accurate information. Meeting these public interest reporting responsibilities is the foundation of a sustainable, functioning reporting system. Report users and reportees communicate with reporters in a feedback loop on how well reporters are meeting their public interest reporting responsibilities.

We can apply this general model to the tax accounting profession. Professional tax accountants (reporters) prepare tax returns (reports) on tax client (reportee) performance for the taxing authority such as the IRS (report users). Tax accounting professionals fill the critical tax reporting role by reporting truthful accurate information to satisfy the reporting public interest responsibilities to clients and the tax system and help create a healthy, functioning, trusted tax system. What complicates matters is that tax accountants also provide tax planning advice to clients which ultimately impacts the amounts reported.

### *2.2.2 The Tax Accounting Professional's Public Interest Foundation and Resulting Tensions*

Serving public interest responsibilities is integral to the notion of profession. Although the concept of profession has been widely debated in the literature, two key characteristics of professions appear to be consistently and widely accepted within the literature (May 2001; Toren 1975). First, there is an intellectual dimension. A profession is marked by "a body of theoretical and technical knowledge" (Toren 1975, 325). Second, there is a moral dimension which requires "a service orientation" (Toren 1975, 325). This public interest role is the distinctive basis for all professions (Scott 1965; Hall 1967, 1968) including the accounting profession (Wilkerson 2010; Cohen and Holder-Webb 2006, 26; Almer et al. 2005, 5; Puxty et al. 1994, 77–78; Dillard 2008).

The AICPA explicitly recognizes the tax professional's dual obligations to the client to act as a client advocate and to the tax system (AICPA 2009) to foster integrity in the tax system by honestly and fairly administering tax laws. It is not sufficient to merely represent private interests. A CPA must place the public interest ahead of those of the client and self-interests. Client advocacy is an acceptable standard in tax practice, but objectivity should not be sacrificed along the way. Similarly, the IRS has repeatedly emphasized the obligations of the tax professional to the tax system and the need for balance. For example, Shapiro (1986) notes:

> The [public interest] responsibility is of pervasive importance…In the normal practitioner-client relationship, both duties are recognized and carried out. However, there are situations in which this is difficult. In those situations, the practitioner is required to decide which obligation prevails and, in so doing, may correctly conclude that *the obligation to the tax system is paramount…The IRS relies on tax practitioners to assist it in administering the tax laws* by being fair and honest in their dealings with the Service and by fostering confidence…in the integrity of the tax system. (136, 139, emphasis added)

In a similar vein, Pickard (2005) states:

> We can't administer the tax system alone. We rely on the work of accountants and attorneys to make sure people get good advice and take the proper tax positions….Individual and business taxpayers rely on their CPAs to give them answers that are correct under the law without causing them to pay more than they have to. It's a delicate balance, and one that requires integrity. (Pickard 2005, 31)

An ideal, healthy, functioning tax system relies on tax accountants who build trust in the tax system by fulfilling their public interest responsibility. This responsibility requires practitioners to balance the commercial, self-interested incentives they face with their responsibilities to clients and the tax system. If tax practitioners focus on commercial interests to the exclusion of the public interest, they risk loss of professional status and self-regulation privileges. Failing to meet public interest reporting responsibilities invites external regulation to curb inappropriate behavior and protect the public interest[1].

There are numerous examples where tax practitioners have ignored their obligation to the tax system. One pertinent example is the use of abusive tax shelters to create artificial losses via mechanisms that serve no business purpose. According to media reports one of the Jenkens and Gilchrist attorneys who pleaded guilty to tax fraud admitted that "she wrote false opinion letters designed to justify complex financial transactions that reduced the potential taxes to be paid by the firm's clients. The overall scheme created more than $400 million in false tax losses" (Bray 2012). It would appear that the accountants who developed these shelters failed to take into account their public interest obligation. Similarly, Henchman (2008) reports on the Sale-in-Lease-out (SILO) transactions in which private corporations (who could use depreciation deductions) "purchased" public transit assets from public authorities (who could not take advantage of depreciation deductions). The private corporations involved immediately leased them back to the public entities and eventually sell them back at the end of the lease term. Again, there is a legitimate question as to whether the accountants who developed and promoted these artificial schemes to move deductions out of the hands of public entities and into the hands of corporations, without any legitimate business change or purpose, simply abandoned their public interest obligations in the interests of profit making.

[1]One example of this might be seen in the role of the PCAOB which serves to limit the professional autonomy of professional accounting firms.

## 2.3 De-professional Erosion (The Current State): A Fraud Triangle Analysis

As noted in the previous chapter (Fogarty 2014), recent developments in the accounting profession suggest that there has been a shift from professional public interest ideals to self-interested business pursuits. Beginning in the mid-1960s, the accounting profession gradually shifted from professionalism to commercialism (Zeff 2003a, b). Big firms transformed from organizations strongly imbued with professional values to ones strongly pursuing commercial and business goals placing added pressure on partners to generate fees and placate clients. Numerous other authors have noted this development among the major accounting firms not only in the US but globally (Sikka 2008; Hanlon 1994). Sikka (2008) cites comments made by former SEC chief accountant Lynn Turner in a PBS interview as follows:

> Today they [major firms] are a business firm, and the CEOs and culture at the top of these firms is, "What can we do [to] make our business more profitable?". (p. 277)

The fraud triangle (Cressey 1953) provides a helpful and well-established framework for analyzing this shift in the tax profession. A fraud, or "trust violation" in Cressey's (1953) terminology, generally involves three elements depicted in Fig. 2.2 below: opportunity, incentives, and rationalization. We use the fraud triangle to analyze the illegal tax shelters that became a significant part of the tax environment in the 1980s and 1990s. We focus on tax shelters because they provide an example of the way the tax profession sacrificed its public interest responsibility in pursuit of commercial gain and each of the Big Four public accounting firms played a widespread, extensive and dominant role in the tax shelter industry (Wang 2003). Understanding this drift helps us to determine ways to restore the public interest focus and thus reverse the deprofessionalization trend.

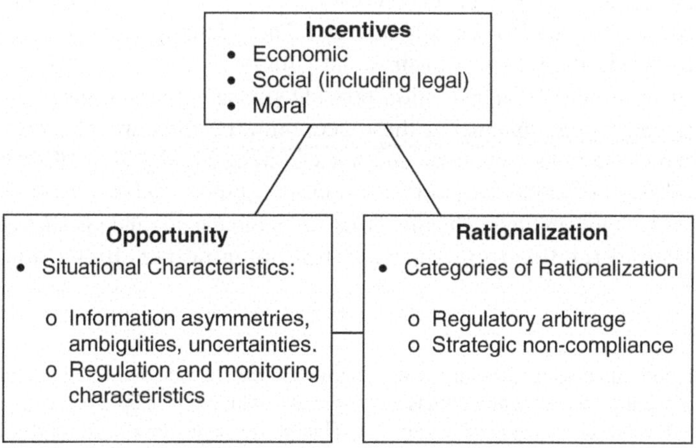


**Fig. 2.2** Fraud triangle model—factors contributing to tax reporting frauds

### 2.3.1 Opportunity[2]

Opportunities for fraud arise from information asymmetries, uncertainty, or ambiguity combined with absent or inadequate monitoring and enforcement mechanisms. Reporters and reportees have an informational advantage over report users because they control the information reported (creating opportunity). The IRS lacks the resources to monitor all tax reporting activity and is often at an informational disadvantage in the tax reporting environment (Smith 2004). "Gray" areas in the tax law require judgment and create opportunities to aggressively exploit so-called loopholes to lower taxes but at the cost of sacrificing tax system integrity and the tax authority's trust in tax accountants.

One example of this tax-law ambiguity is the legal uncertainty surrounding abusive tax shelters and the resulting opportunities for commercial gain. The primary purpose behind abusive or illegal tax shelters is the avoidance or evasion of taxes in a manner not intended by the law (Permanent Subcommittee 2005). This distinction between abusive and legal shelters is not always clear in practice, and this ambiguity made it easier for the Big Four to find lawyers willing to support aggressive shelters (Wang 2003, 1259). Limited tax authority monitoring and enforcement further fueled the opportunity for the use of tax shelters (Wang 2003). The IRS lacked sufficient resources to monitor tax shelter activity (Smith 2004), and this increased the opportunity for fraud.

### 2.3.2 Incentives

It is well established that incentives influence judgment (Watts and Zimmerman 1986) and can motivate fraudulent tax reporting. Incentives take three primary forms: economic, social and moral (Levitt and Dubner 2005, 21). Economic incentives cause individuals to act in their own self-interest. They generally involve cost-benefit considerations and the prospect of financial gain or loss. For example, client fees, client acquisition, and client retention provide strong economic incentives for the tax practitioner. Counterbalancing these economic benefits are the corresponding potential economic risks, penalties, and fines from aggressive fraudulent activity.

In the abusive tax shelter example, economic incentives substantively dominated public interest responsibilities. The immediate economic gains and tax shelter earnings were substantial relative to inconsequential potential penalties (Smith 2004).

---

[2]We present the fraud triangle elements with opportunity first followed by incentives and rationalization. This maintains consistent parallels and symmetry with our proposed practical educational model in Sect. 2.5.1 and presented in Fig. 2.4. This is also consistent with Stuebs (2010) and Stuebs and Thomas (2011). We recognize that the auditing literature often presents the fraud triangle in a different order with incentives first followed by opportunity and rationalization.

Contingent fees elevated the potential return from aggressive tax shelter sales providing additional key economic incentives (Wang 2003). These economic incentives became more salient in an environment of competitive market forces. Contingent fees, market pressures, and other salient economic incentives played a key role in diverting accounting firms' attention away from steadfastly administering their entrusted client advocate and legal administrate responsibilities in favor of commercial gain (Permanent Subcommittee 2005, 88).

Social incentives involve the aversion to being seen by others as engaging in wrongful behavior. They are similar to "subjective norms" or an individual's perception of social pressures in the Theory of Planned Behavior (Ajzen 1985) and can be either formal or informal. Obeying authority (Milgram 1963) and conforming to group norms (Asch 1958) are examples of common social incentives. Legal compliance is a powerful formal social incentive. In addition to pressures to comply, social incentives can also involve pressures to impress by meeting or exceeding perceived social norms and expectations. Social pressures reinforced the use of abusive tax shelters. For example, in the well-known KPMG tax shelter case, superiors placed intense pressure on subordinates to comply with and impress superiors by 'signing-off' on the merits of a proposed product even with serious questions about its legal compliance (Permanent Subcommittee 2005, 22; Minority Staff 2003, 7; Milgram 1963) reflecting strong social pressure to serve commercial interests over the public interest (Smith 2004).

Moral incentives involve individuals' aversion to something they consider wrong. Moral incentives focus on duties, responsibilities and obligations. For example, the tax accountant has dual responsibilities to advocate for the client and to serve the public by maintaining tax system integrity.

In the tax shelter case, there is evidence that firms used their reputations to give legitimacy to tax shelters that were highly questionable. For example, an illustrative internal KPMG e-mail stated: "Our reputation will be used to market the transaction" (Permanent Subcommittee 2005, 20). Essentially, senior executives in the firm were willing to use the firm's reputation (the belief that this firm would not support something unethical) in order to make commercial gain but in a way that was directly opposed to the factors that had created this positive reputation (selling tax shelters that were hard to understand and that were not consistent with basic ethical practices). Instead of being upheld, the public interest reputation of the profession was not only disregarded but used to pursue commercial gain.

### 2.3.3 *Rationalization*

Rationalization involves the individual's internal response to external opportunities and reconciles an individual's moral incentives with economic and social incentives. It involves an erosion of public interest responsibilities in the presence of incentives and occurs when tax preparers justify on a post hoc basis predetermined, aggressive reporting behaviors that fail to meet professional public interest responsibilities.

Since rationalizations respond to incentives, we categorize economically motivated rationalizations, and legally motivated rationalizations. The behavior of firms in the tax shelter example was rationalized with economic concerns and incentives. For example, KPMG increased fees to reflect the increased risk from dubious tax products (Permanent Subcommittee 2005). The economic benefits provided the primary ad hoc rationale for creating and marketing the tax shelters (Permanent Subcommittee 2005, 57–58).

Bratton (2003) identifies two primary legally motivated rationalizations to eliminate the difference between what legally should be done and what is done. Regulatory arbitrage involves "the practice of structuring an inappropriate transaction so it stays within the bounds set by a rule" (Bratton 2003, 1044). In other words, the tax professional modifies the characteristics of the actual transaction to meet the tax law's technical requirements and rationalize *technical* compliance.

In contrast, strategic noncompliance takes advantage of opportunities to exercise judgment in applying tax laws to modify the interpretation and application of tax law to fit the desired transaction. It involves an "action under an interpretation of the law in conflict with the stated interpretation of the regulator" (Bratton 2003, 1044). Although the original intent of the law may not always be clear, strategic noncompliance implies an aggressive use of judgment such that the practitioner distorts the underlying spirit of the law in order to achieve a positive tax result for the client. Accounting firms were aware of the questionable and precarious legality of their tax shelters (Permanent Subcommittee 2005) and often justified actions on the basis that the structures adhered to the technical "letter of the law". For example, KPMG's tax shelters complied with the literal form of the tax law but not the intended substance[3] and even though KPMG staff had identified serious questions about the technical validity of these shelters, they proceeded to market them (Permanent Subcommittee 2005, 1). It is very difficult to see how the tax professionals at KPMG acted in a way that was consistent with their duty to the public interest when they actively promoted a transaction with no economic substance and that internal staff had expressly regarded as being technically questionable.

---

[3]One example of the way that a transaction complied with the letter of the law but not the spirit of the law can be seen in the bond linked issue premium structures (BLIPS) that were sold by KPMG. Hosmer (2008) provides a detailed overview of the way that these transactions operated. Essentially, the taxpayer would take a $50 million 7 year loan with a very high interest rate. As compensation for the excessively high interest rate, the investment bank would provide an offsetting "premium" of $20 million. The benefit of the premium arrangement was that it was classed as equity rather than a liability (because it was not strictly speaking a loan) but at the same time the taxpayer avoided treating it as income because of the risk of forfeiture. Ultimately, when the taxpayer terminated the 7-year $50 million loan, the bank required repayment of the $20 million premium. This resulted in the taxpayer being able to claim a loss of $20 million. There is little doubt that the loss is a paper loss only and that the transaction lacks economic substance. The only real cost is to the tax system. Accordingly, it is difficult to see that the professionals who developed and sold such products were acting in a manner consistent with their public interest obligations.

### 2.3.4 *Results: Deprofessionalization and a Loss of Trust*

Although aggressive tax shelters initially resulted in economic benefits, significant costs accrued to the profession and society as a whole. Aggressive tax shelters signaled a shift from professionalism to commercialism (Permanent Subcommittee 2005) consistent with the commercialization trend within the broader public accounting profession (see for example Fogarty et al. 2006). Firms emphasized customer-driven commercialism and client service rather than public-service responsibilities (Hanlon 1994). Pursuit of financial rewards eclipsed traditional values (Sikka and Hampton 2005; Smith 2004).

This shift from professionalism to commercialism signals a shift from "service interest" to "self-interest" (Toren 1975, 326). For example, self-interested revenue potential received primary consideration and often trumped service-interested ethical considerations relegating them to secondary, ancillary consideration in KPMG's tax shelter approval process (Permanent Subcommittee 2005). KPMG's aggressive marketing tactics also signaled a move away from service-interested professionalism to self-interested commercialism. Tax shelter services were no longer client specific. Instead, generic tax shelters were developed and then methodically and aggressively sold (Wang 2003, 1251) with the goal of creating and encouraging an aggressive sales culture (Permanent Subcommittee 2005, 36, 42). KPMG turned tax professionals into tax product salespersons, pressured tax professionals to meet revenue targets, and used questionable marketing tactics (Permanent Subcommittee 2005, 33). KPMG's own internal documents recommended deceptive hard-sell tactics like using misleading statements to convince uninterested or hesitant clients (Permanent Subcommittee 2005, 42). Instead of serving clients and the tax system, accountants like KPMG used clients and their position in the tax system to further personal gains and increase commercialization in the tax profession.

The tax shelter industry ultimately undermines the public confidence in the tax system and in the tax profession. By placing pursuit of personal gain ahead of client advocate and public interest responsibilities, firms lost the trust of clients, employees, and the public (Smith 2004). Although profitable, the primary consequence of the tax shelter abuses was a loss of public trust. Ultimately, the root of the problem lies in the loss of understanding and subversion of the profession's primary public interest reporting role and responsibilities.

### 2.3.5 *The International Dimension*

The loss of public interest focus and associated problems are not contained to the domestic sphere. Numerous international issues also exist. Sikka (2008) makes reference to the engagement of Big Four accounting firms in schemes to avoid sales tax in the UK, income splitting schemes using trusts in Australia and tax evasion in Russia.

Among others, international tax evasion schemes that have direct implications for the US include the use offshore credit/debit cards, offshore banking secrecy and the role of tax havens.

Ostrander (2003) provides a helpful review of the offshore credit card schemes which entailed hiding income in financial institutions located in tax haven countries and then using credit or debit cards to draw on those funds. Ostrander notes that:

> To engage in an offshore scheme, the individual in the US will *find an offshore professional* to assist in the development of an overall offshore plan. ... Once the offshore structure is created, the next step is devising methods to transfer funds or assets ... These funds or assets may represent profits the US person seeks to hide from US tax authorities. The last step in the process is using techniques to access such funds ... Payment cards are common and at the time were promoted as a purportedly non-traceable method of accessing offshore funds. (emphasis added, p. 114)

These complex structures could not have been developed without the assistance of accounting and legal experts (the professionals). It is apparent that these professionals disregarded the public interest obligations imposed on them by their respective professions.

Tax havens and banking secrecy laws have long been a recognized international tax problem. There is widespread evidence of corporations using offshore tax havens to substantially reduce their worldwide effective tax rates. In a compelling article, Drucker (2010) documented the way that Google was able to secure a 2.4 % effective tax rate via manipulations such as the "Dutch Sandwich" and the "Double Irish." Although the Organization for Economic Cooperation and Development (OECD) countries have primarily taken the lead in fighting tax haven abuses, the OECD (2010) points out that "These issues face not only OECD and G20 jurisdictions, but also those in the developing world, where thc goal of self-sustaining growth depends in large part on securing a stable stream of tax revenue" (p. 21).

## 2.4 Achieving Change: A Structural Change Model

The previous two sections established a normative ideal for the tax profession and contrasted it with the current state of the profession. The comparison makes clear how far the current state deviates from the normative ideal. This is consistent with Fogarty's (2014) analysis concerning the deprofessionalization of accounting more generally. Moving our profession from its current state to its ideal state necessitates understanding how institutions change. In this section, we turn our attention to the sociology literature and the possibilities of structural change.

The notion of structure is well developed in the sociology literature and encompasses "the tendency of patterns of relations to be reproduced, even when actors engaging in the relations are unaware of the patterns or do not desire their reproduction" (Sewell 1992, 3). We can view the tax profession as a form of structure that shapes the behaviors of the professionals within it. The structural shift in thinking from professionalism to commercialism in the tax profession has become so

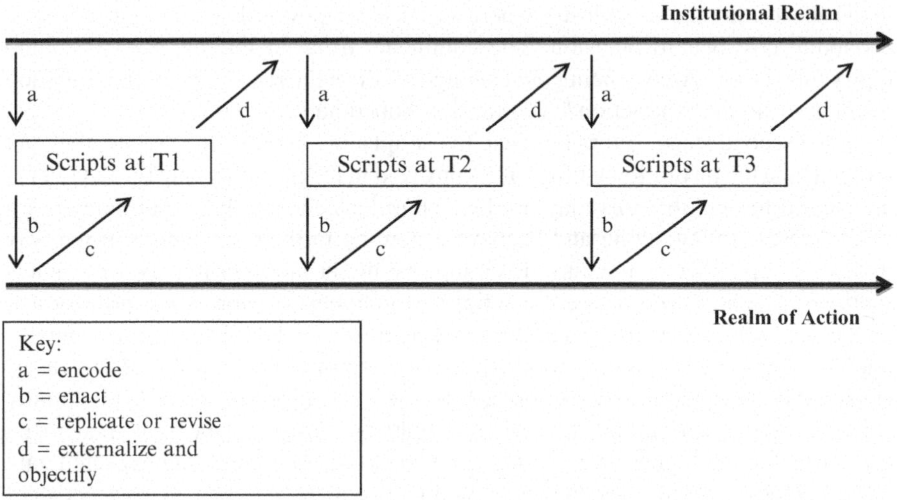


**Fig. 2.3** Barley and Tolbert's (1997) institutional change model (*Source*: Barley and Tolbert 1997)

entrenched that new generations of tax preparers simply follow without challenging the status quo. In other words, patterns of behavior are reproduced over time perpetuating a commercialism status quo.

On one level, this entrenched behavior is discouraging and seems to offer little hope for change. On another level, however, the notion of structure provides the very hope of change. Giddens' suggests that not only does structure place constraints on human behavior but it also enables human behavior (Giddens 1976). Essentially, structure both regulates how people behave but it also provides those same people with the authority and opportunity to achieve certain goals and ends. Sewell (1992) articulates this most clearly in his comment that "if enough people or even a few people who are powerful enough act in innovative ways, their action may have the consequence of transforming the very structures that gave them the capacity to act" (p. 4). In the professional accounting context, the profession restricts certain behaviors but at the same time being a part of the profession gives meaning and power to individuals who are then positioned to make changes to the profession. This gives us hope that change is a legitimate possibility.

The next question then is: how might change be achieved? We focus on the change model developed in the sociology literature by Barley and Tolbert (1997). They depict the structuration process as one which operates continuously. In this model, there are constraints imposed on the action of individual actors, but the behaviors of the actors then serve to reinforce the existing structure or promote change. Their model is shown in Fig. 2.3 and consists of four moments or stages.

In the first stage, institutional principles are encoded into specific "scripts". Barley and Tolbert (1997) define scripts as "behavioral regularities." One possible current institutional script is that commercial gain is the highest priority of the tax professional and that the public interest is secondary. Another example can be seen in the abusive tax shelter industry where a critical script was that compliance was an economic cost-benefit decision. The comments from an internal KPMG memo typify this script: "Are we being paid enough to offset the risks of potential litigation resulting from the transaction?" (Permanent Subcommittee 2005, 20)[4].

In the second stage, actors translate the scripts into actions. In essence, they put into practice the institutional principles conveyed to them. Barley and Tolbert (1997) are careful to note that this may not be a conscious choice; that is, in many cases actors merely follow along and "behave according to their perception of the way things are" (p. 102). In the current setting, we might interpret this as accountants routinely putting into practice the script that commercial gain is the priority and public interest issues are irrelevant. Because superiors model this behavior, accountants operate as employees seeking to maximize the return to the firm. Similarly, in the abusive tax shelter industry example, lower-level employees in the firms blindly followed the commercial-interest-over-public-interest script that had been established at the higher levels of the firms involved. As long as the expected gain exceeded the expected costs, they were willing to pursue transactions irrespective of the cost to the integrity of the tax system.

The third stage involves either replication of or revision to the original scripts. Individual actors either seek out new scripts (revision) or they continue with the current scripts (replication). Replication, however, increases the entrenched nature of the script. Barley and Tolbert (1997) note that actors tend not to seek out new scripts unless there has been some exogenous influence. Such external influences can include technological change, economic crises, changes in regulations, and cross-cultural contacts (Burns 1961; Ranson et al. 1980). Absent such external influences, actors are more likely to follow along with the existing scripts.

In the fourth and final stage, the behaviors of the actors are objectified. Essentially, "the patterns acquire a normative, 'factual' quality and their relationship to the existing interests of different actors becomes obscured" (Barley and Tolbert 1997, p. 103). In essence, when scripts are repeated over and over, people begin to see them as an objective reality of the way things work. The current status of the profession is consistent with this phenomenon. Fogarty's (2014) deprofessionalizaton arguments highlight the fact that there is little understanding among tax professionals of their public interest obligation. Few tax accountants see their role as being any different to other commercial service providers. They believe in a reality that entails getting the best result for the client irrespective of any public interest implications because that is what they are hired to do. This perception of an objective reality then drives the development of scripts in the next iteration, highlighting the dynamic

[4]Although it is true that all pricing invariably takes into account future risks, we suggest that there is a difference between pricing in legitimate risk (that the IRS and firm positions may differ, resulting in some loss) and pricing in risk associated with being caught for engaging in practices that were known ex ante to be highly suspect from a legal standpoint. The latter represents an 'audit lottery' type of thinking; that is, there's a risk we'll get caught but we're making so much that it's worth taking the risk. This type of thinking is contrary to the standards for tax practice prescribed by the AICPA (2009).

nature of the process. It also explains why there is limited concern outside the halls of academia for the current lack of public interest focus in the tax profession: the new normal is that public accounting is simply another form of commerce with no notion of professional responsibilities.

## 2.5 Professionalization and a Return to Public Interest Responsibilities: Applying the Change Model to the Tax Profession

The relevant conclusion for the accounting profession from this sociology literature is that external shocks can provide the impetus and opportunity to affect needed change. Change is unlikely to occur without such external shocks. The recent accounting scandals (e.g., Enron and WorldCom) including the tax shelter scandal represent systemic failures that had the potential to precipitate significant change. Unfortunately, however, the changes they precipitated were not internal but have tended to be external to the system; that is; most of these changes have been regulatory changes. The problem with such changes, however, is that they perpetuate an illusion of control (Rosanas and Velilla 2005) without necessarily inducing real change. Accordingly, there is potentially no internal change but rather a mere accommodating of the external change, which ultimately leads to further failures. In this case, the new regulation simply increases the costs of engaging in tax shelters and thus makes this specific behavior less attractive. However, absent a change in the underlying thought processes or central *scripts* of professional tax accountants that underpinned the tax shelter phenomenon, there are likely to be further failures in other areas. The regulation may fix the tax shelter problem but it won't prevent similarly bad practices in other areas.

We suggest that real change will occur only if practitioners establish and secure a foundational script of the public interest reporting role and responsibilities of the tax profession. Consistent with Barley and Tolbert's (1997) comments, change will need to be intentional and driven by actors with the power to effect change (e.g., public accounting firms and universities) (Sewell 1992).

The actors with the power to effect such change (here, the major public accounting firms) need to act expressly to facilitate such change. These actors must also be shown that it is ultimately in their own best long-run interests to act now to preserve the profession. Although there are short term economic benefits to ignoring the public interest, there is a high long-term cost in the loss of professional status. It is well established that professions are afforded many rights and freedoms[5] but the quid pro quo is that they act in a way that promotes the public interest. As Sellers et al. (2012)

[5]For example, professionals are afforded the right of self-regulation. Increased external regulation in response to scandals such as the abusive tax shelters marketed by KMPG highlights the potential risks from the loss of professional status.

note, the very survival of organizations depends on their ability to balance social fitness with the furtherance of their own advantage. The accounting profession's loss of professional status is not something that should be embraced lightly.

Ultimately, we argue that changing the thinking of tax accountants (such that they embrace the public interest notion) requires two things. First, there must be an acknowledgement by the firms that they have a public interest obligation and that they expect their employees to act accordingly. Second, there must be a change in professional education (Wilkerson 2010). Fogarty (2014) specifically identifies education as a source of potential substantive professional change. We agree with this assessment and propose a process by which this could be operationalized in the next section.

Further, we in the academy must shoulder some considerable responsibility because our research agenda has facilitated the demise of public interest thinking. There is an abundance of evidence that we have pursued an increasingly narrow research agenda dominated by neoclassical economics and limited statistical methodologies (see for example Williams et al. 2006; Reiter and Williams 2002; and Tuttle and Dillard 2007). We have lost sight of our own public interest role, and we have eliminated research into issues such as ethics from the mainstream on the basis that it is not scientific.

This limited research agenda has fed into our teaching. Goshal (2005) points out that business schools have routinely taught agency theory as an acceptable and legitimized fact in a way that has left students with the understanding that they have no moral responsibility beyond self-interest. Ironically, he notes that rather than the theory explaining behavior, the teaching of agency theory has in fact created reality; that is, it has influenced scripts and perpetuated behavior. That is, managers behave exactly as business schools taught them they should behave (by pursuing self-interest above all else, unless there is sufficient monitoring and bonding to curtail such behavior).

A critical response, then, must be script-modifying reform both to accounting research and education in order to re-establish the notion that professionals have a duty to the public that transcends private interest. In the next section, we outline an example of a practical educational model that can address this need. This example model trains students to explicitly consider professional public interest responsibilities when making decisions. By explicitly incorporating consideration of professional ideals and responsibilities, this example decision making model practically applies many of the professional education reforms in Wilkerson (2010). As we outline the model, we specifically use the tax shelter example to show how appropriate training may have equipped tax professionals to act in an alternate manner.

### *2.5.1 An Example of a Practical Educational Model*

The example training and educational model described in this section applies a holistic decision process that facilitates and practices explicit consideration of public interest responsibilities. The model can facilitate and train consideration of public

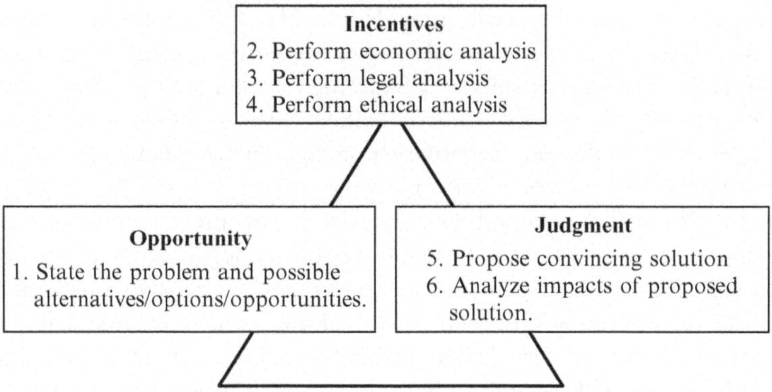


**Fig. 2.4** Judgment decision model

interest responsibilities at both the pre-entry level (that is, at universities) and in professional training (once accountants have entered the profession). With regard to professional training, we advocate that this occur outside the confines of the individual firm; that is, the training be administered by a third party rather than the firm. This is because of Barley and Tolbert's (1997) observation that actors need to experience a change in context before they are able to see and embrace the flaws in the current scripts and initiate change. Thus cooperative efforts between accounting academia and the profession present collaborative opportunities for reversing the current demise in the public interest focus within the accounting profession. The model we propose is consistent with and practically implements many of the professional education suggestions of Wilkerson (2010).

The professional judgment[6] model presented here identifies and explicitly considers responsibilities in the presence of incentives. Such a model provides several educational advantages. It can *improve judgments* in a practical setting. Practicing habits of identifying and meeting professional responsibilities even in the presence of incentives when making decisions prepares the professional to make tough "in the moment" decisions. A decision model can also *communicate judgments* by providing assurance that the process exercised rigor and care in identifying and meeting public interest responsibilities. The decision model in Fig. 2.4 is the holistic incentives-based model in Stuebs and Thomas (2011) and Stuebs (2010) that evolved from the decision-making framework in Hosmer (2008).

This broader framework offers advantages over other less complete decision models because it *explicitly considers ethical professional responsibilities and incentives*: (1) economic incentives to pursue self-interest; (2) legal incentives to comply with regulations; and (3) moral incentives to meet responsibilities to others

[6]Professional judgment is judgment exercised with due care, objectivity, and integrity within a framework of professional standards by experienced and knowledgeable people (Gibbons and Mason 1988, 5; Mintz 2010, 115).

including public interest responsibilities. Notice also that the primary steps in this broader, incentives-based model are also advantageously compatible and consistent with the fraud triangle's elements: (1) State the problem and possible alternatives and *opportunities*; (2) Identify and consider various *incentives*; (3) Exercise *judgment*. Notice also that the incentives-based model can advantageously begin to foster moral development since it considers incentive categories that loosely follow Kohlberg's (1969) primary moral development stages: preconventional (motivated by self-interest), conventional (motivated by social and legal compliance incentives), and postconventional (motivated by identified responsibilities, duties and obligations).

Explicitly incorporating professional ethical public interest responsibilities into a general model that considers different incentives creates an integrative, inclusive, and versatile model with potential to facilitate integration of professional ethical public interest responsibilities into courses across academic curriculum and professional training (Wilkerson 2010). Repeatedly applied, such an approach aids students in habitually realizing professional public interest responsibilities as a primary part of a unified, integrated decision process.

This potential advantage is substantial. This model can aid faculty efforts to consistently and holistically address "ethics whenever possible because it is fundamental to an accounting education" (Mintz 2010, 131). This model can aid efforts to move toward a professional education curriculum founded in professional ideals and identity (Wilkerson 2010) by helping "provide the conceptual and judgment-based skills with an ethics underpinning needed by students" (Mintz 2010, 132).

While Stuebs and Thomas (2011) and Stuebs (2010) provide examples that apply each decision model component in detail, we use the KPMG tax shelter case to summarize how the decision model can be used to help identify incentives and meet responsibilities. A synopsis of the KPMG case is given in Stuebs (2010) and presented below.[7]

**KPMG and the Sale of Tax Shelters: Synopsis**

As one of the "Big 4" accounting firms, KPMG is one of the largest, oldest, most global, and most independent public accounting firms. The issue in this case is whether KPMG's marketing and use of a proprietary set of tax shelters was "right", "just" and "fair". Faced with the threat of criminal prosecution, the senior partners of KPMG negotiated a settlement including payment of $456 million in penalties. There were several notable aspects related to KPMG's tax shelters: (1) The extent of the tax savings created by these

(continued)

[7]The complete, expanded case with detail appears in Hosmer (2008, 83–96). A brief summary of the case is presented here.

(continued)

shelters was enormous—one estimate was $2.5 billion in avoided taxes; (2) Several senior level KPMG employees were involved in the tax shelters; (3) KPMG recorded extensive profits from the tax shelters; (4) KPMG intensely and aggressively marketed its tax shelters; (5) KPMG attempted to deliberately conceal the nature of the tax shelters.

But the most notable aspect of KPMG's tax shelters was that they had never been declared to be illegal in formal court proceedings. The line between improper tax shelters and more legitimate tax avoidance strategies is often blurry. Unlike legitimate tax shelters, abusive tax shelters have no real economic substance. The issue to determine the legal legitimacy of newly designed tax shelters, then, is the existence of a "real economic purpose"—an actual chance for growth and profit from an at risk investment. Senator Levin described four allegedly faulty tax shelters. Two of these four shelters, BLIPS and SC2, were described in detail.[8] Should KPMG sell its proprietary set of tax shelters?

#### 2.5.1.1 Incentives Analyses

After the problem is identified and stated, it can be analyzed on economic, legal and ethical bases, explicitly using respective theories to consider the primary incentives that exist in each category. Each of the economic, legal and ethical theories and analyses affect the identification and fulfillment of public interest responsibilities. Specifically, economic and legal analyses use respective theories to limit and simplify the identification and fulfillment of responsibilities. The ethical analysis uses ethical theory to identify, not limit, professional public interest responsibilities.

Perform an Economic Analysis

Based on economic theory, an **economic analysis** meets public interest responsibilities to maximize society's net benefit by using self-interested incentives to choose the action that maximizes self-interest and/or profit. The assumptions of economic theory limit an individual's public interest responsibilities to self-interest. According to economic theory (Friedman 1962, 133; McKie 1974, 19), open, free and competitive markets assure that individuals acting in their *individual* self-interests

[8]Details of Senator Levin's comments and the BLIPS and SC2 shelters can be found in Hosmer (2008, 89–95).

maximize *society's* net benefit (Hosmer 1984, 2008, 32–34). The individual's only moral responsibility is to act in his/her self-interest *if* the assumptions of economic theory hold. Market controls ensure society benefits from self-interested action and protect the public interest; individual self-controls are unnecessary. The assumptions of economic theory limit and simplify moral responsibility; however, using economic theory, assumptions and incentives to limit professional responsibilities (i.e., professionalism) to commercial self-interests (i.e., commercialism) can create social costs in practice.

In the KPMG case, KPMG should aggressively market and sell tax shelter products to increase profit and reported performance and fulfill self-interested responsibilities according to economic theory. However, market imperfections and legal ambiguities provide imperfect controls in this situation and cannot be relied on to ensure maximum net benefit for society.

The tax system is not open. Information asymmetries exist among tax system parties due to deliberately nontransparent tax shelter disclosures. Questionable tax shelter legality can result in external costs to society in the form of lost tax revenues passed onto U.S. citizens. An economic analysis uses economic theory and relies on market controls to simplify responsibilities. Costs result from these simplifying assumptions in practice.

### Perform a Legal Analysis

Based on legal theory, a **legal analysis** fulfills public interest responsibilities to meet society's moral standards by using legal compliance incentives to choose the alternative that obeys the law. The underlying legal theory assumption is that the law contains and expresses society's collective moral standards (Hosmer 2008, 63–76). As a result, the individual's only moral responsibility is to obey the law. The legal theory assumption limits individual public interest responsibilities to legal compliance. Legal controls ensure society benefits from individual action and protect the public interest; additional individual self-controls beyond legal compliance are unnecessary. The assumptions of legal theory limit and simplify professional moral responsibility (i.e., professionalism) to legal compliance (i.e., legalism).

In the KPMG case, KPMG should obey relevant tax shelter laws and tax position recommendation laws to fulfill legal compliance responsibilities according to legal theory. However, the law is an imperfect control. Costs can result from using the law to simplify responsibility identification. First, political and special interests can influence the formation of the law and threaten whether resulting laws contain and express society's moral standards. The design of many legal loopholes is verifiably rigged in favor of influential taxpayers and creates problems for using the legal justification for certain tax-related practices. Second, applying laws relies on professional judgment that goes beyond compliance with technical form to compliance with underlying substance. While the assumptions of legal theory can simplify and limit the identification of responsibilities, the usefulness of legal compliance responsibilities is limited and incomplete.

### Perform an Ethical Analysis

Based on ethical theory, an **ethical analysis** fulfills professional public interest responsibilities resulting from moral incentives by choosing the action that fulfills ethical duties, in this case professional public interest and client reporting responsibilities (i.e., professionalism). Unlike economic theory and legal theory, moral theory simply identifies responsibilities instead of using assumptions to limit and simplify responsibilities. Individual professional self-controls of competence to identify responsibilities and character to fulfill responsibilities ensure that society benefits from individual action.

The tax professional has a public interest responsibility to clients and the tax system to report truthful, accurate, useful tax advice and information to build trust in the tax system. The virtue ethics approach (Mintz 2010) uses these public interest responsibilities to guide the virtues needed by a tax accountant. Some needed virtues (though not a comprehensive list) can include integrity, objectivity, due diligence, competence and a desire to serve the public interest. Identifying these virtues and the public interest reporting responsibilities of a tax accountant guides the ethical decision. What would a diligent, competent tax accountant with integrity, objectivity, and a sense of public interest do to provide transparent tax information regarding tax shelters to clients and the tax authority? Virtue ethics provides a logical, practical method of identifying responsibilities to guide ethical decisions.

Professional standards can also provide guidance for identifying public interest reporting responsibilities. The AICPA's Statements on Standards for Tax Service (AICPA 2009) impose a requirement on practitioners that they comply with any standards imposed by a tax authority. Regardless of the level of such standards, the Statements require that practitioners at minimum ensure that any recommended tax positions have a "realistic possibility" of being sustained[9]. The danger of such standards, however, is that they can serve as a means of justifying inappropriate behaviors. Even if a transaction can be structured to artificially meet a minimum threshold, the essence of our proposal is that professionals should be able to look deeper than the technical-compliance surface. Serving the public interest extends beyond meeting the letter of a standard and goes rather to meeting the spirit embodied in the standard. It is for this reason that professionals are afforded the

[9] Interpretation No. 1–1, "Reporting and Disclosure Standards" and Interpretation No. 1–2, "Tax Planning" of Statement on Standards for Tax Services No. 1, *Tax Return Positions* (2011) provide further clarification on the meaning of this standard.

benefit of *self-regulation*; that is, they are trusted to go beyond a legalistic approach and adopt a holistic, professional approach that identifies and fulfills public interest reporting responsibilities.

#### 2.5.1.2 Judgment: Propose a Convincing Solution and Analyze Impacts

The economic, legal and ethical incentives, analyses, and resulting decisions should guide and support the eventual solution. Professional responsibilities should not be compromised in reconciling these analyses and arriving at a final decision. In addition, the benefits, costs and other impacts of the final decision can be assessed.

Analyzing impacts can lead to valuable modifications through an iterative process that improves the eventual solution. The final solution is based on reconciliation of economic incentives, legal incentives, moral incentives and analysis of resulting impacts while not compromising professional or public interest responsibilities.

In the KPMG case, one possible solution is to not market or sell abusive tax shelters since this decision is consistent with public interest ideals and ethical professional responsibilities to serve the public and protect the client by providing accurate and reliable information. In this example, the ethical analysis extends professional reporting responsibilities beyond the legal and economic analyses. Primary benefits are that the public and clients can trust KPMG and tax professionals and the tax profession benefits from public trust created by dutiful fulfillment of professional ideals and responsibilities in the tax system.

Applying tax law and meeting professional public interest responsibilities relies on professional judgment. This decision model gives students an opportunity to practice considering and analyzing different economic, legal and ethical incentives and responsibilities when making professional decisions. A key lesson is that substantively fulfilling professional responsibilities is a confining prerequisite to selecting an action. It is not a burden, but a professional privilege and should become a habitual, natural choice.

## 2.6 Conclusion

There can be little doubt that the accounting profession is facing a fundamental problem. The root of the problem can be found in the loss of the public interest focus of the profession. There is ample evidence that this public interest focus has been replaced by an entirely private interest (economically motivated) focus. In our capitalist system, we need to ask ourselves the question: why does this matter? Quite simply, it matters because we are a profession. It is well established in the literature that professions are given very significant privileges (for example, barriers to entry, creating a higher price for the services provided by the profession) but the *quid pro quo* is that the profession will look not only to its own interests but also the interests of the public more generally. If as a profession we fail to deliver on the latter, we might lose the privileges that go along with being characterized as a profession.

In previous chapters the problems of deprofessionalization were identified. In this chapter, we have drawn on the sociology literature to examine a possible way out of the stasis in which we find ourselves as a profession. The sociology literature is quite clear that change from within a structure is unlikely; rather, the likely outcome is continued replication of the existing structure. What is needed is some external influence that results in a disruption of the normal process of reproducing the current structure. Such a disruption offers an opportunity for individuals to reflect on the current "taken for granted" scripts and allows for a re-awakening of personal ethics and virtues that have become suppressed by the current structure. We suggest that education is an external force with the potential to disrupt the current pattern and set change in motion. Although pre-entry education is essential, we concur with Fogarty (2014) that firm training is an integral part of system change. To achieve this, we argue that there is a vitally important role for independent cross firm education. There is little doubt that this may have adverse implications for firm autonomy and power. Nonetheless the sociology literature on structural change suggests that the extent to which the profession can be revitalized is almost certainly linked to the willingness of the major professional accounting firms to willingly and actively embrace change. What we do next will demonstrate to our society whether we really have a legitimate claim to being a "profession."

## References


Ajzen, I. 1985. From intentions to actions: A theory of planned behavior. In *Action control: From cognition to behavior*, ed. J. Kuhl and J. Beckmann. New York: Springer.

Almer, E.D., J.L. Higgs, and K.L. Hooks. 2005. A theoretical framework of the relationship between public accounting firms and their auditors. *Behavioral Research in Accounting* 17: 1–22.

American Institute of Certified Practicing Accountants (AICPA). 2009. *Statement on standards for Tax services No. 1, Tax return positions*. New York: AICPA.

Asch, S. 1958. Effects of group pressure on the modification and distortion of judgment. In *Readings in social psychology*, ed. E.E. Maccoby, T.M. Newcomb, and E.L. Hartley, 566–575. New York: Holt, Rinehart, & Winston.

Barley, S.R., and P.S. Tolbert. 1997. Institutionalization and structuration: Studying the links between action and institution. *Organization Studies* 18: 93–117.

Bratton, W.W. 2003. Enron, Sarbanes-Oxley and accounting: Rules versus principles versus rents. *Villanova Law Review* 48: 1023–1055.

Bray, C. 2012. Lawyer pleads guilty after winning new trial in tax-shelter fraud case. *Wall Street Journal of Accountancy,* September 13.

Burns, T. 1961. Micropolitics: Mechanisms of institutional change. *Administrative Science Quarterly* 6: 257–281.

Cohen, J.R., and L. Holder-Webb. 2006. Rethinking the influence of agency theory in the accounting academy. *Issues in Accounting Education* 21: 17–30.

Cressey, D. 1953. *Other people's money: A study in the social psychology of embezzlement.* Glencoe: The Free Press.

Dillard, J. 2008. An ethic of accountability. *Research on Professional Responsibility and Ethics in Accounting* 13: 1–18.
Drucker, J. 2010. The tax haven that's saving Google billions. *Bloomberg Business Week*, October 25.
Fogarty, T. 2014. The bloom is off the rose: Deprofessionalization in public accounting. In *Accounting for the public interest: Perspectives on accountability, professionalism and role in society*, ed. S. Mintz. 51–72. Heidelberg: Springer.
Fogarty, T.J., V.S. Radcliffe, and D.R. Campbell. 2006. Accountancy before the fall: The AICPA vision project and related professional enterprises. *Accounting, Organizations and Society* 31(1): 1–25.
Friedman, M. 1962. *Capitalism and freedom*. Chicago: University of Chicago Press.
Gibbons, M., and A. Mason. 1988. *Professional judgment in financial reporting no. CICA research study*. Toronto: CICA.
Giddens, A. 1976. *New rules of sociological method: A positive critique of interpretive sociologies*. London: Hutchinson.
Goshal, S. 2005. Bad management theories are destroying good management practices. *The Academy of Management Learning and Education* 4(1): 75–91.
Hall, R.H. 1967. Some organizational considerations in the professional-organizational relationship. *Administrative Science Quarterly* 12(3): 461–478.
Hall, R.H. 1968. Professionalization and bureaucratization. *Administrative Sociological Review* 33: 92–104.
Hanlon, G. 1994. *The commercialization of accountancy: Flexible accumulation and the transformation of the service class*. London: St. Martin's Press.
Henchman, J. 2008. *Transit agencies in bind due to SILO deals and AIG collapse*. Washington, DC: The Tax Foundation.
Hosmer, L.T. 1984. Managerial ethics and microeconomic theory. *Journal of Business Ethics* 3(4): 315–325.
Hosmer, L.T. 2008. *The ethics of management*, 6th ed. New York: McGraw-Hill.
Kohlberg, L. 1969. Stage and sequence: The cognitive developmental approach to socialization. In *Handbook of socialization theory*, ed. D.A. Goslin, 347–480. Chicago: Rand McNally.
Levitt, S.D., and S.J. Dubner. 2005. *Freakonomics: A rogue economist explores the hidden side of everything*. New York: HarperCollins.
May, W.F. 2001. *Beleaguered rulers: The public obligation of the professional*. Louisville: Westminster John Knox Press.
McKie, J. 1974. Social responsibility and the business predicament. In *Changing views*, ed. J. McKie. Washington, DC: Brookings Institute.
Milgram, Stanley. 1963. Behavioral study of obedience. *Journal of Abnormal and Social Psychology* 67: 371–378.
Minority Staff of the Permanent Subcommittee on Investigations. 2003. *U.S. tax shelter industry: The role of accountants, lawyers, and financial professionals. Four KPMG case studies: FLIP, OPIS, BLIPS, and SC2*. Available at http://levin.senate.gov/newsroom/supporting/2003/111803TaxShelterReport.pdf.
Mintz, S.M. 2010. Linking virtue to representational faithfulness in making judgments in a principles-based environment. *Research on Professional Responsibility and Ethics in Accounting* 14: 113–136.
OECD. 2010. *Tax co-operation 2010: Towards a level playing field*. Paris: OECD. http://dx.doi.org/10.1787/taxcoop-2010-en
Ostrander, T.W. 2003. The offshore credit card and financial arrangement probe: Fraught with danger for taxpayers. *Journal of Taxation* 99: 113–119.
Permanent Subcommittee on Investigations of the Committee on Homeland Security and Governmental Affairs, United States Senate. 2005. *The role of professional firms in the U.S. tax shelter industry*, S. Rept. 109–54. Washington, DC: U.S. Government Printing Office.
Pickard, G. 2005. With integrity and fairness: An interview with Mark W. Everson, Commissioner of Internal Revenue. *Journal of Accountancy* April, 27–32.

Puxty, A., P. Sikka, and H. Willmott. 1994. (Re)forming the circle: Education, ethics and accountancy practices. *Accounting Education* 3(1): 77–92.

Ranson, S., R. Hinings, and R. Greenwood. 1980. The structuring of organizational structures. *Administrative Science Quarterly* 28: 314–337.

Reiter, S.A., and P.F. Williams. 2002. The structure and progressivity of accounting research: The crisis in the academy revisited. *Accounting Organizations and Society* 27: 575–607.

Rosanas, J.M., and M. Velilla. 2005. The ethics of management control systems: Developing technical and moral values. *Journal of Business Ethics* 57: 83–96.

Scott, W.R. 1965. Reactions to supervision in a heteronomous professional organization. *Administrative Science Quarterly* 10: 65–81.

Sellers, R.D., T.J. Fogarty, and L.M. Parker. 2012. Unleashing the technical core: Institutional theory and the aftermath of Arthur Anderson. *Behavioral Research in Accounting* 24: 181–201.

Sewell, W.H. 1992. A theory of structure: Duality, agency, and transformation. *The American Journal of Sociology* 98: 1–29.

Shapiro, L.S. 1986. Professional responsibility in the eyes of the IRS. *The Tax Adviser* 17(3): 136.

Sikka, P. 2008. Enterprise culture and accountancy firms: New masters of the universe. *Accounting, Auditing and Accountability Journal* 21: 268–295.

Sikka, P., and M.P. Hampton. 2005. The role of accountancy firms in tax avoidance: Some evidence and issues. *Accounting Forum* 29(3): 325–343.

Smith, H. 2004. Tax me if you can. *Frontline*, Public Broadcasting Service, http://www.pbs.org/wgbh/pages/frontline/shows/tax/

Stuebs, M.T. 2010. Moral confrontation: An essential companion to moral imagination. *Research on Professional Responsibility and Ethics in Accounting* 14: 57–78.

Stuebs, M.T., and C.W. Thomas. 2011. Principles-based accounting: The case for principled judgment. In *Research on professional responsibility and ethics in accounting*, vol. 15, ed. C. Jeffrey, 47–73. Bingley: Emerald Group.

Toren, N. 1975. Deprofessionalization and its sources. *Sociology of Work and Occupation* 2(4): 323–337.

Tuttle, B., and J. Dillard. 2007. Beyond competition: Institutional isomorphism in U.S. accounting research. *Accounting Horizons* 21(4): 387–409.

Wang, B. 2003. Supplying the tax shelter industry: Contingent fee compensation for accountants spurs production. *Southern California Law Review* 76: 1237–1274.

Watts, R.L., and J.L. Zimmerman. 1986. *Positive accounting theory*. Englewood Cliffs: Prentice Hall.

Wilkerson Jr., J.E. 2010. Accounting educators as the accounting profession's trustees: Lessons from a study of peer professions. *Issues in Accounting Education* 25(1): 1–13.

Williams, P.F., J.G. Jenkins, and L. Ingraham. 2006. The winnowing away of behavioral accounting research in the U.S.: The process for anointing academic elites. *Accounting, Organizations and Society* 31(8): 783–818.

Zeff, S.A. 2003a. How the U.S. Accounting profession got where it is today: Part I. *Accounting Horizons* 17(3): 189–205.

Zeff, S.A. 2003b. How the U.S. Accounting profession got where it is today: Part II. *Accounting Horizons* 17(4): 267–286.

# Chapter 3
# The Bloom Is Off the Rose: Deprofessionalization in Public Accounting

**Timothy J. Fogarty**

There is no shortage of accounts of the grand march of accounting toward professional status. These include the semi-official histories of the large international firms (e.g., Grayson and McDermott 1993) that trace origins to the nineteenth Century British islands, and commemorations of the introduction of accountancy to the curriculum of higher education (Langenderfer 1987). The American Institute of Certified Public Accountants' (AICPA) publication of a centennial edition of the *Journal of Accounting* in 1987 suggested quite strongly that accountancy had joined occupations such as law and medicine as fully-formed professions. Most practitioners accept as a matter of faith that they are members of a profession that is qualitatively different and superior to the managers and marketers with whom they routinely rub shoulders.

The question of what constitutes a profession is quite problematic. Most observers continue to frame the question in terms of critical traits that an occupation must possess (Greenwood 1957). The requisite traits are difficult, if not impossible, to precisely enumerate. Millerson (1964) found very little commonality within 21 occupations in their accumulation of characteristics that writers have suggested critical for professionalism. Early studies of necessary traits removed the process from the acquisition of social esteem, and made the effort seem exclusively within the control over the occupation itself. More theoretically, a belief in mandatory traits has always been aligned with social functionalism, a school of thought that was premised in the notion that an occupation that performed an important function would be more or less automatically rewarded with the incremental privileges of professionalism. This view has more recently given way to a conflict orientation that portrays professionalism as a zero-sum ongoing struggle for work and recognition (Abbott 1988; Kultgen 1988; Saks 1983).

T.J. Fogarty (✉)
Department of Accounting, Weatherhead School of Management,
Case Western Reserve University, Cleveland, OH 44106, USA
e-mail: tjf@case.edu

S. Mintz (ed.), *Accounting for the Public Interest: Perspectives on Accountability, Professionalism and Role in Society*, Advances in Business Ethics Research 4,
DOI 10.1007/978-94-007-7082-9_3, © Springer Science+Business Media Dordrecht 2014

The purpose of this chapter is not to again cover this terrain. The idea of a profession is sufficiently debatable to render continued discussion of absolute status somewhat pointless. If one conceives of the important phenomenon as the process whereby occupations must continue to strive for social esteem, it does not matter whether we call some a profession and deny that label to others. All occupations are engaged in a purposeful change process that is well-worthy of study. The extent to which such change accomplishes or frustrates the public interest presents a dimension to which both insiders and outsiders should be attentive.

Moore (1970) asserts that professional identity can be expected to form in proportion to the degree that optimal conditions exist for such a development. One would expect this also would be true for the professional community as a whole. Accordingly, this chapter outlines ideal societal circumstances for specialized knowledge, community, self-regulation, practitioner autonomy and public interest dedication. This template then is used to assess recent developments in the accounting profession, as seen in the practice of public accounting. For present purposes, the accounting profession is limited to its public practice since such a modality represents the purest form of practice (Abbott 1988).

This chapter argues that accounting is no longer in ascendency. Wherever accounting currently is positioned on the professional continuum is less important than the fact that it is deprofessionalizing. The forces that contribute to this conclusion are sufficiently strong and pervasive so as to render our continued belief in classic professionalism a potentially harmful ideology. As deprofessionalization progresses, accounting's service to the public interest is endangered.

The balance of this chapter is organized into six sections. The first five establishes the dimensions of professionalization. This effort organizes the progress in these arenas for the accounting domain. This application features the dedication of accountancy to the public interest. The last section contextualizes the analysis in a broader spectrum, and offers concluding remarks that point toward future research.

## 3.1 Specialized Knowledge

The *sine qua non* of a profession is their ability to solve important problems for a clientele that is willing to pay for their solutions (Freidson 1970). Professionals help the laity understand the nature of their situation in ways that are amenable to the diagnoses proffered by practitioners. At any point in time, the means-ends relationships that are embraced by professional knowledge exist in competition with other occupations that are working toward the acceptability of alternatives (Abbott 1988). Successful professions are those that can, by virtue of the grants of government or by open competition, get the work. Thus, the expertise available to the profession serves as an important and intuitive first dimension of professional claims.

Professions vary in the extent that their knowledge bases are convincing and scientific. In addition to their willingness to use their skills for the public good, those that enjoy a governmentally created monopoly over certain domains needed to have excellent bodies of knowledge that could rationalize the foreclosure of others from operation in those areas (Freidson 1986). One of the hallmarks of such a powerful corpus of expertise is the need that trainees spend a long period of time in formal study to master its intricacies (Larson 1977).

The knowledge of the professions tends not to be exclusively scientific. Since it only exists in the way that it is operationalized by practitioners, knowledge resides in the shared understanding developed in professional socialization. A particularly stylized language that has been sanctioned for use, especially when communicating with the clientele, tends to conform behavior to vested interests (Edelman 1977), as well as mystify the proceedings. Behavior consistent with the language makes the shared understandings of the profession real in ways that the uninitiated fail to grasp (see Fischer 1996; Gill 2009).

The imperfections and inadequacies in the technical knowledge and abilities of the professional may convey an advantage beyond mystification. The indeterminacy of professional knowledge prevents external parties from reducing it to canned protocols that could be efficiently encroached. At the margins of knowledge, professionals must possess the right values. The right values are those believed to be harmonious with the use of technical knowledge (Weber 1968).

Professional knowledge should transmit some degree of client control to the armed practitioner. The exact configuration of this dependency can vary among the professions since they have different structures and activities (Bidwell and Vreland 1963). Nonetheless, a degree of jurisdictional warfare will always exist since professions will naturally overextend their claims to authority. At the periphery, clients have more choices among professionalized providers. How problems are defined by clients often exceed the true diagnostic powers of any professional group.

### *3.1.1 Specialized Accounting Knowledge in Accounting*

On its face, the knowledge possessed by accountants would seem to qualify as simultaneously abstract and specialized (Hodson and Sullivan 1995). Their ability to deploy it on behalf of clients should meaningfully reduce client uncertainty about the classification and consequence of transactions and enhance the usefulness of financial reporting. Accountants would seem to be the classic knowledge professionals who richly deserve their monopoly power over their clients. However, the existence of such knowledge does not preclude its erosion, a usual precondition of deprofessionalization (Toren 1975).

Professions like accounting walk a thin line with regards to their knowledge. Richardson (1988) articulates the central problem in terms of an indeterminacy ratio. Professions are obliged to provide reasonably reliable solutions. However, answers can neither be made too mechanical nor too idiosyncratic. Accounting seems to have done well, simultaneously having a reputation for certainty, but a reality of flexibility. This duality deserves the mystique that accounting possesses (Burns and Haga 1977).

Basic philosophic questions exist about how well accountants have managed the judgments that are needed for their historically primary product, the audit. Dyckman (1974) finds the theoretical canon and application rules to be insufficiently defensible because of their non-optimality. Power (1995) goes further, ironically pointing out that audits are accountability dead ends that ultimately insist that constituents just trust the audit experts.

Most would agree that the profession has not invested adequately to improve audit procedures, a position long since advocated (e.g., Olson 1978). Had more effort been made to make audits more effective would have led to better codification of audit standards. As is, audit standards have not led practice but merely followed its justification of higher degrees of efficiency. Standards do not conclusively express the duties of auditors to the public, and often are only able to document the preferred positions of audit firms more interested in escaping legal liability for their work.

The standard audit report illustrates the forced conformity resorted to by a profession unsure of their knowledge base (see Alvesson 1993). Audit reports, offering only boilerplate conclusions, operate presumably at the symbolic level, communicating an unspoken expertise (Van Maanen and Pentland 1994) that has led some to conjecture about what the audit can actually accomplish (Fogarty et al. 1991; Sikka and Willmott 1995a, b). Periodic proposed revisions to the standard audit report continue to be made, as if they were not only minor changes that still refuse to communicate what knowledge had been brought to bear by the auditors.

Rather than suffering for its knowledge problem, public accounting is able to loosely couple the process from the output, obtaining more power over client as the result (Humphrey and Moizer 1990). Avoiding scientific techniques confers a higher status on the auditor as a risk expert whose expertise is not open to critical scrutiny (Power 1995).

Facing a dubious ability and questionable incentive to make audits more effective, public accounting firms have invested considerable resources in making audits more efficient. Much formal logic, involving budgets for time and the sequence of steps to be taken, have been deployed in the process of ensuring the economy of effort. The process of "taking time out of the audit" continues to be accomplished in a variety of ways that involve depending more on the work done by others and eschewing time-intensive compliance testing. In that judgment is difficult to use in such an environment, auditors may have been partially deskilled. Judgment has been bypassed through many changes that would make today's audit work unrecognizable to Mautz and Sharef (1961). Without fully deployed judgment, auditors are less able to contribute to the highest and best aspects of professional work. As such, to claim that auditors are even knowledge workers (Brint 1997) may be an overstatement. In fact, career advancement in public accounting tends to depend more on economic criteria than on wisdom attained (Hanlon 1996).

The tendency of accountants to stray too far from their core monopoly has also caused deprofessionalization tension. Although some believe that creativity and professionalism can be harmonized (e.g., Al-Beraidi and Rickards 2006), the motif of the profession for many decades has been one of conservatism. The idea that accountants should serve as a constraint upon the reckless tendencies of capitalism is deeply embedded in the public interest elements mapped out for the profession. Although this attribute is often soft-pedalled as objective and reliable information that provides insight into economic substance (e.g., Becker et al. 1961), the work of accountants is expected by external users to be skewed in the conservative direction as a bulwark against those with the most to gain from pushing the reality envelope. Instead of investing in way to better meet these expectations, accountants continuously have attempted to re-engineer the audit as a consulting engagement (Jepperson 1998). The existence of highly profitable work within public accounting has led to the questioning of the value of traditional competencies and the worth of those that possessed them (Wyatt 2004). Although one could argue that a deepening of the skill set for some accountants (consultants) offsets the deskilling of others (auditors), that which is unique to accountants becomes compromised.

The remaking of accounting firms around the dictates of the market also has distinct consequences for the individual. The career value of technical excellence (mastery of the knowledge of the profession) tends to be confined to early stages. Beyond that point, high levels of competence in leveraging the talents of lower wage staff become a currency of the realm. However, the major reward (equity partnership) is reserved for those capable of generating revenue. In a sales culture, social competence and social class are much more valuable than differential technical prowess (Hanlon 1996). To the extent that the public interest only can be furthered by the willingness of accountants to stand up for good accounting, it is diminished when subjugated to client economic interests in their use of accounting (Belkaoui 1989).

In sum, serious questions have developed about the knowledge claims currently made by public accountants, especially as they pertain to audit work. Traditional vectors of commodification-based erosion have combined with idiosyncratic forms of redirection to create a unique deprofessionalizing force.

## 3.2 Community of Practice

The second major attribute of professions is their ability to construct and maintain a community of practice. People in the professions should feel such affinity to each other that they look to each other for patterns of values and beliefs that are needed to supplement and interpret those that have been officially adopted by the community. In other words, true professions form reference groups whose collective judgments are consequential in determining the normative content of behavior (Van Maanen and Bailey 1984).

Like technical expertise, community depends heavily upon formal socialization for its inception. People are not born into the profession but instead must learn its unique ways. Educational experiences that verge toward proverbial "total institutions" (Goffman 1961) are quite powerful in the consequence of creating a community of practice. This effort includes systematic training provided by employing organizations, especially as a prelude to the actual performance of duties. These experiences are important to the extent that they crystalize the values that practitioners are expected to internalize (Merton 1957).

The idea of a professional community has varied in the exclusivity intended. Certainly, each strives to be a world of their own, marking out a symbolic space with customs, practices and a historic legacy (Carr-Saunders and Wilson 1933). Barber (1963) argues that in the wider societal sense, professions are social movements struggling for power, managing their public image, and attempting to control the arenas in which their work is performed.

Professions that function as communities provide members with a personal identity of not only specialness from others, but also superiority (Harring 1976). These perceptions transform the work to be performed into a calling whose righteousness transcends that of the ordinary work performed by outsiders. This state is psychologically facilitated if practitioners share a fellowship of suffering on their journey to membership to in the heroic pursuit of client advantage (Moore 1970).

Many mechanisms play parts in the furtherance of professional community. For some, the legal system provides ongoing monitoring of member adherence to the standards of behavior that were assented to upon admission. Trade associations that sponsor meetings and publish journals are instrumental in fostering colleague consciousness (Gross 1958). More generally, the existence of an in-group language tends to reinforce the knowledge that one has to be an insider to know what transpires in a profession (Moore 1970). Shared language causes the renewed daily commitment of a deeper symbolic appreciation (Barber 1963).

The professional community provides members with an alternative to the formal hierarchy of employing institutions. Professions assert some degree of equality for all members and therefore exist at odds with bureaucracies (Hall 1975). This tension will have different consequences for autonomous professional organizations and for heterogeneous ones. The latter differs from the former most importantly in whether clients need to be pursued from the public. When professionals are asked to serve as a unit of a larger entity, professional culture can be more difficult to sustain (Bloor and Dawson 1994). More generally, organizational formalization may have complex consequences on the attitudes needed for professionalism (Podsakoff et al. 1986).

### *3.2.1 Community of Accounting Practice*

That people selling accounting services to the public join organizations organized for this purpose creates a built-in association of professionals. However, the economic ties between such individuals, be it as co-claimants on residual income or as one paying a salary to others, tends to disqualify such an association as an attribute of professionalism. Voluntary associations among accountants that are financially autonomous produce much stronger evidence that the profession serves as a meaningful basis of affiliation.

As organized by state societies, accountants do involve themselves in the affairs of the profession. Increasingly however, the overall rate of volunteerism has been in decline for some time (Estes 1990). Whereas those activities that pursue some promotional or branding advantages for the profession are over-subscribed, other good causes find little involvement from accountants. Practice development pressure puts a premium on opportunities to associate with potential clients, and therefore limits incentives to form affiliations with fellow accountants. Even more difficulty exists to staff volunteer positions at the national level. As things become more removed from the prospects of clear economic advantage, they become more problematic.

Burrage et al. (1990) attribute the power of a profession to its life time duration for practitioners. Because they have no other reasonable alternative, people in the strongest professions invest heavily into it. Part of this process is surrounding oneself with similarly situated others. As a boundary spanning endeavor, accounting fares poorly in this regard. Accountants are attracted by opportunities in general management, and therefore are drawn away from the community of practice. The possession of specialized accounting ability makes accountants valuable for higher managerial positions. Such a directional alternative tends to reduce accountants involvement in their chosen field as they reach mid-career.

The ability of accountants to form a meaningful collective is limited by the large size differences that exists in their employing organizations. Unlike professions that are usually practiced in rather small groups, accountancy has been marked for many decades by the existence of very large organizations that operate on a global scale. These size disparities have many consequences for the individual. Career management in the large firms becomes a highly bureaucratized exercise with many alternative paths and political quagmires. It bears little resemblance to the quite democratic and non-hierarchical professional ideal. People in the large firms are socialized into a set of professional assumptions quite distinct from other accountants. They are led to believe that they have little in common with practitioners in other practice segments. Rewards and other career outcomes are thus distributed according to one's position in a stratified profession rather than in accordance with performance or merit (see Podolny 1993). This schism tends to erode any meaningful profession-wide community.

All professions need a single organization that represents their collective interests to the outside world. Following some degree of early entity rivalry (see Edwards and Miranti 1987), the mantle of such leadership fell to the American Institute of Certified Public Accountants (AICPA). The task of representing members from all segments of practice with a "big tent" entity is not an easy one, especially as the practice terrain expands. Unfortunately, the AICPA has not been very facile in managing internal tensions. Their inability to recognize the interests of accountants that work outside of public practice has led to the formation of several rival organizations. The AICPA is generally perceived to be overly concerned with the interests of the larger firms (Henry and McNamee 2003).

The global reach of business has not led to progress toward a global accountancy profession. Although big firm practice requires co-ordination across national boundaries, little movement has occurred that would reshape accountancy as a transnational community. The profession still has to employ cumbersome work-arounds to perform basic work in other nations. In fact, US practice still has not resolved multi-state practice. Notwithstanding achievable efficiency advantages, the profession still remains a creature of political jurisdiction.

The large firms have long since stopped believing that they are defined by their common grounding in the accounting discipline. They have formed new types of communities that are organized around what they can sell to their clients. For some time, the large firms have recognized that since problems are multi-dimensional, they needed expertise well beyond accounting They employed experts of all sorts (i.e., lawyers, engineers, actuaries) by offering these people the chance to share in the profits of the firm. Movement away from accounting as the *sine qua non* of fully vested membership has diluted the nature of accounting professionalism (Wyatt 2004). The ability to contribute to gross profit margins has replaced common training or values adherence as the basis of the new brotherhood.

The new community that exists among accountants is not one of equals. Instead, a virtual corporate form of some accountants managing the careers of others has emerged. How this new model embraces professional admission is quite telling. Successful passage of the CPA examination and the obtaining of full certification has become less important to the firm. Firms, rather than being the foremost advocate of the process, now view it as a bothersome constraint or distraction that employees need to attend to early in their careers. Although the completion of the exam still serves as a strong signal of personal accomplishment, the firms have essentially abandoned the belief that it contributes to the value of an employee.

The large firms also have become increasingly corporate in their management of human resources. In order to support an expanded need for partner compensation (see Covaleski et al. 1998), these organizations had to depart further from the apprenticeship ideal wherein junior members of the firm would be carefully groomed for succession. The line between equity holders and employees has hardened with reduced concerns for mentorship and turnover. Public accounting became increasingly like corporations with layoffs and other hardnosed recruitment practices that had never been seen before. Public accounting never had to develop paraprofessions as did law and medicine precisely because those that were recruited each year were seen as junior employees until they proved their right to broader recognition.

In sum, strong reservations exist about how well accounting functions as a professional community. Although economic pressures have played a large role in making such a network of affiliations unaffordable, one is entitled to wonder how successful this field has ever been in this regard. In that the large firms set the tone, the community of accountants has become indistinguishable from the community of any businesses' employees.

## 3.3 Self-Regulation Ideology

The third dimension of a profession is the assertion of self-regulation as a normative feature. Successful professions have achieved the ability to police their own practitioners with a set of rules of their own construction. All professions must assert that self-regulation is superior to control by external groups or through more general societal mechanisms.

The case for self-regulation is grounded in the specialized knowledge of professionals. Those lacking in awareness of diagnostic routines and the limits of prescription should be loathe to declare standards for acceptable work and the protection of the public. Only those fully immersed in the means by which practitioners absorb uncertainty are deemed to have rule-making credibility and the ability to recognize deviant behavior.

Despite this logic, self-regulation is not self-evident as enlightened public policy. Perhaps as a product of their self-contained community, professionals have demonstrated a reluctance to create standards for practices that are effective at balancing the interests of insiders and outsiders. Self-regulation tends to prove the wisdom of George Bernard Shaw's aphorism that all professions are conspiracies against the public. Left to police themselves, professions tend to be quite indulgent of deviations from ideal behavior and very reluctant to deny anyone who has been admitted to the brotherhood, the continued right to practice the trade (Lieberman 1978).

The dispute about self-regulation has far reaching consequences beyond possible punishment for negligent practice. Self-regulation often results in the elimination of alternative modes of practice, including the more casual (e.g., part-time) and hybrid forms (Freidson 1970). This tendency regularizes practice and routinizes control over it. Whether or not self-regulation increases the quality of professional performance is a more complex question. To the extent that self-regulation empowers professionals to coordinate a fragmented task environment, higher levels of effectiveness are possible (Flood and Scott 1978) but not inevitable.

The ability of a profession to establish the very standards by which its performance should be judged is quite consequential to its success. Saks (1983) asserts that this control can be used to shape the external environment to a profession's advantage. The basic strategy is to carve out sufficient room for successful operation while convincing external parties that proper restraints are in place. Unfortunately, societal willingness to defer to experts and to grant them monopolies over critical areas of decision making has reduced over time, and thereby serves as a deprofessionalizing threat (Rothman 1984).

### 3.3.1 Self-Regulatory Ideology in Accounting

Accountants have historically controlled both the standards of acceptable financial reporting and rules regarding the conduct of audits. Although the former could never be more definitive than a "generally acceptable" set of choices, and the latter usually did not do much more than record good practice, they represented a solid expression of professorial expertise over important domains. In normal times, external parties in the public and private sectors were content to cede this control to the accounting profession. However, following the Enron and Arthur Andersen debacles of 2001–2002, the self-regulation privilege was lost. A new era began with external control by the Public Companies Accounting Oversight Board (PCAOB) in charge.

The loss of exclusive control over conduct of practice is a classic indication of deprofessionalization (Toren 1975). The takeover of professional oversight by the government as dictated by the Sarbanes Oxley Act of 2002 amounted to no less. The newly formed PCAOB usurped much of the self-regulation that existed in the profession. Although the body will be hard-pressed to materially improve the process of auditing, the symbolic loss of self-determination was a bellwether moment. Even the most favorable interpretation of this change would leave one with the idea that a harsh rebuke of accounting self-regulation occurred.

Financial accounting standards had long since stopped being a pursuit of the best ways to report economic reality, although such remained as a constraint and as an official ideology. The realization that sizeable economic consequences were at stake meant that accounting standards became highly political (Zeff 1978). Accounting organizations, in such an environment, did not act as the voice of reason, but instead took positions known to be favored by existing or potential clients. In that the professional community did not often initially push for good standards, retroactive complaint about them by public accounting firms have fallen on deaf ears (Wyatt 2004).

Auditing standard setting might appear to outsiders as a deductive exercise utilizing the collective wisdom to find the best means to obtain sufficient evidence to support an audit opinion. However, they often are revealed to be exercises in rationalizing existing practice. Only with great reluctance did the public accounting firms that participated in this process consent to reduce their degrees of freedom by mandating a particular procedure. More attention was paid to the documentation of decisions than in clarifying the ways in which decisions should be made. Auditing standards were sufficiently flexible so as to not preclude the high levels of risk taken by audit firms in client selection and ultimate opinion choice.

For many years, the oversight of quality had been an important function of the profession. Peer review had been accepted as a response to audit failures, wherein accounting firms submitted to a program of quality review managed by the profession. That great efforts were taken to avoid public disclosure of results and to minimize sanctioning power illustrate the ambivalence of this consent. With the overthrow of self-regulation, a potentially coercive and more public process has been instituted. In the hands of the PCAOB, quality would aspire to more than the ability to keep the corporate clientele returning for an ever-expanding set of services.

The self-regulation process in professions includes the obligation of disciplining members that fall from the straight and narrow path. To do this, professions maintain and enforce a code of ethics that supplements the conduct expected of the laity. The belief that every group effectively polices themselves inspires confidence and justifies non-intervention. The accounting profession has long been known as particularly reluctant to discipline its members (Abraham 1978). For some time, external pressure has been needed to generate significant prosecution (Dyckman 1974). As enforced, the code of ethics tends to protect accountants from excess competition (Loeb 1972) and to deflect criticism from the profession (Canning and O'Dwyer 2001). Although the externalization of regulation as it relates to publicly held clients has the potential to curb some of the worse abuses, the situation exhibits inadequate professionalism at its core. The myth that all accounting practitioners have competence and integrity well above the acceptable level continues to be strong.

In summary, the story of self-regulation in accounting is a rather sad one. Disruptive economic events triggered crises of confidence that exposed the fragility of how accounting choice was constrained and how auditing was conducted. The wide net of reform also cast question upon the ongoing effort to improve firm quality and sanction individual deviance. The idea that external parties are more likely to pursue the public interest has brought about a severe deprofessionalization.

## 3.4 Autonomy Demands

Self-regulation at the profession-wide level translates into the demand for autonomy at the individual practitioner level. Classic professionalism entails vesting full authority to the individual to use the knowledge of the discipline on behalf of clients, and to be unfettered by a supervision that tempers such exercises of judgment, especially from those not cut from the same cloth (Hall 1968).

That professionals should be given maximum autonomy rests upon the premise that a large proportion of professional work is non-standard (Hall 1975). Unlike the tasks performed by many occupations, a mechanical solution cannot be accessed when so much indeterminacy is inevitable. The very idea of a profession is so closely intertwined with the exercise of judgment that the ability to do so is essential to organizational commitment (Wallace 1995). The autonomy to exercise judgment is also believed to be essential to the job satisfaction of the professional (Raelin 1989; Meiksins and Watson 1989). Thus, in a perfect world, individual practitioners are primarily motivated by their ability to pursue the goals of the profession, most notably as they further the public interest.

Our very imperfect modern world has strongly attached the practice of the professions to their ability to organize as businesses. Rather than being incidental to the practitioner, the organizational form imposes bureaucratic control. To some extent, the autonomy at the heart of professionalism is incompatible with the hierarchical discipline that bureaucracies entail. Undeniably however, the latter brings levels of quality control needed for the guarantee of organizational predictability (Ross and Duff 1978). Modern professional socialization must blend the commonality of the profession with the specificity of the employing organization. The organization offers many rewards, including career advancement, in exchange for surrendering degrees of autonomy (Van Maanen and Bailey 1984). The orientation toward the role configured by the needs of the organization is likely to diminish the professional orientation over time (Corwin 1961). Rather than continue to suffer role conflict, practitioners are likely to forget the autonomy claims that came with their status as professionals (Wade 1967). As autonomy is diminished, the distinctiveness of the profession declines, perhaps to the point when the transcendent obligation of being a moral actor seems quaint and superfluous.

### 3.4.1 Autonomy Demands of Accountants

Classic professionalism wears thinnest in the modern world when the autonomy demands of individual practitioners are concerned. Our conception of the modern accountant is more likely to be as an employee in a large firm, and less likely to be a sole-practitioner. In other words it has become increasingly difficult to imagine an accountant that is not subject to the autonomy-limiting demands of the firm that they represent.

The gravitation of accountants to larger group practice modes now makes the notion that professionalism might be unable to thrive in bureaucratic settings seem a rather dated inquiry. Nearer in time to the start of this trend, researchers investigated the conflict between the two, measuring deprivation in their perception of adequate professionalism (e.g., Sorensen 1967; Sorensen and Sorensen 1974). Now that bureaucratic professional organizations are much better accepted, such a conflict is much less likely to be expressed. Accordingly, subsequent work has questioned the extent that individual accountants even want autonomy as a decision-maker (Norris and Niebuhr 1983). Nonetheless, the loss of autonomy is part of professional deskilling (Shaw 1987), that is more extreme in accounting because it is so unproblematic.

The epitome of professional autonomy in accounting occurs when a practitioner refuses to cooperate with a client who wants a particular treatment that is inconsistent with authoritative guidance. In addition to incurring the displeasure of the client, this accountant may have to confront resistance from firm members regarding this stand. When all practitioners invoke a personal set of standards that delineates lines that they what they will not cross, the firm's reputation cannot be determined. Thus, full personal autonomy does not appear to be a profit maximizing strategy (Brooks 1999) in a world that thrives on firm branding.

Firms of professionals can be expected to establish collective positions by attempting to anticipate the tension between client preferences and their appreciation of what is correct. This effort will be both imperfect and incomplete, often forcing the individual to choose between the dictates of their conscience and the profit-maximizing outcome. The struggle in accounting is likely to be extreme, given the dearth of clarity in standards and ethical codes (see Gill 2009).

Accountants in public practice tend to be supervised by other accountants, and therefore have a sympathetic audience for their judgment dilemmas. The growing segments of practitioners employed by corporations often do not have that luxury. This employment situation maximizes the difficulty for even limited professional autonomy (Hall 1975). Accountants are likely to have to enter into power struggles with other groups for whom the integrity of accounting is not a central concern (Montagna 1974).

The real autonomy concern in the accounting profession involves the problem of excessive connection to the client. This presents itself as a manifestation of the unique institutional separation between the entity benefiting from the service and the entity purchasing it. For audit engagements, independence represents the essential value offered by the professional to society. Accordingly, the greatest image problem suffered by the profession involves independence compromises (Strier 2006). Independence by auditors can also be in the best interests of clients, offering them protection from their tendencies to self-destruct in the pursuit of fleeting short-term advantages (Wyatt 2004).

A variety of circumstances conspired to make audit independence difficult to maintain. As clients increasingly looked toward Wall Street and subjected themselves to the task of meeting earnings expectations, auditors became co-conspirators who championed client interest, usually by allowing management to put the best possible face on corporate performance. For such loyalty accounting firms were rewarded handsomely, in part with the opportunity to be the favored provider of an ever-increasing panoply of non-audit services (Hanlon 1996; Stevens 1991). The deviation of effort from the core societal monopoly privilege tends to weaken professional status (Toren 1975). However, for accountants the opportunity to share corporate wealth on an unprecedented level for other services has been more than compensatory.

Independence as a historically espoused value could not be disavowed, and therefore had to be redefined. Essentially, the public was instructed to ignore the appearances of conflicts of interest (Jepperson 2002). At the same time, the profession challenged external parties to produce empirical evidence of actual losses caused by independence compromises (Fogarty and Rigsby 2010). The new version of independence tended to be subscribed to by younger accountants and by those in public accounting (Gendron et al. 2006). Although the aggressive posturing of the new thinking about independence event fell into abeyance following the accounting crisis of the early 2000s, the circumstances that make it economically advantageous continue to exist.

In summary, the idea that accounting firms had to have a size commensurate with their clientele has altered the usual meaning of autonomy within the profession. Autonomy demands are still made by individuals that perceived the conflict between the needs of their firms and the normative position taken by the profession (Shafer et al. 2002). However, the unique social purpose of the audit calls for the revision of our conceptualization of autonomy. In this appreciation, we should include the profession's connections to its clientele.

## 3.5 Public Interest Dedication

The final, and perhaps most important criteria of the classic view on professionalism involves the expectation that practitioners make positive contributions to the public interest. Professions invariably operate in areas of great concern and sensitivity for those they serve. That much depends upon the caliber of professional services illustrates the trust that is invariably involved. Work in furtherance of the public interest can range from the minimal "do no harm" to a more proactive expectation of *pro bono* contributions to the disenfranchised.

Most of the difficulty with the pursuit of the public interest lies in its problematic juxtaposition with private interests. Most professionals have made extensive investments in their education and skill development, and therefore feel entitled to ample pecuniary returns. Such a pursuit consumes large amounts of the professional's time and attention. However, this striving may also cause a shift in values that allow less room for serving the good of the whole society, even on a theoretical basis. Often the public interest is amorphous and can be redefined so that it is not at odds with private interests. When the rhetoric that supports such a merger of convenience colonize the mainstream discourse, the degree to which the social contract, wherein society must be made better by the actions of its professionals, is legitimately put at issue.

### *3.5.1 Public Interest Dedication of Accountants*

Accountants tend to be honorable citizens who work tirelessly, avoid legal trouble and pay their taxes. However, to the extent that their chosen profession has been given special privileges, accountants can be expected to make larger societal contributions.

Collectively, accountants should work toward the protection of the integrity of the capital markets. Ensuring that information is reliable prevents capitalism from its own worse tendency, and safeguards the operation of Adam Smith's invisible hand. However, casting accountants in the role as the guardians of a sacred trust became more precarious when they started to see corporate managers as their true clients. This subtle shift justified resolving the benefit of the doubt in accounting and auditing judgments in favor of management (Olson 1978) and being unable to admit that alternative perspectives on the public interest are possible (Abraham 1978). Given the existence of many stakeholders who are influenced by corporate actions, this alignment cannot be taken as anything but partisan. The support of a nominally independent, highly respected profession such as accounting legitimizes current management, but tends to put accounting at risk in the process.

The public interest, however ambiguously defined, tends to be trotted out following the more egregious shortfalls by professionals. The aftermath of "Enron et al." was no exception, led by the declaration of a "new accounting culture" that would restore the pursuit of an unsullied and unvarnished public interest (see Melancon 2002). The effort that the Financial Times (2003) called "chasing the moral high ground" was compromised from its inception by accounting firm reluctance to shed consulting arms. Subsequent analyzes revealed significant undercurrents wherein accountants, also attempted to evade responsibility and diminish the offensiveness of their actions (Rogers et al. 2005).

The furtherance of the public interest may no longer be part of the culture of public accounting. Unlike other professions such as the law (see Schmedemann 2008), accounting does not attract talent predisposed toward *pro bono publico*. Public interest contributions are not well articulated during the formal education and training of accountants (Olson 1978). How much room exists for these notions in an atmosphere that prioritizes technical expertise (see Hanlon 1996) is debatable. A more profound inconsistency resides in subsequent occupational socialization. For many firms, the cultural dictum that the worst evil is a lost client (Abraham 1978) reduces the space for alternative expressions of the public interest. The prevailing attitude that only those elements of the public interest that can be pursued profitably deserve to survive illustrate that more expansive ideas about the public interest will have an uphill struggle in today's public accounting.

## 3.6 Discussion

The classic view of professionalism invites consideration of its ongoing relevance in the modern world. If we can assume that five attributes considered in this section adequately surround the concept of professionalism, one can readily observe some degree of tension with other aspirations of social organization that we currently prefer. If we need to step back and ask what set of dimensions would do better, we would likely find a similar oppositional tendency. The decline of traditional professionalism in accounting appears to be so pervasive as to call for broader rationales. Social change of such proportion and parallelism is likely to be a response to broader alterations in cultural organization.

Bledstein (1967) argues that professionalism protects the middle class against corporate capitalism by conferring a degree of honor, dignity and security upon its members. By providing the economy with the deep expertise valued by many, the professions coexisted with corporate wealth in the modern economy (Halliday 1983). This arrangement appears to have ruptured in the case of accounting. Accounting knowledge and those that sell it have been excessively subjugated to economic interests to the point that accounting becomes more of a tool of capital, and less a body of external fact.

Many writers have suggested that changes in economic organizations represent fundamental reasons for the alterations that have been discussed in this chapter. For example, Belkaoui (1991) argues that accounting has had to respond to escalating contradictions grounded in globalization, situationalization and proletarianism. Along these lines, postmodern economists have suggested that we have entered a phase of "flexible accumulation" in the extraction of profits from activity (see Hanlon 1996). A full examination of this question is beyond the scope of this chapter. Suffice it to say that the economic and social realms that had been carefully intertwined by professionalism have now been more tightly coupled.

Ritzer and Walczak (1988), in a study of the medical world, offer the spread of formal economic rationality as the main cause of modern deprofessionalization. In subsequent work, Ritzer (1993, 2002) proposed a more formal theory about modern capitalism that he called McDonaldization whose core dimensions involve the pursuit of efficiency, the transition to calculatability, the insistence upon predictability across operations, and the emergence of control through non-human technology. These ideas may form the larger picture of how accounting professionalism now is being reshaped.

Another broad societal trend that has some explanatory power is the privatization of public goods. Gradually, people in positions of power have come to the realization that the organization of the accounting profession could be reconfigured to produce higher amounts of wealth for those who could engineer such a transition. The first stage of this change was the emergence of a small number of large firms that could form a collective will that simultaneously would be different than the unorganized masses of accountants, but also leverage their normative status. Fueled by a globalization that legal reform facilitated, mergers and acquisitions created concerns that never before existed for an increasingly full time set of managers of these enterprises (e.g., CPA Partners Report 2000). Those who spoke on behalf of the profession could only exist if they directly or indirectly contributed to the new agenda of making profit, sometimes in novel ways (see MacDonald 2002).

This chapter focuses on developments at the highest level of analysis. Professions are large scale organizations that exist in a field with the business organizations that buy their services. At the same time, professionalism also has meaning at the individual level. For example, Palmer (1914) asserted that professionalism is principally a state of mind. More recently, several writers have professionalism as an orientation that may be implicated in the nomological network of outcomes such as satisfaction, organizational commitment and turnover (Bartol 1979; Hall et al. 2005; Goetz et al. 1991). The integration of these levels represents the challenge for the literature. Whereas individuals are provided interaction possibilities as defined by organizational and institutional structure, they also enact that structure (Giddens 1984). Thus, professionalism is neither completely a given state to the staff accountant, nor are they completely free to reinvent it for themselves (see also Regan 1999).

The events described in this chapter are a small part of the larger evolution of the place of systemic accounting knowledge in society. Because depictions of early times in accounting professionalism are virtually unrecognizable to us today (e.g., Walker 2000), we should expect that future changes will also render today's arrangements historically limited. We should expect globalized redefinition of the business professions. As part of the next stage, we might also anticipate a more active role of government. As long as states are able to dictate the proper degree of competition between private sector entities, there will be consequences for the profitability of accounting activity. In many ways, the enhanced legitimacy of wide-open competition in a financial sector has undergirded the deprofessionalization we have witnessed in recent times. Because this mandate has not been accompanied by diminished compensation (but see Rothman 1984), few in accounting have complained.

Alternatively, the deprofessionalization of accounting implies the end of the accounting profession as a construct separate from, and transcendent above, accounting firms. To the extent that wealth can be converted into power, movement to burnish the elements of accounting professionalism that are inconvenient, or just non-contributory to further wealth creation, can be expected. If, as Cooper and Robson (2006) argue, the sites of professionalization have been relocated to the firms, we continue to miss the point by even speaking of professionalism in terms that are broader than these businesses. We should instead study how the firm's enact their self-serving versions of professionalism.

This chapter has not stressed the role of education. However, people come to believe some things and disbelieve others not by magic or because the truth has been revealed to them. Students could learn to crave the rare and intrinsic joys of professional status just as much as the more tangible and extrinsic rewards of organizational position. A more sustained focus on socialization is needed if we are to get past the mere fact that people believe some things, and not others, about their roles. We need to reach the questions of why they believe it. Formal education could serve as a counterbalance to the deprofessionalism observed in this chapter by resisting trends that would squeeze out ethicality and reinterpret independence. A first step would be to better appreciate how firm training either enhances or contradicts pre-recruitment education (Fogarty 2000; Anderson-Gough et al. 2002). Although this work threatens to widen the schism between accounting professors and practitioners, such a consequence would seem preferable to being part of the machinery bringing about an inhospitable new world order.

This chapter addressed the practice of public accounting. Although it often spoke of the accounting profession as if no other sector existed, the chapter did not explicitly intend to generalize to other modalities of practice. People doing accounting work, some of whom are fully licensed, may be found in many occupational classifications, and may be paid by many types of entities. That some sectors might be experiencing their highest level of professionalism is entirely possible. Such an analysis needs to be left to other authors.

The attempt to resurrect professionalism as a serious academic inquiry is itself rather retrograde. Most younger academics would be surprised by the volume of writing that appeared in both the practitioner (e.g., Olson 1978; Thompson 1982; Black 1982) and the academic (e.g., Burns and Haga 1977; Smith 1990) literatures a generation ago. That professionalism is the rhetorical divide now used to understand and deflect crises within the industry (e.g., Carmichael 2003; Wyatt 2004) suggests that the construct still possesses "juice" worthy of academic pursuit.

Every profession has its own story to tell, as it attempts to negotiate its power and privilege. One could argue that accounting's role in the modern economy makes it uniquely important to appreciate (Abbott 1988). However, its study is made more difficult by how thoroughly it is intertwined with both economic and political forces (Burchell et al. 1980).

Writing about the profession always risks engaging in a wishful fantasy about a bygone era that may have never occurred. Calls to restore such a time would be self-defeating. The profession is an ideal type from which movement and processes can be measured. A large amount of language, writing and myth-making can be understood as efforts to reinforce or dislodge the status quo. For these purposes, professionalism is ammunition.

Although this chapter argues that a pervasive deprofessionalization is occurring, a deterministic resolution is not necessary. Such a field of constant struggle is capable of new syntheses or novel hybrid rationalities. The broader environment may serve up changes in the economic and social contexts of the profession. Because accounting is far from a homogeneous body of practitioners, the front that it is able to present to the world may also change. New technologies can also act as power-shifting intrusions in accounting contexts (Fischer and Dirsmith 1995). Dyckman (1974) was probably not correct in asserting that full professional status was necessary for accounting. Its expertise is inherently contingent (Knights and Vurdubakis 1994). Progressive internationalization may constitute another source of change.

The study of deprofessionalization confronts the continued tendency to think of the traits that occupations assemble as displays that they are professions. If traits were the *sine qua non* of being a profession, deprofessionalization would be so much more difficult. Instead as a process, we need to understand how certain values become embedded in everyday social practices. If such a view facilitates our appreciation of how accounting becomes a profession (see West 1996), it can also enlighten the other slope. Harrington (2005) may have understated professional change when she recommended that we "fasten our seatbelts."

## References


Abbott, A. 1988. *The system of professions*. Chicago: University of Chicago Press.

Abraham, S. 1978. *The public accounting profession*. Lexington: Lexington Books.

Al-Beraidi, A., and T. Rickards. 2006. Rethinking creativity in the accounting profession. *Journal of Accounting and Organizational Change* 2: 25–41.

Alvesson, M. 1993. The play of metaphors. In *Postmodernism and organizations*, ed. J. Hassard and M. Parker, 114–131. London: Sage.

Anderson-Gough, F., C. Grey, and K. Robson. 2002. Accounting professionals and the accounting profession: Lurking conduct and context. *Accounting and Business Research* 32: 41–56.

Barber, B. 1963. Some problems in the sociology of the professions. *Daedalus* 92: 42–59.

Bartol, F. 1979. Professionalization as a predictor of organizational commitment, role stress and turnover: A multidimensional approach. *Academy of Management Journal* 22: 815–821.

Becker, H., B. Geer, E. Hughes, and A. Strauss. 1961. *Boys in white: Student culture in medical school*. Chicago: University of Chicago Press.

Belkaoui, Ahmmed. 1989. *The coming crisis in accounting*. Westport: Quorum Books.

Belkaoui, A. 1991. The context of the contemporary accounting profession. *Advances in Public Interest Accounting* 4: 83–97.

Bidwell, C., and R. Vreland. 1963. Authority and control in client servicing. *The Sociological Quarterly* 4(3): 231–242.

Black, T. 1982. The professionalization of accounting. *Management Accounting*, November, pp. 21–25.

Bledstein, B. 1967. *The culture of professionalism*. New York: Norton Books.

Bloor, G., and P. Dawson. 1994. Understanding professional culture in organizational context. *Organizational Studies* 15: 275–295.

Brint, S. 1997. *Professionals and the 'knowledge economy': Rethinking the theory of post-industrial society*. Paper presented at the American Sociological Association Meetings, Toronto.

Brooks, I. 1999. Managerialist professionalism: The destruction of a nonconforming subculture. *British Journal of Management* 10: 41–52.

Burchell, S., C. Clubb, A. Hopwood, J. Hughes, and J. Nahapiet. 1980. The roles of accounting in organizations and society. *Accounting, Organizations and Society* 5(1): 5–28.

Burns, D., and W. Haga. 1977. Much Ado about professionalism: A second look at accounting. *The Accounting Review* 52(3): 705–715.
Burrage, M., K. Jarausch, and H. Siegrist. 1990. An actor-based framework for the study of the professions. In *Professions in theory and history*, ed. M. Burrage and R. Torstandahl, 203–225. London: Sage.
Canning, M., and B. O'Dwyer. 2001. Professional accounting bodies' disciplinary procedures: Accountable, transparent and in the public interest? *The European Accounting Review* 10: 171–197.
Carmichael, D. 2003. *Professionalism is primary*. Speech at the annual SEC/AICPA conference, New York.
Carr-Saunders, A., and P. Wilson. 1933. *The profession*. Oxford: Oxford University Press.
Cooper, D., and K. Robson. 2006. Accounting, professions and regulation: Locating the sites of professionalization. *Accounting, Organizations and Society* 31: 415–444.
Corwin, R. 1961. The professional employee: A study in conflict in nursing roles. *The American Journal of Sociology* 66: 604–614.
Covaleski, M., M. Dirsmith, J. Heian, and S. Samuel. 1998. The calculated and the avowed: Techniques of discipline and struggles over identity in big six public accounting firms. *Administration Science Quarterly* 43: 293–327.
CPA Partners Report. 2000. *Why firm culture makes mergers succeed-or not*. 11(November), 1: 13–15.
Dyckman, T. 1974. Public accounting: Guild or profession? In *Institutional issues in public accounting*, ed. R. Sterling, 189–210. New York: Scholars Books.
Edelman, J. 1977. *Political language: Words that succeed and policies that fail*. New York: Academic.
Edwards, James Don, and Paul J. Miranti Jr. 1987.The AICPA: A professional institution in a dynamic society. *Journal of Accountancy* (May): 22.
Estes, R. 1990. Publics or privates: Pro whose bono? *Advances in Public Interest Accounting* 3: 33–42.
Financial Times. 2003. *Gloves are off as auditors chase moral high ground*, May 2, pp. 5–6.
Fischer, M. 1996. 'Real-izing' the benefits of new technologies as a source of audit evidence: An interpretive field study. *Accounting, Organizations and Society* 21(2/3): 219–242.
Fischer, M., and M. Dirsmith. 1995. Strategy, technology and social processes within professional cultures: A negotiated order, ethnographic perspective. *Symbolic Interaction* 18: 381–412.
Flood, A., and W.R. Scott. 1978. Professional power and professional effectiveness. *Journal of Health and Social Behavior* 19(3): 240–254.
Fogarty, T. 2000. Socialization and organizational outcomes in large public accounting firms. *Journal of Managerial Issues* 12: 13–33.
Fogarty, T., and J. Rigsby. 2010. A reflective analysis of the "new audit" and the public interest: The revolutionary innovations that never came. *Journal of Accounting and Organizational Change* 6: 300–329.
Fogarty, T., J. Heian, and D. Knutson. 1991. The rationality of doing nothing: Auditors' responses to legal liability in an institutionalized environment. *Critical Perspectives on Accounting* 3: 201–226.
Freidson, E. 1970. *Profession of medicine: A study of the sociology of applied knowledge*. New York: Harper & Row.
Freidson, E. 1986. *Professional powers: A study of the institutionalization of formal knowledge*. Chicago: University of Chicago Press.
Gendron, Y., R. Suddaby, and H. Lam. 2006. An examination of the ethical commitment of professional accountants to auditor independence. *Journal of Business Ethics* 64: 169–193.
Giddens, A. 1984. *The constitution of society*. Berkeley: University of California Press.
Gill, M. 2009. *Accountants' truth: Knowledge and ethics in the financial world*. Oxford: Oxford University Press.
Goetz, J., P. Morrow, and J. McElroy. 1991. The effect of accounting firm size and member rank on professionalism. *Accounting, Organizations and Society* 16: 159–165.

Goffman, E. 1961. *Asylums: Essays on the social situation of mental patients and other inmates*. New York: Doubleday.
Grayson, A., and K. McDermott. 1993. *Accounting for success: A history of price Waterhouse in America 1890–1990*. Boston: Harvard University Press.
Greenwood, E. 1957. Attributes of a profession. *Social Work* 6: 44–45.
Gross, E. 1958. *Work and society*. New York: Crowell and Co.
Hall, R. 1968. Professionalization and bureaucratization. *American Sociological Review* 33: 92–104.
Hall, R. 1975. *Occupations and the social structure*. Englewood Cliffs: Prentice Hall.
Hall, M., D. Smith, and K. Langfield-Smith. 2005. Accountants' commitment to their profession: Multiple dimensions of professional commitment and opportunities for future research. *Behavioral Research in Accounting* 17: 89–109.
Halliday, T. 1983. *Professions, class and capitalism*. London: Arch Europe Social.
Hanlon, G. 1996. "Casino capitalism" and the rise of the "Commercialized" service class – an examination of the accountant. *Critical Perspectives on Accounting* 7(2): 339–363.
Harring, S. 1976. The Development of police institutions in the United States. *Crime and Social Justice* 5: 44–59.
Harrington, C. 2005. The accounting profession: Looking ahead. *Journal of Accountancy* 200(4): 43–48.
Henry, D., and M. McNamee. 2003. Bloodied and bowed. *Business Week*, January 20, pp. 56–57.
Hodson, R., and T. Sullivan. 1995. *The social organization of work*. Belmont: Wadsworth.
Humphrey, C., and P. Moizer. 1990. From technique to ideology: An alternative on the audit profession. *Critical Perspectives on Accounting* 1: 217–238.
Jepperson, J. 1998. Reinventing auditing, refining consulting and independence. *The European Accounting Review* 7(3): 527–538.
Jepperson, R. 2002. Political modernities: Disentangling two underlying dimensions of institutional differentiation. *Social Theory* 20: 61–85.
Knights, D., and T. Vurdubakis. 1994. Foucault, power, resistance and ALL that. In *Resistance and power in organizations: Agency, subjectivity and the labor process*, ed. J. Jermier, D. Knights, and W. Hard. London: Routledge.
Kultgen, J. 1988. *Ethics and professionalism*. Philadelphia: University of Pennsylvania Press.
Langenderfer, H. 1987. Accounting Education's history – a 100 year search for identity. *Journal of Accountancy* 163(5): 302–337.
Larson, M. 1977. *The rise of professionalism*. Berkeley: University of California Press.
Lieberman, J. 1978. Same reflections on self-regulation. In *The professions and public policy*, ed. P. Slayton and M. Trebelock, 89–94. Toronto: University of Toronto Press.
Loeb, S. 1972. Enforcement of the code of ethics: A survey. *The Accounting Review* 43: 1–10.
MacDonald, E. 2002. *The man with nine lives*. Forbes.com. Available at http://www.forbes.com/forbes/2002/1125/060a_print.html
Mautz, R., and H. Sharef. 1961. *The philosophy of auditing*. New York: American Accounting Association.
Meiksins, P., and K. Watson. 1989. Professional autonomy and organizational constraint: The case of engineers. *The Sociological Quarterly* 30: 561–588.
Melancon, B. 2002. A new accounting culture. *Journal of Accountancy* 194(4): 27–32.
Merton, R. 1957. Science and economy of the 17th century England. In *Social theory and social structure*, ed. R. Merton, 607–627. Glencoe: Free Press.
Millerson, G. 1964. *The qualifying associations*. London: Routledge & Kegan Paul.
Montagna, P. 1974. Public accounting: The dynamics of occupational change. In *The institutional issues in public accounting*, ed. R. Sterling, 3–24. New York: Scholar's Books.
Moore, W. 1970. *The professions: Roles and rules*. New York: Russell Sage.
Norris, D., and R. Niebuhr. 1983. Professionalism, organizational commitment and Job satisfaction in accounting organizations. *Accounting, Organizations and Society* 8: 49–59.
Olson, W. 1978. Is professionalism dead? *Journal of Accountancy* 156: 78–82.
Palmer, G. 1914. *Trades and professions*. Boston: Houghlin Mifflin.

Podolny, J. 1993. A status-based model of market competition. *The American Journal of Sociology* 98: 929–972.
Podsakoff, P., L. Williams, and W. Todor. 1986. Effects of organizational formalization on alienation among professionals and Non-professionals. *Academy of Management Journal* 29: 820–831.
Power, M. 1995. Auditing, expertise and the sociology of technique. *Critical Perspectives on Accounting* 6: 317–339.
Raelin, J. 1989. The anatomy of autonomy: Managing professionals. *The Academy of Management Executive* 3: 216–228.
Regan, M. 1999. Law firms, competition penalties and the values of professionalism. *Journal of Legal Ethics* 13(1): 1–74.
Richardson, A. 1988. Accounting knowledge and professional privilege. *Accounting, Organizations and Society* 13: 381–398.
Ritzer, G. 1993. *The McDonaldization of society*. Thousand Oaks: Pine Forge Press.
Ritzer, G. 2002. An introduction to McDonaldization. In *McDonaldization: The reader*, ed. G. Ritzer, 7–23. Thousand Oaks: Sage.
Ritzer, G., and D. Walczak. 1988. Rationalization and the deprofessionalization of physicians. *Social Forces* 67(1): 1–22.
Rogers, R., J. Dillard, and K. Yuthas. 2005. The accounting profession: Substantive change and/or image management. *Journal of Business Ethics* 58: 159–176.
Ross, C., and R. Duff. 1978. Quality of outpatient pediatric care: The influence of Physicians' background, socialization and work informational environments on performance. *Journal of Health and Social Behavior* 19(4): 348–360.
Rothman, R. 1984. Deprofessionalization: The case of law in America. *Work and Organizations* 11: 183–206.
Saks, M. 1983. Removing the blinkers? A critique of recent contributions to the sociology of the professions. *The Sociological Review* 31(1): 1–21.
Schmedemann, D. 2008. Priming for pro bono publico: Inculcating a norm of public service in new lawyers. *William Mitchell Law Review* 35: 977–1026.
Shafer, W., L.J. Park, and W. Liao. 2002. Professionalism, organizational-professional conflict and work outcomes. *Accounting, Auditing, and Accountability Journal* 15: 46–68.
Shaw, K. 1987. Skills, control and mass professionalization. *The Sociological Review* 35: 775–794.
Sikka, P., and H. Willmott. 1995a. The power of "independence": Defending and extending the jurisdiction of accounting in the United Kingdom. *Accounting, Organizations and Society* 20: 547–581.
Sikka, P., and H. Willmott. 1995b. Illuminating the state-profession relationship: Accounting acting as department of trade and industry investigations. *Critical Perspectives on Accounting* 6: 341–369.
Smith, G. 1990. Privileged communications, independence, and client advocacy: A perspective on professionalism. *Journal of Accounting and Public Policy* 9: 135–158.
Sorensen, J. 1967. Professional and bureaucratic orientations in the public accounting firm. *The Accounting Review* 42: 553–566.
Sorensen, J., and T. Sorensen. 1974. The conflict of professionals in bureaucratic organizations. *Administrative Science Quarterly* 19: 98–106.
Stevens, M. 1991. *The big six: The selling out of America's top accounting firms*. New York: Simon & Schuster.
Strier, F. 2006. Proposals to improve the image of the public accounting profession. *CPA Journal* 76: 67–70.
Thompson, R. 1982. Professionalism in a large corporation. *Georgia Journal of Accounting* 4: 1–9.
Toren, N. 1975. Deprofessionalization and its sources. *Sociology of Work and Occupations* 2: 323–337.
Van Maanen, J., and S. Bailey. 1984. Occupational communities: Culture and control in organizations. In *Research in organizational behavior*, vol. 6, ed. B. Staw, 287–365. Greenwich, CT: JAI Press.

Van Maanen, J., and B. Pentland. 1994. Cops and auditors: The rhetoric of records. In *The legalistic organization*, ed. S. Sitkins and R. Bies, 53–90. Thousand Oaks: Sage.
Wade, L. 1967. Professionals in organizations: A neoteric model. *Human Organization* 26: 40–46.
Walker, S. 2000. Benign sacerdotalist a pious assailant. The rise of the professional accountant in British management. *Accounting, Organizations and Society* 25: 313–322.
Wallace, J. 1995. Organizational and professional commitment in professional and nonprofessional organizations. *Administrative Science Quarterly* 40: 228–255.
Weber, M. 1968. *Economy and society*. Totowa: Bedminster Press.
West, B. 1996. The professionalization of accounting. *Accounting History* 1: 77–102.
Wyatt, A.R. 2004. Accounting professionalism—they just don't get it! *Accounting Horizons* 18: 45–53.
Zeff, S. 1978. The rise of economic consequences. *Journal of Accountancy* 146(6): 56–63.

# Part II
# An Ethic of Accountability, Societal Responsibilities, and Accounting for the Public Interest

# Chapter 4
# Taking Pluralism Seriously Within an Ethic of Accountability

**Jesse Dillard and Judy Brown**

## 4.1 Introduction

The work reported herein is part of a larger research project directed toward the democratization of accounting by "taking pluralism seriously" (Brown 2009; Dillard and Brown 2012; Dillard and Roslender 2011; Dillard and Yuthas 2011; Söderbaum and Brown 2010) as a means for developing a more critically enabling accounting. Democratization involves making accounting "relevant" beyond the mantra of providing information for investors. We propose that accounting and accountability systems can, and should, provide support not only to investors and managers but also to a wide and diverse set of generally under-represented constituencies (labor, ethnic minorities, feminists, indigenous peoples, etc.) as they strive to articulate their perspectives and/or influence socio-political processes so that their perspectives become a viable and recognized part of the debate and deliberations.

Accounting gains its professional legitimacy from its claim to act in the public interest. Acting in the *public* interest means to act in such a way as to enhance the human condition. Enhancing the human condition refers to the collective well-being of the community of people and institutions that support the community, not simply benefitting a privileged subset of the community at the expense of the

J. Dillard (✉)
School of Management, Queen's University Belfast, Belfast, UK

Victoria University of Wellington, Wellington, New Zealand
e-mail: jdillard@pdx.edu

J. Brown
School of Accounting and Commercial Law, Victoria University of Wellington, PO Box 600, Wellington, New Zealand
e-mail: judy.brown@vuw.ac.nz

S. Mintz (ed.), *Accounting for the Public Interest: Perspectives on Accountability, Professionalism and Role in Society*, Advances in Business Ethics Research 4,
DOI 10.1007/978-94-007-7082-9_4, © Springer Science+Business Media Dordrecht 2014

other members.[1] Kant provides one set of criteria whereby our actions can be evaluated: "Act in such a way that you treat humanity, whether in your own person or in the person of any other, always at the same time as an end and never merely as a means to an end" (Kant 1993/1785). From this perspective, we consider the context and process for acting in the public interest.

It seems fair to ask why we, as academics, take the time to engage in such reflective and communicative activities as lecturing and writing; specifically, what does it mean to act in the public interest, what are our responsibilities, and how do we rationalize the effort expended? Our motivation is to communicate our ideas and experiences.[2] We undertake these engagements with the conviction that such interactions will lead to understanding the world differently. By understanding the world differently, we can *choose* to live our lives differently, both professionally and personally and, as a result, we can have an enlightening, enabling, and transforming effect on our world. Our professional part of that world comprises the study and practice of business and accounting, in the broadest sense. Therefore, the possibility exists for *changing* the understanding and practice of accounting and business. The challenge, and that of any society, is to act, based on a value set that increases the social welfare rather than furthering the interests of only a privileged subset of society.

Having accepted membership in the accounting and business academy, we have a responsibility to develop and disseminate expert knowledge and professional responsibilities to current and future professionals. We should also facilitate and engage in an ongoing conversation among constituencies regarding public interest responsibilities associated with an ethic of accountability. In addition, we are in a position to act as conscience, critic,[3] and advisor to accounting and business professionals, organizational management, and society. Not to do so abdicates our societal responsibilities as members of the academy.

It is within this spirit of conscience, critic, and advisor that we take pluralism seriously within the context of an ethic of accountability. The discussion is organized as follows. First, we present an ethic of accountability as a general framework for articulating the responsibilities of economic institutions[4] within a democratically

[1] See other chapters in this monograph for specific critiques of accountants and the accounting profession.

[2] Initially, in our deliberations the motive is to communicate ideas. Then we began to recognize the creative component of our vocation, and we became aware that the motivation might be more of a desire to communicate *one's own* ideas and experiences. Then, in reflecting on the lack of influence of one's own ideas on improving the human condition and the need for multi-directional learning, we have come to realize that a more appropriate and promising objective might be creating a space wherein the ideas of those with whom we engage can emerge.

[3] In New Zealand the responsibility of conscience and critic is codified into law. See New Zealand Education Act (1989).

[4] We use the term economic institutions as a collective to refer to business organizations within western democratic capitalism; however, as discussed below, it includes responsibility of the social and ecological as well as the economic implications of their actions. Further, we recognize that these institutions, especially corporations are, and impact, social, political and cultural institutions as well.

**Table 4.1** Principles of pluralistic accounting and accountability systems

1. Include all interested parties by being aware of the multiple assumptions, values, and perspectives held by the participants and to consider alternative techniques for identifying and representing the differences
2. Recognize the constraints imposed by the exclusive reliance on quantitative, especially monetary, valuation
3. Recognize the subjective and contestable nature of the calculations underlying traditional and emergent representations
4. Make the representations, decision rules, and implications understandable to all participants
5. Ensure the efficacy of the participatory process
6. Be cognizant of power relationships
7. Recognize the transformative potential of dialogical accounting within the context of agonistic pluralism
8. Resist the new forms of monological discourse

governed society. Next we consider the context wherein these debates and deliberations might be legitimately undertaken, theorizing the process using agonistic pluralism. We apply eight principles (summarized in Table 4.1) derived from agonistic pluralism and critical dialectics within an ethic of accountability that facilitate taking pluralism seriously, our ultimate objective being enhancing the human condition through sustainable economic, social and environmental systems. The chapter concludes with brief closing remarks.

## 4.2 An Ethic of Accountability

In this section, we summarize and refine ideas related to an ethic of accountability (Dillard 2007, 2008, 2011). Given that our focus is business and accounting and the public interest, it seems appropriate to have some idea as to the purpose of economic institutions (business) in society. The traditional response is to maximize shareholder value. A more reflective response might be that the purpose is to provide goods and services, employment, and investment opportunities for members of the community/society. At a more fundamental level, we might argue that the purpose of business in society is to act in a socially responsible way, that is, to act in the public interest. Acting in the public interest means recognizing that as a primary societal institution, *business (economic organizations) has a central role in facilitating the long term viability of a democratically governed society grounded in values such as justice, equality, and trust, supported by a sustainable economic system.*[5]

While all members of society have a moral responsibility to act in the public interest, corporate management is specifically granted a fiduciary responsibility over society's economic resources (financial assets, human resources assets, technology, and natural resources). The fiduciary relationship entails certain rights and

[5] As will be discussed later, a sustainable economic system presumes a sustainable social system that presumes a sustainable natural system.

responsibilities for the actors involved. Rights are deemed to be privileges accruing to a member of society. Responsibilities are obligations accruing from societal privilege. Both provide the criteria by which actions are legitimated. An ethic of accountability within the fiduciary relationship between society and organizational management presumes that granting a right and accepting the associated responsibilities entails an ongoing relationship wherein the grantor has the right and responsibility to hold the actor accountable for the use of the resources.

Accountability is the duty to give an intelligible account(ing) of one's actions to another and is a necessary condition for the functioning of a just, equitable, and trustworthy society. Regarding the relationship between corporate management and society, accountability is the linchpin of a legitimate, sustainable, and just economic system. Accounting and accountability systems reside at the interface between organizational management (controllers of economic assets) and the citizens to whom they furnish goods and services and provide a medium for communication among the various societal actors. An ethic of accountability provides a contextual framework wherein the various rights and responsibilities can be actualized, and the results evaluated.

An ethic of accountability considers the relationships among various social actors and their representatives: business, government and the citizens. The government gains legitimacy to govern from the sovereign will of the citizens and is designated to administer the affairs of the society. As such, government gains administrative responsibility for society's economic assets.[6] Ideally, within a democratically governed society, if the government's actions are not consistent with the norms and values of the society, the citizens can bring about change though the established democratic processes. If the actions of business are not consistent with the expectations of the citizens, they, through their government, can impose sanctions and bring about change. Currently, within the context of global market capitalism, control of a significant portion of society's economic assets is granted to organizational management and is operationalized through various means associated with private property arrangements. In assigning these assets, government accepts the responsibility to provide the necessary social, political, and material infrastructure to successfully employ society's assets. Within the current context, these include security, a judicial system that enforces the execution of contracts, an education system that provides the requisite skilled employees, and facilitating banking, transportation and communication systems. Citizens themselves also ideally actively participate in governance activities within the private and public sectors (which, for example, is why education must crucially also be thought of as preparing students for active citizenship not merely providing employment skills).

Having been granted the right to use society's economic assets, organizational management accepts the associated fiduciary responsibilities regarding the entrusted

[6] This is a complex process as individuals have overlapping and at times contradictory roles and needs. Thus "administration" should not be read in a narrow instrumental sense; what we envisage is more akin to the participatory governance models being developed in interpretive and critical policy analysis (see e.g., Hillier and Healey 2010; Bond 2011).

assets that include rendering their actions transparent and understandable by providing relevant, timely, and accurate information. This suggests that instead of obfuscating indicators of their performance, management consciously and proactively provides information that best reflects the short term and long term implications of their activities as they relate to the economic, social and natural systems.

Society has the right to hold organizational management accountable for the use of society's economic assets. Relatedly, society has the responsibility to specify and clearly communicate the reporting and performance criteria to which organizational management is held accountable. In the United States, the Securities and Exchange Commission (SEC) is an example of a governmental regulatory institution formed to specify criteria by which organizational management is evaluated as well as to hold corporations accountable for meeting these criteria. Developing reporting and evaluation criteria is a dynamic, political process in which the citizens of the society should take an active part. This requires that the citizens engage in discussions and decisions about the purpose of economic institutions in society. These deliberations may include such questions as: what is meant by democracy and how can it best be implemented; what would facilitate the long term viability of such a society; what are the core values of the society and how should they be defined and operationalized; what form should reporting and accountability take; and what are the necessary and sufficient conditions associated with sustainable natural, social, and economic systems? In other words, acting in the public interest, and thus reporting and evaluation criteria associated with economic institutions, should reflect the overall objectives of the society that have emerged from ongoing debate and dialogue as to what this means and the necessary and sufficient conditions for its implementation. Arguably, engagement with civil society in the dialogue of setting criteria has been the greatest failure. The current democratic institutions do not seem to motivate and facilitate such dialogue.[7]

We do not conceptualize an ethic of accountability strictly as a social contract between society and its various members. The obligations emerge from a preexisting sense of duty or responsibility (Levinas 1998). Thus, the relationship is not one of an "exchange" of equal "commodities", but one of rights and responsibilities that reflect emergent dimensions of preexisting relationships and are the means and outcomes of social integration. Social integration takes place within the context of the extant social structures and the socio-physical and historical situatedness of the actors (Niebuhr 1963; Dillard and Yuthas 2001). Responsible actions result from the actors identifying themselves as members of an ongoing community. For example, as corporate management and members of civil society contemplate what constitutes appropriate evaluation criteria and action, they both recognize the community and their ongoing membership therein. As a reflective member of the community, there is an awareness and understanding of the effects of past actions on the community and its members. In light of this historical knowledge, there is

[7] Habermas (1984, 1987) would characterize the communicative lacuna as the colonization of the lifeworld by interested groups as a result of asymmetrical power distributions. His solution is communicative action.

reasoned anticipation of the consequences of the contemplated action, and there is an expectation by management and the community that management will be held accountable for their actions by the community. In the next section, we consider a framework wherein meaningful discourse could be undertaken.

## 4.3 Communicative Action: The Ideal

Ideally, the implementation of an ethic of accountability is facilitated by an open, honest, and ongoing dialogue among the various interested parties. This dialogue emerges within a set of democratic processes. The dialogue is seen as a process for arriving at an appropriate course of action consistent with the norms and values of the community. The purpose is not to discover the "good" from a utilitarian perspective or the "right" from a deontological one, but to engage in a process whereby both are part of a polylogical discourse. Previous work (e.g., Dillard 2011) has proposed Habermas' (1984, 1987) ideal speech situation as a set of criteria for engaging in the facilitating discourse wherein trust among the community members is developed through an ongoing honest and open dialogue. The participants in the discourse are called on to satisfy three validity claims. The first is propositional validity, which refers to establishing the objective validity or "truth" of the statement. The second is normative validity, which concerns the correspondence between the claim and the degree to which it conforms to the community's social norms. That is, grounds are to be presented that establish the "rightness" of the claim. The third is subjective authenticity, which refers to the "truthfulness" of the claim and the extent to which the statement corresponds to the actual intent of the speaker. According to Habermas, these three validity claims provide the necessary and sufficient conditions for undistorted communication and as a result, alternatives will be identified and chosen based on the strength of the better argument.[8] Habermas' ideal speech situation represents an ideal model for engaging in, and evaluating, meaningful discourse.

At a more concrete level, an ethic of accountability provides a context or framework within which alternative political and ideological systems and/or perspectives can be evaluated as they relate to business organizations. An ethic of accountability makes no presumption as to a political or ideological system's legitimacy, but it does provide a framework for considering the implications of a particular system within the context of an ongoing community. The process begins with the presumption that the purpose of business is to facilitate the long term viability of a democratically governed society based on justice, equity, and trust supported by a sustainable economic system.

Society requires goods and services, employment and investment opportunities for its members. One way of meeting these needs is to allow the state to control the economic resources of the society in the production of the goods and services.

[8] As discussed further below, Habermas' communicative action is not without its problems. Also see Brown and Dillard (2012) for a more complete discussion.

Alternatively, society could decide to assign the task to some other group(s). For example, an economic system could be implemented such that the control over the economic resources would be granted to a group perceived to have requisite skills for the efficient and effective transformation of the resources into the needed goods and services. At this point, we are confronted with political decisions and judgments about which system and/or group might best meet the afore-mentioned objectives.

If one is inclined to traditional neoclassical economic theories of markets, private property, and laissez faire capitalism, then to demonstrate this economic system to be superior, a case would have to be made showing that it provides the best opportunity of facilitating the long term viability of a democratically governed society, upholding the society's values, and not destroying the natural and social environment. The claim that would have to be validated is that the market allocation of resources within the context of private property rights provides goods and services in a sustainable context that facilitates the values of justice, equity, and trust. To support the claim that markets are superior, evidence would have to be presented that could be compared with alternative ideologies and their expected implications. On the one hand, markets are seen to allocate scarce resources in an unbiased and objective way following from the perceived needs or desires of the individual. On the other hand, if the individual's perceived needs or desires are contrary to the public interest in that one group is privileged over another or sections of the community do not have access to the resources required to participate fully in markets, then the ability to meet the societal objectives becomes questionable. However, if one accepts the assumption of the effect of enlightened self-interest, which is a major underlying assumption of the neoclassical ideology, then one can argue that, in fact, this system provides the best available means by which to enhance the human condition. Again, the proposed framework related to an ethic of accountability provides a structure within which to evaluate, compare, and debate alternative applications. One repeatedly returns to the question of how, and based on what assumptions, does the action facilitate a sustainable democratically governed society. According to the theory of communicative action ideals, if a more convincing argument can be made in light of the recognized assumptions required, then the ideology would be accepted as a (the) viable alternative and implemented through the democratically appointed governmental institutions. The communicative action criteria would be applied in making these decisions as well.

However, from a more realistic, and pragmatic point of view, we see the choices associated with facilitating a "better" society committed to enhancing the human condition to be an ongoing, dialectical process that pits autonomy of the economic institutions against control by an external entity such as the state. Concerns about corporate autonomy are commonly associated with the concentration of power and wealth and the abuse thereof. Concerns about external control are commonly associated with stifling innovation and creativity and the inefficient allocation and use of scarce resources. In the contemporary neo-liberal context, there is much concern about the control business exercises over the state, making it highly problematic to assume the state acts on behalf of its citizens and suggesting the need for exploration of alternative governance arrangements. Differentials in knowledge, expertise, resources, communicative capability, and power more generally underlie the ongoing antagonistic relationships among the interested parties. Some have argued that attaining Habermas' ideal speech situation is difficult if not impossible and continuing to pursue this apolitical course reinforces the status quo (e.g., Purcell 2009). While we see merit in aspects of Habermas' ideas as an ideal toward which we should strive, we propose agonistic pluralism as a more realistic approach given the current disparities among the interested parties. It is that to which we now turn our attention.

## 4.4 Agonistic Pluralism: A Realistic Alternative

Agonistic pluralism is a critical political philosophy emerging from the writings of Laclau and Mouffe's (2001) *Hegemony and socialist strategy: Towards a radical democratic politics*. Difference arises from "ineradicable dimensions of undecidability and antagonism" (Mouffe 1997, 27). Agonist pluralism explicitly recognizes these irresolvable differences and antagonisms among the interested parties and focuses on democratic processes for deliberations and decision making wherein the differences may be fully recognized and expressed. The objective of their program has been to move radical democratic politics beyond the outmoded conceptualizations of modernity and to explore possibilities provided by a more realistic linguistically grounded post-structural materialism. Social and political identities are constructed as participants articulate and give meaning to their world through discursive interactions. The emerging ideas provide an alternative to deliberative modernists such as Habermas as to ways of understanding, deciding, and acting, fostering democratic processes wherein the effect of difference and asymmetrical power relationships are not assumed away but are explicitly recognized and addressed.[9]

In comparing Habermas' communicative action and agonistic pluralism, Bond (2011) argues that the post-structuralist approach of agonistic pluralism provides a more realistic context by recognizing the political nature of the decision making processes and the inherent contingencies and antagonisms in social relationships.[10] Such a perspective makes it easier to question dominant, taken for granted discourses and to develop alternatives that question the extant asymmetrical power relationships that challenge the status quo. The antagonistic relationships arising out of opposing interests and asymmetrical power relationships are translated into agonistic relationships where instead of enemies trying to eliminate each other, the antagonists adamantly defend their positions but recognize the opponent's right

[9] Much debate and scholarship surrounds the work of deliberative democrats (Habermas) and agonistic democrats (Laclau and Mouffe). See Gaffikin and Morrissey (2011), Hillier and Healey (2010), and Kapoor (2008, Chapter 6) for reviews.

[10] See for example Glynos and Howarth (2007), Howarth (2010), Laclau and Mouffe (2001), Torfing (1999).

to defend their position as well.[11] Out of this ongoing struggle and debate, new, or as yet unrecognized, alternatives emerge providing a richer understanding of the issues being considered and of the implications for the effected groups. However, unlike Habermas' communicative action, it is not necessary for such deliberations to culminate in a consensus among all parties. Here a more complex view of public interest arises, which engages ideas of *multiple publics* – with divergent and sometimes incommensurable frames, values and interests – in pluralistic societies.

We contend that agonistic pluralism foregrounds pluralism and diversity by theorizing difference and conflict, facilitating our quest for a more enabling and political accounting and providing a theoretical base for dialogical/polylogical accountings (Bebbington et al. 2007a, b; Brown 2009; Dillard and Brown 2012; Söderbaum and Brown 2010). We propose a polylogical accounting theoretically grounded in agonistic pluralism as providing a framework for considering the issues associated with an ethic of accountability. For example, the trade-off between organizational autonomy and external control would recognize the inherent conflict among the various interested groups such as management, labor, investors, competitors, environmental interests, civil society, the state, indigenous peoples, etc. Acting in the public interest, accounting would provide accountings *of* and *for* each of the interested groups. Here we argue that accounting as a profession must recognize a broader audience if it is to maintain its relevance and viability in an ever more complex polylogic world with ever-increasing demands for information across various constituencies.

Deliberative debate and dialogue predicated on reaching a consensus based on the strength of better argument carried out within an environment wherein differential power relationships are suspended seems an unlikely proposition within the current socio-political setting. Agonistic pluralism assumes that identity and understanding among democratic subjects arises from differentiation. Pluralism is recognized and alternatives evaluated through processes whereby contingency, difference, and conflict are not only explicitly recognized but also facilitated. Participants are seen as socio-political agents acting within discursively constructed systems of understanding. Different agents or groups of agents[12] can have very different understandings of broadly recognized concepts such as democracy, justice, equality, trust, responsibility, rights, accountability, etc. To implement an ethic of accountability, some level of shared commitment to improving the human condition within democratic governing structures is necessary; however, the specific meaning of, and means to, the socio-political principles such as justice or equality are open to legitimate debate.

Given the current dominance of neo-liberal market logics, it is likely that the fiduciary responsibilities of management would be defined in terms of existing power inequalities. Consensus driven processes such as communicative action are

[11] Limits may be put on this right where positions are constructed on the subordination of others (Brown 2009, 323).

[12] It is important to recognize that there may be significant diversity within apparently homogenous groups. For example it cannot be assumed that even all shareholders seek simply to maximize their monetary return on investment.

more likely to subordinate alternative arguments, claims and possibilities through co-opting the debate and downplaying power asymmetries (Bond 2011, 167; and Murtagh and Ellis 2011). One of the primary assumptions of agonistic pluralism is that what appears to be consensus is always incomplete and temporary, resulting from a provisional stabilization of power (Mouffe 1999, 756). As such, it is better thought of as a "conflictual consensus" or a pause between discussions allowing different constituencies to group and/or regroup. Any agreement is thus viewed as a negotiated political achievement involving conflict and compromise. Collective decisions unavoidably exclude less powerful interested groups by labeling their claims as illogical or unreasonable. Resisting closure even after action is taken provides a means whereby the democratic processes can continue to function (Brown 2009, 321).

Taking pluralism seriously requires that accounting and accountability be thought about in new ways that emerge from and are supported by effective and realistic participatory processes. Fostering agonistic relationships among the participants increases the likelihood of utilizing new ways of thinking and facilitates the recognition of new alternatives. The challenge for accounting and accountability systems is to facilitate agonistic engagement among the interested parties recognizing and encouraging their diverse interests, values, conceptualizations of reality, and knowledge bases. For example, Purcell (2009, 140) points out the constraining effect of market logics and competitive discipline, both valorized by the prevailing neoclassical economic model. By not questioning the assumptions underlying the neoclassical hegemony, neither existing power relationships nor the status quo are not seriously challenged. In fact, the prevailing power relationships are likely to be reinforced due to the perceived enhanced political legitimacy.

Alternatively, taking an agonist perspective encourages the interrogation of market rationality and its place in creating and maintaining power asymmetries among the interested groups. The challenge for accounting is to aid in understanding the contingent and historic nature of the social spaces within which events take place. Doing so necessitates a relational understanding and representation of the economic, social, and political activities and implications, especially as they involve power and resistance. We suggest that an agonistic pluralism framework can provide insights into how meanings are constructed and identities are established through complex discursive practices, how they can change as the result of differentiation, and the effect of these changes on the representational and evaluative frameworks.[13] The associated accountings and accountability systems need to challenge the dominant knowledge systems (e.g., neoclassical market based discourses) and practices (e.g., privileging owners/investors) by providing alternative representations, paying particular attention to power relationships within particular contexts. These new imaginings need to provide support of the various disadvantaged social actors by, for example, recognizing the power-directed processes by which certain privileged meanings become dominant (Gray 2002; Bond 2011).

[13] See Bond (2011), Glynos and Howarth (2007), Griggs and Howarth (2008), and Howarth (2010) for a discussion.

Accounting and accountability systems construct and legitimate what issues are privileged, how they are framed, and the resulting actions taken. The privileged meanings and taken for granted understandings reinforce power asymmetries and create and maintain various social inequalities. The challenge of accounting and accountability systems is to interrogate and make transparent the various parties affected, who wins, who loses, what qualifies as a "legitimate" argument, and who decides. Greater transparency surrounding the political process, for example in terms of the funding behind publicly espoused positions (e.g. medical research sponsored by pharmaceutical companies), also becomes important in terms of identifying, understanding and evaluating the motivations of different actors. Recognizing and supporting the conflict and contestation among the interested groups facilitates the dialectical engagements that may lead to social reform and/or new understandings of social norms such as accountability.

In the context of urban planning, Bond (2011, 178) illustrates the type of relevant questions that might be motivated by applying the principles of agonistic pluralism to accounting and accountability systems:

- What interests (owners/investors) are involved and how do they interact?
- What power relationships and differentials become evident from studying the interactions among the interested parties?
- What totalizing ideologies (e.g., neoclassical economics) attempt to dominate the debate for contestable terrain?
- What tactics are used by the various dominating attempts?
- What concepts (e.g., sustainability) take on a universal posture, becoming devoid of meaning, and how are they redefined by the various interested groups in support of their position?
- When a decision is made, what advantages and disadvantages accrue to the various parties, what possibilities have been terminated and why were they subordinated?

We propose that such a process is useful as we consider how accounting might be employed in implementing an ethic of accountability given the current network of interests and their unequal power relationships.

## 4.5 Applying Agonistic Pluralism Within an Ethic of Accountability

The implementation of an ethic of accountability is predicated on ongoing and open dialogue among the interested parties recognizing the inherent tensions and power differentials among them. Following from a review of the critical dialogics literature, Brown (2009, esp. 314–329) provides a set of eight principles or guidelines useful in contemplating possibilities for alternative accountings applied with an ethic of accountability analyzed within an agonistic framework. We propose these as necessary conditions for the design and implementation of effective pluralist accounting and accountability systems.

The first principle recognizes the need to include all interested parties by being aware of the multiple assumptions, values, and perspectives held by the participants and to consider alternative techniques for identifying and representing these differences. For example, workers, the local community, public interest groups, local government, suppliers, and customers would have an equal opportunity for recognition as would organizational management, stockholders, and creditors. Different information needs, expectations, and values not reflected in traditional accounting and accountability systems might be associated with each group. The alternative accountings and accountability systems are developed consistent with alternative logics of each constituency that would reflect their alternative moralities, needs, expectations, and values. These alternative systems require new and imaginative approaches to accountings and accountability systems. The remaining principles concern the development of these systems such that they meet the needs of organizational management as well as the governing bodies and various other segments of society.[14]

The second principle concerns the constraints imposed by the reductionist inclinations of traditional accounting's instrumental rationality based accountings reflected in their exclusive reliance on quantitative, especially monetary, valuation when considering the appropriate criteria for providing transparent and understandable representations of the economic entity's actions. These traditional measures may be presented together with alternative, nonmonetary, nonfinancial representations that might include measures in nontraditional areas such as environmental reporting, social responsibility reporting, third party shadow/contra accounts, worker self accounts, accounts from members of civil society, local resource needs statements, and community norms and values. Here, we recognize the need to question and make more transparent the taken for granted primacy of instrumental logic and its tangible manifestations within the traditional accounting and accountability systems. The remaining six principles refer to specific areas for expanding our perspective to include more subjective and contestable understandings facilitated by dialogical engagement.

The third principle states that the participants need to be open about the subjective and contestable nature of the calculations underlying both the traditional and emergent representations. The socially constructed and contested nature of any measure or representation is recognized. One obvious example is the current privileging of equity accounting over all other possible accountings and, thus, the calculation of income from this perspective. Within this context of asymmetrical power relationships and differing social logics and needs, we want to be sensitive to the extent that the representations facilitate or inhibit attaining societal values such as justice, equity, and trust within an ethic of accountability. Agonistic pluralism recognizes and enhances the possibilities associated with the contestable nature of these values as a means of creating space for new imaginings.

[14] However "society" is arguably more realistically recognized as constituted of *multiple* publics rather than *one* homogenous group.

The fourth principle recognizes the need to make the representations, decision rules, and implications understandable to all participants. Organizational management has a responsibility to recognize the information needs of the various constituencies and make a concerted effort to meet them. The citizens have a responsibility to attain a level of understanding such that the differing groups can develop meaningful reporting and evaluation criteria relevant to their various interests. Within an agonistic context, the various interested groups attempt to better understand the nature of the communications provided and the positions taken by their adversaries as a means for gaining insights into the core contestations among them. According to Brown (2009), this requires having access to and calling on the requisite expertise. "Organic" experts assist the affected groups to develop and articulate representations and evaluation criteria that embody the group's needs, values and norms. Here, the accounting profession(als) and academics could provide the expertise to a wide range of constituencies instead of their current primary focus on investors and business through workshops or involvement with groups such as labor unions or indigenous peoples. Likewise, "border crossing" experts initiate and sustain understanding and assist polyvocal dialogue and debate among different perspectives. Brown (2009) also points out that we need to recognize the different viewpoints both within and between areas of expertise as well as the centrality of learning. Ideally, experts learn from one another and from non-experts as well as non-experts learning from the experts. Part of this process includes recognizing that the legitimacy of expertise and technique emanate from values and assumptions that mirror the extant relationships among knowledge, power, and expertise.

Principle five pertains to ensuring the efficacy of the participatory process. Not inconsistent with Habermas' theory of communicative action, each participant is ensured the opportunity and facility to speak and be heard. Access to information necessary for supporting debate is presumed. Agonistic pluralism moves beyond the expectation of consensus, recognizing that the deliberations represent unfolding understandings emerging through the ongoing dialogue among the interested groups. The multiple accountings provide a facilitating means for this dialogical process and the assessable outcomes primarily relate to the efficacy of the participatory process whereby all are granted the right to speak, or not, and the right to disagree. Societal groups need legally enforceable rights to information and participation rather than having to rely on voluntarist managerial-controlled initiatives. Social and environmental accounting is an example of the dynamics involved in expanding the participatory process through alternative reportings.

Principle six recognizes the need to be cognizant of power relationships. For an ethic of accountability to be realistically considered, the reality of differences in power among the interested groups must be recognized. Accounting and accountability systems embody, formulate, and modify power relationships by directing the allocation of resources. Agonistic pluralism recognizes the unavoidable and ongoing, though possibility changing, power differentials among the interested groups. The objective is not to eliminate the differences but to make visible the decision processes as well as the related distributional effects of the power differentials. As marginalized voices are identified, representations (e.g., accounting techniques and practices) need to be developed so that the different, often conflicting positions can be recognized and understood. For example, labor might be provided with financial information that would enable them to determine whether they are getting a fair return for their productive efforts and non-financial information relating to working conditions.

Principle seven recognizes the transformative potential of dialogical accounting within the context of agonistic pluralism. Within an ethic of accountability, we recognize the potential for accounting and accountability systems to be used pluralistically for agonistic discussion, debate, and reflection. Dialogical accounting and accountability systems construct, reinforce, and modify the facilitating practices of organizational management, government, and civil society. An ethic of accountability provides the context for action as structures merge from the dynamic and ongoing structuration processes that construct, reconstruct, and modify the institutions and discourses that foster identification with democratic values. While the transformative potential of dialogic accounting within the context of agonistic pluralism has not been achieved, we see social and environmental accounting as one of the emerging areas in which these ideas should be constructively applied.

Principle eight concerns the need to resist new forms of monologic discourse within an ethic of accountability. Once new polylogic accounting and accountability systems, techniques, and practices are developed and implemented, the agonistic debate, discussion, and reflection must be vigorously renewed so that a new tyranny does not replace the old ones. Explicitly recognizing and articulating the multiple and competing discourses that arise from the inherent agonistic tensions and power differentials indicate the ongoing contestability of the representational technologies. For example, if some set of social and environmental accounting standards were agreed upon, they should be immediately opened to question, critique, and possibly change, recognizing the voices not heard and the inevitable unequal power relationships that subordinated those voices.

## 4.6 Closing Remarks

Developing the capacity to "live our lives differently" is part of an ongoing, dialectical process whereby we become aware of new, or as yet unrecognized, alternatives. By becoming aware of the expanded alternative set, we recognize that we have choices in the way we live our lives, do our research, and teach and practice business and accounting. Applying agonistic pluralism within the context of an ethic of accountability can help evaluate the actions of interested parties in light of their ability to facilitate the long term viability of a democratically governed society based on values such as justice, equality, and trust and supported by a sustainable economic system. Agonistic pluralism provides a realistic framework wherein we can interrogate the extent to which the various parties engage their rights and fulfill their responsibilities as members of an ongoing community. Taking pluralism seriously within an ethic of accountability means that accountings, as part of the information and decision making systems, should be designed so as to provide timely, relevant, and understandable information of and to the various interested groups. We propose agonistic pluralism as a facilitating possibility.

**Acknowledgement** We wish to thank the Royal Society of New Zealand Marsden Fund for supporting this research as part of a funded project on "Dialogic Accounting: The Challenge of Taking Multiple Perspectives Seriously", Contract No. VUW1011.

## References

Bebbington, J., J. Brown, and B. Frame. 2007a. Accounting technologies and sustainability assessment models. *Ecological Economics* 61(2/3): 224–236.

Bebbington, J., J. Brown, B. Frame, and I. Thomson. 2007b. Theorizing engagement: The potential of a critical dialogic approach. *Accounting, Auditing and Accountability Journal* 20(3): 356–381.

Bond, S. 2011. Negotiating a 'democratic ethos': Moving beyond the agonistic – Communicative divide. *Planning Theory* 10(2): 161–186.

Brown, J. 2009. Democracy, sustainability and dialogic accounting technologies: Taking pluralism seriously. *Critical Perspectives on Accounting* 20(3): 313–342.

Brown, J., and J. Dillard. 2012. Critical accounting and communicative action: On the limits of consensual deliberation. *Critical Perspectives on Accounting*. http://dx.doi.org/10.1016/j.cpa.2012.06.003 doi:10.1016/j.cpa.2012.06.003#doilink

Dillard, J. 2007. Legitimating the social accounting project: An ethic of accountability. In *Sustainability accounting and accountability*, ed. J. Unerman, B. O'Dwyer, and J. Bebbington, 37–53. London: Routledge.

Dillard, J. 2008. An ethic of accountability. *Research on Professional Responsibility and Ethics in Accounting* 13: 1–18.

Dillard, J. 2011. Framing sustainability within an ethic of accountability. In *Sustainable business practices: Challenges, opportunities, and practices*, vol. I, ed. S. McNall, J. Hershauser, and G. Basile, 107–125. Santa Barbara: Praeger.

Dillard, J., and J. Brown. 2012. Agonistic pluralism and imagining CSEAR into the future. *Social and Environmental Accountability Journal* 32(1): 3–16.

Dillard, J., and R. Roslender. 2011. Taking pluralism seriously: Embedded moralities in management accounting and control systems. *Critical Perspectives on Accounting* 22(2): 135–147.

Dillard, J., and K. Yuthas. 2001. A responsibility ethic of audit expert systems. *Journal of Business Ethics* 30: 337–359.

Dillard, J., and K. Yuthas. 2011. Critical dialogics, agonistic pluralism and accounting information systems. *International Journal of Accounting Information Systems*. http://dx.doi.org/10.1016/j.accinf.2011.07.002 doi:10.1016/j.%20accinf.2011.07.002.

Gaffikin, F., and M. Morrissey. 2011. *Planning in divided cities: Collaborative shaping of contested space*. Chichester: Wiley-Blackwell.

Glynos, J., and D. Howarth. 2007. *Logics of critical explanation in social and political theory*. London: Routledge.

Gray, R. 2002. The social accounting project and *Accounting Organizations and Society*: Privileging engagement, imaginings, new accountings and pragmatism over critique? *Accounting, Organizations and Society* 27(7): 687–708.

Griggs, S., and D. Howarth. 2008. Populism, localism and environmental politics: The logic and rhetoric of the stop Stansted expansion campaign. *Planning Theory* 7(2): 123–144.

Habermas, J. (1984). *The theory of communicative action. Vol. 1: Reason and rationalisation of society*. Trans. T. McCarthy. London: Heinemann.

Habermas J. (1987). *The theory of communicative action. Vol. 2: The critique of functional reason*. Trans. T. McCarthy). London: Heinemann.
Hillier, J., and P. Healey. 2010. *The Ashgate research companion to planning theory*. Surrey: Ashgate.
Howarth, D. 2010. Power, discourse, and policy: Articulating a hegemony approach to critical policy studies. *Critical Policy Studies* 3(3): 309–335.
Kant, I. (1993/1785). *Metaphysics of morals*, 3rd ed. Trans. J. Ellington. Indianapolis: Hackett.
Kapoor, I. 2008. *The postcolonial politics of development*. London: Routledge.
Laclau, E., and C. Mouffe. 2001. *Hegemony and socialist strategy: Towards a radical democratic politics*, 2nd ed. London: Verso.
Levinas, E. 1998. *entre nous: On thinking-of-the-Other*. New York: Columbia University Press.
Mouffe, C. 1997. Decision, deliberation and democratic ethos. *Philosophy Today* 41(1): 24–30.
Mouffe, C. 1999. Deliberative democracy or agonistic pluralism. *Social Research* 66(3): 745–758.
Murtagh, B., and G. Ellis. 2011. Skills, conflict and spatial planning in Northern Ireland. *Planning Theory and Practice* 12(3): 349–365.
New Zealand Education Act 1989. Section 162 (4)(a)(v).
Niebuhr, R. 1963. *The responsible self*. San Francisco: Harper Press.
Purcell, M. 2009. Resisting neoliberalization: Communicative planning or counter-hegemonic movements? *Planning Theory* 8(2): 140–165.
Söderbaum, P., and J. Brown. 2010. Democratizing economics: Pluralism as a path towards sustainability. *Annals of the New York Academy of Sciences* 1185: 179–195.
Torfing, J. 1999. *New theories of discourse. Laclau, Mouffe and Žižek*. Oxford: Blackwell.

# Chapter 5
# Social and Economic Implications of Increasing Income Inequality: Accountability Concerns

**Sue Ravenscroft and Christine A. Denison**

## 5.1 Introduction

> We can either have democracy in this country, or we can have great wealth concentrated in the hands of a few, but we cannot have both.
>
> • Louis Brandeis

> An imbalance between the rich and the poor is the oldest and most fatal ailment of all republics.
>
> • Plutarch

One of the roles of accounting is to provide a narrative of accountability over how societal resources are being managed (Bayou et al. 2011; Merino et al. 2010). We believe that the accounting narrative produced by US corporations omits information crucial to understanding our country's current economic and social conditions. We shall argue that corporations are responsible to a great extent for the dramatic increase in income inequality over the last four decades. Because corporations[1] disclose only what is required by Generally Accepted Accounting Principles (GAAP), accounting narratives have been silent on corporations' role in expanding income inequality, a phenomenon which causes significant problems for individuals, and could threaten the survival of our tradition of democratic institutions (Fukuyama 2012; Phillips 2002, 2008). We argue that the public interest is undermined when disclosure requirements are too narrow, thus allowing corporations to behave unethically (though legally), without sufficient scrutiny, and as a result, without adequate accountability. Theoretically, the most direct path to change corporate behaviors

[1] We do not mean to reify corporations or assign them agency, but find that speaking of corporations as if they are agents is widely accepted in academic discourse and is a trope without obvious alternatives. When we speak of corporations as agents, we are referring to decision-makers (usually executives) within corporations.

S. Ravenscroft (✉) • C.A. Denison
Department of Accounting, Iowa State University, Ames, IA, USA
e-mail: sueraven@iastate.edu; caw@iastate.edu

S. Mintz (ed.), *Accounting for the Public Interest: Perspectives on Accountability, Professionalism and Role in Society*, Advances in Business Ethics Research 4,
DOI 10.1007/978-94-007-7082-9_5, © Springer Science+Business Media Dordrecht 2014

would be through a change in law. However, a number of factors such as recent gridlock in Congress and the powerful influence of corporate interests on the political process make such a route impractical. We therefore advocate that accountants expand mandated disclosure through GAAP to include information about corporate transactions which contribute to current severe income inequality. Thus, the public would be provided with greater information to make decisions regarding corporate behavior as it impacts income inequality. We begin with a brief look at how social responsibility accounting has been defined within academia and applied in practice. Next, we examine income inequality in the US, which increased dramatically with a shift from Keynesian to neoliberal government policies. We note some of the problematic social phenomena associated with income inequality. We next propose new disclosure requirements relating to compensation, taxation and non-business expenditures that would help render the role of corporations in promoting income inequality more transparent.

## 5.2 Corporate Social Responsibility

### *5.2.1 A Broader Definition of Corporate Social Responsibility*

> Corporate social responsibility is a hard-edged business decision. Not because it is a nice thing to do or because people are forcing us to do it… because it is good for our business
>
> • Niall FitzGerald, Former CEO, Unilever

Corporate social and environmental responsibility (CSR) has been extensively discussed, measured, and evaluated, although many definitional and pragmatic issues remain unresolved by academic researchers (e.g. Owen 2008; Parker 2005; Tinker and Gray 2003). In this chapter, we assume that any discussion of CSR must include the actions taken by corporations which promote income inequality. Accountants provide information that helps society allocate resources. We believe that if corporations disclosed and reported more information in a straightforward manner within financial statements themselves, such increased disclosure could enable citizens to make better-informed decisions about choices regarding public resources and shape measures the public might take to construct more socially desirable policies and communities.

### *5.2.2 Corporate Social Responsibility – A Look Back*

> We have the most crude accounting tools. It's tragic because our accounts and our national arithmetic doesn't [sic] tell us the things that we need to know.
>
> • Susan George

Only 50 years ago – during the era in which the Great Society policies were formulated and enacted – social accounting was discussed in *The Accounting*

*Review* and in professional pronouncements. Gray (2002, 690) characterizes this as a time of "anxiety about corporate ethics, corporate power, social responsibility and ecological degradation" which generated arguments for a brave new world of accounting. In that vein, Rappaport argues that society at large has a public interest in corporate accounting reports based on the relationship between corporations and "the fundamental ideals or values of society" (1964, 951) which shape the objectives of accounting reports. While economic progress is desired, it cannot impinge on other basic values, such as the "equitable sharing" of increases in productivity amongst labor, management, and capital providers. Although the relative contribution of each of those groups may be difficult to delineate, there is a strong argument in favor of promoting "an improved distribution of income" (Rappaport 1964, 958). Financial information that helps evaluate how profits are distributed is essential, as is information that calls attention to monopoly profits, which should be avoided in order to preserve a pluralistic society.

Rappaport notes that "no form dominates the American scene as does the large business corporation," (1964, 959) and asks whether, given the extreme influence of corporations on daily life, we can truly call corporations "a 'private' affair." He concludes that because of corporations' pervasive influence "corporate accountability solely to stockholders is inconsistent with the contemporary model of the large business corporation" (1964, 961). Though the phrase 'corporate social responsibility' had not become part of the academic discourse in 1964, Rappaport is clearly arguing for broad-based accountability that helps inform social policies designed to promote a more equitable and less skewed distribution of wealth.

Ten years later, the American Accounting Association established a social accounting committee, noting that "no corporation has yet designed or implemented anything approaching a systematic information system for its socially relevant actions" (AAACSC 1975, 64). The following year, Ramanathan (1976) argued that the social contract between society and corporations should encompass both the productive function of firms and the distributive effect of firms on society. While financial reports focus on the productive function, they must, Ramanathan argues, be expanded to include externalities and account for the distributive effects of corporate actions on society. These early authors are clearly arguing for a stakeholder perspective on financial reporting.

Gray's history of social and environmental accounting reveals that interest in accounting for stakeholders (rather than only shareholders) died fairly rapidly in the US in the 1980s, and was replaced by neoliberal ideology[2] and a focus on designing financial statements primarily for investors and creditors (2002). The academic discussion of social and environmental accounting shifted almost entirely to the UK and Australia, and plays out currently in journals such as *Accounting, Organizations and Society* and *Accounting, Auditing and Accountability*. In practice, moreover, corporations fairly quickly realized how CSR could be used as a vehicle for positive

[2] Neoliberalism is an ideology that advocates greater privatization and deregulation, and a greater reliance on markets.

impression management and publicly embraced the concept.[3] Cho et al. (2012) provide an example of negative correlation between environmental reputation and environmental actions of 92 US firms in environmentally sensitive industries. Shamir (2004, 671) notes that the embrace of CSR is associated with "a voluntary – at times altruistic and at times utilitarian – meaning of the term" which has vitiated its more significant possibilities. He describes how even the CSR reporting monitoring agencies have become part of the corporate platform, and labels them MaNGOs, market oriented non-governmental organizations, which often fail to serve a critical and independent role. Corporations have used CSR as a way to conflate doing good works (i.e., being good corporate citizens according to their self-imposed criteria) with doing well financially (Shamir 2004). This union of behaving responsibly with generating positive earnings is particularly clever. Once that identity is established in the public's mind, excessive profits become not a sign of a corporation's failure to contribute to society in proportion to the benefits it receives, but rather a sign that the firm has been particularly virtuous, a reflection both of Puritanism and modern prosperity Christianity.

Bayou, Reinstein, and Williams argue that accountants have too narrowly defined our responsibilities within a democratic society. In an examination of how truthfulness relates to ethics within accounting, they conclude that "the important social function of accounting, particularly in democracies, is informing on the affairs of powerful institutions, i.e. situating them in the present so that decisions may be made about them" (2011, 122). They urge accountants to expand accounting from a narrow focus on investors' and creditors' concerns for future cash flows to more broadly-conceived and socially significant information. In a related vein, Merino et al. (2010) call on accounting academics to assume a more active role as public intellectuals and to lead an examination of the consequences of neoliberalism, one of which is increased income inequality.

## 5.3 Income Inequality in the US

### *5.3.1 The Fall and Rise of Income Inequality in the US*

It's no longer an exaggeration to say that middle-class Americans are an endangered species.
• Arianna Huffington

In response to the Great Depression of 1929, the US government instituted programs which increased national prosperity and simultaneously created a more equal

[3] Despite widespread insistence that shareholder value maximization is a legal mandate for corporate officers, large corporations (e.g. British Petroleum, Exxon, General Electric, and Archer Daniels Midland) promulgate commercials in both print and electronic format that focus almost exclusively on their social welfare activities and general concern for the planet.

distribution of that prosperity.[4] Galbraith describes the period from the 1930s through the 1970s as one in which organized labor, large corporations, and governmental policy formed a three-legged stool of countervailing powers that provided balance and stability, allowing labor and corporate profits to grow while government enlarged its role in ways that fostered productivity, expanded public education, and created greater security for citizens through programs such as Social Security and Medicare (Galbraith 2008).

The "basic bargain" of that period was that the rise in US prosperity would be widely shared; those workers who helped create higher corporate earnings would receive a "proportionate share of the fruits of economic growth" (Reich 2011, 31). The idea of the basic bargain, or equitable sharing (Rappaport 1964), has historic roots in modern capitalism. Adam Smith explains, "The produce of labour constitutes the natural recompence or wages of labour" (1776, Book I, ch. VIII). Smith's support for the basic bargain and a concern for equity led him to argue that workers should be paid more than maintenance wages.

During the period of the 1930s through mid-late 1970s, the basic bargain was observed to a significant extent, although minorities suffered significantly relative to the majority white population. As national productivity rose, so did working class and middle class incomes, more rapidly in percentage terms than did upper-class incomes (Adler 2010; Reich 2011; Saez 2012).

In constant 2007 dollars, average family income rose from $25,000 to $55,000 (Reich 2011, 43). The GI bill significantly increased the percentage of adults who were college-educated. Overtime pay was instituted for work beyond 40 hours per week, unemployment benefits were initiated, and unionization grew. By the mid-1950s, roughly one-third of US workers were in unions, helping to ensure workers' pay reflected employers' productivity growth. In 1965, Medicare was signed into law, increasing seniors' life expectancy and access to health care, and contributing to lower poverty rates. During this period, top marginal tax rates on individuals never dropped below 70 %, and rose during World War II to 94 %; top marginal corporate tax rates averaged 49 %. The overall effect was of a rising middle and working class.

During the 1970s, efforts to change the direction of government policies gained momentum. A neoliberal movement towards smaller government, greater militarism, domestic fiscal stringency, and deregulation began (Harvey 2005; Pollin 2003; Powell 1971). The premise of the neoliberal movement was that unrestricted markets offer efficiency in allocation of resources, and the implied promise was that "more prosperity for all citizens" would result (Soederberg 2008, 663).

Although support for neoliberalism had begun in the 1970s, with Reagan's election in 1980, neoliberalism became the ruling ideology of Washington politics.[5] Harvey notes that despite promises of broadly shared improved well-being, "the main

[4] This was also the era known by some economists as The Great Compression (i.e., of incomes) (Phillips 2002, 76). Reich (2011) calls this period The Great Prosperity.

[5] Margaret Thatcher's rise to power in the UK gave rise to neoliberal policies there at the same time.

substantive achievement of neoliberalism, however, has been to redistribute, rather than to generate, wealth and income," (2005, 159). Neoliberal economics resulted in enormous gains, but only for those at the top of the income spectrum. The top 10 % of earners claimed about 45 % of all earnings from the 1920s until 1940, after which time that percentage hovered around 33 % until 1975. Since then, their share has increased rapidly, to 49.7 % of all earnings in 2007, a level which is "higher than any other year since 1917, and even surpasses 1928, the peak of (the) stock market bubble in the 'roaring' 1920s" (Saez 2012, 2).

Meanwhile, with the rise of neoliberalism, income in the middle of the spectrum took a hit (Congressional Budget Office (CBO) 2011). Median wages in constant dollars were lower in 2007 than they were in 1977 (Reich 2011, 19). Although average income rose from 1975 to 2008, 94 % of the total gain went to the top 10 % of the population. Even within the top 10 % of the income distribution there is strong skew; the CBO observes that the top 1 % had substantially higher income growth than the remaining 9 % of that group (CBO 2011). By contrast, during the 1970s, the top 1 % of income earners received the lowest share of total income since 1913 (Saez 2012).

The basic bargain has been violated since the rise of neoliberalism. In J. P. Morgan's "Eye on the Market" member newsletter, the editors explain historically high profit margins. They note that "*reductions in wages and benefits explain the majority of the net improvement in margins*. This trend has continued; as we have shown several times over the last 2 years. US labor compensation is now at a 50-year low relative to both company sales and US GDP," (2011, 1, emphasis in original). Corporate profits are going up because wages and benefits are not. From 1947 to the early 1970s, productivity gains and average hourly compensation increased simultaneously, but since then, the two have diverged with accelerating speed. While productivity has continued to rise, average compensation has stagnated. Figure 5.1 illustrates the critical role that lower wages play in increasing inequality. Those at the top are gaining disproportionately across all income categories – active or passive earnings – so the increasing inequality cannot be attributed primarily to growth in the stock market, where assets are disproportionately held by the wealthy.[6]

Within corporate America, CEOs and other high-level executives receive ever-rapidly-increasing salaries (Adler 2010; Chang 2010; Martin 2011; Reberioux 2007). In 1950, Charles E. Wilson, CEO of General Motors, was the best-paid executive in the US; his gross income was $626,300, and if he had paid taxes on that without any unusual deductions his take-home pay would have been $164,300.[7] In the 1960s and 1970s, CEO pay was 30–40 times the average worker's compensation. Now it is 300–400 times the average worker's compensation (Chang 2010). If the

[6]Although our focus is on income inequality, the closely-related problem of wealth inequality is even more severe and worsening. In 2010, households in the bottom half of the net worth distribution owned only 1.1 % of the nation's household wealth (Levine 2012).

[7]The inflation factor since then is 9.33, which would yield an income of $5,843,379 in 2011 dollars. By comparison, the CEO of McKesson Medical earned over $145,000,000 in 2010.

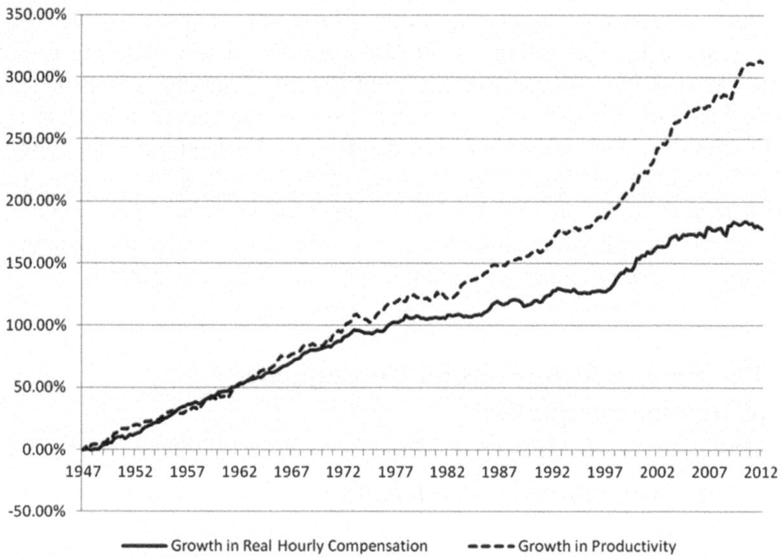


**Fig. 5.1** Growth of real hourly compensation for production/nonsupervisory workers and productivity, 1948–2011. (*Source*: Bureau of Labor Statistics)

minimum hourly wage in the US had kept pace with the growth in CEO pay, it would have been $23.03 in 2005 instead of $5.15 (Sahadi 2005).

Furthermore, income inequality in the US is increasing more quickly than in most other countries. The US pattern of rapidly increasing income inequality is paralleled in India and China, but not in European countries (Atkinson et al. 2011). The extraordinary gap between executive pay and average pay does not hold true overseas. Japanese workers receive 91 % of what the average US worker receives, while Japanese CEOs receive 5 % of what the average CEO of a similar US company receives (if stock options are included in US pay figures, 25 % if options are excluded). The global village that sets competitive wages for US workers does not appear to encompass the executive suite, where pay is clearly not equalized globally.

Martin compares average total CEO compensation earned to net income earned by the CEO's firm over time. From 1960 to 1980, CEO compensation per firm dollar earned dropped by 33 %. But since then, CEO compensation per dollar of firm income has gone up eightfold. Martin reports that between 1933 and 1976 the "total real compound annual return on the S & P 500" (Martin 2011, 63) was 7.5 %; since 1976 the return has been 6.5 %. The neoliberal justification for very high executive salaries is that the executives have created very high values for shareholders; however, average market returns have been lower while executive compensation has risen significantly higher. Considering historical trends and the pay of their international colleagues, Chang concludes that "US managers are over-priced" (2010, 153).

Classical economists, such as Adam Smith, argued that wages are the result of power rather than of strict supply and demand (Adler 2010). Agency theory would imply that executives, as agents, act in their own self-interest, with the board of directors responsible for setting executive compensation and imposing discipline. However, Martin asks, "How does the employment of another group of agents – called the board of directors – discipline the first group of agents and reduce agency costs?" (2011, 39). Directors often lack the detailed, in-depth knowledge required to detect and curtail self-interested managerial behavior. Thus, "entrenched managers can design dysfunctional or excessive compensation plans," (Baber et al. 2012, 221). Furthermore, when shareholders become aware of earnings management, they do not have the power to correct dysfunctional behavior (Chang 2010).

## 5.4 The Economic and Social Consequences of Income Inequality

### *5.4.1 Macro-economic Considerations*

> Inequality is not simply a description of how the pie of things is divided. It is also a force that determines how big the pie is…we will see that inequality itself causes the pie of things to be smaller.
>
> • Moshe Adler

Increased income inequality in the US is concentrated and driven to a great extent by a greatly expanded financial sector. "More than half of all the money that the top one-tenth of 1 % of American earners reported on their 2001 taxes represented the combined incomes of the top *five* executives at the 500 largest American companies. Almost all the rest were financial traders and hedge-fund managers" (Reich 2011, 56). Furthermore, "in 2009, the 25 best-paid hedge-fund managers together earned $25.3 billion" (Reich 2011, 57).

Phillips (2008) takes a historical view of the consequences of increasing financialization, drawing parallels from the fall of seventeenth century Spain, eighteenth century Netherlands, and the nineteenth (and early twentieth) century British Empire to the current US situation. Spain, the Netherlands, and Britain were leaders in important industries and services; as their wealth increased, so did the well-being of workers in those trades or industries. But the wealthy classes shifted from production of actual goods and services in basic areas to engage increasingly in financialization, a shift accompanied by increased income inequality. Phillips notes a repeated pattern of subsequent economic decline. An "enlarged vulnerability that comes with financial preoccupation and a *rentier* culture – nonchalance towards humdrum-seeming production, tendencies to acquire buildups of debt, and increasingly transnational loyalties," (Phillips 2002, 197) leads to a failure to invest and maintain technology, infrastructure, and an industrial base. Phillips (2008, viii) observes that the "1980s can be identified as the launching pad of a decisive financial sector takeover of the US economy, consummated by turbocharged, relentless expansion of financial debt," and warns that "moving money around instead of making things is always dicey, and the U.S. transformation has been the most grandiose to date."

Phillips (2008) describes the money generated by the increasingly-dominant, loosely-regulated financial sector as "bad," in part because of the negative effects of extreme income inequality on individual well-being, which we explore in the next section.

### *5.4.2 Social Consequences of Inequality*

> Our inequality materializes our upper class, vulgarizes our middle class, brutalizes our lower class.
>
> • Matthew Arnold

In *The Spirit Level* (2010), Wilkinson and Pickett provide comparative data from 23 of the countries within the Organization for Economic Cooperation and Development (OECD) as well as comparative data, when available, on the 50 states within the US. They find striking and consistent evidence that income inequality is associated with a broad array of social problems, including health effects. The strongest correlation of the incidence of social problems with other markers is with that of income inequality, defined as the ratio of the top 20 % of income earnings to the bottom 20 %. This is a very forgiving measure that understates the extent of income inequality, because incomes become more and more skewed as one moves higher up the income distribution (Hacker and Pierson 2010; Reich 2011). Even with this fairly broad and forgiving measure, the US is second only to Singapore in income inequality.

Wilkinson and Pickett describe some of the psychological and biological mechanisms by which inequality causes stress to individuals. They posit an increase in anxiety occasioned by interpersonal comparison, which – even if unconscious – creates shame, social anxiety, and threats to one's self-esteem, all of which can be shown to have biological effects that form a downward vicious cycle. In addition, more conscious cognitions of these comparisons lead to self-defeating behaviors, loss of optimism, anger and resentment, and less trust in others, and may at the extreme result in criminal behavior, but can at the least lead to lives of less satisfaction and fulfillment.

Wilkinson and Pickett's data show that even the best-off in highly unequal societies suffer; in several of their analyses those at the lower income level in more equal societies do better than those at the top levels of unequal societies. This conclusion is reinforced by sociobiologists D. S. and E. O. Wilson, who summarize a lifetime of research by saying," Selfishness beats altruism within groups. Altruistic groups beat selfish groups. Everything else is commentary" (2007, 345). Selfish behavior may be advantageous for the individual in the short run, but a society of the generous outlasts a society of the greedy.[8]

---

[8]Axelrod's famous computerized Prisoner's Dilemma experiment showed this effect quite dramatically when Anatol Rappoport won with a generous strategy called Tit for Tat (1984).

In the late 1970s the US Gross Domestic Product (GDP) and indicators of social health and well-being rose together. Then divergence between the financial and social measures began; the national GDP continued rising while indexes of social health declined significantly (Phillips 2002, 166). As income inequality began to increase, poverty among children, homicides among teen-agers, poverty amongst the elderly, and unemployment did as well. Looking at a more granular data set allowing comparison of states and metropolitan areas, Phillips found that health and life expectancy were "more closely linked to *relative* than *absolute* income, with rising inequality meaning higher mortality," (Phillips 2002, 346). In making that comparison, Phillips foreshadows the work of Wilkinson and Pickett. They find that the following social and health phenomena are lower in countries where income inequality is higher:

- Trust in others
- Women's status
- Life expectancy (and that is NOT related to health expenditures)
- Math and literacy scores of 15-year-olds in the international comparison and 8th graders in the US state comparison
- Teen-age aspirations
- Social mobility
- Child well-being
- Innovation
- Spending on foreign aid[9]

The following social and health phenomena increase with increased income inequality:

- Mental illness
- Use of illegal drugs
- Infant mortality
- Adult and child obesity
- High school dropout rates
- Teen pregnancies and births
- Homicides
- Reported bullying in schools
- Blood pressure and diabetes
- Imprisonment rates
- Carbon emissions
- Environmental damage

Other researchers report similar findings. Bezruchka demonstrates that the US has fallen behind in key health measures compared to other countries, and concludes that "income and economic inequality are important factors in a wide range of social and health outcomes," (2012, 167). Collison et al. (2007) report that mortality of children under 5 years of age is correlated with income inequality, even when the US (an outlier on the income inequality scale) is excluded from the analysis.

[9]These lists are not exhaustive.

Fukuyama bemoans the takeover of politics by neoliberal economics and notes that the "benefits of the new order accrued disproportionately to a very small number of people in finance and high technology" (2012, 58). He observes that a stable democracy requires a "broad middle class and that societies with extremes of wealth and poverty are susceptible either to oligarchic domination or populist revolution" (2012, 55). Interestingly, Fukuyama, whose past conservative credentials are well-established, urges Democrats to create an alternative narrative to the neoliberal promises that all will be enriched if markets are ever-freer and governments and states ever-smaller. Clearly, the neoliberal promises have not been fulfilled. Economic evidence shows that when a nation hews more closely to the neoliberal ideology, inequality of income, wealth and opportunity are greater (Adler 2010; Chang 2010; Merino et al. 2010; Phillips 2002, 2008).

We turn next to the issue of how some of the policies that foster income inequality could be disclosed within annual financial reports so the public can be better informed about the allocation of societal resources.

## 5.5 Accounting for Income Inequality

> One big part of the reason we have so much inequality is that the top 1 % want it that way.
> • Joseph Stiglitz

We argue that the accounting profession should change required disclosures in three areas – compensation, taxation, and non-business expenses, such as charitable giving, political donations, and lobbying. This is a modest step towards informing the public, which could affect their decisions as customers, investors, and citizens, and could possibly lead to pressure to change laws that currently promote extreme income inequality. We focus on these three areas because they have the greatest impact, direct or indirect, on income inequality. Shifting compensation patterns are – as we have shown – the direct cause of increasing income inequality. Taxation policies are also implicated in increasing income inequality (CBO 2011). Those who argue for lower taxation claim that the result will be greater job creation. Having clear, available, and transparent information on taxes paid by corporations will allow both citizens and government officials to weigh those claims more knowledgeably. Finally, non-business expenses (which include lobbying and campaign contributions) are used to shape legal policies that further income inequality (and represent a ursurpation of shareholder rights, as we shall argue later).

We are not proposing the use of complex models which involve assumptions about future interest rates or stock market volatility, such as those which corporations must create when complying with reporting stock option expenses or goodwill impairment, for instance. We are calling only for greater detail and transparency on actual cash transactions, expenditures corporations engage in routinely and which, in some instances, generate refunds from local governments. Thus, providing this information does not require costly expertise and should be relatively unburdensome.

We argue for increased information within the financial statements themselves. Accountants can and should revise Generally Accepted Accounting Principles to encompass a fuller accounting of the distributive effects corporations have (e.g. Bayou et al. 2011; Ramanathan 1976). The free market depends on information, and we are arguing that the public's information set should include data on how corporations have fostered income inequality through compensation, taxation, and social expenditures. This is a change that accountants have the power to enact.

We suggest the additional data we call for can be used as measures of a corporation's impact on income inequality in the US – measures of its "inequality footprint," if you will. This list is tentative and represents an initial effort. Information to construct some of these measures may be obtained given current publicly-available information. Other measures cannot, and would require new disclosures by corporations, many of which would require accountants to change the requirements of GAAP, because corporations would not be likely to disclose such information voluntarily.[10] Even if some limited information is currently available to the public, we argue it should be compiled into annual financial reports to be consistent across firms, making comparisons easier for users of the financial statements.

### *5.5.1 Compensation Issues*

> The institutions in which we are employed are, after all, the main source of income inequality. It is there that value is created and divided between the various gradations of employees. It is there that the inequities which necessitate redistribution are set up.
>
> • Richard Wilkinson and Kate Pickett

#### 5.5.1.1 Pay Disparity

The income inequality created by or resulting from corporate actions and decisions takes many forms. Corporations create inequality by distributing payouts differently among their different stakeholders: wage-earning labor, executives, and shareholders. Corporations exacerbate income inequality by their compensation practices *within* their workforces. "The gap between what workers and top executives make helps explain why income inequality in the United States is reaching levels unseen since the Great Depression," as executive pay in the last 40 years has quadrupled while non-supervisory worker pay has dropped over the same time period (Whoriskey 2011). Firms are not required to disclose the details of compensation costs other than limited executive compensation, post-retirement benefits, and structures such as employee stock-option plans, so information on compensation patterns is

[10] The information we propose gathering may be easier to obtain for companies that are registered as benefit corporations or B-Corporations, which are required to provide expanded disclosure about their social impact. As this is a relatively new and small category of companies, however, we do not discuss these types of companies or the disclosures they provide separately from more traditional companies.

difficult to obtain from a firm's financial statements. We suggest providing detail on average compensation and benefits by decile of employee and providing total compensation and details of deferred compensation for the ten top-paid executives. This information is readily available from corporate Human Resource departments and would help the public understand the benefits in job provision provided by companies in their communities.

Even the limited disclosure of Dodd-Frank Section 953(b), which requires public firms to provide the ratio of executive pay to median employee compensation, has not yet been implemented, and has been resisted by members of Congress and groups such as the US Chamber of Commerce. We recommend that far greater detail concerning ranges of compensation and the numbers of workers within each range should be included in the annual financial report.

#### 5.5.1.2 Employee Benefits

According to the US Bureau of Labor Statistics, benefits make up 29.9 % of employee compensation. Slottje et al. (2000) find that benefits are more unevenly distributed than base pay is; when health and pension benefits are included in total compensation, income inequality increases. Thus, when looking at the impact of the benefits paid by a firm on income inequality, we must consider not only the dollar amount of those benefits in total, but also the distribution of those benefits across the firm's employees. This information is not publicly available, but could be easily compiled by publicly-traded companies. Some firms voluntarily disclose the cost of employee benefits in total, but usually not how those benefits are distributed across their workforces. In any comparison of compensation, all forms of providing employee wealth (such as stock options, deferred compensation, moving allowances, etc.) must be considered, and given the various ways to enrich high-level executives, defining compensation is not always straightforward. Accountants can and should, however, help firms to formulate public reporting that is more transparent and comprehensible for readers.

#### 5.5.1.3 Employee Turnover

Research has shown that employee turnover is higher at firms that pay less (Cotton and Tuttle 1986; Guthrie 2000), and that one of the biggest reasons employees leave their jobs is that they are unsatisfied with the pay and benefits they receive (Robison 2008). As such, a firm's employee turnover rate may serve as a measure of the level of pay at a firm and how satisfied the firm's employees are with their compensation. While employee turnover rates are available publicly by industry from the Bureau of Labor Statistics, data for individual firms are not currently available publicly, but could be easily provided as part of firms' annual audited reports. If communities are asked to give tax abatements or cash incentives to companies for expanding in or moving to their communities, then the communities should have more comprehensive information related to firms' employment patterns in order to make well-informed decisions.

#### 5.5.1.4 Ratio of Full-Time Employees to Part-Time Employees

Part-time employment has been on the rise in the United States over the last few years, according to Bureau of Labor Statistics data. Full-time employment is more stable and pays more on a per-hour basis than part-time employment (Rani 2008; Tilly 1990). In addition, typically, part-time employees do not earn benefits (Tilly 1990). Furthermore, when more part-time workers are employed in an industry, the pay of the *full*-timers employed in that industry is lower as well (Tilly 1990). Research has shown that as the proportion of jobs in an economy that are non-standard (part-time and temporary) increases, so does income inequality in that economy (Rani 2008; Tilly 1990).

Firms that employ a higher percentage of their workforce as part-time workers, therefore, are contributing to increasing income inequality in the economy. As such, the lower the ratio of full-time to part-time employees within a given company, the more that company is likely to contribute to income inequality. The number of full-time workers employed by a publicly-traded firm is usually included in its company profile on financial websites, but it is difficult to find information on how many workers are employed at a company on a part-time basis. However, companies could easily provide information on how much of their workforce is part-time or temporary as part of their annual reports.

#### 5.5.1.5 Relationship with Unions

> Unions – the folks who brought you the weekend
> • Bumper sticker

Union membership in the United States has declined fairly steadily over the past 40 years, from 34 % of employed men to 8 %, and from 16 % of employed women to 6 % (Western and Rosenfeld 2011). Western and Rosenfeld (2011) argue that the decline in union membership can account for between a fifth and a third of the growth in income inequality, due to two effects. First, wages for workers who belong to unions are, on average, higher than their counterparts at firms that are not unionized (see also Anderson et al. 2008). Second, when unions are more prevalent in society, norms for fair pay tend to increase, resulting in higher pay for those who are not unionized.[11] Union membership is also information that could be easily provided by firms.

#### 5.5.1.6 Offshoring

> We cannot keep outsourcing our future to low-wage countries.
> • Bernie Sanders

[11] Galbraith makes a similar argument in *The Predator State* (2008).

In the 2000s, multinational firms based in the US eliminated 2.9 million jobs in their home country, and added 2.4 million jobs outside the country (Wessel and Greenberg 2011). When jobs are moved overseas, a practice called offshoring, short-term unemployment goes up in the U.S. as those who have lost their jobs search for new work. Those who do find new work typically do so at lower pay; manufacturing workers lose on average 12 % of their earnings, and nonmanufacturing workers lose on average 4 % of their earnings after such a shift (Garner 2004). While some economists argue that offshoring is actually good for the American economy because it generates savings for companies and stimulates the economies of countries we trade with, it is not good for the American workers whose jobs are terminated (Bivens 2005).

Firms engaged in offshoring contribute to income inequality by taking income away from US workers while increasing savings, and thus profit, to themselves. A good measure of the extent to which a firm has engaged in offshoring would be the ratio of jobs added by the company overseas to jobs eliminated in the US. It is currently difficult to find this information, however, as US companies are required to report only their total employment. Several bills have been introduced in Congress to require disclosure of employment by country, at least in some industries, but none have yet been made law, so we recommend that it become GAAP disclosure.

## 5.5.2 *Taxation Information*

### 5.5.2.1 Income Tax

> We now live in a world in which profitable companies perfectly legally pay nothing in taxes at precisely the same moment that we are saying to young people, 'You're going to have to take on debt to get a college education' and we're saying to seniors, 'You're just going to have to learn to live on less.'
>
> • Elizabeth Warren

The best measure of a firm's true federal income tax expense is its actual cash paid to tax authorities (Sloan 2011; Citizens for Tax Justice 2012). While a great deal of arcane language and at least one complicated footnote purport to offer this information to readers of financial statements, the amount companies actually pay cannot be determined from information currently required on annual reports. Sloan reports that he worked with a distinguished tax professor who tried unsuccessfully to determine the amount General Electric actually paid in taxes from information on the financial statements (2011). Another expert reported that General Electric paid a tax rate of approximately 2.3 % over the last decade. While disputing that, General Electric did not counter with a different actual rate paid. Cash payments, as accounting faculty repeat to students, are easier to audit because they are not subject to accrual. Determining the amount of checks that were written to tax authorities of various governments (Federal, state, and local) is not a theoretically difficult task. Such information should be made available in annual financial reports in order to help stakeholders know what companies are contributing to the national and local treasury.

When corporations take advantage of tax loopholes to pay less than the nominal federal corporate income tax rate, the overall tax burden is shifted towards individuals. Effective federal taxes are particularly low. "..If corporations paid the same effective tax rate that they paid in 1961, the additional tax revenue would total $485 billion" (Collins et al. 2011, 1). Since 1961, the amount of total federal tax revenues contributed by corporations has declined from 22.2 to 9.1 % (Collins et al. 2011, 8). Such a dramatic change would imply that corporations today consume (and should therefore pay for) only 40 % of the social goods, infrastructure, and other governmental benefits they did in 1961. We have seen no studies supporting such a radical shift. As such, when a firm pays lower rates or is eligible for credits based on favorable laws and regulations (often lobbied for by business interests), it contributes to income inequality.

#### 5.5.2.2 Corporate Subsidies, Abatements, Tax Incentives, and Other Tax Expenditures

> Roseanne: "So they get a tax break? Well, who's gonna pay the taxes that they ain't paying?"
> Congressman: "Well…you will."
> • *Roseanne* episode "Aliens"

Many exceptions to stated corporate income and property tax rates exist. Firms often receive economic incentives, subsidies, or tax abatements from state or local governments to either relocate facilities into their jurisdictions, or not relocate outside their jurisdictions.[12] These subsidies amount to almost $50 billion annually (Thomas 2011). Despite proponents' claims, relocation subsidies do not create jobs, as jobs created in a new location result in jobs lost in another location (Thomas 2011). Such transfers of wealth to firms from state or local government represent a shifting of the tax burden from those firms to individual taxpayers within those jurisdictions, and contribute to income inequality nationwide (Zimmerman 2011). In 16 states, incentives for relocating or for job creation of various sorts are collected by corporations who are allowed to retain all or some of their employees' state and local income tax withholdings (Mattera et al. 2012). Estimates are that about $700 million per year is being diverted, all of it without notice to employees on their pay stubs.

Many forms of tax abatement and subsidies do not require careful auditing to ensure that the public purpose behind the subsidy was fulfilled. An appropriate measure of a firm's impact on the tax burden in the communities in which it operates would be the ratio of total subsidies received in a jurisdiction to the total tax revenues collected in that jurisdiction. This ratio would measure the percentage of tax revenues diverted from other government purposes to that specific firm. We suggest that companies disclose the individual and total tax subsidies and incentives they receive as part of their audited annual reports.

[12] In Iowa, for example, the state actually gives refundable tax incentives, so some of the largest corporations receive refunds that exceed their tax liability.

#### 5.5.2.3 Transfer Pricing

> Transfer pricing is the corporate equivalent of secret offshore accounts of individual tax dodgers.
> • Carl Levin

In addition to shifting jobs overseas, firms are also shifting income overseas. When multinational firms engage in internal transactions or transactions with closely related firms, they do so using transfer pricing, in which they set a price for such transactions that is supposed to be a price that would be set in an arm's length transaction, according to US law. However, numerous studies suggest such prices are not always arm's length; instead, they are set so that higher profits are reported in countries where the tax rate is lower, and consequently lower profits accrue in countries where the tax rate is higher (see the JCT 2010 for a review of these studies). To take advantage of the tax benefits of such abuses of transfer pricing, or transfer mispricing, the corporation must intend to permanently reinvest those funds outside the United States. Consistent with this, earnings reinvested abroad by US multinationals have increased (JCT 2010).

Engaging in transfer mispricing can have detrimental effects on income inequality in the US. First, it shifts tax revenues from the US to other, lower-rate countries, which results in a higher tax burden on individual taxpayers of $28 billion dollars annually (Sullivan 2010). Second, it encourages investment in foreign countries, which contributes to the previously-mentioned offshoring of jobs. It is difficult to judge the extent to which multinational corporations engage in transfer mispricing. However, this mechanism is available only to multinational corporations, but not to wholly domestic corporations. It is thus reasonable to assume that on average, multinationals contribute more to income inequality than do wholly domestic corporations. We suggest that corporations clearly indicate how much of their earnings have been retained outside US tax jurisdictions.

### *5.5.3 Non-business Expenses – Social, Lobbying and Political Contributions*

> Washington now works for those who can hire an army of lobbyists.
> • Elizabeth Warren

Milton Friedman famously proclaimed that a corporation's sole responsibility is to maximize profits, presumably to create shareholder value.

> ...A corporate executive is an employee of the owners of the business. He has direct responsibility to his employers. That responsibility is to conduct the business in accordance with their desires, which generally will be to make as much money as possible while conforming to the basic rules of the society, both those embodied in law and those embodied in ethical custom. (Friedman 1970)

Friedman speaks of law as an exogenous force, independent of business, and separately formed and authorized. He continues by saying that a corporate executive who spends money for social purposes, which includes lobbying, imposes taxes and "becomes in effect a public employee, a civil servant, even though he remains in name an employee of a private enterprise." Friedman strongly condemns executives who assume this civil role and says it is "intolerable" for civil servants to be selected in such a private manner. If corporate executives "impose taxes and make expenditures to foster 'social' objectives, then political machinery must be set up to make the assessment of taxes and to determine through a political process the objectives to be served." Friedman asks how a corporate executive could know any better than his three key constituent groups – employees, customers, and shareholders – how to spend those constituents' money on social ends the constituents have no voice in selecting.

Lobbying is "the attempt to persuade legislators to propose, pass, defeat legislation, or change existing laws to provide benefits to parties with special interests" (Hill et al. 2011). Ignoring Friedman, corporations now influence legislators to such an extent that lobbying and campaign contributions have become a profit center, and laws are written at the behest of and in some cases by corporate agents. Neither the government nor unions is a reliable and consistent counterbalance to corporate influence and power (Hacker and Pierson 2010). Income inequality is exacerbated by lobbying, public interest campaigns, and other pressures exerted by corporations outside of the public eye, activities which are not typically included in the glossy, public-relations oriented CSR reporting companies issue to the public. The amount corporations have spent on lobbying in recent years has skyrocketed; Hacker and Pierson (2010) report that $3.5 billion annually is probably a minimum. Because of the Citizens United ruling by the Supreme Court, this number will definitely increase.

Researchers have found that firms that engage in lobbying experience increased accounting income and returns to shareholders relative to firms that do not lobby, firms that lobby less, the firm's industry, and the market overall (Chen et al. 2010; Hill et al. 2011; Kim 2008). Former SEC chairman Levitt notes, "With laserlike precision, groups representing Wall Street firms, mutual fund companies, accounting firms, or corporate managers would quickly set about to defeat even minor threats. Individual investors, with no organized labor or trade association to represent their views in Washington, never knew what hit them" (2002, 250).

The increased returns firms experience from lobbying come from a number of sources: direct subsidies, lower taxes, government contracts, limited competition, entry into previously protected markets, and relaxed regulatory oversight (Chen et al. 2010; Faccio 2006; Stigler 1971; Yu and Yu 2011). Either directly or indirectly, these benefits to firms contribute to income inequality. For instance, when firms increase their lobbying expenditures, they experience significantly lower effective tax rates in the following year (Richter et al. 2009). Thus, data from the Center for Responsive Politics (2012) shows taxes are one of the top issues lobbyists discuss with government officials (see also Richter et al. 2009). Campaign and political action committee contributions are lucrative. Chirinko and Wilson (2010, 20) find that "the economic value of a $1 business campaign contribution in terms of lower state corporate taxes is approximately $6.65." We are unaware of a similar study of the economic return of lobbying and campaign contributions in terms of federal tax avoidance.

The overall purpose of lobbying and political contributions is to influence government outside of the electoral process and without input from shareholders, and ultimately divert government resources to the firm. We suggest that all such social influence payments by corporations be provided in detail and total in annual financial statements. This disclosure would include more traditional philanthropic payments, as well as payments to independent expenditure committees (Super PACs), think tanks, business/trade groups such as the Chamber of Commerce, and political campaigns. Some limited information about payments to these recipients is publicly available on various websites, but fuller disclosure has been resisted, as the 2012 Congressional vote against the Disclose Act reveals.

### 5.5.4 *Shadow Reports*

We are supportive of shadow reports on income equality as a second information outlet, but do not argue for them explicitly as they are beyond the scope of this proposal. Such reports would be prepared by outsiders and would expose the activities corporations engage in that promote greater income inequality. Such reports have been attempted by the Centre for Social and Environmental Accounting Research (CSEAR) in the United Kingdom. Professional accountants do not have the authority to mandate shadow reports, but various non-profit groups are currently gathering information that could be useful for such reports. Aggregating that information into a single report could enhance its information value significantly.

## 5.6 Summary and Concluding Remarks

Increasing income inequality emerged in the US in the late 1970s and has accelerated since. We have described some of the serious negative individual, social, and macroeconomic consequences of income inequality, which we consider one of the most pervasive and consequential of social issues. We support the early work of Ramanathan and Rappaport and recent work (e.g. Adams 2004; Bayou et al. 2011; Dey 2007) arguing that the scope of corporate reporting should include distributive effects in addition to the current focus on predicting future cash flows from production or service activities. We offer a tentative list of data related to compensation, taxation and non-business expenses that should be included in annual financial reports. We believe that a focus on the distributive effects of corporate behavior is broader and more liberating than arguing for the inclusion of identified additional stakeholders in various corporate governance roles. We believe that accountants have a unique professional role and responsibility – we define generally accepted accounting principles and the content of annual reports. We have a responsibility to expand the information in those reports to address the public interest. In addition to our narrow (and intellectually confused) focus on helping investors and creditors predict future cash flows, we suggest that accountants require expanded information to help the public understand current cash flows. Citizens need more information to evaluate current tax policies, compensation patterns, and involvement by corporations in setting legal and social policies.

In addition to providing information that will enable the public to better understand the role corporations play in the allocation of societal resources, additional disclosure can help inform discussions as to alternative approaches to organizing businesses. Such alternatives include cooperatives, employee-owned business, and benefit corporations. By serving different goals and differently-defined stakeholders than traditional corporations do, such groups will provide different information sets to the public. They can directly and by example slow down the increase of income inequality and provide possibilities that help citizens understand that the status quo is not the result of inevitable forces, but can be altered to better serve the public good.

## References


AAACSC (American Accounting Association Committee on Social Costs). 1975. Report of the committee on social costs. *The Accounting Review, 50*(Suppl), 50–89.

Adams, C.A. 2004. The ethical, social and environmental reporting-performance portrayal gap. *Accounting, Auditing & Accountability Journal* 17(5): 731–757.

Adler, M. 2010. *Economics for the rest of us: Debunking the science that makes life dismal*. New York: The New Press.

Anderson, S., J. Cavanagh, C. Collins, S. Pizzigati, and M. Lapham. 2008. *Executive excess 2008: How average taxpayers subsidize runaway pay*. Washington, DC: Institute for Policy Studies and United for a Fair Economy. http://www.faireconomy.org/files/executive_excess_2008.pdf. Accessed 29 Mar 2012.

Atkinson, A.B., T. Piketty, and E. Saez. 2011. Top incomes in the long run of history. *Journal of Economic Literature* 49(1): 3–71.

Axelrod, R. 1984. *The evolution of cooperation*. New York: Basic Books.

Baber, W.R., L. Liang, and Z. Zhu. 2012. Associations between internal and external corporate governance characteristics: Implications for investigating financial accounting restatements. *Accounting Horizons* 26: 219–237.

Bayou, M.E., A. Reinstein, and P.F. Williams. 2011. To tell the truth: A discussion of issues concerning truth and ethics in accounting. *Accounting, Organizations and Society* 36: 109–124.

Bezruchka, S. 2012. The hurrieder I go the behinder I get: The deteriorating international ranking of U.S. health status. *Annual Review of Public Health* 33: 157–173.

Bivens, J. 2005. *Truth and consequences of offshoring: Recent studies overstate the benefits and ignore the costs to American workers*. Washington, DC: Economic Policy Institute, August 1. http://www.epi.org/publication/bp155/. Accessed 29 Mar 2012.

Chang, H. 2010. *23 things they don't tell you about capitalism*. New York: Bloomsbury Press.

Chen, H., D. C. Parsley, and Y. Yang. 2010. *Corporate lobbying and ginancial performance*. Available at SSRN: http://ssrn.com/abstract=1014264. Accessed 29 Mar 2012, doi:10.2139/ssrn.1014264

Chirinko, R.S., and D.J. Wilson. 2010. Can lower tax rates be bought? Business rent-seeking and tax competition among U. S. states. *National Tax Journal* 63: 967–993.

Cho, C.H., R.P. Guidry, A.M. Hageman, and D.M. Patten. 2012. Do actions speak louder than words? An empirical investigation of corporate environmental reputation. *Accounting, Organizations and Society* 37(1): 14–25.

Collins, C., A. Goldberg, S. Klinger, and S. Pizzigati. 2011. *Unnecessary austerity, unnecessary shutdown*. Washington, DC: Institute for Policy Studies, April 7. http://www.ips-dc.org/reports/unnecessary_austerity_unnecessary_government_shutdown. Accessed 29 Mar 2012.

Collison, D., C. Dey, G. Hannah, and L. Stevenson. 2007. Income inequality and child mortality in wealthy nations. *Journal of Public Health* 29(2): 114–117.

Congressional Budget Office (CBO). 2011. *Trends in the distribution of household income between 1979 and 2007*. Washington, DC: Congress of the United States.

Cotton, J.L., and J.M. Tuttle. 1986. Employee turnover: A meta-analysis and review with implications for research. *The Academy of Management Review* 11(1): 55–70.

Dey, C. 2007. Developing silent and shadow accounts. In *Sustainability accounting and accountability*, ed. J. Unerman, J. Bebbington, and B. O'Dwyer, 327–344. London: Routledge.

Faccio, M. 2006. Politically connected firms. *American Economic Review* 96(1): 369–386.

Friedman, M. 1970. The social responsibility of business is to increase profits. *The New York Times Magazine*, September 13.

Fukuyama, F. 2012. The future of history. *Foreign Affairs* 91(1): 53–61.

Galbraith, J.K. 2008. *The predator state: How conservatives abandoned the free market and why liberals should too*. New York: The Free Press.

Garner, C. A. 2004. Offshoring in the service sector: Economic impact and policy issues. *Economic Review*. 89(3): 5–38 [Third Quarter, Federal Reserve Bank of Kansas City]

Gray, R. 2002. The social accounting project and *Accounting Organizations and Society* privileging engagement, imaginings, new accountings and pragmatism over critique? *Accounting, Organizations and Society* 27(7): 687–708.

Guthrie, J.P. 2000. Alternative pay practices and employee turnover: An organization economics perspective. *Group & Organization Management* 25(4): 419–439.

Hacker, J.S., and P. Pierson. 2010. *Winner-take-all politics: How Washington made the rich richer – and turned its back on the middle class*. New York: Simon and Schuster.

Harvey, D. 2005. *A brief history of neoliberalism*. Oxford: Oxford University Press.

Hill, M. D., G. W. Kelly, G. B. Lockhart, and R. A. Van Ness. 2011. *Determinants and effects of corporate lobbying*. Available at SSRN: http://ssrn.com/abstract=1420224. Accessed 29 Mar 2012, doi:10.2139/ssrn.1420224

JCT (Joint Committee on Taxation). 2010. *Present law and background related to possible income shifting and transfer pricing*, July 20, Washington, DC: Joint Committee on Taxation.

Kim, J. 2008. Corporate lobbying revisited. *Business and Politics* 10(2): 1–23.

Levine, L. 2012. *An analysis of the wealth across households, 1989–2010*. Washington, DC: Congressional Research Service. Available at www.crs.gov

Levitt, A. 2002. *Take on the street: How to fight for your financial future*. New York: Vintage.

Martin, R.L. 2011. *Fixing the game: Bubbles, crashes, and what capitalism can learn from the NFL*. Boston: Harvard Business Review Press.

Mattera, P., K. Tarczynska, L. McIlvaine, T. Cafcas, and G. LeRoy. 2012. *Paying taxes to the boss*. Washington, DC: Good Jobs First. Available at www.goodjobsfirst.org

Merino, B., A.G. Mayper, and T. Tolleson. 2010. Neoliberalism, deregulation and Sarbanes-Oxley: The legitimatisation of a failed corporate governance model. *Accounting, Auditing, and Accountability Journal* 23: 774–792.

Morgan, J.P. 2011. Profits. *Eye on the Market*, July 11, 1.

Owen, D. 2008. Chronicles of wasted time? a personal reflection on the current state of, and future prospects for, social and environmental accounting research. *Accounting, Auditing & Accountability Journal* 21(2): 240–267.

Parker, L.D. 2005. Social and environmental accountability research: A view from the commentary box. *Accounting, Auditing & Accountability Journal* 18(6): 842–860.

Phillips, K. 2002. *Wealth and democracy: A political history of the American rich*. New York: Broadway Books.

Phillips, K. 2008. *Bad money: Reckless finance, failed politics, and the global crisis of American capitalism*. New York: Viking.

Pollin, R. 2003. *Contours of descent*. London: Verso.
Powell, L. F. Jr. 1971. *Confidential memo: Attack on the American free enterprise system*. http://law.wlu.edu/powellarchives/page.asp?pageid=1251
Ramanathan, K.V. 1976. Toward a theory of corporate social accounting. *The Accounting Review* 51(3): 516–528.
Rani, U. 2008. *Impact of changing work patterns on income inequality*. Geneva: International Institute for Labour Studies. http://www.ilo.org/public/english/bureau/inst/publications/discussion/dp19308.pdf. Accessed 29 Mar 2012.
Rappaport, A. 1964. Establishing objectives for published corporate accounting reports. *The Accounting Review* 39(4): 951–962.
Reberioux, A. 2007. Does shareholder primacy lead to a decline in managerial accountability? *Cambridge Journal of Economics* 31: 307–324.
Reich, R.B. 2011. *Aftershock: The next economy & America's future*. New York: Vintage.
Richter, B.K., K. Samphantharak, and J.F. Timmons. 2009. Lobbying and taxes. *American Journal of Political Science* 53(4): 893–909.
Robison, J. 2008. Turning around employee turnover. *Gallup Business Journal*, (May 8). http://gmj.gallup.com/content/106912/turning-around-your-turnover-problem.aspx. Accessed 29 Mar 2012.
Saez, E. 2012. *Striking it richer: The evolution of top incomes in the United States (updated with 2009 and 2010 estimates)*, March 2. http://elsa.berkeley.edu/~saez/saez-UStopincomes-2010.pdf. Accessed 29 Mar 2012.
Sahadi, J. 2005. *CEO pay: Sky high gets even higher*. CNN Money, Last modified August 30. http://money.cnn.com/2005/08/26/news/economy/ceo_pay/.
Shamir, R. 2004. The de-radicalization of corporate social responsibility. *Critical Sociology* 30(3): 669–689.
Sloan, A. 2011. Big corporations need to show us how much they pay in taxes. *Fortune* 164(9): 79.
Slottje, D.J., S.A. Woodbury, and R.W. Anderson. 2000. Employee benefits and the distribution of income and wealth. In *Employee benefits and labor markets in Canada and the United States*, ed. W.T. Alpert and S.A. Woodbury, 349–378. Kalamazoo: W.E. Upjohn Institute for Employment Research.
Smith, A. 1776/2000. *An inquiry into the nature and causes of the wealth of nations*. New York: Modern Library Paperback Edition.
Soederberg, S. 2008. A critique of the diagnosis and cure for 'Enronitis': The Sarbanes-Oxley Act and neoliberal governance of corporate America. *Critical Sociology* 34(5): 657–680.
Stigler, G.J. 1971. The theory of economic regulation. *Bell Journal of Economics and Management Science* 2(1): 3–21.
Sullivan, M. A. 2010. Transfer pricing costs U.S. at least $28 Billion. *Tax Notes*, March 29.
Thomas, K.P. 2011. *Investment incentives and the global competition for capital*. New York: Palgrave Macmillan.
Tilly, C. 1990. *Short hours, short shrift: Causes and consequences of part-time work*. Washington, DC: Economic Policy Institute. http://epi.3cdn.net/c6374dfbf045a10c38_9gm6ivu46.pdf. Accessed 29 Mar 2012.
Tinker, T., and R. Gray. 2003. Beyond a critique of pure reason: From policy to politics to praxis in environmental and social research. *Accounting, Auditing & Accountability Journal* 16(5): 727–761.
Wessel, D., and S.L. Greenberg. 2011. Big U.S. firms shift hiring abroad. *Wall Street Journal* 257(90): B1–B2.
Western, B., and J. Rosenfeld. 2011. Unions, norms, and the rise in U.S. wage inequality. *American Sociological Review* 76(4): 513–537.
Whoriskey, P. 2011. *Cozy relationships and 'peer benchmarking' send CEOs' pay soaring*. The Washington Post Online, October 3. http://www.washingtonpost.com/business/economy/cozy-relationships-and-peer-benchmarking-send-ceos-pay-soaring/2011/09/22/gIQA-gq8NJL_story.html. Accessed 29 Mar 2012.
Wilkinson, R., and K. Pickett. 2010. *The spirit level: Why equality is better for everyone*. London: Penguin.

Wilson, D.S., and E.O. Wilson. 2007. Rethinking the theoretical foundation of sociobiology. *The Quarterly Review of Biology* 82(4): 327–348.

Yu, F., and X. Yu. 2011. Corporate lobbying and fraud detection. *Journal of Financial and Quantitative Analysis* 46: 1865–1891.

Zimmerman, J. I. 2011. *The folly of corporate relocation incentives*. The Atlantic Cities, December 16. http://www.theatlanticcities.com/jobs-and-economy/2011/12/folly-corporate-relocation-incentives/737/. Accessed 29 Mar 2012.

# Chapter 6
# Professionalism, the Public Interest, and Social Accounting

**Gordon Boyce**

## 6.1 Introduction: Bringing the Social into Accounting

The role of accounting in the occurrence (and recurrence) of corporate and business scandals and the associated crises of public confidence highlights the importance of clarifying our understanding of the relationship between accounting and the public interest and of addressing any deficiencies in that relationship. This chapter critically considers how the developing domain of **social accounting** may contribute to such an understanding and to a strengthening of the relationship between accounting and the public interest. The analysis in the chapter is premised on an initial acceptance that this task may necessitate questioning our established and taken-for-granted ways of doing things:

> Our conceptions, practices, and beliefs are not to be regarded as fixed and timeless, but rather as hypotheses in use … [thus] highlight[ing] their impermanence and allow[ing] us to more readily accept the importance of periodically examining their "goodness" by carefully attending to the consequences that they produce. (Young 2005: 10)

Through social accounting, a range of non-financial[1] considerations may be integrated and prioritised in accounts that may be asked for and provided in the context of relationships of accountability between social actors (including, but not limited

---

[1] Defining social accounting as revolving around non-financial concerns encompasses a very broad domain of social and environmental issues. This is consistent with the approach now adopted by many researchers in this growing field (see Gray 2002a, 2006a, 2007; Gray and Laughlin 2012). Therefore, for the purposes of the discussion in this chapter, the more specific endeavours, and, to some degree, more established sub-disciplinary field, of environmental accounting, or sustainability accounting, may be considered under the broad rubric of social accounting. Although the particular focus of the chapter is on the social dimension, the considerations of the chapter also broadly relate to what is sometimes referred to as social and environmental accounting.

G. Boyce (✉)
Department of Accounting, La Trobe University, Melbourne, Australia
e-mail: g.boyce@latrobe.edu.au

S. Mintz (ed.), *Accounting for the Public Interest: Perspectives on Accountability, Professionalism and Role in Society*, Advances in Business Ethics Research 4,
DOI 10.1007/978-94-007-7082-9_6, © Springer Science+Business Media Dordrecht 2014

to, agency relationships) (see Boyce et al. 2009: 65). Social accounting recognises the effects and consequences of traditional accounting worldviews and practices, and can be applied at the level of entities, organisations, and other units of interest, including society as a whole (Boyce et al. 2012; Gray 2006a, 2007). Processes (practices) and products (outputs) of social accounting are likely to include or involve, as central elements, various forms of information about impacts on, and consequences for, society and environment. The related discourse and debate that may be prompted or infused by social accounting contributes to social processes of accountability (Boyce 2000). Therefore, social accounting constitutes an element of social interaction that need not be limited to, or necessarily expressed in, financial terms.

In considering the relationship between accounting and the public interest, the overarching objective of the chapter is to look beyond the conventionally conceived boundaries of accounting to consider how the discipline might be further developed and operationalised in ways that are more attentive to the public interest. It is suggested that key contributions of social accounting may be to expose values and priorities, to challenge accepted understandings, to generate visibilities, and to highlight the perspectives of neglected and marginalised segments of society. By so doing, social accounting has the potential to refocus and strengthen the relationship between accounting and the public interest.

It is recognised that the public interest is a contestable concept that is not reducible to a singular, all-encompassing, or universally accepted definition or approach (see Dellaportas and Davenport 2008, for some analysis of how this plays out in accounting). While this observation informs the analysis in the chapter, it is not possible to resolve the difficulty in settling upon an agreed and encompassing definition of the public interest within the scope of the chapter. Instead, key themes that are readily related to the public interest will be drawn out to examine how the development of accounting in more social forms may contribute to the achievement of public interest commitments.

The discussion and analysis in the chapter proceeds in the following way: In Sect. 6.2, the professional status of accounting is considered in the contemporary context of business and accounting scandals, critiquing the tendency towards self-interest and an increasingly commercial orientation. Changes in corporate and accounting regulation prompted by the Enron/Arthur Anderson and related scandals are considered, with a focus on their potential to lead to a revitalisation (or establishment) of a public interest ethos within accounting. Section 6.3 focuses on teasing out the relationship between accounting professionalism and the public interest by considering different views on what this means (or may mean). This analysis provides a possible opening for recognising the social within accounting, as a means to addressing public interest dimensions. Section 6.4 explores the nature of social accounting and canvasses ways in which the public interest agenda in accounting may be advanced through social accounting. These ideas are further fleshed out in Sect. 6.5, which analyses various emergent technologies of social accounting, focusing on silent, shadow, and counter accounting. Conclusions and implications are brought together in the final section.

Overall, the chapter seeks to contribute to our thinking about accounting and the public interest by explicitly addressing the importance of *the social* in this domain.

Specifically, social accounting is advocated as an activity (or set of activities) that is currently positioned on the margins of accounting, but which has significant potential to address public interest concerns from within the accounting discipline.

## 6.2 Accounting as a Profession

### *6.2.1 Professionalism and Society*

Professions and their associated forms of expertise dominate the contemporary world, yet the creation, ongoing existence, and social role of professions is often taken for granted (Abbott 1988). In studies of professions and professionalism, there has been a tension between functionalism that sees professional organisation as a natural outcome of attempts to undergird knowledge and expertise, and critical analysis that interprets it as an attempt to monopolise and dominate identified areas of social activity, principally for the benefit of the members of the professional group itself (Larson 1977). Critical insights into the power of professions have shifted the focus of the debate from a narrow analysis of ostensible professional traits or characteristics to a much broader perspective on the organisation, power, status and privileges of professional groups (see Scott 2008).

It is not the purpose of the present chapter to resolve the debate regarding the nature of professions (see Baker's chapter for an analysis of accounting professionalism from several different perspectives). It is noted, however, that themes of expertise, ethics, and pursuit of public interest are central to both of the broad perspectives on professionalism outlined above – either as posited or targeted professional characteristics, or as points of critique of claims to professional status and authority and of the social power and functions of professional groups.

The generalised crisis of confidence in business and the accounting profession and a widespread decline in citizen confidence in professions and public officials in recent decades (e.g. Nolan et al. 1995; Organisation for Economic Co-operation and Development 2005) provides a significant impetus for a re-examination of professionalism and the social functioning of accounting. In whatever way professions are viewed, it seems clear that the decline in public confidence in the accounting profession has coincided with an overall historical move from "social trustee professionalism", which centres on an explicit public interest orientation, to "expert professionalism", which centres on specialist skills and knowledge (Brint 1994).

In many senses, expert professionalism has largely come to be regarded as a sufficient meta-narrative to justify professional status, yet it remains the case that professional ideology continues to have both technical and socio-ethical dimensions. At the technical level, the training, skills, competence, and knowledge of professional experts delineate them from others outside recognised professional groupings. Yet, professional status and prestige and the socioeconomic and political power that often attach to professionalism are integrally tied with the influential idea that professions serve important societal ends and can be trusted to contribute to the furtherance of general social welfare.

### *6.2.2 Accounting: Industry, Business, or Profession?*

Explicit claims that the accounting profession served the public interest and acted independently of sectional and self-interests were significant in the accounting occupation's historical ascension to the status of profession, which brought with it social cache and the privileges of self-regulation (Sikka et al. 1989; Willmott 1990). However, it has also been argued that the pursuit of the public good was used ideologically to legitimate the pursuit of professional self-interest (Preston et al. 1995) and that the profession's notion of, and approach to, the public interest thereby became intertwined with its own self-interest (Parker 1994). Parker concluded his analysis of the profession's approach to the development and enforcement of codes of ethics with the observation that "The private interest is ever present. The public interest remains to be served" (p. 523).

Whether or not it has been broadly recognised, the accounting profession has always been characterised, to differing degrees, both by the pursuit of professional self-interest and the public interest. Young (2005) suggests that the marked tendency towards self-interest within both the corporate world and the accounting profession presents a key problem for contemporary accounting, particularly insofar as it lies at the root of many of the accounting scandals (see also Parker 1987, 1994; Willmott 1990; Lee 1995; Lindblom and Ruland 1997; Canning and O'Dwyer 2001; Baker 2005). Analysis suggests that as the self-interest of the profession has come to the fore, the ethos of social service and public interest has waned (Sikka 2008; Cooper and Robson 2006; Hanlon 1997b).

It is noteworthy that some writers have more recently come to use the term "accounting industry" in preference to "accounting profession" (e.g. Preston et al. 1995; Willmott and Sikka 1997; Cooper and Taylor 2000).[2] This reflects developments within the major professional accounting firms, which have reinvented themselves as multidivisional businesses with an increasingly commercial orientation (Hanlon 1996, 1997a; Perera et al. 2003; Brock and Powell 2005; Cooper and Robson 2006; Neu and Green 2006). Evidence suggests that the commercialised culture that has emerged has resulted in a dissipation of traditional professional values, particularly among the Big Four international accounting firms, and higher executive ranks within these firms (Suddaby et al. 2009).

The developments within accounting may be partly a product of the era of neoliberalism and globalisation in which "enterprise culture" (Sikka 2008) has triumphed, but the accounting profession has not just *responded* to neoliberalism. Major accountancy firms have played an important role in legitimating neoliberal ideas and practices, and they "simultaneously share and shape much of the contemporary entrepreneurial culture" (Sikka 2008: 269).[3] Accountants have played a significant

[2] Without drawing conclusions about the appropriateness of the terminology, the chapter will continue to use the term "accounting profession" whilst recognising that "accounting industry" may, indeed, be more appropriate.

[3] This is not entirely surprising, because accounting exists not just *in* but *because of* its environment. However, it is part of a symbiotic process through which it mutually legitimates, and is in turn legitimated by, particular modes of economic activity (see Cooper et al. 1989; Strange 1996: Ch. 10).

role "as a political mediator" in the alignment of ostensibly socially responsible organisational practices with dominant market rationality (Malsch 2013: 165).

At the same time, there has been a generalised decline in public confidence in accounting. This is partly a consequence of a range of corporate and business scandals in the last decade of the twentieth century and early twenty-first century in the United States of America, Europe, Asia, and Australia, in which accounting played a prominent role. There is likely to be something of a cumulative effect resulting from similar scandals over preceding decades (see Clarke et al. 2003; Sykes 1996, 1998).[4]

Although, to some degree the debate about accounting and the public interest has been overtaken by developments within the profession itself (see above), the crisis in public confidence in the profession presents both a challenge and opportunity to rethink directions and developments within the profession. It remains the case that there is a set of generally accepted "professional values, beliefs and aspirations woven into the very fabric of professional firms and organizations" (Brock et al. 1999: 4; see also Lander et al. 2013), even when professions wield enormous socioeconomic power under contemporary neoliberal capitalism. As they seek to deliver business and client-focused service, "[w]hat professionals sell is [still] primarily technical assistance and trust or reputation", and this is what the public still expects (Hanlon 1997b: 127). There is some evidence that, within some accounting firms, the tension between of market or commercial logics is played out in resistance to the dominance of commercial cultures and profit maximisation (Lander et al. 2013). It is suggested that "... professionals in smaller firms continue to draw on much of the social service ethos and rhetoric and are hostile to managerialism" (Lander et al. 2013: 144).

### *6.2.3 Pulling up the Profession's SOX*

The corporate and accounting scandals of recent years – most notably the Enron/Arthur Anderson case – may have acted as a wake-up call for the accounting profession. The scandals catalysed a range of legislative responses in many countries, including, most prominently, the Sarbanes–Oxley Act (SOX) in the USA. Analysis of the intent behind SOX, its effects and outcomes, subsequent legal developments, and the effects on the accounting profession, have been mixed.

On one account, a "perfect storm" created by the combination of accounting and financial scandals and intense public and media scrutiny allowed SOX to pass with investor and public interest provisions intact – principally relating to financial reporting transparency, corporate governance provisions, and auditor independence

[4] The role of the accounting profession in a range scandals and corporate misdeeds has been significant. For example, in exposés of the background to many corporate collapses in Australia, the professions were singled out for particular criticism, with accounting and auditing receiving prominent attention. See, for example, Sykes (1996) and Main (2003), who singled out the professions – notably accounting and auditing – as key culprits.

(Canada et al. 2008). Thus, the interests and established power behind the "accounting lobby [and] the business lobby" (Canada et al. 2008: 995) could not overcome the momentum that enabled SOX to pass the US Congress. Baker (2008) concluded that the effect of SOX was a progressive change that contributed to greater financial reporting transparency and auditor independence, although on the latter point, and in relation to audit failure generally, more remains to be done (Baker 2007; Cullinan 2004). In other respects, however, the provisions of SOX have been under attack and are not necessarily entrenched in the corporate and regulatory framework (Sy and Tinker 2008).

SOX represented some improvements for the public position of the accounting profession – particularly in relation to auditor independence. However, the impetus behind these changes was predominantly an attempt to maintain the functioning of the existing capitalist system and restore credibility and public confidence in capital markets (Baker 2008; Baker et al. 2006). Symbolic and rhetorical strategies minimised the threat to existing vested interests while placating the public demand for action (Conrad 2004). Overall, it has been concluded that SOX maintained, and further entrenched, what Merino et al. (2010) referred to as a "failed corporate governance model" that rests on self-regulation and financial deregulation. They concluded that:

> Sarbanes-Oxley preserved the status quo; it reflects an effort to maintain shareholder primacy in the face of ever-growing evidence that the traditional model, corporate self-regulation and financial deregulation, has been detrimental from a societal perspective. Neoliberals successfully diverted attention from the systemic failures of deregulated markets. (Merino et al. 2010: 786)

Thus, although SOX and similar post-Enron legislative changes brought improvements in corporate governance, accountability, and auditor independence, there has not been serious action to address issues that may be of greater relevance to advancing the broader relationship between accounting and the public interest. Similarly, the accounting profession's response has primarily been to seek to buttress its own position, repair its legitimacy in the broader institutional context, and protect its own commercial interests (Dwyer and Alon 2008; Baker et al. 2006). Ironically, "many of the provisions of the Sarbanes-Oxley Act have resulted in additional billable services that must be performed by independent accountants" (Baker et al. 2006: 32), thus benefitting the profession considerably.

In terms of the effect on corporate ethics and codes, there have undoubtedly been some enhancements in corporate practices, but evidence relating to the corporate Codes of Ethics that are mandated under SOX and related requirements suggests a largely symbolic response that is designed to allow "decoupling of the organization's public response from the internal workings of the firm" (Holder-Webb and Cohen 2012). Although SOX-style "legislated ethics" (Rockness and Rockness 2005) may diminish the attractiveness of engaging in corporate fraud by changing the risk and payoff dynamics, the compliance perspective that results may tend to limit action to minimal adherence to the requirements of written rules (Gaa 2007). In such a business environment, the pursuit of a more encompassing sense of integrity and the public interest within accounting may become secondary or may be lost altogether.

### 6.2.4 *Prospects*

Overall, the legislative, professional and related responses to accounting crises have been reactive rather than proactive; focused primarily on dealing with individual miscreants rather than dealing with systemic problems (Boyce 2008). On its own, this conclusion does not bode well for any effort to recover the public interest priority traditionally associated with professionalism.

Whilst recognising the advances and shortcomings represented by SOX, a socially productive outcome may yet emerge from the accounting scandals of the first decade of the twenty-first century. Specifically, accounting can no longer be automatically assumed to be an independent, technical, expert professional activity. Accordingly, the ostensible triumph of (the presumption of) technical and specialist expertise (Brint 1994) may come further into question. The presumption that professionals speak and act to enhance the public good is likely to come under continuing scrutiny.

Taking an optimistic stance, these developments may lead to a deeper consideration of the nature of professional expertise, ethos, and commitments, and the ways in which, and ends to which, the expertise of the profession is exercised in the public interest.

## 6.3 Accounting Professionalism and the Public Interest

Miller (1998) shows how the conception of what constitutes accounting is itself a social accomplishment, "formed and re-formed" as "accounting comes to be linked up to the demands, expectations and ideals of diverse social and institutional agencies" (p. 174). He demonstrates how the boundaries of accounting are neither fixed nor inflexible; they are constantly changing, and it is often at the margins of accounting that the most interesting developments within the discipline are at play.

### 6.3.1 *The Accounting Profession and the Public Interest*

As noted earlier in the chapter, there is ongoing uncertainty and about what the concept of the public interest means in accounting (see Neu and Graham 2005; Dellaportas and Davenport 2008). To some extent, this situation also pertains to society generally where there is no universal agreement on what the public interest means or how it should be measured (Held 1970), and courts have been reluctant to develop a definitive formulation (Chandler 1991). It is not the purpose of this chapter to provide a definitive resolution of this question, but some exploration of the concept in relation to the (potential) domain of social accounting is warranted.

Debate around the meaning of public interest in accounting includes competing ideas of how the public interest may be served, such as:

- through the unbiased application of accepted accounting practices (e.g. Brooks 2001);
- via the development of accounting knowledge (e.g. Sikka et al. 1989);
- through the provision of sound information to capital markets and the investing public (e.g. Public Interest Oversight Board 2010);
- by considering the social effects of accounting practice and of the economic practice that is accounted for (e.g. Gray 2002a);
- by considering how social outcomes may be related to socioeconomic systems (e.g. Collison et al. 2010); or
- through active engagement to bring about social change (e.g. Lehman 2005).

Despite apparent ambiguity and uncertainty, public interest obligations are explicitly accepted by the accounting profession in national jurisdictions and internationally. The International Federation of Accountants (IFAC) Code of Ethics, upon which many national-body codes are based, prominently states that "A *distinguishing* mark of the accounting profession is its acceptance of the responsibility to act in the public interest …" (International Ethics Standards Board for Accountants 2010: 9, emphasis added). However, as Dellaportas and Davenport (2008) point out, the final inclusion of this statement in the Code was a significantly watered-down compromise over earlier proposals. They note that IFAC originally proposed a stand-alone definition of the public interest in a separate section of the Code; in a later draft, the definition was subsumed in the introduction section; and in the final version of the Code, the definition was withdrawn and only a minor reference to the term was made in the introduction.

The accounting profession has been willing to explicitly recognise the importance of the public interest, but this has often been accompanied with attempts to constrain the application of the concept. The earlier version of the IFAC Code explicated a notion of "the accountancy profession's public" that was very limited:

> *The accountancy profession's public* consists of clients, credit grantors, governments, employers, employees, investors, the business and financial community, and others who rely on the objectivity and integrity of professional accountants to maintain the orderly functioning of commerce. This reliance imposes a public interest responsibility on the accountancy profession. The public interest is defined as the collective well-being of the community of *people and institutions the professional accountant serves*. (IFAC Ethics Committee 2001: 10, emphasis added)

This notion that "the public" and therefore, "the public interest" relates to a more restricted set of *users of financial statements* is consistent with the stated mission of the IFAC:

> … to serve the public interest, continue to strengthen the accountancy profession worldwide, contribute to the development of strong international economies by establishing and promoting adherence to high-quality professional standards, furthering the international convergence of such standards, and speaking out on public interest issues where the profession's expertise is most relevant. (e.g. see: International Ethics Standards Board for Accountants 2010: 7)

This construction places emphasis on the technical and expert dimensions of accounting practice rather than on a broad and encompassing notion of public interest (indicative of the move from "social trustee professionalism" to "expert professionalism" as discussed earlier in this chapter – see Brint 1994). This approach also implicitly arranges stakeholders hierarchically: shareholders as "primary stakeholders", holders of direct economic interests (such as managers, lenders, and suppliers) as "secondary stakeholders", and those without direct economic interests (such as members of the general public) as "tertiary stakeholders" (see Accountancy Foundation Review Board 2002). Despite public interest rhetoric, the practical focus has consistently been on the needs of primary and secondary stakeholders (those with private economic interests), while the broader public interest has repeatedly been marginalised (Baker 2005; see also Sikka et al. 1989).

### 6.3.2 *Holding Out Hope?: Recent Developments*

Recent developments from with the accounting profession provide some insights into elements in the current thought process that may hold out hope for a broader perspective on accounting and its interactions with society and the public interest. For example, IFAC and the ICAEW (UK) have each issued substantial discussion papers related to efforts to more clearly define and enact the public interest in accounting (IFAC 2010, 2012; ICAEW 2012).

IFAC (2012) now defines the public interest as "the net benefits derived for, and procedural rigor employed on behalf of, all society in relation to any action, decision or policy". The IFAC Policy Position contains some expansive discussion on key elements of the public interest, including a broad discussion of "the public" and those who have an "interest" in accounting. However, rather than taking an integrated view of "the public interest", the concept is split into two constituent notions – public and interest – and it is deemed that "the accountancy profession helps realize certain interests of society, many of which are economic in nature and related to the efficient management of resources" (IFAC 2012: 3). This rather crude position implies that the "interests" of the public are the private interests of identifiable individuals and groups, and that the "public interest" is effectively an aggregation of individual private interests. The notion of common good is recognized but not addressed in depth; rather, there is a prior understanding that:

> The responsibilities of the profession are designed to protect certain "interests" of the public. These interests include, amongst many others, the soundness of financial reporting, the comparability of financial information across borders, fiscal prudence in public expenditures, and the contributions that accountants make to corporate governance and organizational performance. (IFAC 2010: 4)

The ICAEW has taken a slightly different approach by seeking to limit the usage of the concept of public interest. Rather than a commitment to the public interest being a defining characteristic of the profession, it is said that "the concept of the public interest should be used sparingly" (ICAEW 2012: 4). This is set in the context of posited situations "when governments, regulators and others seek to intervene in the public interest" (*ibid.*). Overall, like the IFAC Policy Position, the ICAEW framework for analysing the public interest treats the "public" and its "interests" separately and incorporates a generally private, individual, and additive approach to the public interest that is, surprisingly, based on the economic notion of "wants". Although constraints on wants are to be recognised, they are, nevertheless, regarded as the primary criterion of public interest:

> … the proponent of the public interest action's first consideration in determining what is in their interest should be what their wants are and whether the action is consistent with those … popular opinion must be relevant. (p. 7; see also Ch. 6)

Thinking about the future of accountants, the Pathways Commission on Accounting Higher Education, under the auspices of the American Accounting Association and American Institute of CPAs has also considered the "role of accounting in society". Its "Value Proposition for a Broadly Defined Accounting Profession" (Ch. 2) reflects traditional professional rhetoric about accounting and the public interest by enunciating the role of accounting in society in the following terms:

> The definition of any profession begins with a commitment to provide a benefit to the public. This commitment to public trust and service represents one side of a social contract. In return, society grants the profession a measure of autonomy to govern its own affairs. (Behn et al. 2012: 21)

Like IFAC and the ICAEW, the Pathways Commission takes a predominantly economistic and technical approach to accounting. It continues:

> … In accounting, this commitment requires members of the profession to consistently provide accurate and reliable information to members of the public, which enables them to make sound investment decisions, and to managers to facilitate the efficient and productive use of resources. For accounting education, this commitment requires the preparation of accountants to encompass not just technical accounting knowledge, effective thinking and problem solving, and professional practice skills, but also a deep understanding of the accountant's public role. (Behn et al. 2012: 21)

Drawing these recent developments in thought within the accounting profession together, it is apparent that the positions of IFAC, the ICAEW, and the Pathways Commission represent a traditional accounting mindset, and are framed within the constrictions of shareholder (or investor) primacy. The earlier concerns of Merino et al. (2010) in relation to SOX and corporate/accounting regulation are equally applicable to these developments. Key pronouncements and papers are underpinned by a neoliberal ideology. Where a more inclusive view of "the public" is recognised, the influence of economistic approaches to the public interest remains apparent and the social dimension seems largely absent. Nevertheless, there are some elements of these emergent framework documents that may provide an opening for a more expansive approach. For instance, the "interests" of the public are said by IFAC to include:

- increased economic certainty in the marketplace and throughout the financial infrastructure (e.g., banking, insurance, investment firms, etc.);
- sound, decision-useful financial and non-financial reporting for stakeholders, investors, and all parties in the marketplace (directly or indirectly) impacted by such reporting;

- a high degree of comparability of financial and non-financial reporting and auditing across different jurisdictions;
- sound and transparent financial and non-financial information and decision making on the part of governments and public sector organizations to their constituents;
- sound corporate governance and performance management in private and public sector organizations; and
- increased efficiency (i.e., less costly) and/or the minimization of natural resource depletion in the production of goods and services, thereby enhancing the welfare of society by their greater availability and accessibility. (IFAC 2012: 3)

At first appearance, these points largely reflect traditional accounting practice and ideology, therefore presenting little that is likely to challenge or change accounting. The key expressed concern of the profession continues to revolve around financial accounting practice, standards, standard-setting. However, the inclusion of references to non-financial reporting and the "minimization of natural resource depletion" provide some recognition of a push within accounting to expand the purview of what is deemed to be important within the discipline. This may represent an opening for the greater recognition of the social dimension within accounting.

## 6.4 Enter the Social

### *6.4.1 Broader Views of the Public Interest*

The developments examined in Sects. 6.2 and 6.3 reflect a particular approach by the profession that has effectively treated conventional (financially dominated and denominated) approaches to accounting and the concept of the public interest as mutually constitutive. In this light, it has been suggested, in effect, that accounting "does not *serve* the public interest so much as *generate* a peculiar and hyperreal version of it" (Neu and Graham 2005: 585, emphasis added). Within the profession, accounting is "widely understood to serve the public interest" merely by producing and presenting information that is thought to reflect underlying "facts" (Willmott 1990: 315). Then, "[t]he question of whether accounting itself serves the public interest is excluded from consideration" (*ibid*., p. 316). This approach validates particular forms of accounting that are (perhaps unsurprisingly) largely in the image of extant practice. Willmott's analysis suggests that a significant ongoing challenge is presented by this situation:

> The practical value and significance of the concept of 'public interest' resides precisely in its capacity to stimulate and articulate debate upon some of the most fundamental political issues … It begs what is perhaps the most central question of politics: do the objectives, procedures and policies embodied in the structure and resolution of social and economic relations benefit the 'many'; or do they, in the name of public interest, disproportionately advantage a minority of unnecessarily privileged individuals, members of powerful interest groups or a dominant class? (Willmott 1990: 318)

The meaning of public interest will inevitably be contested, but this does not obliterate a practical capacity to inform debate that can, in turn, inform decisions and actions within and about accounting and that which is accounted for. These are questions, issues, and debates that must be ongoing; they "need to be asked again and again, in different contexts and at different times" (Young 2005: 11). In this sense, the commitment of the accounting profession to serve the public interest ought not be assumed, but should be seen as a constant challenge, particularly when the public interest may conflict with the self-interests of the profession, the private interests of clients, or the sectoral interests of business in general (see Parker 1994).

Clearly, serving the public interest is not a straightforward concept, and different views are not necessarily commensurable. It is interesting to reflect on the different *interests* that underlie the various approaches in the list presented in Sect. 6.3.1 – some are clearly more *public* than others, and it is perplexing how easily some approaches are able to conflate private interests and the public interest (for example, the Public Interest Oversight Board's focus on the "investing public", which, despite the word "public" clearly relates to private interests of investors!). Clarity and clarification is undoubtedly needed; the developments outlined in Sect. 6.3.2 may offer some hope that this agenda could be advanced.

Whatever approach is taken, it is possible to discern a common thread that is necessary to connect any approach to public interest: it must imply a focus on the *collective* interest of the *community as a whole* rather than on particular sectional interests or individual wants per se. A focus on community rather than sectional interests lies at the core of an encompassing approach to public interest (see Cochran 1974), requiring attention to material,[5] intellectual, moral, and spiritual wellbeing (see Douglass 1980).

Thus, a professional ethos to serve the public interest requires a fundamentally social approach, rather than an exclusively economically-centred one, paying heed to the concerns of any and all members of society rather than subsections and particular groups. The remainder of this chapter explores how social accounting offers and avenue through which these issues may be addressed.

### 6.4.2 Making Accounting Social

In their recent reflection on the development of social accounting research and practice, Gray and Laughlin (2012: 240) suggest that accountability provides a mechanism by which "relationships between (and within) civil society, the market and the state" are "negotiated, articulated and developed". Seen in this light, social accounting is:

> … concerned with exploring how the social and environmental activities undertaken (or not, as the case may be) by different elements of a society can be – and are – expressed … how they are made speak-able – even knowable. (Gray and Laughlin 2012: 240)

This encapsulates an endeavour to clarify and negotiate (and renegotiate) relationships in ways that transcend the dominance of the economic; to accommodate and prioritise the social and the environmental dimensions of relationships; and

[5] "Material" may include *financial*, here.

surmount the calculative forms that dominate more established approaches to accounting and accountability (Gibbon 2012; Boyce 2000; Chua 1996). Social accounting "offers a means whereby the non-financial might be created, captured, articulated, and spoken" (Gray and Laughlin 2012: 240).

### *6.4.3 Expanding the Gaze: Thinking Beyond the Financial*

In extending thinking beyond extant financial accounting, social accounting recognises that "the giving and receiving of accounts is a ubiquitous part of human existence" (Gray 2002a: 364). The notion of "accounts" is construed broadly – they need not be financially or numerically denominated. Many writers such as Gray (2002a, 2010) have powerfully problematised attempts to force social (and environmental) accounting into conventional financial accounting frames, in part because such efforts may seek to reconcile the irreconcilable (see also Chua 1996). Gray argues that a key problem faced by those seeking to develop alternative and social forms of accounting has been the combined effect of an inherent conservatism within accounting, and perceived disciplinary boundaries that have conventionally placed "the social" beyond the scope of the discipline. Together with a melange of "power, pragmatism, self-interest, idealism and so on" (Gray 2002a: 362), these factors have tended to suppress the development and acceptance of social accounting.[6]

The above analysis suggests that both the problematisation of existing accounting practices and the development of new ones reflect different sets of interests that are themselves articulated and modified through this process. Although Miller's (1998) focus is on how "calculative technologies and rationales" are added to the repertoire of accounting from other "knowledges and ideals" (p. 190), his analysis may be regarded as equally applicable to the development of the largely non-calculative practices under the rubric of social accounting.

Although there has been some interest in developing social accounting calculative practices that are able to be articulated with conventional financial accounting (see, for example, Bebbington and Gray 2001; Fraser 2012), overall, these projects have produced disappointing results, and have not yet significantly advanced the sustainability agenda with which they have been primarily associated. It could be that a significant difficulty lies in the focus on a desire to financialise or monetise social dimensions. Owen (1992: 23) suggests that "the accountant's traditional obsession with, and insistence on, objectively verifiable and largely financially based measurement

[6] In attempts to develop social accounting, where there has been a focus on financial quantification, this has seriously limited the endeavour because such an approach admits only a relatively narrow perceptual field: "… the accountant's perceptual field is constrained by reference to events that … can generally be described in financial terms" (Owen 1992: 24). Owen (2005: 397) concluded that much of the present practice of "social reporting amounts to little more than a smokescreen, diverting attention away from core issues of ethical and moral accountability". Gray (2006a: 798) argued that accounting in this vein actually "produces a social construction of a world of precision and accuracy, of measurement and rationality, of bleakness and inhumanity …".

techniques" has presented a major stumbling block to the social relevance of social accounting and that it may lead to self-deception and/or the deception of others (see also Owen 1993).

Thus, social accounting does not exclude quantitative approaches, but recognises that attempts to fit into the calculative and financial paradigms of extant accounting frameworks and approaches are problematic and may in fact defer the advancement of attempts to develop a more public interest oriented accounting. To overcome the continual tension that arises when attempts are made to force non-economic values into economic and accounting calculus, "a fundamental re-examination of the marginalist and neo-classical economic underpinnings of the accounting craft" (Owen 1992: 24) is necessary. This requires that the "perceptual field" (*ibid.*) of accounting be unfettered by economic events that directly impinge on a particular economic entity and are amenable to description in financial terms. This, of course, takes the analysis into the realm of social accounting.

It is suggested that if accountants are prepared to move beyond their possibly "overestimate[d] … abilities in the realm of attaching financial numbers to various aspects of business activity" (Owen 1992: 7), they may bring valuable skills to the processes of constructing and interpreting environmental and social accounts in various forms. These skills (developed or incipient) include "the design and implementation of information systems, articulation of the links between information and decisions, verification of the links between evidence and reports, explication and description of values, and presentation of information in ways that make it meaningful to users" (Boyce 2000: 54).

Thus, the task for a multilingual (Chua 1996) and multi-logical (Crowther and Hosking 2005) social accounting is to instil and instantiate communication though the presentation, provision, and interpretation of information in ways that are intended to inculcate debate and dialogue through "intelligible, actionable insights" (Boyce 2000: 55). The resultant prevention of premature closure on issues which merit such debate and dialogue should also generate a greater potential for genuine and informed citizen participation in democratic processes (see also Gray 1998; Brown 2009). The intention here is not to deny the place of financial logics, financial calculation, and financial reporting in relation to such processes, but to suffuse them with wider social logics and reporting. This can make a significant contribution to the advancement of a public interest orientation within accounting. In so doing, social accounting needs to "look as far and as wide for understanding and insights as we are humanly capable" (Gray 2010: 25).

## 6.5 The Importance of Social Accounting at the Margins

### *6.5.1 Contingency*

As noted earlier in the chapter, Miller (1998: 190) suggested that "[t]he criteria for what can count as accounting are historically contingent and only temporarily established". More broadly, the current state of accounting and its socioeconomic role is a part of the intellectual and practical inheritance of contemporary society. However, neither the nature of the future role of accounting, nor the nature of the broader society, is pre-determined or inevitable. The future, just as the present, is historically contingent and determined and is thus created by people in given circumstances:

> Men make their own history, but they do not make it just as they please; they do not make it under circumstances chosen by themselves, but under circumstances directly found, given and transmitted from the past. (Marx 1982: 116, originally published 1852)

Accounting as it exists is thus a historical product of our past; and presently dominant forces and tendencies within accounting reflect that contingent past. Despite this, accounting and other social phenomena may *appear* to be the objective results of natural processes of social evolution and development. Marcuse's (1964) analysis drew attention to the role of social choice in determining future societal development. Social organisation is itself a historical choice between alternatives that are "determined by the inherited level of the material and intellectual culture", but the choice itself reflects "the play of the dominant interests" (Marcuse 1964: xvi). Thus, the future development of accounting knowledge and of accounting professionalism, is strongly influenced by present socioeconomic and political tendencies but is neither inevitable nor determined. Developments in social accounting represent one set of "demands, expectations and ideals" (Miller 1998: 174) that may move accounting towards a more explicit and practical public interest orientation.

Whilst it is still possible to characterise accounting in the traditional way as the *language of business*, it is now generally recognised that the domain of the accounting discipline is much broader than is captured by this epithet. Accounting has real effects across all social domains and has become a *language of politics and society*. Accounting, together with related technologies such as audit, is increasingly recognised to be an important element of the material and intellectual culture of society. This draws attention to a much broader setting that must be addressed to appreciate the richness of accounting as a social technology with political, moral, and ethical dimensions.

### *6.5.2 Forms of, and Approaches to, Accounting Knowledge*

The significant role of accounting in creating, sustaining, and reproducing particular social realities, and its function, in this context, as a tool of sociopolitical power is now broadly recognised and well-accepted in the accounting literature (see, for example, Hines 1988; Tinker 1980; Miller and O'Leary 1987; Munro and Mouritsen 1996; Boyce 2008). Accounting, as part of social processes of reality construction (that themselves are a reflection of broader context), "is a human construction" (Boyce et al. 2012: 59) and the accounting profession does not simply apply specialist, technical, and/or expert knowledge.

Therefore, social reality and the understanding of it that is created through accounting is not to be regarded as a set of objective "facts" external to the individual knower or to the social processes that produce knowledge (Berger and Luckmann 1984). It follows that knowledge is not transformed by chance, but through "reflection and action upon the world in order to transform it" (Freire 1996: 33), that is, through praxis as a relationship between theory and practice. This kind of practical knowledge emerges only "through … the restless, impatient, continuing, hopeful inquiry human beings pursue in the world, with the world, and with each other" (Freire 1996: 53).

### *6.5.3 Technologies of Social Accounting*

For some time, accounting researchers have recognised accounting's implication in the creation and perpetuation of many contemporary environmental and social problems (see Boyce 2008; Boyce et al. 2012). It is increasingly recognised within the social accounting literature that radical change is required to address current and continuing threats such as those outlined earlier (e.g. Boyce 2000; Tinker and Gray 2003; Gray 2002a, 2006a, b; Boyce et al. 2009). There is a clear resonance here with some approaches to the public interest, as canvassed earlier in the chapter.

Thinking about practical ways that this agenda is being, or might be, pursued, Gray (2010) has suggested that a social accounting that embraces social, environmental, and ethical responsibility might be concerned with:

- the social and environmental (including sustainability) impacts and effects arising from conventional accounting practice;
- ameliorating the social and environmental impacts arising from conventional accounting practice (including seeking ways to reduce the negative impacts and looking for ways to encourage positive social and environmental effects); and
- deriving and developing new methods of accounting that might be implicated in more benign social and environmental effects and which, typically, would advance the case of accountability … (Gray 2010: 12)

At the margins of the accounting discipline, social accounting is itself an attempt at reality construction, in part through its "… quite different, even antagonistic, relationship" with the assumptions and practices of conventional accounting (Gray 2006a: 794). Gray suggests that a radical re-working of accounting is needed in order to influence change. Social accounting is definitionally *radical* to the extent that it reflects efforts to carve out a distinct approach and new methodologies, rather than merely to supplement extant financial and management accounting. The latter are regarded as inevitably deficient, because:

> Financial accounting still tends to see the environmental and social issues as just another potential cost or liability … Management accounting similarly has responded only at the edges – typically around "the business case" … (Gray and Laughlin 2012: 237)

A number of emergent approaches to social accounting are under development. These include silent, shadow, and counter accounting (see Gray 1997; Boyce 2000; Dey 2003, 2007; Dey et al. 2010; Gallhofer et al. 2006; Sikka 2006; Ruffing 2007; Collison et al. 2010). *Silent accounting* involves the reconstruction of readily-available "nuggets" (Gray 1997: 204) of social and environmental data about an entity or activity – as made available by the relevant organisation itself (for example, in the case of a corporation, such information may be readily available in annual reports and other corporate publications). Although such information is freely available (and is thus not generated as part of the social accounting process), it may not be presented in a way that depicts a holistic social (or environmental) perspective (for example, it may be dispersed or presented obliquely and not be readily amenable to critical analysis). Silent accounting therefore also re-presents such information in a more meaningful and "fuller social account" (Gray 1997: 204), effectively creating (or depicting) "a different social reality" (Boyce 2000: 57) from that represented by conventional accounting reports. This highlights social dimensions and raises awareness of the social dimensions of organisations and activities. Silent accounting effectively gives voice and visibility to that which was previously silent (hence the name), despite being formally and publicly available. It does not explicitly seek to present an alternative perspective on an organisation or activity, but an alternative presentation of data that permits a different reading.

*Shadow accounting* takes a similar approach to silent accounting but draws on a wider variety of sources of information, including those direct sources that are used in silent accounting and a range of external and alternative sources. The information is freely available, and may include media reports, statement from employees or ex-employees, trade unions, local citizens, suppliers, public information offices, non-governmental organisation reports, published scientific reports, court reports, and the like (Dey et al. 2010). In general, shadow accounting seeks to problematise and possibly de-legitimate established perspectives and discourse by challenging the formal, official narrative presented by currently dominant players. The perspective of less powerful social groups is explicitly adopted:

> … shadow accounts … systematically creat[e] alterative representations, new visibilities, and knowledge of existing situations in order to problematise, act as a catalyst for intervention, and typically represent the views of oppressed social groups or ecological systems. (Dey et al. 2010: 64)

This approach shifts the focal point of accounts from the control of the organisation to create space for an independent (or alternative), critical interpretation of social impacts, issues, and performance in contested arenas.

*Counter accounting* can be defined as being constituted by "information and reporting systems employed by groups such as campaigners and activists with a view to promoting their causes or countering or challenging the prevailing official and hegemonic position" (Gallhofer et al. 2006: 681–682). Thus, in addition to adopting alternative perspectives or to delegitimise established perspectives, as with shadow accounting, counter accounting explicitly seeks to confront existing narratives and approaches.

Silent, shadow, and counter accounting share the objective of problematising existing institutional conduct and creating space for alternative conceptions, primarily through the creation of visibilities and the construction of different representations, which:

> … may be valuable as a basis for problematising and challenging dominant forms of economic organisation and the rhetoric which privileges certain interests as well as a commensurately selective approach to accountability mechanisms … (Collison et al. 2010: 964)

Taking a combined silent and shadow accounting approach, social indicators have been used by Collison et al. (2007, 2010) to analyse – and account for – the relationship between income inequality and child mortality in a manner that also provides a wider basis for the creation of:

> ... new visibilities that challenge the dominant and contestable values and rationalities underlying shareholder oriented capitalism ... the social account supporting such a challenge could be important in confronting the assumptions and spurious rationalities embodied in the theory and practice of Anglo-American accounting and finance. (Collison et al. 2010: 973)

Thus, these approaches provide an avenue through which existing knowledge and understanding may be challenged, opening a space for the development of new knowledge and understanding, without necessarily pre-determining what the content or implications of that knowledge and understanding will be.

### *6.5.4 Insights from the Margins*

It is evident from the foregoing that social accounting is "increasingly informed by the alternative/critical project(s) and seeks evolutionary and emancipatory moment within current possibilities" (Gray 2002b: 692). For Gray, social accounting work is motivated by feelings of "outrage, engagement, passion" and aspirations for "disruption and empowerment" (p. 700).[7] Collison et al. (2010: 974) conclude that social accounting may find resonance "because it may be possible to strike a chord with a (reassuringly persistent) level of public sentiment towards notions of equality and a 'common good'".

Silent, shadow and counter accounting thus have the potential to energise and give voice to public interest concerns within accounting. They represent practical developments within social accounting that may facilitate the operationalisation of public interest. It may be that it is here, at the social accounting "margins of accounting" (c.f. Miller 1998), that the discipline is at its most innovative, interesting, and important, in terms of the prospective contribution of accounting to the future of human society and the planetary environment (see, for example, Gray 2002a, 2010). It is – perhaps only – at the interface of social accounting that it is possible to clearly grasp accounting in the broader context in which it operates (see Hopwood 1983), in part because it is that context itself that is of central importance to social accounting.

[7] Although Gray (1998: 213) stresses that the aim of social accounting is to change the world, much social accounting research has been criticised as representing "political quietism" (Tinker et al. 1991), subject to capture by those opposed to real social change. In this light, it has been compared with "rearranging the deck chairs on the Titanic" (Puxty 1986: 107).

## 6.6 Conclusions and Implications: Social Accounting and the Public Interest

> … the definition and defence of the *public interest* – which whether one likes it or not, will never, even by juggling the figures, be produced by the accountant's view of the world … (Bourdieu 1998: 105, original emphasis)

The concept of the public interest "directs our attention beyond the more immediate and toward the often-ignored interests … that might be forgotten or overlooked" (Sorauf 1957: 639). If "being part of a profession implies having a concern for the public interest, and therefore being prepared to address the main issues facing society" (Owen 1992: 26), then social accounting seems destined to become a necessary part of any accounting that aspires to retain professional status.

Professional accounting has always, in some sense, been a business, but "the business dimensions have existed in tension with the ideal of public service … What has differed from time to time is the strength of these two pulls within the profession" (Neu and Green 2006: 159, emphasis added). It may be that the idea of serving the public interest has always provided a powerful legitimating rhetoric behind which the accounting profession has been able to serve its private economic interests (Parker 1994; Lee 1995; Baker 2005), but the ideals of public interest professionalism have not altogether succumbed to the challenge of contemporary neoliberal beliefs. Broadbent et al. (1997: 3) argue that the "ideas of professions still linger in our collective consciousness", advocating that this should be channelled to the "development of a new professionalism" and a "reinstitutionalised sense of social responsibility" (p. 7). By contrast, Brint's (1994) analysis of the contemporary move to "expert professionalism" leads him to conclude that "powerful social and economic forces have brought the older idea of professionalism linking social purposes and knowledge-based authority close to an end" (p. 17). Nevertheless, Brint does suggest that improvement in the capacity of professionals must be connected in some way "to long-term societal interests, important cultural values and traditions, and the requirements of a decent public life" (1994: 18; see also Neu and Green 2006: 163). The scale of the challenge this represents to accounting should not be underestimated. As Malsch (2013) has noted:

> As a symbol of genuine political power, the mediating role of the accounting industry is conducive to the deployment of an individualistic and instrumental moral rationality, reinforcing the fragmentation of the social body into a multitude of stakeholders and undermining the prospect of a collective agreement on the definition and protection of a common good such as the preservation of natural resources or the maintenance of social protection for the most vulnerable groups in society. (Malsch 2013: 165)

Addressing this situation necessitates a fundamental consideration of the nature of the accounting craft and of the profession and its commitments. The kind of change advocated by Broadbent et al. (1997) necessitates an initial recognition that the contradiction between the private interests largely served by the accounting profession and the public interest that is essential to the idea and practice of professionalism is a significant element of the current crisis of confidence in accounting.

Professional ideology will continue to have technical and moral aspects, and the profession must recognise that a consequence of the diminution in the sense of social purpose for professions is a loss of their "distinctive voice" in public debates (cf. Brint 1994: 17). It is likely that future public perceptions of, and trust in, the profession will be shaped in large measure by the way the profession addresses the social dimension of public interest.

Although the characterisation of accounting as the language of business, together with the aura of neutrality that accompanies this characterisation, has tended to mask the wider socio-political functioning of accounting, the current situation presents an opportunity for change. Accounting is increasingly understood to be a significant determinant of the manner in which societies think about, organise, and conduct economic, social, and political activity. The key contribution of social accounting may lie in its potential to infuse discourse and debate via the creation of new forms of social visibility – the capacity to help see things which may otherwise remain hidden or unknown (Boyce 2000). Such visibilities have the capacity to inculcate social, environmental, and political discourses and to, thereby, generate a greater sensitivity to the interrelation between them. Therefore, the inherently communicative process at the core of social accounting includes the "exposure of values and priorities" and "outputs which are contestable and open to debate" (Boyce 2000: 53). Any "desire to meaningfully engage with the interrelations of the social, environmental, and economic domains in a more critically pluralistic fashion" (Brown and Dillard 2013: 15) is likely to require "a multiplicity of social and environmental accountings and accountabilities" (Gray and Laughlin 2012: 241).

Emergent and incipient approaches to social accounting as exemplified by silent, shadow and counter accounting, and Brown and Dillard's chapter in the present volume and other recent work (Brown 2009; Dillard and Brown 2012; Brown and Dillard 2013) exemplifies current efforts being made to advance this agenda. If these directions and developments can be sustained, social forms of accounting can make an important contribution to the manner in which "human society attempts to reconstitute its economic relationships within nature and between its peoples and species" (Gray and Laughlin 2012: 241). As Arrington (1990) points out, addressing the issue of quality of life must be on the agenda of the accounting profession if it is to meaningfully address public interest. Arrington offers an alternative to the neoliberal economic dominance of accounting by suggesting that the concept of "solidarity" should underpin accounting knowledge that is "useful in the construction of a good community—useful in the public interest". He notes that "[a]ccounting as a human construction is certainly capable of taking whatever form we desire … we can account for anything we choose" (p. 12).

Broader conceptions and broader understanding of accounting that are highlighted in and by social accounting draw attention to the need for a "change in societal mindset from an embracing of self-interest to a greater concern for the social good … to a consideration of the kind of society we are creating …" (Moore and Loewenstein 2004: 200). The further development and recognition of social accounting as a domain that lies within the boundaries of accounting may prove to be an important element in rekindling accounting as a profession that is committed to the public interest and is prepared to address the key issues facing society.

## References

Abbott, A. 1988. *The system of professions: An essay on the division of expert labor*. Chicago: University of Chicago Press.

Accountancy Foundation Review Board. 2002. *Protecting the public interest: Introducing the work programme of the review board*. London: The Accountancy Foundation.

Arrington, E. 1990. Intellectual tyranny and the public interest: The quest for the grail and the quality of life. *Advances in Public Interest Accounting* 3: 1–16.

Baker, C.R. 2005. What is the meaning of "the public interest"?: Examining the ideology of the American public accounting profession. *Accounting, Auditing and Accountability Journal* 18(5): 690–703.

Baker, C.R. 2007. The contested concept of auditor independence. *Advances in Public Interest Accounting* 12: 17–26.

Baker, C.R. 2008. Ideological reactions to Sarbanes–Oxley. *Accounting Forum* 32(2): 114–124.

Baker, R.L., W.E. Bealing, D.A. Nelson, and A.B. Staley. 2006. An institutional perspective of the Sarbanes-Oxley act. *Managerial Auditing Journal* 21(1): 23–33.

Bebbington, J., and R. Gray. 2001. An account of sustainability: Failure, success and a reconceptualization. *Critical Perspectives on Accounting* 12(5): 557–587.

Behn B. K., W. F. Ezzell, L. A. Murphy, M. Stith, J. Rayburn, and J. R. Strawser. 2012. *The pathways commission: Charting a national strategy for the next generation of accountants*. Sarasota, FL and Durham, NC: American Accounting Association and American Institute of CPAs.

Berger, P., and T. Luckmann. 1984. *The social construction of reality: A treatise in the sociology of knowledge*. Pelican: Harmondsworth.

Bourdieu, P. 1998. *Acts of resistance: Against the new myths of our time*. Cambridge: Polity.

Boyce, G. 2000. Public discourse and decision-making: Exploring possibilities for financial, social, and environmental accounting. *Accounting, Auditing and Accountability Journal* 13(1): 27–64.

Boyce, G. 2008. The social relevance of ethics education in a global(ising) era: From individual dilemmas to system crises. *Critical Perspectives on Accounting* 19(2): 255–290.

Boyce, G., W. Prayukvong, and A. Puntasen. 2009. Social accounting for sufficiency: Buddhist principles and practices, and their application in Thailand. *Advances in Public Interest Accounting* 14: 55–119.

Boyce, G., S. Greer, B. Blair, and C. Davids. 2012. Expanding the horizons of accounting education: Incorporating social and critical perspectives. *Accounting Education: An International Journal* 21(1): 47–74.

Brint, S. 1994. *In an age of experts: The changing role of professionals in politics and public life*. Princeton: Princeton University Press.

Broadbent, J., M. Dietrich, and J. Roberts (eds.). 1997. *The end of the professions? The restructuring of professional work*, Routledge studies in business organization and networks. London/New York: Routledge.

Brock, D.M., and M.J. Powell. 2005. Radical strategic change in the global professional network: The "Big Five" 1999–2001. *Journal of Organizational Change Management* 18(5): 451–468.

Brock, D.M., M.J. Powell, and C.R. Hinings. 1999. *Restructuring the professional organization: Accounting, health care and law*. London/New York: Routledge.

Brooks, L.J. 2001. Conflict of interest in the accounting profession. In *Conflict of interest in the professions*, ed. M. Davis and A. Stark, 92–111. New York: Oxford University Press.

Brown, J. 2009. Democracy, sustainability and dialogic accounting technologies: Taking pluralism seriously. *Critical Perspectives on Accounting* 20(3): 313–342.

Brown, J., and J. Dillard. 2013. Agonizing over engagement: SEA and the "death of environmentalism" debates. *Critical Perspectives on Accounting* 24(1): 1–18.

Canada, J., J.R. Kuhn, and S.G. Sutton. 2008. Accidentally in the public interest: The perfect storm that yielded the Sarbanes-Oxley act. *Critical Perspectives on Accounting* 19(7): 987–1003.

Canning, M., and B. O'Dwyer. 2001. Professional accounting bodies' disciplinary procedures: Accountable, transparent and in the public interest? *The European Accounting Review* 10(4): 725–749.

Chandler, R.A. 1991. "Guardians of knowledge and public interest": A reply. *Accounting, Auditing and Accountability Journal* 4(4): 5–13.
Chua, W.F. 1996. Teaching and learning only the language of numbers—monolingualism in a multilingual world. *Critical Perspectives on Accounting* 7(2): 129–156.
Clarke, F.L., G.W. Dean, and K.G. Oliver. 2003. *Corporate collapse: Regulatory, accounting and ethical failure*. Cambridge: Cambridge University Press.
Cochran, C.E. 1974. Political science and "the public interest". *Journal of Politics* 36(2): 327–355.
Collison, D., C. Dey, G. Hannah, and L. Stevenson. 2007. Income inequality and child mortality in wealthy nations. *Journal of Public Health* 29(2): 114–117.
Collison, D., C. Dey, G. Hannah, and L. Stevenson. 2010. Anglo-American capitalism: The role and potential role of social accounting. *Accounting, Auditing and Accountability Journal* 23(8): 956–981.
Conrad, C. 2004. The illusion of reform: Corporate discourse and agenda denial in the 2002 "corporate meltdown". *Rhetoric and Public Affairs* 7(3): 311–338.
Cooper, D.J., and K. Robson. 2006. Accounting, professions and regulation: Locating the sites of professionalization. *Accounting, Organizations and Society* 31(4–5): 415–444.
Cooper, C., and P. Taylor. 2000. From Taylorism to Ms Taylor: The transformation of the accounting craft. *Accounting, Organizations and Society* 25(6): 555–578.
Cooper, D., T. Puxty, T. Lowe, and H. Willmott. 1989. The accounting profession, corporatism and the state. In *Critical perspectives in management control*, ed. W.F. Chua, T. Lowe, and T. Puxty, 245–270. London: Macmillan.
Crowther, D., and D.M. Hosking. 2005. Accounting in Babel? Constructing social accounting as a multi-logical performance. *Critical Perspectives on Accounting* 16(5): 535–550.
Cullinan, C. 2004. Enron as a symptom of audit process breakdown: Can the Sarbanes-Oxley Act cure the disease? *Critical Perspectives on Accounting* 15(6/7): 853–864.
Dellaportas, S., and L. Davenport. 2008. Reflections on the public interest in accounting. *Critical Perspectives on Accounting* 19(7): 1080–1098.
Dey, C. 2003. Corporate 'silent' and 'shadow' social accounting. *Social and Environmental Accounting* 23(2): 6–9.
Dey, C. 2007. Developing silent and shadow accounts. In *Sustainability accounting and accountability*, ed. J. Unerman, J. Bebbington, and B. O''Dwyer, 307–326. Abingdon/New York: Routledge.
Dey, C., S. Russell, and I. Thomson. 2010. Exploring the potential of shadow accounts in problematising institutional conduct. In *Social accounting and public management: Accountability for the public good*, ed. A. Ball and S.P. Osborne, 64–75. New York/Abingdon: Routledge.
Dillard, J., and J. Brown. 2012. Agonistic pluralism and imagining CSEAR into the future. *Social and Environmental Accountability Journal* 32(1): 3–16.
Douglass, B. 1980. The common good and the public interest. *Political Theory* 8(1): 103–117.
Dwyer, P.D., and A. Alon. 2008. In whose interests? An examination of the professional ideology revealed in the AICPA's State Cascade Project. *Accounting and the Public Interest* 8(1): 77–93.
Fraser, M. 2012. "Fleshing out" an engagement with a social accounting technology. *Accounting, Auditing and Accountability Journal* 25(3): 508–534.
Freire, P. 1996. *Pedagogy of the oppressed*. London: Penguin.
Gaa, J.C. 2007. Integrity, auditor independence, and the protection of investors. *Advances in Public Interest Accounting* 12: 27–47.
Gallhofer, S., J. Haslam, E. Monk, and C. Roberts. 2006. The emancipatory potential of online reporting: The case of counter accounting. *Accounting, Auditing and Accountability Journal* 19(5): 681–718.
Gibbon, J. 2012. Understandings of accountability: An autoethnographic account using metaphor. *Critical Perspectives on Accounting* 23(3): 201–212.
Gray, R. 1997. The practice of silent accounting. In *Building corporate accountability: Emerging practices in social and ethical accounting, auditing and reporting*, ed. S. Zadek, P. Pruzan, and R. Evans, 201–217. London: Earthscan.

Gray, R. 1998. Imagination, a bowl of petunias and social accounting. *Critical Perspectives on Accounting* 9(2): 205–206.
Gray, R. 2002a. Of messiness, systems and sustainability: Towards a more social and environmental finance and accounting. *The British Accounting Review* 24(4): 357–386.
Gray, R. 2002b. The social accounting project and *Accounting Organizations and Society*. Privileging engagement, imaginings, new accountings and pragmatism over critique? *Accounting, Organizations and Society* 27(7): 687–708.
Gray, R. 2006a. Social, environmental and sustainability reporting and organisational value creation?: Whose value? Whose creation? *Accounting Auditing and Accountability Journal* 19(6): 793–819.
Gray, R. 2006b. Taking a long view on what we now know about social and environmental accountability and reporting. *Electronic Journal of Radical Organisation Theory* 9(1): 6–36.
Gray, R. 2007. Taking a long view on what we now know about social and environmental accountability and reporting. *Issues in Social and Environmental Accounting* 1(2): 169–198.
Gray, R. 2010. A re-evaluation of social, environmental and sustainability accounting: An exploration of an emerging trans-disciplinary field? *Sustainability Accounting Management and Policy Journal* 1(1): 11–32.
Gray, R., and R. Laughlin. 2012. It was 20 years ago today: Sgt pepper, *Accounting, Auditing & Accountability Journal*, green accounting and the Blue Meanies. *Accounting, Auditing and Accountability Journal* 25(2): 228–255.
Hanlon, G. 1996. "Casino capitalism" and the rise of the "commercialised" service class—an examination of the accountant. *Critical Perspectives on Accounting* 7: 339–363.
Hanlon, G. 1997a. Commercialising the service class and economic restructuring—a response to my critics. *Accounting, Organizations and Society* 22(8): 843–855.
Hanlon, G. 1997b. A shifting professionalism: An examination of accountancy. In *The end of the professions? The restructuring of professional work*, ed. J. Broadbent, M. Dietrich, and J. Roberts, 123–139. London/New York: Routledge.
Held, V. 1970. *The public interest and individual interests*. New York: Basic Books.
Hines, R.D. 1988. Financial accounting: In communicating reality, we construct reality. *Accounting, Organizations and Society* 13(3): 251–261.
Holder-Webb, L., and J. Cohen. 2012. The cut and paste society: Isomorphism in codes of ethics. *Journal of Business Ethics* 107(4): 485–509.
Hopwood, A.G. 1983. On trying to study accounting in the contexts in which it operates. *Accounting, Organizations and Society* 8(2/3): 287–305.
ICAEW. 2012. Acting in the public interest: A framework for analysis. In *Market foundations initiative*. London: Institute of Chartered Accountants in England and Wales.
IFAC. (2010). *A public interest framework for the accountancy profession*. IFAC Policy position paper. New York: International Federation of Accountants.
IFAC. (2012). *A definition of the public interest*. IFAC Policy Position. New York: International Federation of Accountants.
IFAC Ethics Committee. 2001. *IFAC code of ethics for professional accountants*. New York: International Federation of Accountants.
International Ethics Standards Board for Accountants. 2010. *Handbook of the code of ethics for professional accountants*. New York: International Federation of Accountants.
Lander, M.W., B.A.S. Koene, and S.N. Linssen. 2013. Committed to professionalism: Organizational responses of mid-tier accounting firms to conflicting institutional logics. *Accounting, Organizations and Society* 38(2): 130–148.
Larson, M.S. 1977. *The rise of professionalism: A sociological analysis*. Berkeley: University of California Press.
Lee, T. 1995. The professionalization of accountancy: A history of protecting the public interest in a self-interested way. *Accounting, Auditing and Accountability Journal* 8(4): 48–69.
Lehman, C.R. 2005. Accounting and the public interest: All the world's a stage. *Accounting, Auditing and Accountability Journal* 18(5): 675–689.
Lindblom, C.K., and R.G. Ruland. 1997. Functionalist and conflict views of AICPA code of conduct: Public interest vs. self interest. *Journal of Business Ethics* 16(5): 573–582.

Main, A. 2003. *Other People's money: The complete story of the extraordinary collapse of HIH*. Sydney: HarperCollins.
Malsch, B. 2013. Politicizing the expertise of the accounting industry in the realm of corporate social responsibility. *Accounting, Organizations and Society* 38(2): 149–168.
Marcuse, H. 1964. *One dimensional man: Studies in the ideology of advanced industrial society*. London: Routledge & Kegan Paul.
Marx, K. 1982. The eighteenth brumaire of Louis Bonaparte. In *The Marxist reader: The most significant and enduring works of Marxism*, ed. E. Burns, 116–131. New York: Avenel Books.
Merino, B.D., A.G. Mayper, and T.D. Tolleson. 2010. Neoliberalism, deregulation and Sarbanes-Oxley: The legitimation of a failed corporate governance model. *Accounting, Auditing and Accountability Journal* 23(6): 774–792.
Miller, P. 1998. The margins of accounting. In *The laws of the markets*, ed. M. Callon, 174–193. Oxford/Malden: Blackwell/The Sociological Review.
Miller, P., and T. O'Leary. 1987. Accounting and the construction of the governable person. *Accounting, Organizations and Society* 12(3): 235–265.
Moore, D.A., and G. Loewenstein. 2004. Self-interest, automaticity, and the psychology of conflict of interest. *Social Justice Research* 17(2): 189–202.
Munro, R., and J. Mouritsen (eds.). 1996. *Accountability: Power, ethos and the technologies of managing*. London: International Thompson Business Press.
Neu, D., and C. Graham. 2005. Accounting research and the public interest. *Accounting, Auditing and Accountability Journal* 18(5): 585–591.
Neu, D., and D. Green. 2006. *Truth or profit? The ethics and business of public accounting*. Halifax/Calgary: Fernwood and Centre for Public Interest Accounting, University of Calgary.
Nolan, M., C. Boulton, A. King, T. King, P. Shore, Thomson of Monifieth, W. Utting, A. Warburton, and D. Warwick. 1995. *Standards in public life: First report of the committee on standards in public life*. London: HMSO.
Organisation for Economic Co-operation and Development. 2005. OECD guidelines for managing conflict of interest in the public service. In *Policy brief*. Paris: OECD.
Owen, D. 1992. The implications of current trends in green awareness for the accounting function: An introductory analysis. In *Green reporting: Accountancy and the challenge of the nineties*, ed. D. Owen. London: Chapman and Hall.
Owen, D. 1993. The emerging green agenda: A role for accounting? In *Business and the environment: Implications of the new environmentalism*, ed. D. Smith. London: Paul Chapman.
Owen, D. 2005. CSR after Enron: A role for the academic accounting profession? *The European Accounting Review* 14(2): 395–404.
Parker, L.D. 1987. An historical analysis of ethical pronouncements and debate in the Australian accounting profession. *Abacus* 23(2): 122–140.
Parker, L.D. 1994. Professional accounting body ethics: In search of the private interest. *Accounting, Organizations and Society* 19(6): 507–525.
Perera, H.B., A.R. Rahman, and S.F. Cahan. 2003. Globalisation and the major accounting firms. *Australian Accounting Review* 13(1): 27–37.
Preston, A.M., D.J. Cooper, D.P. Scarbrough, and R.C. Chilton. 1995. Changes in the code of ethics of the U.S. accounting profession, 1917 and 1988: The continual quest for legitimation. *Accounting, Organizations and Society* 20(6): 507–546.
Public Interest Oversight Board. 2010. *Fifth public report of the PIOB*. Madrid: PIOB.
Puxty, A.G. 1986. Social accounting as immanent legitimation: A critique of technicist ideology. *Advances in Public Interest Accounting* 1: 95–111.
Rockness, H., and J. Rockness. 2005. Legislated ethics: From Enron to Sarbanes–Oxley, the impact on corporate America. *Journal of Business Ethics* 57(1): 31–54.
Ruffing, L. 2007. Silent vs. Shadow reports: What can we learn from BP's sustainability report versus the financial times? *Social and Environmental Accounting Journal* 27(1): 9–16.
Scott, W.R. 2008. Lords of the dance: Professionals as institutional agents. *Organization Studies* 29(2): 219–238.

Sikka, P. 2006. The internet and possibilities for counter accounts: Some reflections. *Accounting, Auditing and Accountability Journal* 19(5): 759–769.

Sikka, P. 2008. Enterprise culture and accountancy firms: New masters of the universe. *Accounting, Auditing and Accountability Journal* 21(2): 268–295.

Sikka, P., H. Willmott, and T. Lowe. 1989. Guardians of knowledge and public interest: Evidence and issues of accountability in the UK accountancy profession. *Accounting, Auditing and Accountability Journal* 2(2): 47–71.

Sorauf, F.J. 1957. The public interest reconsidered. *Journal of Politics* 19(4): 616–639.

Strange, S. 1996. *The retreat of the state: The diffusion of power in the world economy*. Cambridge: Cambridge University Press.

Suddaby, R., Y. Gendron, and H. Lam. 2009. The organizational context of professionalism in accounting. *Accounting, Organizations and Society* 34(3–4): 409–427.

Sy, A., and T. Tinker. 2008. Sarbanes-Oxley: An endangered specie? *Critical Perspectives on Accounting* 19(7): 927–930.

Sykes, T. 1996. *The bold riders: Behind Australia's corporate collapses*. St Leonards: Allen & Unwin.

Sykes, T. 1998. *Two centuries of panic: A history of corporate collapses in Australia*. St Leonards: Allen & Unwin.

Tinker, A.M. 1980. Towards a political economy of accounting: An empirical illustration of the Cambridge controversies. *Accounting, Organizations and Society* 5(1): 147–160.

Tinker, T., and R. Gray. 2003. Beyond a critique of pure reason: From policy to politics to praxis in environmental and social research. *Accounting, Auditing and Accountability Journal* 16(5): 727–761.

Tinker, T., C. Lehman, and M. Neimark. 1991. Falling down the hole in the middle of the road: Political quietism in corporate social reporting. *Accounting, Auditing and Accountability Journal* 4(2): 28–54.

Willmott, H.C. 1990. Serving the public interest? A critical analysis of a professional claim. In *Critical accounts*, ed. D.J. Cooper and T.M. Hopper, 315–331. London: Macmillan.

Willmott, H., and P. Sikka. 1997. On the commercialization of accountancy thesis: A review essay. *Accounting, Organizations and Society* 22(8): 831–842.

Young, J. 2005. Changing our questions: Reflections on the corporate scandals. *Accounting and the Public Interest* 5: 1–13.

# Part III
# Defining the Public Interest in Accounting

# Chapter 7
# Alternative Perspectives on Accounting in the Public Interest

C. Richard Baker

## 7.1 Introduction

Similar to other professional groups, the accounting profession has asserted that it serves the 'public interest' (Anderson-Gough et al. 2002; Robson et al. 1994). However, the definition of exactly what constitutes the 'public interest' has been subject to considerable debate and there is no general agreement on its meaning (Baker 2005; Sikka et al. 1989). The purpose of this chapter is to illustrate that there have been and continue to be differing perspectives regarding accounting in the public interest. For example, during the last 30 years, the interpretive and critical strands of the academic accounting literature have contributed various reflections regarding the co-opting of accounting rhetoric, philosophical perspectives, and discourse in an age of neoliberalism[1]. A lack of similar research in the 'mainstream' accounting literature[2] may indicate that there is a lack of interest regarding accounting in the public interest on the part of mainstream researchers. However, one reason for this difference may involve the definition of the 'public interest'.

The 'public interest' has been defined as "the interests of third parties who rely on the opinions and advice delivered by the members of the accounting profession" (Parker 1987, p. 509). This definition implies three things in particular: First, that there is an accounting profession that is seeking to serve the public interest; second, that the public interest involves the interests of third parties (i.e. those who are not in direct contact with the accounting professional); and third, that the public interest is served when the accounting professional provides opinions and advice. Thus, the

[1] A later section of this chapter will discuss this point in greater detail.

[2] See for example: *The Accounting Review*, *Journal of Accounting Research*, *Journal of Accounting and Economics.*

C.R. Baker (✉)
School of Business, Adelphi University, Garden City, NY 11530, USA

Department of Accounting, Rouen Business School, Rouen, France
e-mail: Baker3@adelphi.edu

S. Mintz (ed.), *Accounting for the Public Interest: Perspectives on Accountability, Professionalism and Role in Society*, Advances in Business Ethics Research 4,
DOI 10.1007/978-94-007-7082-9_7, © Springer Science+Business Media Dordrecht 2014

accounting profession's claim to serve the public interest can be viewed as focusing on providing opinions and advice to third parties (e.g. shareholders and creditors) who rely upon such opinions and advice.

The claim to serve the public interest might also be seen as a form of 'symbolic discourse', involving an interplay between the profession's ideology and the efforts of its members to expand the market for their labor (Robson et al. 1994). Therefore, a profession could be viewed as not merely a group of occupational practitioners who seek to serve the public interest, but also as an institutionalized form of social control. This institutionalized form of social control seeks to secure a monopoly of practice in a specific occupational area in order to advance the economic interests of its members.

Finally, it could be argued that unlike other professions, the accounting profession plays an important role in the regulation and distribution of economic resources, and that this role has a significant impact upon a wide range of individuals (i.e. the 'public interest' more broadly defined). Consequently, it would be important to consider accounting in the public interest from a broad perspective.

In summary, then, the definition the public interest with respect to accounting can range from an obligation by accounting professionals to provide reliable opinions and advice to third parties (e.g. audited financial statements), to a symbolic discourse that protects the accounting profession from outside interference, to a role for the profession in determining the regulation and distribution of economic resources. In essence, then, the definition of the public interest becomes the starting point for helping the reader to gain a better understanding about this topic. It is important to define what the public interest is in order to determine whether the accounting profession is serving the public interest or not. The primary argument of this chapter is that there have been and there continue to be alternative perspectives regarding accounting in the public interest, and that these alternative perspectives need to be understood in order to gain a better comprehension of the topic.

The following section presents a brief historical summary of certain cleavages that have taken place in the academic accounting discipline which may have led to alternative perspectives on accounting in the public interest.

## 7.2 Brief Historical Sketch of the Cleavage in Accounting Research[3]

Prior to the 1970s, there were few divisions in accounting research. Scholars were expected to be conversant with all significant issues and topics in different parts of the discipline whether the topic involved financial accounting, auditing, or managerial accounting. By the end of the 1980s, a major transformation had taken place

[3] This section is based on the author's experiences as a doctoral student and professor at various American universities in the 1970s through 1990s and as a Visiting Senior Lecture at a British University in the mid 1990s.

in the accounting discipline in the United States, one which was characterized by an emphasis on positivist, numerical research.

The first indication of this transformation was revealed by a growing rigidity in doctoral programs and a tendency for there to be little connection between accounting research and accounting practice. The second trend in doctoral education was that doctoral students in accounting were required to complete their minor fields in finance, economics or statistics, or in some cases, psychology. Collateral fields such as sociology or history were excluded. The third trend was the emergence of distinct sub-disciplines such as financial, managerial, auditing, taxation, governmental, and information systems. Finally, there was a proliferation of journals. Prior to 1970, there were only a few accounting research journals; by the end of the 1980s, there were dozens. Each of these trends led to a growing emphasis on positivist research methodologies focusing on the testing of hypotheses through the collection and statistical analysis of numerical data. It was assumed that the accounting researcher would teach and do research in a particular sub-discipline, and that the researcher would attempt to publish in "high-quality" journals (i.e. *The Accounting Review, Journal of Accounting Research, Journal of Accounting and Economics*).

This focus on statistical analysis of numerical data has been called "positivist". It should be noted, however, that it is called positivist primarily because the underlying philosophical assumption of this line of research is that rigorous scientific studies should be based on numerically measureable data. Positivism arose as a reaction to speculative academic articles that were not anchored in actual observations. Positivism was designed to test specific hypotheses asserted in advance (usually based on a prior theoretical framework), which were then tested using real data. While the well-known article by Watts and Zimmerman (1978), entitled "Towards a Positive Theory of the Determination of Accounting Standards", has often been referred to as "positivist", that article is positivist only because it is based on numerical data. The Watts and Zimmerman (1978) article represents only one example in a large body of positivist, numerical accounting research that has been produced over the last 40 years primarily by North American scholars who follow the positivist tradition.

In contrast to developments taking place in the United States during the 1970s and 1980s, there was a different approach to accounting research taking place in countries outside the United States. In the United Kingdom, for example, although some accounting researchers followed the American example of using positivist, numerical research methods other researchers took an interpretative or critical approach to accounting research. These interpretive and critical studies usually employed theories and methodologies from well-known philosophers and social theorists like Giddens, Foucault, Habermas, Marx, Derrida and others. Accounting researchers would become identified as experts regarding these social theorists, and they would seek to collaborate with scholars having similar perspectives, while simultaneously rejecting the positivist perspective on accounting research.

Thus, by the end of the 1980s, there was a distinct cleavage in the accounting research discipline, not only into sub-disciplines in the United States, but also into the paradigmatically separate fields: "positivist" and "critical" accounting research.

In the intervening period these two fields have had little interaction with one another, with scholars in one field largely unfamiliar with the work of scholars in other fields. In particular, the positivist field, which by the 2000s encompassed virtually all American accounting research, had come to define quality research to include only articles appearing in a few "top" journals (e.g. *The Accounting Review, Journal of Accounting Research, Journal of Accounting and Economic*), as well as a select number of other journals such as *Contemporary Accounting Research; Review of Accounting Studies; Journal of Business, Finance and Accounting; Journal of Accounting, Auditing and Finance.*

In response to the growing domination of the accounting research discipline by the positivist paradigm, certain scholars began searching for alternative paradigm and perspectives. The initial and most prominent example of this search for alternative perspectives was begun by Anthony Hopwood who founded *Accounting, Organizations and Society* (AOS) in 1976. Over the intervening period, AOS has published a wide spectrum of positivist, critical and interpretive research, and as a journal it is included among the top tier in most league tables. Consequently, AOS has emerged as the premier outlet for critical and interpretive research in accounting. Subsequently, there has been a growth in the number of journals that publish alternative accounting research, including journals such as *Accounting, Auditing and Accountability Journal* and *Critical Perspectives on Accounting*, and *Accounting Forum.*

In summary, then, differences in approaches to accounting research constitute a primary reason for the existence of alternative perspectives regarding accounting in the public interest. These differing approaches to accounting research will be discussed in the following sections of the chapter.

## 7.3 Social Science Approaches to Accounting Research

As a profession and an academic discipline, accounting has been influenced to a great extent by economics. In addition, the academic accounting profession has been influenced by psychology and to a lesser extent by sociology. As will be seen in the following sections, these different social science disciplines have led to alternative perspectives on accounting in the public interest.

### *7.3.1 Economics Based Approaches*

Theories derived from neo-classical economics underpin most accounting research[4], and it has been often observed that economics based models tend to crowd out other approaches to accounting research (Williams et al. 2006). In terms of economics

[4] As an academic discipline, accounting evolved out of economics and most of its primary metaphors are derived from neo-classical economic theory.

based research in accounting, a search using the phrase 'public interest' in *The Accounting Review* produced more than 50 articles; however, virtually all of these articles define the public interest as "the interests of third parties who rely on the opinions and advice delivered by the members of the profession" (Parker 1987, p. 509). A sample of economics based research related to accounting in the public interest is discussed in the following paragraphs.

One seminal economics paper that has had a great deal of influence on the accounting discipline is Jensen and Meckling (1976). This paper integrated elements from the theory of agency, the theory of property rights and the theory of finance to develop a theory of the ownership structure of the firm. Effectively this paper established the use of agency theory in accounting research, a theory which has provided one of the primary theoretical underpinnings for economics based research in accounting. Essentially agency theory states that there is a conflict between the goals of agents (i.e. managers) and those of principals (i.e. shareholders), and that shareholders will create monitoring mechanisms (e.g. auditing) to control agent/managers so that they will act in the interests of the shareholders and not in their own interests. Agency theory is widely accepted in the economics, accounting and finance literatures, but it has sometimes been misinterpreted by critics who claim that agency theory argues that the only purpose of a business firm is to maximize the wealth of its shareholders. In fact, agency theory does not say what the interests of shareholders should be; shareholders might in fact be interested in seeing that managers act in both the interests of shareholders and the public interest. Thus, agency theory is completely congruent with the definition of the public interest that considers the 'public interest' to be "the interests of third parties who rely on the opinions and advice delivered by the members of the accounting profession" (Parker 1987). A need for reliable information would exist regardless of the purpose of the firm, and the professional accountant has an obligation to serve the public interest by providing reliable information.

An example of an economics based perspective regarding research on accounting in the public interest is Noreen (1988). Noreen used an agency theory model to explain the existence of altruistic behavior in capitalist organizations. Noreen suggested that the existence of ethical behavior in markets can be explained not only through social variables, but also through variables inherent to individuals, such as altruism, and that altruistic behavior has the desirable effect of making markets more efficient. Even though there are instances of opportunistic self-interested behavior, "it is does not follow that businessmen generally are or should be opportunistic…at least some varieties of ethical behavior are not to be scorned; they are a necessary lubricant for the functioning of markets" (Noreen 1988, p. 369).

In a second economics based study, Lev (1988) argued that the public interest of role of accounting should be to enhance efficiency and equity in financial markets. Such a policy would favor the interests of less informed investors over those of more informed investors. Lev argued that this could be accomplished, for example, by requiring the public disclosure of management's forecasts of earnings. Lev maintained that accounting in the public interest should focus on enhancing investor and creditor decision making for the purpose of helping markets to become more efficient and effective.

In a third economics based study, Hope and Langli (2010) indicated that a distinguishing mark of the accounting profession is its acceptance of a responsibility to act in the public interest, which the authors define as compliance with the code of ethics of the profession, and that the purpose of the code of ethics is to enhance the reliability and credibility of audited financial statements. In a similar way, McGuire et al. (2012) define the public interest from an auditing perspective as the validation the accuracy of financial statements in order to aide investor and creditor decision making. Finally, Schmidt (2012) defines the public interest in relation to auditor independence for the purpose of enhancing the reliability and credibility of audited financial statements.

Consequently, it can be seen that the primary focus of economics based research in accounting with respect to the public interest involves a concentration on the interests of third parties who rely on the opinions and advice delivered by the members of the profession. Implicitly, the primary measure of serving the public interest is the degree of reliability of audited financial statements.

The following sections will discuss some alternative approaches to accounting research beyond the dominant economics based approach.

### *7.3.2 Psychological Approaches*

Social science approaches to research on accounting have also been conducted using methodologies derived from psychology. Because of its focus on variables such as attitudes, beliefs, values, opinions and behaviors, which are inherent to individuals, the psychological approach to accounting research examines correlations between accounting variables and psychological variables in order to test various hypotheses about human behavior in business and other organizational settings. With respect to accounting in the public interest, the psychological approach to accounting research often examines the ways that individuals can be selected or trained in order to act in the public interest, without actually defining what the public interest may be.

The 'moral development paradigm' is a particular psychological theory that addresses accounting in the public interest from a moral perspective (Kohlberg 1981). The moral development paradigm focuses on an individual's beliefs and how the individual's belief system controls conflict resolution and moral decision making. Kohlberg's studies of beliefs about moral behavior were based on a theoretical model derived from Piaget (1932). According to Piaget, an individual's moral sense develops through a series of stages over time as the person matures. Kohlberg (1958) elaborated upon the stages of moral development formulated by Piaget in order to explain the processes that cause an individual to act in accordance with a set of certain moral principles. According to Kohlberg's model, a person's moral judgment develops in stages, and at any given point in time, a person will be situated at particular stage and then proceed to the next stage depending upon the person's education and maturity level.

In the accounting literature, many researchers[5] have employed the Kohlbergian model in empirical studies of individual accountants. These studies have produced a wide range of findings, such as: individuals at higher level positions in public accounting firms do not necessarily demonstrate higher levels of moral development as measured by the Defining Issues Test (Ponemon 1990; Rest 1979); that female professional accountants are more sensitive to moral issues than male accountants (Arnold et al. 2007); that cheating behavior is associated with lower levels of moral development (Bernardi et al. 2008); and that there may be a difference in moral development based on political orientation (Sweeny 1995).

Because of its focus on the individual person as the locus of moral development, the Kohlbergian psychological approach to accounting research deals with behavior at the individual level rather than at the social level. In this way, it is similar to the economics based approach to accounting research; however, the difference is that the moral development paradigm emphasizes the importance of higher levels of moral development, and in particular, how higher levels of moral development among practicing professional accountants might serve the public interest. While the unstated assumption of most research based on the moral development paradigm is that the public interest would be served in a general sense if the accounting profession provided reliable opinions and advice, it is potentially the case that the public interest could be defined in a much broader manner within the moral development paradigm.

## *7.3.3 Sociological Approaches*

Accounting research has also been influenced by theories and methodologies derived from sociology. The general assumption underlying sociology is that social structures determine human behavior. Within the framework of sociology, researchers have taken distinctly different approaches to professional ethics and accounting in the public interest, ranging from the highly structural-functionalist theories put forth in the *sociology of professions and professional self-interest* literatures to the more critical *organization theory* literature.

### 7.3.3.1 The Sociology of Professions and Professional Self Interest Literatures

The *sociology of professions* literature focuses on identifying social structures that define a profession and seek to explain how these structures serve the functions of

[5] See for example: Arnold and Ponemon (1987), Ponemon (1990), Ponemon and Gabhart (1990), Shaub (1994), Sweeny (1995), Fisher and Ott (1996), Thorne (2000), Bay and Greenberg (2001), Massey (2002), Jones et al. (2003), Arnold et al. (2007), Bernardi et al. (2008) and Ariall et al. (2012).

both advancing the interests of the profession and serving the public interest. The *sociology of professions* literature defines a profession as having among other attributes: a defined body of knowledge; specific recognition by society; a code of ethics; and a defined cultural tradition (Abbot 1983; Greenwood 1957). Historically, individuals have become members of a profession by joining guilds or institutes which impose codes of conduct upon their members. These codes of conduct address both technical and ethical issues, and violations of the code constitute grounds for taking disciplinary actions against the offending member. The disciplinary actions could range from warnings and reprimands to harsher penalties including expulsion from the guild or institute. Threats of expulsion from the professional guild or institute and the corresponding loss of status and income generally suffice to cause the members of the profession to abide by the written and unwritten codes of conduct (Durkheim 1933, 1957).

One issue that arises when discussing accounting in the public interest is whether accounting actually is a profession (Zeff 1987). The auditing services provided by the accounting discipline have generally been regarded as constituting a profession because the regulation of this aspect of accounting corresponds to the characteristics of a profession as defined by the *Sociology of Professions* literature (Greenwood 1966; Abbott 1983; Burns and Haga 1977). However, there have been many critical commentaries on the role of professional accountants with respect to auditing and other professional accounting practices. These criticisms tend to focus on the lack of credibility of the public accountant's claim to serve the public interest[6], arguing that the codes of ethics of the accounting profession are often "smoke-screens" for actions that are actually intended to foster the private interests of the profession (see for example: Sikka 2008; Sikka and Hampton 2005; Sikka and Wilmott 1995; Sikka et al. 1989).

Closely related to the sociology of professions literature is a body of research which deals with *professional self-interest*. In this line of research, codes of ethics are viewed as mechanisms designed to enhance the interests of the profession or to secure monopoly control of a particular economic activity (Parker 1994; Preston et al. 1995). Parker indicates that the accounting profession has often issued statements emphasizing its professional status and its role in serving the public interest. While the codes of ethics of the accounting profession have usually been expressed in terms of advancing the public interest, it can be seen that these codes are inextricably linked with the profession's private interests (Willmott 1986; Preston et al. 1995). In a study of ethical pronouncements issued by the Australian public accounting profession, Parker (1987) identified protection of the private interests of the profession as a primary rationale underlying many of the ethical pronouncements. Parker (1994) also found that the majority of disciplinary actions for code of ethics violations taken by the professional accounting institutes in Australian during the period 1961–1987 were oriented towards the private

[6] See for example: Adams (2004). Anderson-Gough et al. (2002), Cooper and Neu (2006) and Merino et al. (2010).

interests of the profession rather than the public interest. Parker's findings in Australia support some earlier findings of Briloff (1978) and Montagna (1974) concerning the public accounting profession in the United States, by Quick (1994) in Germany, by Bédard (2001) in Canada, and by Canning and O'Dwyer (2006) in Ireland, to the effect that disciplinary practices for code of ethics violations tend not to address the public interest role of professional accounting (Baker 2005, 2007, 2008).

The underlying assumption of the *sociology of professions* approach to the study of accounting in the public interest is that the moral dilemmas faced by accountants can be resolved by creating appropriate social structures. However, the conclusion from this approach is that the accounting profession serves the public interest best when it provides opinions and advice to third parties who rely upon such opinions and advice, hence this approach does not differ substantially from the economics based approach or the psychological approach. In contrast, the *professional self-interest* perspective tends to view the claims of the accounting profession to serve the public interest as self-serving (Sikka 2008; Sikka and Hampton 2005; Sikka and Willmott 1995; Sikka et al. 1989), thus questioning the basic assumption underlying the public interest claims of the accounting profession. Unfortunately, while this approach to accounting research is powerful as a critique, it offers very little in terms of suggestions for change or reform.

#### 7.3.3.2 Organization Theory Approaches

Another approach to accounting research within sociology is based on *organization theory*. There have been a number of studies that have approached the ethical conduct of accountants from an organization theory perspective[7]. These studies often focus on the ethical dilemmas faced by accountants and investigate how organizational structure variables act to determine the outcome of these dilemmas. These studies argue that organizational and cultural variables have an impact on ethical behavior regardless of the beliefs, attitudes, values, personalities, or levels of moral development of the actors. The conclusion is that the organizational settings in which the accountants find themselves determine their behavior regardless of individual ethical and moral beliefs (Hunt and Vitell 1986; Ajzen and Fishbein 1973; Frankena 1963). Thus, the conclusion is that in order to improve accounting in the public interest, organizations must be changed to take the public interest more into consideration. This idea permeates much of the critical perspectives and corporate social responsibility literature that will be discussed in the following sections.

[7] For examples see: Aranya et al. (1981), Baker (1977, 1993, 2005, 2007, 2008), Gaa and Smith (1985), Knapp (1985), Lightner et al. (1982), Loeb (1971, 1972), Schilit (1984), Adams (2004), Anderson-Gough et al. (2002), Cooper and Neu (2006) and Merino et al. (2010).

### 7.3.4 Non-conventional Approaches to Accounting Research

In recent years, a large and growing literature on *Critical Perspectives on Accounting* and *Corporate Social Responsibility* has emerged in the accounting literature which has produced insightful reflections on accounting rhetoric, philosophical perspectives, and discourse in the age of neoliberalism. In contrast to the economics, psychological and sociological approaches discussed in the previous sections of this chapter, this literature has developed important examinations of public discourse, and debates regarding normative and positive accounting philosophies and what this means for accounting and the public interest. The perspective taken in these studies is that the privileged position of the accounting profession in contributing to economic decision making determines the nature and outcomes of social conflicts. Consequently, unlike other professions, there is a significant role for the accounting profession in the regulation and distribution of economic resources, which can be seen as having an impact on the public interest, broadly defined.

#### 7.3.4.1 Critical Perspectives Approaches to Accounting Research

The critical perspectives approach to accounting research began as a reaction to positivist, numerical accounting research. The efforts of Anthony Hopwood in founding *Accounting, Organizations and Society* were mentioned previously as being instrumental in opening up an opportunity for critical accounting research (see Gendron and Baker 2005). The Critical Accounting Perspective pointed to the need for consideration of alternatives to mainstream research. One of the bases for this line of research was that financial statements were traditionally drafted to show returns to equity or capital, and therefore minimized the return for labor. It was thought that there may be alternatives to rectify this traditional focus of accounting.

Among the first reactions to mainstream, positivist accounting research put forth by critical accounting scholars was a commentary of Lowe et al. (1982), which appeared in the *Journal of Accounting and Public Policy*. This commentary offered a critique of a mainstream, positivist article by Watts and Zimmerman (1979), which had appeared *The Accounting Review*. In their article, Watts and Zimmerman (1979) had questioned why most accounting theories are normative and they concluded that accounting theories are economic goods that are produced in response to a demand for such theories, with most of the demand coming from government regulation. Lowe et al. (1982) criticized Watts and Zimmerman (1979) for using a simplified model to capture and predict complex social phenomena. Lowe et al.'s criticism took three forms: (1) the methodology and testability used by Watts and Zimmerman was suspect; (2) the applicability of the evidence used by Watts and Zimmerman was questioned; (3) Lowe et al. provided contrary evidence is to rebut the theory put forth by Watts and Zimmerman.

This attempt by Lowe et al. (1982) to offer a critique of the mainstream, positivist accounting literature did not lead to a dialogue between the differing paradigms.

After this initial attempt there was a gradual retreat into the specific journals of respective paradigms, with occasional efforts to advance arguments in favor of one position or another. An example of this attempt to advance a particular position, was the book written by Tinker and Puxty (1995), entitled *Policing Accounting Knowledge: The Market for Excuses Affair*, in which the authors illustrated how the mainstream positivist journals excluded critical accounting research. Tinker and Puxty (1995) argued that what becomes "knowledge" in accounting research is primarily what is published in top-tier journals. While the Watts and Zimmerman (1979) article received the American Accounting Association's Notable Contribution to Accounting Theory Award, various critical commentators on Watts and Zimmerman were unable to have their research published in top-tier journals, primarily because it was claimed that critical accounting research did not meet the standards of scientific rigor. Consequently, Tinker and Puxty's book was the only way to provide an analysis of the way in which accounting knowledge is controlled by academic elites.

In another attempt to provide a critical analysis of the mainstream positive accounting approach to research, Tinker et al. (1982), published an article in Accounting, Organizations and Society, which was solicited by Anthony Hopwood, the editor of AOS. In this article, Tinker et al. argued that "positivist" and "empirical" theories are frequently promoted as being more realistic, factual and relevant than normative and critical approaches. However, they argued that "positive" or "empirical" theories are also normative and value-laden in that they usually mask a conservative ideological bias in their accounting policy implications. They maintained that labels such as "positive" and "empirical" emanate from a realist theory of knowledge, which they claim is an inadequate epistemological basis for social science (hence the disputes about what social science is or is not). The authors attempt to use an alternative philosophical position (i.e. Historical Materialism) together with a historical review of the concept of value to illustrate first, the partisan role played by theories and theoreticians in questions concerning social control, social conflict and social order; second, the ideologically conservative underpinnings of positive accounting theories; and last, some indications of alternative (radical) approaches to accounting policy.

Despite these attempts to confront the mainstream literature, there continued to be a virtual exclusion of critical and interpretive accounting research from top-tier journals. However, a large critical accounting research literature has developed through the auspices of other journals such as *Accounting, Organizations and Society*, *Accounting, Auditing & Accountability Journal* and *Critical Perspectives on Accounting*. This literature is highly diverse, touching on such subjects such as the accounting profession in relationship to racism, colonialism, globalization, corruption, money-laundering, environmental degradation and many other topics[8].

[8] See for example: Annisette and Trivedi (2011), Armstrong (1985), Anderson-Gough et al. (2002), Baxter et al. (2008), Bayou et al. (2011), Broadbent and Laughlin (2005), Catchpowle et al. (2004), Chwastiak (2001), Chwastiak and Lehman (2008), Cooper and Neu (2006), Dillard (2003, 2008), Everett (2003), Gallhofer and Haslam (2006), Macintosh (1993, 1995), Merino et al. (2010), Puxty et al. (1987) and Sikka (2008).

An example of some of the work done in the critical perspectives on accounting literature is the work of Laughlin and Broadbent (1996). See also: Broadbent and Laughlin (1995, 2005). The central concern of this research is with accounting in the public interest. What these studies reveal is the complex interplay between accounting systems and the steering media of society. If accounting systems are not designed in an open and freely discursive manner (i.e. an ideal speech situation), then they are likely to be used by the controlling interests in a way that reduces human freedom. This is probably the central argument of the critical accounting research paradigm, which is, that accounting can be used in ways that are contrary to the public interest, and that there is a constant need to be aware of this possibility.

Evolving out of the critical perspectives approach to accounting research, there has been a growing aspect of accounting in the public interest which focuses on *Corporate Social Responsibility*. This strand of accounting research focusing on Corporate Social Responsibility follows the recommendations of Adams (2002), Larrinaga et al. (2001) and O'Dwyer (2002) that researchers should focus more of their attention on effectuating change in organizations rather than merely describing and criticizing problems. As a result of these recommendations, the topics of sustainability and sustainable development have become increasingly prominent.

Sustainable development is conceived of as a process through which there is satisfaction of human wants and needs while simultaneously preserving the quality of the natural environment. The most commonly employed definition of sustainable development can be summarized as development which meets the needs of the present generation without compromising the ability of future generations to meet their own needs. It is now generally recognized that sustainable development does not focus entirely on the environment. The notion of sustainable development encompasses at least three areas: the economic, the social, and the environmental. A significant amount of accounting research is now being devoted to this subject, for example: Adams (2002, 2004), Buhr (2007), Farneti and Guthrie (2009), Gray and Gray (2011), Gray and Milne (2004), Owen et al. (2001).

## 7.4 Summary and Conclusion

It can be seen that the subject of accounting in the public interest can range from providing reliable opinions and advice to third parties who rely on audited financial statements, to a symbolic discourse which seeks to protect the accounting profession from outside interference, to a role in determining the outcome of social conflicts through the regulation and distribution of economic resources. One of the goals of this chapter has been to illustrate that the alternative perspectives on accounting in the public interest may be traceable to the definition of the public interest. The chapter has examined a number of social science approaches to accounting in the public interest ranging from economics based approaches, to psychological based approaches, to sociological based approaches, to critical approaches and corporate social responsibility approaches. What appears to be obvious is that each of these approaches to accounting research has different underlying philosophical presuppositions and assumptions, which may make a common approach to accounting in the public interest unlikely.

Accounting has evolved into an integral component of modern capitalist societies. Codes of conduct within the accounting profession have evolved in order to define the duties that accountants owe to their clients, to third party beneficiaries, and to society generally and to provide assurances of an adequate level of technical and ethical conduct on the part of professional accountants. Ethical issues and conflicts faced by accountants are continuing despite the considerable amount of effort that has gone into the study of ethical issues. The financial and competitive pressures experienced by professional accountants have often led them to seek revenues through expansion of their services into non-traditional areas. This raises the question of whether codes of conduct which defined the duties of accountants in individual practice units continue to be able to effectively control practices that transcend all former boundaries. Beyond this issue, there lies the question of accounting's role in determining the outcome of social conflicts such as those discussed by the Critical Perspective and Corporate Social Responsibility literatures.

It therefore remains an open question as to whether the primary purpose of accounting in the public interest involves the obligation of accounting professionals to provide reliable opinions and advice to third parties, or is it merely a symbolic discourse that protects the accounting profession from outside interference, or is there an important role for the accounting profession in determining the regulation and distribution of economic resources. The definition of the public interest therefore is central to gaining a better understanding about this topic. The primary argument of this chapter has been that there are alternative perspectives towards accounting in the public interest, and that these alternative perspectives need to be considered in order to gain a better understanding of the topic.

## References

Abbott, A. 1983. Professional ethics. *American Journal of Sociology* 88: 855–885.

Adams, C. 2002. Internal organisational factors influencing corporate social and ethical reporting: Beyond current theorising. *Accounting, Auditing and Accountability Journal* 15(2): 223–250.

Adams, C. 2004. The ethical, social and environmental reporting-performance portrayal gap. *Accounting, Auditing and Accountability Journal* 17(5): 731–757.

Ajzen, I., and M. Fishbein. 1973. Attitudinal and normative variables as predictors of specific behaviors. *Journal of Personality and Social Psychology* 27: 41–57.

Anderson-Gough, F., C. Grey, and K. Robson. 2002. Accounting professionals and the accounting profession: Linking conduct and context. *Accounting and Business Research* 32: 41–56.

Annisette, M., and U. Trivedi. 2011. *Globalization, conflicting logics and the underemployment of Indian chartered accountants in Canada*. Critical perspectives on accounting conference, Clearwater.

Aranya, N., J. Pollock, and J. Amernic. 1981. An examination of professional commitment in public accounting. *Accounting, Organizations and Society* 6: 271–280.

Ariail, D., M. Abdolmohammadi, and L.M. Smith. 2012. Ethical predisposition of certified public accountants: A study of gender differences. In *Research on professional responsibility and ethics in accounting*, vol. 16, ed. C. Jeffrey, 29–56. Bingley: Emerald Group.

Armstrong, P. 1985. Changing management control strategies: The role of competition between accountancy and other organisational professions. *Accounting, Organizations and Society* 10: 129–148.

Arnold, D., and L. Ponemon. 1987. *Moral judgment prospective for various auditing judgment issues*. Proceedings of the British Accounting Association's Annual Meeting, Glasgow University, Glasgow.

Arnold, D., R. Bernardi, P. Neidermeyer, and J. Schmee. 2007. The effect of country and culture on perceptions of appropriate ethical actions prescribed by codes of conduct: A western European perspective among accountants. *Journal of Business Ethics* 70(4): 327–340.

Baker, C.R. 1977. Management strategy in a large accounting firm. *The Accounting Review* 52(3): 576–586.

Baker, C.R. 1993. Self-regulation in the public accounting profession: The response of the large, international public accounting firms to a changing environment. *Accounting, Auditing, and Accountability Journal* 6(2): 68–80.

Baker, C.R. 2005. What do we mean by accounting for the public interest? *Accounting Auditing and Accountability Journal* 18(5): 690–703.

Baker, C.R. 2007. The contested concept of auditor independence. *Advances in Public Interest Accounting* 12: 17–26.

Baker, C.R. 2008. Ideological reactions to Sarbanes-Oxley. *Accounting Forum* 32(2): 114–124.

Baxter, J., C. Boedker, and V. Chua. 2008. The future(s) of interpretive accounting research – A polyphonic response from beyond the Metropolis. *Critical Perspectives on Accounting* 19: 880–886.

Bay, D.D., and R. Greenberg. 2001. The relationship of the DIT and behavior: A replication. *Issues in Accounting Education* 16(3): 367–380.

Bayou, M., A. Reinstein, and P. Williams. 2011. To tell the truth: A discussion of issues concerning truth and ethics in accounting. *Accounting, Organizations and Society* 36: 109–124.

Bédard, J. 2001. The disciplinary process of the accounting profession: Protecting the public or the profession? The Quebec experience. *Journal of Accounting and Public Policy* 20(4–5): 399–437.

Bernardi, R., A. Baca, K. Landers, and M. Witek. 2008. Methods of cheating and deterrents to classroom cheating: An international study. *Ethics and Behavior* 18(4): 373–391.

Briloff, A. 1978. Codes of conduct: Their sound and their fury. In *Ethics, free enterprise and public policy: Original essays on moral issues in business*, ed. R. De George and J. Picher. London: Oxford University Press.

Broadbent, J., and R. Laughlin. 1995. *Developing empirical research: An example informed by a Habermasian approach*, Working Paper No. 95/08. Colchester: Department of Accounting and Financial Management, University of Essex.

Broadbent, J., and R. Laughlin. 2005. The role of PFI in the UK governments modernisation agenda. *Financial Accountability & Management* 21(1): 75–97.

Buhr, N. 2007. Histories of and rationales for sustainability reporting. In *Sustainability accounting and accountability*, ed. J. Unerman, J. Bebbington, and B. O'Dwyer, 57–69. New York: Routledge.

Burns, D., and W. Haga. 1977. Much ado about professionalism: A second look at accounting. *The Accounting Review* 52: 705–715.

Canning, M., and B. O'Dwyer. 2006. The influence of the "organisation" on the logics of action-pervading disciplinary decision making. *Accounting Auditing and Accountability Journal* 19(1): 17–46.

Catchpowle, L., C. Cooper, and A. Wright. 2004. Capitalism, states and ac-counting. *Critical Perspectives on Accounting* 15: 1037–1058.

Chwastiak, M. 2001. Taming the untameable: Planning, programming and budgeting and the normalization of war. *Accounting, Organizations and Society* 26: 501–519.

Chwastiak, M., and G. Lehman. 2008. Accounting for war. *Accounting Forum* 32: 313–326.

Cooper, D., and D. Neu. 2006. Auditor and audit independence in the age of financial scandal. *Advances in Public Interest Accounting* 12: 1–15.

Dillard, J. 2003. Professional services, IBM, and the Holocaust. *Journal of Information Systems* 17: 116.

Dillard, J. 2008. A political base of a polyphonic debate. *Critical Perspectives on Accounting* 19: 894–900.

Durkheim, E. 1933. *The division of labor in society*. Trans. G. Simpson. New York: Free Press.

Durkheim, E. 1957. *Professional ethics and civic morals*. Trans. C. Brookfield. New York: Routledge and Kegan Paul.

Everett, J. 2003. Globalization and its new spaces for (alternative) accounting research. *Accounting Forum* 27: 400–424.

Farneti, F., and J. Guthrie. 2009. Sustainability reporting by Australian public sector organisations: Why they report. *Accounting Forum* 33: 89–98.

Fischer, D., and R. Ott. 1996. A study of the relationship between accounting student's moral reasoning and cognitive styles. *Research on Accounting Ethics* 2: 51–72.

Frankena, W. 1963. *Ethics*. Englewood Cliffs: Prentice-Hall.

Gaa, J., and C. Smith. 1985. Auditors and deceptive financial statements: Assigning responsibility and blame. *Contemporary Accounting Research* 1: 219–241.

Gallhofer, S., and J. Haslam. 2006. The accounting-globalisation interrelation: An overview with some reflections on the neglected dimension of emancipatory potentiality. *Critical Perspectives on Accounting* 17: 903–934.

Gendron, Y., and C.R. Baker. 2005. Interdisciplinary movements: The development of a network of support around Foucaultian perspectives in accounting research. *The European Accounting Review* 14(3): 525–569.

Gray, R., and S. Gray. 2011. Accountability and human rights: A tentative exploration and a commentary. *Critical Perspectives on Accounting* 22(8): 781–789.

Gray, R., and M. Milne. 2004. Towards reporting on the triple bottom line: Mirages, methods and myths. In *The triple bottom line: Does it all add up?: Assessing the sustainability of business and CSR*, ed. A. Henriques and J. Richardson, 70–80. London: Earthscan.

Greenwood, E. 1957. Attributes of a profession. *Social Work* 2(July): 45–55.

Greenwood, E. 1966. The elements of professionalization. In *Professionalization*, eds. H. Vollmer and D. Mills. Englewood Cliffs: Prentice-Hall.

Hope, O.K., and J.K. Langli. 2010. Auditor independence in a private firm and low litigation risk setting. *The Accounting Review* 85(2): 573–605.

Hunt, S., and S. Vitell. 1986. A general theory of marketing ethics. *Journal of Macromarketing* 6(1): 5–16.

Jensen, M., and W. Meckling. 1976. Theory of the firm: Managerial behavior, agency costs and ownership structure. *Journal of Financial Economics* 3(4): 305–360.

Jones, J., D.W. Massey, and L. Thorne. 2003. Auditors' ethical reasoning: Insights from past research and implications for the future. *Journal of Accounting Literature* 22: 45–103.

Knapp, M. 1985. Audit conflict: An empirical study of the perceived ability of auditors to resist management pressure. *The Accounting Review* 60: 202–211.

Kohlberg, L. 1958. *The development of modes of moral thinking and choice in the years ten to sixteen*. Unpublished Ph.D. dissertation, Chicago: University of Chicago.

Kohlberg, L. 1981. *The meaning and measurement of moral development*. Worcester: Clark University Press.

Larrinaga-Gonzalez, C., F. Carrasco-Fenech, F.J. Caro-Gonzalez, C. Correa-Ruiz, and J.M. Paes-Sadubete. 2001. The role of environmental accounting in organizational change: An exploration of Spanish companies. *Accounting, Auditing and Accountability Journal* 14(2): 213–238.

Laughlin, R., and J. Broadbent. 1996. *The 'accounting turn' in steering media in organisations and society with specific reference to the public sector in the U.K*, Working Paper No. 96/03. Colchester: Department of Accounting and Financial Management, University of Essex, January.

Lev, B. 1988. Toward a theory of equitable and efficient accounting policy. *The Accounting Review* 63(1): 1–22.

Lightner, S., S. Adams, and K. Lightner. 1982. The influence of situational, ethical, and expectancy theory variables on accountants' underreporting behavior. *Auditing: A Journal of Practice and Theory* 2: 1–12.

Loeb, S. 1971. A survey of ethical behavior in the accounting profession. *Journal of Accounting Research* 9(2): 287–306.
Loeb, S. 1972. Enforcement of the code of ethics: A survey. *The Accounting Review* 47: 1–10.
Lowe, E., A. Puxty, and R. Laughlin. 1982. Simple theories for complex processes: Accounting policy and the market for myopia. *Journal of Accounting and Public Policy* 2(1): 19–42.
Macintosh, N. 1993. *A research proposal to investigate the possibility of poststructuralist accounting thought*, Working Paper. Queen's University Kingston, Ontario.
Macintosh, N. 1995. The ethics of profit manipulation: A dialectic of control analysis. *Critical Perspectives on Accounting* 6: 289–315.
Massey, D. 2002. The importance of context in investigating auditors' moral abilities. *Research on Accounting Ethics* 8: 195–247.
McGuire, S., T. Omer, and D. Wang. 2012. Tax avoidance: Does tax-specific industry expertise make a difference? *The Accounting Review* 87(3): 975–1003.
Merino, B.D., A.G. Mayper, and T. Tolleson. 2010. Neo-liberalism deregulation and Sarbanes-Oxley: The legitimation of a failed corporate governance model. *Accounting, Auditing and Accountability Journal* 23: 774–792.
Montagna, P. 1974. *Certified public accounting: A sociological view of a profession in change*. Houston: Scholars Books.
Noreen, E. 1988. The economics of ethics: A new perspective on agency theory. *Accounting, Organizations and Society* 13: 359–369.
O'Dwyer, B. 2002. Managerial perceptions of corporate social disclosure: An Irish story. *Accounting Auditing and Accountability Journal* 15(3): 406–436.
Owen, D., T. Swift, and K. Hunt. 2001. Questioning the role of stakeholder engagement in social and ethical accounting, auditing and reporting. *Accounting Forum* 25(3): 264–282.
Parker, L. 1987. An historical analysis of ethical pronouncements and debate in the Australian accounting profession. *Abacus* 23: 126–140.
Parker, L. 1994. Professional accounting body ethics: In search of the private interest. *Accounting, Organizations and Society* 19: 507–525.
Ponemon, L. 1990. Ethical judgments in accounting: A cognitive-development perspective. *Critical Perspectives on Accounting* 1(2): 191–215.
Ponemon, L., and D. Gabhart. 1990. Auditor independence judgments: A cognitive-developmental model and experimental evidence. *Contemporary Accounting Research* 7: 227–251.
Preston, A., D. Cooper, D. Scarbrough, and R. Chilton. 1995. Changes in the code of ethics of the U.S. accounting profession, 1917 and 1988: The continual quest for legitimation. *Accounting, Organizations and Society* 20(6): 507–546.
Puxty, A., H. Willmott, D. Cooper, and T. Lowe. 1987. Modes of regulation in advanced capitalism: Locating accountancy in four countries. *Accounting, Organizations and Society* 12: 273–291.
Quick, R. 1994. *Disciplinary actions against auditors in Germany*. Fourth Maastricht Auditing Research Symposium, University of Limburg, Maastricht, The Netherlands, October.
Rest, J. 1979. *Development in judging moral issues*. Minneapolis: University of Minnesota Press.
Robson, K., H. Willmott, D. Cooper, and T. Puxty. 1994. The ideology of professional regulation and the markets for accounting labour: Three episodes in the recent history of the UK accountancy profession. *Accounting, Organizations and Society* 19: 527–553.
Schilit, H. 1984. Deviant behavior and misconduct of professionals. *The Woman CPA* 46(2): 20–24.
Schmidt, J. 2012. Perceived auditor independence and audit litigation: The role of nonaudit services fees. *The Accounting Review* 87(3): 1033–1065.
Shaub, M.K. 1994. An analysis of the association of traditional demographic variables with the moral reasoning of auditing students and auditors. *Journal of Accounting Education* 12(1): 1–26.
Sikka, P. 2008. Enterprise culture and accountancy firms: New masters of the universe. *Accounting Auditing and Accountability Journal* 21(2): 268–295.
Sikka, P., and M.P. Hampton. 2005. The role of accountancy firms in tax avoidance: Some evidence and issues. *Accounting Forum* 29(3): 325–343.
Sikka, P., and H. Willmott. 1995. The power of "Independence": Defending and extending the jurisdiction of accounting in the United Kingdom. *Accounting, Organizations and Society* 20(6): 547–581.

Sikka, P., H. Willmott, and T. Lowe. 1989. Guardians of knowledge and public interest: Evidence and issues of accountability in the U.K. *Accountancy Profession, Accounting, Auditing and Accountability Journal* 2(2): 47–71.

Sweeny, J. 1995. The moral expertise of auditors: An exploratory analysis. *Research on Accounting Ethics* 1: 213–234.

Thorne, L. 2000. The development of two measures to assess accountants' prescriptive and deliberative moral reasoning. *Behavioral Research in Accounting* 12: 139–169.

Tinker, A., and A. Puxty. 1995. *Policing accounting knowledge: The market for excuses affair*. New York: Markus Weiner.

Tinker, A., B. Merino, and M. Neimark. 1982. The normative origins of positive theories: Ideology and accounting thought. *Accounting, Organizations and Society* 7(2): 167–200.

Watts, R., and J. Zimmerman. 1978. Towards a positive theory of the determination of accounting standards. *The Accounting Review* 53(1): 112–134.

Watts, R., and J. Zimmerman. 1979. The demand for and supply of accounting theories: The market for excuses. *The Accounting Review* 54(2): 273–305.

Williams, P.F., J. Jenkins, and L. Ingraham. 2006. The winnowing away of behavioral accounting research in the U.S.: The process for anointing academic elites. *Accounting, Organizations and Society* 31: 783–818.

Willmott, H. 1986. Organising the profession: A theoretical and historical examination of the development of the major accountancy bodies in the UK. *Accounting, Organizations and Society* 11: 555–580.

Zeff, S. 1987. Does the CPA belong to a profession? *Accounting Horizons* VI: 65–68.

# Chapter 8
# The IFAC Framework: International Accounting and the Public Interest

**Paul F. Williams**

## 8.1 Introduction

The purpose of this chapter is to discuss accounting and public interest within an international context with particular reference to the International Federation of Accountants (IFAC) Framework. Currently IFAC has proposed the most explicit plan for developing a system of public interest accounting and reporting on an international scale; this chapter begins with a description of that proposed framework. This will be followed by an explanation of why professions have a special connection to the public interest and why, because of this special connection, the IFAC framework falls short of providing for a genuine public interest accounting. I will then develop an alternative perspective on public interest accounting based on corporate accountability rather than facilitating of capital market functioning in order to augment the limitations of the IFAC Framework. Some concluding remarks will end the chapter.

### *8.1.1 The IFAC Proposal*

The International Federation of Accountants (IFAC) is an organization comprised of organizations of accounting professionals from around the world. Founded in 1977 at the 11th World Congress of Accountants in Munich, Germany, IFAC represents over 160 groups from 127 countries (IFAC 2012a). According to IFAC:

> IFAC's mission is to serve the public interest by: contributing to the development, adoption and implementation of high quality international standards and guidance; contributing to the development of strong professional accountancy organizations and accounting firms,

P.F. Williams (✉)
Poole College of Management, North Carolina State University, Raleigh, NC, USA
e-mail: paul_williams@ncsu.edu

S. Mintz (ed.), *Accounting for the Public Interest: Perspectives on Accountability, Professionalism and Role in Society*, Advances in Business Ethics Research 4,
DOI 10.1007/978-94-007-7082-9_8, © Springer Science+Business Media Dordrecht 2014

> and to high-quality practice by professional accountants; promoting the value of professional accountants worldwide; speaking out on public interest issues where the accountancy profession's expertise is most relevant. (IFAC 2012a).[1]

In a succession of documents produced over the past few years IFAC outlines how it intends to organize and regulate the global accounting profession and direct it via standards of education, ethics, and professional practice. According to IFAC, the mission of a global profession organized to serve the public interest will not occur without regulation (IFAC 2011). According to IFAC Policy Position One:

> Like other professions, the sustainability of the accounting profession depends upon the quality of the services provided by its members and on the profession's capacity to respond effectively and efficiently to the demands of the economy and society. *Regulation seeks to ensure the right quality and, where appropriate, consistency in the quality of accountancy services* (emphasis added) (ibid, p. 1).

Good regulation aimed at serving the public interest "…must be proportionate, transparent, non-discriminatory, targeted, implemented consistently and fairly, and subject to regular review" (ibid). Thus does IFAC state its intent to operate as a global regulatory body of the accounting profession to assure quality of accounting services that serve the public interest worldwide by setting explicit standards of accounting education, professional practice, and professional ethics.

### *8.1.2 IFAC Policy on International Standard Setting in the Public Interest*

To achieve its mission of standard-setting in the public interest, IFAC developed a policy statement designed to provide the normative framework whereby the shared responsibility between public and private sectors "…for setting international standards for auditing and assurance, ethics and accounting education…" (IFAC 2008, p. 1) may be accomplished. The regulatory framework proposed by IFAC may be found in the first appendix of IFAC's Policy Position 3 (2008). The key element in the public interest mission is the Public Interest Oversight Board.[2] The proposed IFAC framework is designed to insure that the boards created to set standards for education, ethics, practice, and public sector will operate with a process that produces standards

---

[1] Post Sarbanes-Oxley the role of IFAC closely resembles that of the PCAOB, that is, an overarching body to oversee the conduct of accounting professionals that sets standards of conduct for those professionals. Unlike PCAOB, IFAC has no enforcement power other than moral suasion.

[2] The ten members of the PIOB are appointed by the Monitoring Group (MG). Four members are nominated by the International Organization of Securities Commission; one by the International Association of Insurance Supervisors; one by the Basel Committee; one by the World Bank; and two by the European Commission. One member is selected by the MG from nominations submitted by IFAC. Striking is the absence from the PIOB of any representation from groups other than those from the finance industry, i.e., there is no "public" representation on the PIOB. There is no representation from investors, labor, consumers, academe, the religious community, public sector, etc.

that are deemed to be legitimate. The process proposed is similar to the one currently employed by the U.S. Financial Accounting Standards Board (FASB). To gain legitimacy the FASB-like process is constructed to ensure that standard-setters are independent, i.e., free from "inappropriate pressure" (IFAC 2008, p. 3).

The process by which standards will come into effect will conform to the due process procedure currently utilized by FASB and IASB in the promulgation of financial reporting standards. Standards will be developed and put into exposure draft form and be made publicly available for a period of comment. At the completion of this "due process" procedure the standard will be finalized and approved by the PIAC. The notable exception to the FASB/IASB process seems to be that there is a formal monitoring process for continuous assessment of the efficacy of standards. Thus, standards may be more quickly adapted to changing circumstances than can current financial reporting standards, which indicates the IFAC process is a bit more open one, under less control by the profession.

### 8.1.3 The Public Interest

To serve the public interest IFAC has developed a working definition of "public interest" to guide the standard-setting process. In a working document titled "IFAC Policy Position X (IFAC 2012b) the definition of public interest is: "IFAC defines the public interest as the net benefits for, and procedural rigor employed on behalf of, all society in relation to any action, decision or policy" (IFAC 2012b, p. 1). This definition varies from the definition contained in the Exposure Draft "A Public Interest Framework for the Accountancy Profession," which "…considers that the "public interest" is the common benefit that all citizens share from the services provided by the accountancy profession" (IFAC 2010, p. 4). At the time this chapter is being written there remains ambiguity about what "public interest" means in the context of IFAC's public interest framework. The definition in Policy Position X emphasizes a cost/benefit consideration for evaluating the profession's activities. The Exposure Draft definition implies a less dynamic approach in that the public interest re accounting is simply the common benefit from accounting services that the public shares. This could, of course, be a null set. Given what services the profession provides at the moment, there may be no common benefit shared by all members of society. Though IFAC's efforts to attach professional accounting to service of human welfare are laudatory, the two definitions of public interest share a common heritage, which makes the proposed public interest framework appear more as a strategy to legitimize what the profession does rather than a genuine effort at self-examination and transformation of the profession into a practice that serves the general welfare. The reason this is the case has historical roots in the manner in which the *profession* of accounting has come to regard the *function* of accounting in society. The role that accounting has to play in promoting the public interest must be understood in terms of the function that accounting performs, not necessarily in what the profession deems accounting needs to be to serve its commercial interest.

## 8.2 Professions and the Public Interest

According to Kultgen (1988), the idealized purpose of every true profession is to contribute to improving the general well-being of human kind or to serve the public interest.[3] The public interest purpose of professions is based on a principle of equality in that each individual member of society is regarded as equal with respect to the need for and benefits of a particular professional expertise. This principle of equality is the foundation of the widely recognized feature of professional service as altruistic (Kultgen 1988, p. 60). The equality principle is notably present in the two oldest and most universally recognized professions: medicine and law. The equality principle is the basis for one of the more universally agreed upon characteristics that separates a profession from a vocation which is "Professional service is indispensible for the public good" (Kultgen 1988, p. 60). This indispensability is the basis for the functionalist theory of professions, i.e., what professions do is not optional if a society is to flourish. Medicine is the paradigmatic example of an activity with this essential functionality: physicians are morally bound to care for the ill regardless of their social or economic status. The full-flourishing of every human being requires some minimal level of health. Thus, in every society there emerges a function performed in that society aimed at restoring health or avoiding death. This caring function is unique to the human species and perhaps develops from the fear of death, which has been identified by anthropologists as one of the universal human traits (Brown 1991).

Though what has comprised the corpus of medical knowledge has changed radically over the centuries (the only thing remaining from ancient Greek medicine is the Hippocratic Oath) there is still a distinct activity performed by certain learned people whose purpose is to allay sickness among the members of society. Thus, the practitioner of medicine, who needn't be a licensed, certified member of a professional organization of doctors (Williams 2004), serves a public interest by plying his or her expertise to each individual of society without regard to the status of that individual. The public interest role of the medical practitioner is performed directly by the mere provision of medical service to individual patients or "clients." Allaying sickness is in the public interest and the act of allaying it for each member of society one-on-one is a service to the public interest.

Law serves the public interest in a different manner. In most societies every person is entitled to expect equal treatment before the law and lawyers are obliged to provide legal counsel even to those who are not able to afford it. Indeed, the word "law" contains within its definition the connotation of universality of application. However, unlike the physician who provides for the public interest by

[3] Other theories of professions that are critical of this public interest functionalist approach emphasize the group efforts by professionals to gain jurisdiction over certain activities for the purpose of extracting economic rents (e.g., Larsen 1977; Abbott 1988 ). Professional testimonies of their concern for the public, interpreted within these theories, is merely a strategic form of rhetoric to persuade the public that the professional group has the public's interest as paramount in their functioning.

service directly to individual clients, the lawyer serves the public interest not by her service to a client per se but by the opposition of legal practitioners representing the interests of their respective clients in a contest of the better proof. Legal proceedings involve parties in opposition to each other. Indeed one essential function of law is to resolve conflicts "justly" because members of society have an interest in justice being served.[4] Each adversary in a legal proceeding is represented by an attorney who is duty bound to present the best legal case for his or her client before an independent judge and/or jury. It is the adversarial process that in law is deemed to provide for the realization of justice. Thus, even though an attorney doesn't deliver justice directly to a client as the physician delivers health care directly to her client, justice is served by the attorney advocating for her client because of the legal process.

Professional accounting is unlike medicine and law because providing accounting services to clients does not directly lead to serving the public interest. IFAC acknowledges this indirectly in an example to clarify cost/benefit analysis: "It is feasible for an action to have a positive net benefit for a company, while it has a net cost to society as a whole. In the public interest context, this assessment refers to the impact on society as a whole, rather than to the company (IFAC 2012b, p. 7)." This statement is an open acknowledgement that conflict exists between the localized interests of a single company and the overall interests of society. So if a professional accountant was providing this company with services to increase its net benefits, this professional is not necessarily serving the public interest; the service could be actually detrimental to the public interest. The clients served by professional accountants are mainly ones seeking through those services an advantage over everyone else. What is distinctive about accounting clients that is different from medicine or law is that they have the means to acquire accounting services and the interests to need them. Any person may get sick and need a physician; any person may get "in trouble with the law" and need an attorney who will be provided to them whether they can afford one or not. But clients seeking accounting services seek them to pursue interests that bear no ***necessary*** relationship to what society deems in its interest.[5] Thus, for accountants "service to clients" does not automatically provide for the public interest; as IFAC notes, in many cases it leads to outcomes that are detrimental to it.

[4]There is a growing body of evidence that indicates a "public good urge" is a universal human value which is innate in human beings and that fairness is a central consideration in judging social outcomes (Basu 2011). People will incur substantial costs to themselves in order to punish wrongdoers who violate social norms of just behavior (Ariely 2008).

[5]A most obvious example is the tax services public accountants provide to very wealthy people. Society has an interest in everyone paying to support the necessary public goods, e.g., legal system, public safety, education, etc., and a fundamental principle of taxation is proportionality (Smith 1937). Tax avoidance schemes devised by accountants permit the most well-to-do to escape paying proportional tax. If society is to maintain the same levels of public goods, this shifts the burden of paying for them to people less able to afford them, but also not able to pay for the services of a professional accountant. Of course, one important way people "pay" for these services is to be deprived of those services.

## 8.3 The Shortcomings of the IFAC Framework

Since there is no necessary connection between serving clients and the public interest, IFAC argues that the public interest served by accountants is derived rather than direct. As in the case of law it is the attorney serving the interest of his client in a ***process*** that results in a socially desirable outcome, so it is the accountant serving her client in a ***process*** by which the public interest is served. Throughout the IFAC documents there is a particular rhetoric employed that indicates how accountants' service to public interest is derived. Simply put, accountants serve the public interest by serving an idealized version of the market system. The ontological assumptions that underlie the world in which accountants' services serve the public interest are those of conventional neoclassical economics (Williams 2010; Marglin 2008).

Throughout the relevant IFAC documents the serving-markets- equates-with-the-public-interest rationale prevails. Below are some explicit examples of such rhetoric.

- High-quality performance by professional accountants benefits the economy and society by contributing to the efficient allocation and management of resources in both the private and public sectors and to the operation of financial and capital markets, and through both of these to the production of goods and services (IFAC 2011, p. 1).
- …professional accountants contribute to the growth of economies and ultimately to the well-being of society (ibid)
- Competition in a market is, generally, a powerful force in driving improvements in product or service quality and value. The *market* (emphasis added) for accountancy services, which appears to be quite active, is clearly one mechanism to ensure overall quality and consistency as professional accountants compete to offer the best value services (ibid, p. 2).
- Global regulatory convergence of the accountancy profession … enhances the ability of capital markets to work globally, allows investments to move more efficiently across borders, and reduces the risks and uncertainties in capital markets (ibid, p. 6).
- … the "public" includes the widest possible scope of society: individuals and groups sharing a *marketplace* (emphasis added) for goods and services, including those provided by government (IFAC 2012b, p. 2).
- The accountancy profession helps realize certain interests of society, many of which are economic in nature and related to the efficient management of resources (ibid, p. 3).
- … it is critical for individuals and groups at all levels of society to possess confidence in the accountancy profession as an element in the *efficient functioning of markets* (emphasis added) and the legitimacy of their regulatory mechanisms (ibid, p. 9).
- The "public" includes all users of financial information and decision-makers in the financial reporting supply chain: financial preparers, corporate boards, stakeholders, auditors, governments, and financial industries…(IFAC 2010, p. 5).

These references to markets, efficiency, etc. indicate IFAC subscribes to the conventional view of economics that Sen characterizes as the "engineering view." According to Sen:

> This approach is characterized by being concerned with primarily logistic issues rather than with ultimate ends and such questions as what may foster 'the good of man' or 'how should one live.' The ends are taken as fairly straightforwardly given, and the object of the exercise is to find the appropriate means to serve them. Human behavior is typically seen as being based on simple and easily characterizable motives (Sen 1988, p. 40).

This engineering view is the standard neoclassical model of contemporary conventional economic theory. The world is divided into groups of people (stakeholders), e.g., investors, creditors, managers, employees, customers who are all deemed to have specified interests within a social context dominated by market organization. Accounting is deemed to serve the public interest via the services it provides that allegedly make the context in which interests are expressed – markets – perform more "efficiently."

From a public interest perspective there is much wrong with this engineering view. It is premised on the belief that we actually know a great deal about market systems and that economic science is sophisticated and provides a sound basis for making public policy. The engineering view also presumes that the distribution of economic output is not a significant consideration. From an international perspective distribution is the most critical issue in public interest. A sizeable proportion of the world's population is deficient in the basic necessities of life, so much so that they lack sufficient wherewithal to live fully capable lives. Affecting the "efficiency" of global capital markets provides no automatic assurance that the international public is better served. As the chapter by Ravenscroft and Denison in this monograph demonstrates exclusively serving capital markets can operate to the material detriment of the majority even in a society like the United States. No group that purports to serve the public interest by facilitating economic activity can put the issue of distribution out of its professional purview. Indeed one concept that separates the classical economists like Pigou from the neoclassicists is the differing notions of utility central to economic science. For the classicists utility was an objective concept measurable in terms of the material welfare of citizens – how well fed, how well educated, how well sheltered, how healthy, etc. (Walsh 1996).[6]

It is from this confidence in economic understanding that IFAC presumes it will be able to set standards for education, practice and ethics for the accounting profession, i.e., IFAC expresses its confidence that "… economic theory knows how a market economy works and how it can be made to work better, to everyone's ultimate benefit" (Keen 2001, p. 3). What is problematic about this engineering

[6] "But of one fault the economists who developed the 'old' welfare economics cannot be justly accused: they did not suffer from the delusion (not the pretense if not deluded) that what came to be called "welfare economics" can be constructed without facing up to the necessity for making judgements (sic) (at one and the same time judgements (sic) of moral philosophy and of political economy) about the distribution of wealth and of income in society" (Walsh 1996, p. 177).

view is the belief that it is ***sound***. It isn't, or as Keen puts it more poetically, it is "Bunkum" (Ibid, p. 4). Were this belief in the wisdom of markets efficiently to guide society to the optimal good as well understood as IFAC seems to presume, the current financial crisis would have been averted, starvation would be non-existent, and everyone would have their interests fulfilled. As Keen notes, "... for over a century *economists* (emphasis in original) have shown that economic theory is replete with logical inconsistencies, specious assumptions, errant notions, and predictions contrary to empirical data (ibid)."[7] Thus, the edifice upon which rests IFAC's claim to serve the public interest is built largely out of economic folk psychology.[8]

So if economics is not a science that permits the engineering of society to a maximal state, what is it? According to Rosenberg (1992) economics is not a science, but is a branch of mathematics.

> Much of the mystery surrounding the actual development of economic theory – its shifts in formalism, its insulation from empirical assessment, its interest in proving purely formal, abstract possibilities, the controversies about its cognitive status – can be comprehended and properly appreciated if we give up on the notion that economics any longer has the aims or makes claims on an empirical science of human behavior (ibid, p. 247).[9]

In other words, economics is a mathematical politics, a system of value judgments about how society ought to be organized and governed. Thus, "markets" are not a devise for ensuring social optimality but a metaphor for a preferred way of social organization, one which even Adam Smith, the alleged father of the self-regulating market system, would not accept as the way to order society (Wolfe 1989). Economics has become a rigorous means for naturalizing a set of value judgments about the proper organization of society (Ravenscroft and Williams 2009). It is this set of value judgments that guides IFAC to deciding how accountants contribute to the public interest. The flaw in this view is that a particular value judgment about what is in the public interest is already contained within the view. If what is in the public interest is contrary to or at odds with such a view, then it will remain elusive to the profession, i.e., the profession will never be able to identify it, thus, the public interest served by the profession will merely be the particular "public interest" the profession is willing to serve.

---

[7] Robert Nelson has demonstrated the theological (faith like) nature of conventional economics, i.e., "The religious purpose of the market is to ensure maximal efficiency in the use of material resources of society, and thus the rapid movement of American society along a route of economic progress in the world (Nelson 2001, p. 8)."

[8] A further complication is the presumption that accounting possesses the expertise to actually provide accurate, transparent, and reliable information that leads to capital markets being more "efficient." In spite of claims that accounting produces "decision useful information", there is no persuasive evidence that the capability to do so actually exists (Williams and Ravenscroft 2012; Young 2006).

[9] The Cambridge University economist Ha-Joon Chang (2010) reaches the same conclusion following a different line of argument, e.g.: "Recognizing that the boundaries of the market are ambiguous and cannot be determined in an objective way lets us realize that economics is not a science like physics or chemistry, but a political exercise (ibid, p. 10)."

## 8.4 An Alternative Perspective

Sen (1988) identified two origins of economics. One is the engineering approach associated with current neoclassical economic theory and the view of economics that underlies IFAC's perspective on public interest. The other is of a much older origin and is related more to ethics than to engineering efficiency. Sen (ibid) traces this view back to Aristotle. Quoting *The Nicomachean Ethics:* "The life of money-making is one undertaken under compulsion, and wealth is evidently not the good we are seeking; for it is merely useful and for the sake of something else" (quoted by Sen, ibid, p. 3 from Ross 1980). This older view takes economics to be ultimately related to the study of ethics and politics where the concern is also about ends, i.e., in what ways are humans to lead good lives.

From this view the relationship between the accounting profession and the public interest is inverted. Under the engineering view of economics where the public interest role of accounting is defined merely as what the profession already does, the political economy view establishes the public interest as pre-eminent and the role of the profession is to adapt itself to serving that interest. This perspective requires a more genuine commitment to serving the public interest since it contemplates the potential for substantial alteration in the way accounting is practiced. It means accountants must serve the public interest by actually serving the public interest, not merely by providing the services accountants currently provide and rationalizing how they serve the public interest.

To operationalize this political economic view the profession will need to re-examine its feasible social function abstracted from its economic interests as an organized profession. Over the past half-century the profession has formally adopted the "decision usefulness" perspective as the rationale for what it provides to society. This is evident in the IFAC quotes about the role of the profession in serving markets, helping economic decision makers, and improving the efficiency of organizations and capital markets (none of which it is capable of empirically demonstrating that it does (Williams and Ravenscroft 2012). Performing a little thought experiment based in historical reflection is helpful in understanding what the implications of functionalist rather than a professional view of accounting means with respect to how the function of accounting, rather than the profession of accounting, serves the public interest.

There is substantial historical evidence that the function of accounting can be traced back to Mesopotamia as much as 8,000 years ago. Accountants are familiar and prideful of the role that the accounting function played in the development of number systems and in written languages. According to Schmandt-Besserat (1992) the activity of accounting, using tokens as counting devices emerged at the time that societies developed ranks (ibid, p. 170). In hunter-gatherer societies the means of subsistence were garnered daily and shared among the small group of individuals that comprised the social group. With the invention of sedentary agrarianism the social group became much larger and also became ranked. According to Schmandt-Besserat: "The most important aspect of these social changes for this study consists on the creation of an elite overseeing the redistributive economy. It is assumed that ranked societies had redistribution as a major element in their economy, with the headman acting as central collector and redistributor (sic)" (Schmandt-Besserat 1992, p. 170). Thus, at the origination of accounting as a function it was focused on the problems of civic administration, i.e., to collect resources and redistribute those resources to members of the social group. Within the social group organized around the temple each member of the society had a tribute to be paid, which in turn was redistributed. The function of accounting in its earliest manifestation was centered on relationships among the members of society and the accountability relationships among them that existed in that society.

The ancient system of accounting developed by the Incans consisting of knotted strings called khipus performed a similar function to the early Mesopotamian system of tokens. According to two Harvard researchers, Gary Urton and Carrie J. Brezine (2005), the khipu was a devise constructed for administering a labor tax on all citizens. Tribute in the Inka state was levied in the form of a labor tax. Each "taxpayer" (state laborer) was required to work a specified number of days each year on state projects. Using data recorded in khipu (knotted-string devices used for bureaucratic recording and communication), Inka accountants assessed tribute levels and assigned tasks to different numbers of local workers (ibid, p. 1065).

Thus, the Incan system of accounting was also constructed to reflect the relationships within Incan society that required each citizen to provide labor for communal projects. In both the token system of Mesopotamia and the knotted-string system of Incan civilization the function of accounting was civic administration, i.e. insuring that the obligations of citizenship of one citizen to another were fulfilled. Accounting provided information, but information of a particular kind – whether an accountability relationship had been properly fulfilled.

The double-entry system purportedly invented by Venetian merchants has as its foundation the reporting about an accountability relationship. The balance sheet equation, which accounting professors still teach in principles of accounting, emphasizes the notion of what is owned (controlled) by an entity is simultaneously owed to parties to the commercial arrangement. The architecture of accounting information systems up to this day follow the basic design lain out by Pacioli in the fifteenth century. As Ijiri has eloquently argued:

> Though the fundamental principles of accounting have not changed, we are new *interpreting* (emphasis in original) the same principles from a more user-oriented viewpoint. Thus, what has changed is our interpretation of accounting methods and not the fundamental substance of accounting (Ijiri 1975, p. 31).

The elaborate procedures of accounting make little sense if informing markets is the purpose of accounting. Statistical sampling could substitute for recording every transaction. Articulating financial statements aren't necessarily the required medium of delivering decision-useful information. Ijiri notes the oddity of the accounting system if its purpose is to facilitate only economic decision making in markets:

> Why do you keep records and provide information for the benefit of someone else? Either you want to do this voluntarily in order to impress, appeal to, and solicit certain actions by others, or you do so involuntarily under force.

> Why force? Because there is an underlying accountability relation between you and someone else. Based on that relation, you are expected to account for your activities and their consequences to a certain person. You are required to do so, whether you like it or not, and most cases in accounting seem to fall under this category (Ijiri 1983, p. 75).

This view of accounting as mediating relationships has profound implications for accounting in serving the public interest. It focuses the purpose of accounting away from a technical discipline concerned only with providing useful information to stereotypical investors and creditors competing for advantage in self-regulating markets to a purpose of mediating relationships of responsibility among various parties. Ijiri emphasizes this aspect of an accountability view: "In an accountability-based framework, the objective of accounting is to provide a *fair* (emphasis added) system of information flow between the accountor and the accountee" (ibid, p. 75). Rather than deferring to the "market" to create whatever society happens to result from the actions of unmitigated market forces, the accountability view requires accounting practice explicitly to concern itself with the public interest per se. Indeed, in developing its definition of the public interest IFAC consulted resources that contain the philosophical underpinnings of Western civilization (IFAC 2012b). In Appendix 1 of IFAC Policy Position X referred to the work of St. Augustine and Thomas Aquinas, which concerned themselves with the obligations of individuals to society. According to IFAC, "These values and rights play into the collective functions of society. An effective example would be society's role in *ensuring justice*" (emphasis added) (ibid, p. 1 of Appendix 1). Combining this allusion to the second judgment criterion in the exposure draft of its public interest framework – adherence to democratic principles (IFAC 2011, p. 7) – IFAC seems to acknowledge that a fair society is a paramount public interest concern.[10]

Sen addresses the essential role of information in making any society fairer. A corollary is that ascertaining what is in the public interest in a democratic society requires information about states of affairs, particularly those about relationships among various members of society. Sen is emphatic about the importance of information, "What is, in contrast, indispensably important is an adequate understanding of the informational basis of evaluation – the kind of information we need to examine in order to assess what is going on and what is being seriously neglected" (Sen 1999, p. 286). Research in various fields (e.g., anthropology, neurobiology, sociology, cognitive psychology and behavioral economics) is changing our understanding about "human nature." A significant result of this research for accounting and the public interest is that the human nature that thousands of years of evolution have given human beings is not compatible with the "... value system of modern market capitalism..." (Corning 2011, p. 39). The view of society that emerges from

---

[10] The notion of fairness is deeply embedded in human nature (Shermer 2004). Corning (2011, pp. 25–26) identifies three components to substantive fairness: (1) equality, i.e., equal shares; (2) equity, i.e., giving one her due; and, (3) reciprocity, i.e., giving in return for getting. Ariely (2008) has shown that people will incur substantial costs to themselves to punish the cheater and to restore a just order.

this research is that "… human society can accurately be called a 'collective survival enterprise'" (ibid, p. 38). The implication of this view is that:

> The deep purpose of human society is not, after all, about achieving growth, or wealth, or material affluence, or power, or social equality, or even about the pursuit of happiness…. It is about how to further the purpose of the collective survival enterprise (ibid, p. 153).

Obviously accounting can provide but a limited amount of the information needed to assess the state of the collective survival enterprise; auditors could perhaps attest to a greater amount of information germane to the task. The key point is that for the profession of accounting to substantively contribute to serving the public interest, the view of public interest currently adopted by IFAC is inadequate. It expresses a pronounced preference for a particular social order in which the life prospects of individuals in society are to be left to economic forces and that, so long as accounting provides information useful to the "efficient functioning" of those market forces, it is fulfilling a public interest mission. This is not the case. A more fruitful perspective argued for in this chapter is to adopt a more ancient view of accounting's function in society, i.e., the mediation of relationships among members of society by providing the necessary information to assess whether the requisite mutual obligations among people have been fulfilled. In a recent report by the Commission on the Measurement of Economic and Social Progress (Stiglitz et al. 2010) the authors noted the importance of accounting frameworks at both the corporate and national levels and the need to improve them so as to "…enhance the quality of information that forms the bases for decision making in our economic and *political* (emphasis added) systems" (ibid, p. xxix) The advantage of this view is that the public interest dictates the service that accountants provide rather than the service being provided determining what public interest the profession will serve. Bayou et al. (2011, p. 122) suggest one possibility for accounting that is consistent with the alternative view: "The important social function of accounting, particularly in democracies, is informing on the affairs of powerful institutions, i.e., situating them in the present so that decisions may be made about them." The public interest is a political and moral problem, not merely an economic one and the information the public needs from accounting to pursue its interests should be useful for political and moral decisions as well.

For example, there are extensive subsidies provided to private firms from governments (taxpayers) at all levels – local, state, and federal. These subsidies take many forms but none of them are currently reported by GAAP for what they are. Instead they show up as higher income for the recipient, misrepresenting equity provided by taxpayers as income generated by the firm. Alperovitz and Daley provide an example:

> A good example is Taxol: the General Accounting Office (sic) estimates that the National Institutes of Health spent a total of $484 million on the development of this drug between 1977 and 2002. Bristol-Myers Squibb – the firm that obtained the patent and marketing rights – achieved world wide sales of $9 billion between 1993 and 2002, but the government received only $35 million in royalties from the earnings (Alperovitz and Daly 2008, p. 84).

Investors are not the only constituency in a democracy that needs information vital to making decisions about corporate behavior.

## 8.5 Concluding Remarks

IFAC's effort to focus explicitly on the public interest role of the accounting profession is a laudatory one. It succeeds in legitimizing discussion of the accounting function performing something other than a service that has only private benefit. The shortcoming of the framework IFAC proposes is that it is far too reliant on a simplistic view of a market economy. Market economies depend on governments; without the regulatory function performed by the law maker, market systems would not function; they are not self-regulating as the recent experience with financial markets so emphatically illustrates (Posner 2010). The accounting profession through its auditing monopoly and standard-setting role are part of the regulatory framework. Accounting is, in an important sense, part of the justice system of any society. As such its professional province cannot be circumscribed to passively providing information to allegedly self-regulating markets. Accountants are the publics' eyes and ears within the many private and public organizations that affect the welfare of everyone in significant ways. To be a profession that serves the public interest, it would best report on all that it sees and hears.

## References

Abbott, A. 1988. *The system of professions*. Chicago: The University of Chicago Press.
Alperovitz, G., and L. Daly. 2008. *Unjust deserts*. New York: The New Press.
Ariely, D. 2008. *Predictably irrational*. New York: Harper Collins.
Basu, K. 2011. *Beyond the invisible hand*. Princeton: Princeton University Press.
Bayou, M.E., A. Reinstein, and P.F. Williams. 2011. To tell the truth: A discussion of issues concerning truth and ethics in accounting. *Accounting, Organizations and Society* 36: 109–124.
Brown, D.E. 1991. *Human universals*. New York: McGraw-Hill.
Chang, H. 2010. *23 Things they don't tell you about capitalism*. New York: Bloomsbury Press.
Corning, P. 2011. *The fair society*. Chicago: The University of Chicago Press.
IFAC. 2008. IFAC policy position 3: International standard setting in the public interest. December, 2008. New York: International Federation of Accountants.
IFAC. 2010. IFAC policy position paper #4: A public interest framework for accountancy profession. Exposure Draft, November, 2010. New York: International Federation of Accountants.
IFAC. 2011. IFAC policy position 1: Regulation of the accounting profession. September, 2011. New York: International Federation of Accountants.
IFAC. 2012a. Our mission. http://www.ifac.org/about-ifac
IFAC. 2012b. IFAC policy position X: A definition of the public Interest. New York: International Federation of Accountants.
Ijiri, Y. 1975. *Theory of accounting measurement*, Studies in accounting research #10. Sarasota: American Accounting Association.
Ijiri, Y. 1983. On the accountability based conceptual framework of accounting. *Journal of Accounting and Public Policy* 2(2): 75–81.
Keen, S. 2001. *Debunking economics*. Anandale: Pluto Press Australia Ltd.
Kultgen, J. 1988. *Ethics and professionalism*. Philadelphia: University of Pennsylvania Press.
Larsen, M.S. 1977. *The rise of professionalism: A sociological analysis*. Berkeley: The University of California Press.

Marglin, S.A. 2008. *The dismal science*. Cambridge: Harvard University Press.
Nelson, R.H. 2001. *Economics as religion*. University Park: The Pennsylvania State University Press.
Posner, R.A. 2010. *The crisis of capitalist democracy*. Cambridge, MA: The Harvard University Press.
Ravenscroft, S., and P.F. Williams. 2009. Making imaginary worlds real: The case of expensing employee stock options. *Accounting, Organizations and Society* 34(6–7): 770–786.
Rosenberg, A. 1992. *Economics – Mathematical politics or science of diminishing returns*. Chicago: The University of Chicago Press.
Ross, D. (ed.). 1980. *Aristotle: The Nicomachean ethics*. Oxford: Oxford University Press.
Schmandt-Besserat, D. 1992. *Before writing*, vol. I. Austin: The University of Texas Press.
Sen, A. 1988. *On ethics and economics*. Malden: Blackwell Publishing.
Sen, A. 1999. *Development as freedom*. New York: Anchor Books.
Shermer, M. 2004. *The science of good & evil*. New York: Times Books/Henry Holt and Company.
Smith, A. 1937. *The wealth of nations*. New York: Random House, Inc.
Stiglitz, J.E., A. Sen, and J.-P. Fitoussi. 2010. *Mis-measuring our lives*. New York: The New Press.
Urton, G., and C.J. Brezine. 2005. Khipu accounting in ancient Peru. *Science* 309(5737): 1065–1067.
Walsh, V. 1996. *Rationality, allocation, and reproduction*. Oxford: Oxford University Press.
Williams, P.F. 2004. Recovering accounting as a worthy endeavor. *Critical Perspectives on Accounting* 15(4–5): 513–517.
Williams, P.F. 2010. The focus of professional ethics: Ethical professionals or ethical profession? *Research on Professional Responsibility and Ethics in Accounting* 14: 15–35.
Williams, P.F., and S. Ravenscroft. 2012. Rethinking decision usefulness. Working paper, North Carolina State University.
Wolfe, A. 1989. *Whose keeper?* Berkeley: University of California Press.
Young, J.J. 2006. Making up users. *Accounting, Organizations and Society* 31(6): 579–600.

# Part IV
# Corporate Social Responsibility and Environmental Reporting

# Chapter 9
# Developing Corporate Reporting in the Public Interest: The Question of Mandatory CSR Reporting and the Potential for Its Integration with Financial Reporting

**Cynthia Jeffrey and Jon D. Perkins**

## 9.1 Introduction

Corporate social responsibility (CSR) reporting is a business trend emerging in response to demands from both stockholders and a broader set of stakeholders that includes communities, customers, and employees (see, for example, Brown and Fraser 2006; Buhmnan 2006; SIF 2009). CSR is the idea that companies have obligations to act in ways that are compatible with society's values and so serve the public interest, and refers to how a business develops, implements, and monitors strategies with respect to the spirit of the law, ethical standards, and international norms.

The accountancy profession gains its legitimacy from its claim to act in the public interest, and so professional responsibility must extend beyond the needs and preferences of a single stakeholder group. Dillard (2008, 3–4) states that "society entrusts organizational management the right to use its economic assets (natural, human and technical) in order to provide goods and services for the citizens of the society … In return, management accepts a fiduciary responsibility with respect to those assets … [and] accepts an obligation to provide an account of, and to be held accountable for, its actions." Indeed, the International Federation of Accountants (IFAC) released a draft of a position paper on the role of accounting with respect to the public interest that defines three criteria (IFAC 2010): (1) consideration of costs and benefits for society as a whole, (2) adherence to democratic principles and processes, and (3) respect for cultural and ethical diversity. These criteria make salient the profession's duty to promote reporting and disclosure practices that go beyond shareholder interests, rather than promoting disclosure standards designed to benefit a subset of the community at the expense of other community members.

C. Jeffrey (✉) • J.D. Perkins
Department of Accounting, Iowa State University, Ames, IA, USA
e-mail: cjeffrey@iastate.edu; jperkins@iastate.edu

S. Mintz (ed.), *Accounting for the Public Interest: Perspectives on Accountability, Professionalism and Role in Society*, Advances in Business Ethics Research 4,
DOI 10.1007/978-94-007-7082-9_9, © Springer Science+Business Media Dordrecht 2014

Bebbington et al. (2007) state that as corporations have increased in power and influence, concerns about accountability of the corporation to society at-large have led to demands for increased disclosure about a broad range of behaviors. The range of topics covered by CSR includes organizational governance, the environment, human rights (including civil and political rights, cultural and social rights, and fundamental rights), labor practices, fair operating practices, and community involvement (Slob and Oonk 2007). For a business to take responsibility for its actions, that business must be fully accountable to the public, and CSR reporting is the effort to disclose the social and environmental effects of a company's economic actions to particular interest groups within society and to society at large (Gray et al. 1987).

Further, there is some evidence that CSR information is used by stakeholders. Stengel (2009) reports anecdotal evidence that Americans are increasingly willing to change their consumer behavior for environmental reasons even in recessionary periods. High levels of CSR are associated with firms that have higher levels of growth and a higher return on equity than conventional firms (Artiach et al. 2010), and firms with strong environmental management generate positive market returns while firms with weak environmental management generate negative market returns (Klassen and McLaughlin 1996). Investors in the $10 trillion Investor Network on Climate Risk have pressured businesses to improve their analysis and disclosure of climate-related risks (Leonard 2008), and Goldman Sachs's GS Sustain report asserts that the equity market is only beginning to recognize the potential impact of sustainability initiatives on companies' competitive positions (GS Sustain 2009, 2).

We begin by discussing the importance of mandatory reporting of CSR disclosures. Next, we develop a framework to evaluate the potential for integrated corporate reporting that incorporates both financial reporting and CSR disclosure. We examine the underlying conceptual frameworks for financial reporting and CSR reporting to determine whether it is feasible or desirable for CSR reporting to be integrated with financial reporting, followed by an examination of assurance and implications for assurance if CSR were to be integrated with financial reporting. We then discuss our recommendations for the continued development of CSR reporting, and summarize our analysis and recommendations in the conclusion.

## 9.2 Mandatory vs. Voluntary Disclosures

Global corporations are voluntarily disclosing more information about a range of social, environmental, and governance activities. In 1999, approximately 39 % of the Global Fortune 250 companies issued some form of CSR report; by 2011, the percentage had increased to 95 % (KPMG 2011). To date, CSR reports have generally been voluntary, and are often presented as stand-alone reports or as an addendum to traditional annual reports (Jensen and Berg 2012), but there are growing demands for greater regulation of CSR reporting to facilitate both the existence and the comparability of CSR disclosure. Jurisdictions around the world are responding;

at least 34 countries currently require, recommend, or are considering requiring aspects of CSR reports, although not necessarily in conjunction with the corporate annual report (IRI 2012).[1] Not only are countries adopting mandatory CSR reporting requirements, standard setters and regulators have shown increased interest in the information disclosures typically included in CSR reports (see, for example, IASB 2010; SEC 2010).

Mandated disclosure would ensure a minimum level of comparable information across companies. When disclosure is voluntary, corporations may or may not choose to make full and complete disclosures, and stakeholders have no way to evaluate voluntary disclosure for completeness.[2] To the extent voluntary disclosure is incomplete or nonexistent, stakeholders cannot make reliable comparisons of CSR performance across industries, across companies within industries, or for a given company over a period of time. The lack of comparability makes it difficult to assess performance and to hold corporations accountable for their performance.

Mandated disclosure is necessary for stakeholder groups to be assured of timely access to appropriate information. In addition to being responsive to potentially divergent norms of broad-based stakeholder groups, for norms to be effective in shaping behavior so that it is acceptable to society there must be a mechanism that allows different stakeholder group to obtain the information necessary to evaluate the behaviors, hold an entity accountable, and impose sanctions for non-compliance. Indeed, a significant weakness of CSR reporting today is its limited availability across companies and even within companies across time. While providers of capital can withhold resources for noncompliance with financial reporting, the potential sanctions of societal groups seem both less immediate and less well-defined. Mandated disclosure is needed to ensure availability by imposing sanctions for non-compliance; without such a mechanism, reporting cannot adequately serve the needs of stakeholders.

## 9.3 A Framework for Integrated Corporate Reporting

As the movement toward mandatory disclosure accelerates, significant attention has focused on whether CSR reporting should continue to be presented in a stand-alone report, or whether CSR and financial reporting should be integrated.[3] There is

[1] As of 2010, the following countries had some form of mandatory CSR reporting requirements: Australia, Austria, Belgium, Brazil, Canada, China, Denmark, Ecuador, Finland, France, Germany, Greece, Hungary, India, Indonesia, Italy, Japan, Luxembourg, the Netherlands, Norway, Portugal, South Africa, Spain, Sweden, the United Kingdom, and the United States.

[2] In another chapter, Patten (2014) explores the notion that one reason corporations may not choose to make full and complete disclosures is that they are using disclosure as a tool to increase their legitimacy in society. He examines how environmental disclosures can function as legitimation tools.

[3] A stand-alone CSR report would likely be included as a section of the Annual Report as this is a major component of a corporation's activities. Separating the CSR report from financial reporting does not preclude parallel presentation.

substantial pressure to integrate CSR reporting into financial reporting using a "top down" approach whereby written standards are promulgated and enforced by a regulator and with a focus on economic decision-making and firm valuation. The International Federation of Accountants (IFAC) states that a key challenge facing accountants is to "incorporate environmental issues into financial statements in a way that supports an organization's stewardship role and enables users to make economic decisions regarding environmental and social impacts on assets, liabilities, income, and expenditure".[4] IFAC quotes Ramona Dzinkowski, Director of the Canadian Financial Executives Research Foundation, who states, "…with the widespread adoption of IFRS [International Financial Reporting Standards], there is a hope that a uniform framework for environmental and sustainability accounting will emerge, which will tie information on environmental costs and benefits, and sustainability to the financial statements – beyond the box of current thinking."

Standardization of CSR reporting and its integration into financial reporting was also a major theme of the 2010 conference, "When CSR and Financial Reporting Must Meet: Integrated Reporting," organized by BSR, an organization that promotes social responsibility in business.[5] In remarks at the conference, Adam Kanzer, managing director and general counsel of Domini Social Investments and a member of an SEC advisory committee on sustainability reporting standards, emphasized the issue and his belief that the SEC will move towards setting rules regarding determination of the "materiality" of sustainability issues to earnings and financial reporting (Kanzer 2010). Kanzer believes that if material to business, CSR information should be included in a company's annual report. He also claims that financial analysts are more likely to integrate CSR information into their recommendations when CSR factors and conventional financial metrics are presented concurrently and suggests that CSR issues are more likely to be ignored if they are presented in stand-alone reports. This theme was echoed at the 2010 conference sponsored by the Global Reporting Initiative (GRI), a non-profit organization that works towards a sustainable global economy by providing sustainability reporting guidance. At the conference, "speaker after speaker lauded the idea of companies consistently integrating sustainability thinking with a reporting framework that naturally encompasses both financial and sustainability information. What's required for such a paradigm shift, they noted, is a clear and comprehensive set of reporting standards that are widely accepted and implemented. Consensus at the conference seemed to be that standards development for sustainability had moved far beyond the realm of the theoretical" (Deloitte 2010, 3).

[4] http://web.ifac.org/sustainability-framework/ip-impact-on-financial-statements.

[5] BSR was founded in 1992; it defines its mission as working with businesses to create a just and sustainable world. Membership in BSR is open to all companies interested in CSR, and currently has over 300 global members ranging from Fortune 100 companies to non-public corporations. Associate membership is open to non-business organizations, such as nongovernmental organizations/nonprofits, government agencies, academic institutions, foundations, and trade associations. Information on BSR, including their membership list, can be found at their website, https://www.bsr.org/.

The potential for the integration of CSR and financial reporting moved forward when, on August 2, 2010, The Prince's Accounting for Sustainability Project (A4S)[6] and the GRI announced the formation of the International Integrated Reporting Committee (IIRC), which is charged with facilitating the convergence of environmental, social, and corporate governance reporting with financial reporting (Eccles and Serafeim 2011). The mission of the IIRC is "[t]o create a globally accepted integrated reporting framework which brings together financial, environmental, social and governance information in a clear, concise, consistent and comparable format... [to] help businesses make more sustainable decisions and enable investors and other stakeholders to understand how an organization is really performing".[7] The IIRC defines integrated reporting as a report that "brings together material information about an organization's strategy, governance, performance and prospects in a way that reflects the commercial, social and environmental context within which it operates" (IIRC 2011, 6). The goal is to develop a framework for a primary corporate report that *replaces* existing corporate reports. To accomplish this goal, the IIRC aims to develop an international integrated reporting framework that captures interdependencies between strategy, financial, and nonfinancial performance, governance and performance, and both an organization's own performance and its performance within a value chain (IIRC 2011, 5). An organization's business model and its ability to create and sustain value in the short, medium and long term are the central themes of the Framework.

The IIRC has developed five underlying principles for the Framework (IIRC 2011, 3):

1. Strategic focus
2. Connectivity of information
3. Future orientation
4. Responsiveness and stakeholder inclusiveness
5. Conciseness, reliability, and materiality

The IIRC believes that application of these principles should both define the elements to be presented in a report and make the interconnections clear to both companies and users.

As the move to an integrated corporate report moves forward, it is important to evaluate the potential to integrate financial information and nonfinancial metrics consistent with the proposed IIRC framework. The conceptual challenge is to determine if it is feasible and efficient to develop a framework for combining the different information items. Further, integration implies not only an ability to report these different metrics, but also to define and measure linkages between the elements. Because such linkages are difficult to define and measure, integration may be

[6]The Prince's Accounting for Sustainability Project (A4S) was founded by His Royal Highness, the Prince of Wales, in 2004 with the objective of bringing together governments, organizations and businesses working on improved performance measurement systems for CSR disclosure.

[7]http://www.theiirc.org.

problematic because, as Biondi et al. (2012) note, if all constructs of interest were both observable and measureable, few reporting controversies would arise.

### *9.3.1 Conceptual Frameworks of Financial Reporting and CSR Reporting*

To be effective, reporting, and standards for reporting, must be built on an established body of concepts and objectives (Kieso et al. 2010, 32). The IIRC hopes to build on existing reporting requirements and specifically notes the importance of the efforts of the IASB and the FASB to converge financial reporting standards in an effort to create a single set of high-quality financial reporting standards to be used internationally.[8] Indeed, while the IIRC believes that an integrated report should replace, rather than add to, existing reporting requirements (including financial reporting requirements), the IIRC also notes that, "The initial focus is on reporting by larger companies and on the needs of investors" (IIRC 2011, 3). As part of the efforts to converge financial reporting, the IASB and the FASB have jointly developed a project to converge and improve the conceptual frameworks of underlying U.S. Generally Accepted Accounting Principles (GAAP) and International Financial Reporting Standards (IFRS).

If CSR reporting and financial reporting are to be meaningfully integrated and linkages developed and reported, the underlying conceptual frameworks for these two reporting paradigms must either be consistent or it must be possible to converge them. The GRI is a partner in the IIRC initiative, and has developed the Sustainability Reporting Framework (GRI 2011). The GRI, pioneered by the Coalition for Environmentally Responsible Economies and the Tellus Institute, was launched in 1998 and has emerged as a dominant force in shaping voluntary CSR reporting. According to the GRI's website, its vision is that reporting on economic, environmental, and social performance by all organizations is as routine and comparable as financial reporting.[9] The GRI's legitimacy was enhanced and its reach expanded in 1998 when it partnered with the United Nations Environment Programme (UNEP). As of 2011, thousands of companies from more than 60 countries, including 95 % of the Global 250, used the GRI's reporting framework (GRI 2011) to produce CSR reports (KPMG 2011), and more than 84 % of the reports came from large companies. Noble and Kotevski (2008) identify the GRI's framework as particularly useful for CSR reporting because it has achieved international support and acceptance, it enables investors as well other

[8] International Financial Reporting Standards are now mandated or allowed by approximately 120 countries around the world (http://www.ifrs.com/ifrs_faqs.html). To the extent that the IIRC wishes to build a global reporting initiative that draws from work already in progress and to focus on the needs of investors and creditors, the work of the IASB and the convergence effort with the FASB is a critical starting point.

[9] http://www.globalreporting.org/ReportingFramework/G3Guidelines/G3GlossaryOfTerms.htm.

information users to compare information across companies, and a broad-base of stakeholders are actively involved in its development.

The GRI's reporting framework recommends specific information to be produced and disclosed related to environmental, social, and economic performance. The GRI's evolution from a confluence of consumer, investor, and shareholder interests into a multi-stakeholder network has allowed it to develop its current reporting framework and allows its stakeholder base to revise the framework via consensus among participants from business, society, labor, and the professions. Over the years, thousands of individuals and organizations have participated in the development of the GRI's reporting framework (Brown et al. 2009).

The IIRC has stated a desire to build on developmental efforts already in progress. Because the GRI is a partner in the IIRC, the GRI conceptual framework is relevant to the potential for integration. To determine the potential for a corporate report that integrates financial reporting, CSR reporting, and potentially other aspects of corporate performance, a comparison of the underlying conceptual frameworks for the IASB/FASB and the GRI is an appropriate starting point. An evaluation of the objectives of reporting, the identified users, the qualitative characteristics of the information, the elements being reported, and measurement are particularly relevant considerations in determining the potential for integrating CSR reporting into financial reporting. See Table 9.1 for a listing of the features of these two frameworks.

#### 9.3.1.1 Objectives and Users of Financial Reporting and CSR Reporting

The IASB and the FASB completed the first phase of the project to produce a converged conceptual framework on September 28, 2010 and jointly issued *Chapter 1, The Objective of General Purpose Financial Reporting* and *Chapter 3, Qualitative Characteristics of Useful Financial Information*. To reflect the Phase 1 convergence, the IASB officially revised portions of its existing framework, and the FASB issued Statement of Financial Accounting Concepts No. 8 (FASB 2010a). In this joint release, the boards identify the objective of financial reporting and the targeted user groups, stating that "[t]he objective of general purpose financial reporting forms the foundation of the Conceptual Framework" (FASB 2010a, OB1, p. 1) and the defined objective of financial reporting is to "provide financial information about the reporting entity that is useful to existing and potential investors, lenders, and other creditors in making decisions about providing resources to the entity" (FASB 2010a, OB2, p. 1). The Statement notes that this information encompasses the entity's prospects for future net cash inflows, including "how efficiently and effectively the entity's management and governing board have discharged their responsibilities to use the entity's resources" (FASB 2010a, OB4, p. 2). A broad interpretation of this purpose might include an evaluation of how well management has managed assets with respect to any perceived fiduciary responsibility to society and with respect to societal assets. The boards note that SFAC No. 8 establishes an objective of financial reporting, not just of financial statements, broadening the

**Table 9.1** Comparison of conceptual reporting frameworks

| Item | IASB conceptual framework for financial reporting (2010) | GRI sustainability reporting guidelines V3.1 (2011) |
|---|---|---|
| Objective | To provide financial information about the reporting entity that is useful to users in making decisions about providing resources to the entity | To provide information desired by stakeholders and explain how the information is responsive to the reasonable needs and expectations of stakeholders |
| Users | Existing and potential investors, lenders, and other creditors | See *Stakeholder Inclusiveness* below |
| Qualitative characteristics | | |
| *Accuracy* | Financial information must faithfully represent what it purports to represent (i.e., it must be complete, neutral, and free from error) | The reported information should be sufficiently accurate and detailed for stakeholders to assess the reporting organization's performance |
| *Balance* | See *Accuracy* above | The report should reflect positive and negative aspects of the organization's performance to enable a reasoned assessment of overall performance |
| *Clarity* | The usefulness of financial information is enhanced if it is comparable, verifiable, timely, and understandable | Information should be made available in a manner that is understandable and accessible to stakeholders using the report |
| *Comparability* | See *Clarity* above | Issues and information should be selected, compiled, and reported consistently. Reported information should be presented in a manner that enables stakeholders to analyze changes in the organization's performance over time, and could support analysis relative to other organizations |
| *Completeness* | See *Accuracy* above | Coverage of the material topics and indicators and definition of the report boundary should be sufficient to reflect significant economic, environmental, and societal impacts and enable stakeholders to assess the reporting organization's performance in the reporting period |
| *Context* | The report should present the organization's performance in the context of financial decision making | The report should present the organization's performance in the wider context of sustainability |
| *Materiality* | See *Relevance* below | The information in a report should cover topics and indicators that reflect the organization's significant economic, environmental, and societal impacts or that would substantively influence the assessments and decisions of stakeholders |

(continued)

**Table 9.1** (continued)

| Item | IASB conceptual framework for financial reporting (2010) | GRI sustainability reporting guidelines V3.1 (2011) |
|---|---|---|
| *Relevance* | Financial information must have predictive value and confirmatory value, based on the nature or magnitude, or both, of the item to which the information relates in the context of an individual entity's financial report | Sustainability information must have predictive value and confirmatory value, based on the nature or magnitude, or both, of the item to which the information relates in the wider context of sustainability |
| *Reliability* | This is now believed to be captured by other constructs (see *Clarity* above and *Verifiability* below) | Information and processes used in the preparation of a report should be gathered, recorded, compiled, analyzed, and disclosed in a way that could be subject to examination and that establishes the quality and materiality of the information |
| *Stakeholder inclusiveness* | See *Users* above | The reporting organization should identify its stakeholders (e.g., communities, customers, consumers, governments, society-at-large, etc.) and explain in the report how it has responded to their reasonable expectations and interests |
| *Timeliness* | See *Clarity* above | Reporting occurs on a regular schedule and information is available in time for stakeholders to make informed decisions |
| *Verifiability* | See *Clarity* above | See *Reliability* above |
| Elements | | |
| *Asset* | A resource controlled by the entity as a result of past events and from which future economic benefits are expected to flow to the entity | Elements defined by stakeholders' emerging information needs (see *Core Indicators* and *Additional Indicators* below) |
| *Liability* | A present obligation of the entity arising from past events, the settlement of which is expected to result in an outflow from the entity of resources embodying economic events | |
| *Equity* | The residual interest in the assets of an entity after deducting all its liabilities | |

(continued)

**Table 9.1** (continued)

| Item | IASB conceptual framework for financial reporting (2010) | GRI sustainability reporting guidelines V3.1 (2011) |
|---|---|---|
| *Income* | An increase in an economic benefit during an accounting period in the form of an inflow or enhancement of an asset or decrease of a liability that results in an increase of equity, other than that relating to a contribution from an equity participant | |
| *Expense* | A decrease in an economic benefit during the accounting period in the form of an outflow or depletion of an asset or incurrence of a liability that results in a decrease in equity, other than that relating to a distribution to an equity participant | |
| *Core indicators* | | Those indicators identified in the GRI Guidelines to be of interest to most stakeholders and assumed to be material unless deemed otherwise on the basis of the GRI Reporting Principles; the six general categories of indicators are Environmental, Human Rights, Labor Practices and Decent Work, Society, Product Responsibility, and Economic |
| *Additional indicators* | | Those indicators identified in the GRI Guidelines that represent emerging practice or address topics that may be material to some organizations but not generally for a majority |
| Measurement | The process of determining the monetary amounts at which the elements of the financial statements are to be recognized and carried in the balance sheet and income statement; this involves the selection of the particular basis of measurement | Measurement is not constrained by monetary unit; some items may not even be quantitative. Reported data should be presented using generally accepted international metrics (e.g., kilograms, tonnes, litres) and calculated using standard conversion factors. Where specific international conventions exist (e.g., GHG equivalents), these are typically specified in the indicator protocols |

scope of the framework (FASB 2010a, BC1.4). Further, the growth in investment in socially responsible funds indicates that investors find CSR information useful in making financial decisions.

However, both the purpose and the targeted user group defined for financial reporting are narrower than how those constructs are defined for CSR reporting, where stakeholders are defined as including employees, legislators, regulators, local communities, investors, suppliers, customers and consumers, industry associations, environmental groups, and the media (UNEP 1996). Gray et al. (1996) suggest that management, trade unions, government, competitors, peers, industry groups, and society in general are also stakeholders. GRI's reporting guidelines state that an organization reporting CSR activities should identify its stakeholders and explain how it has responded to their reasonable expectations and concerns (GRI 2011).

While the user base is generally broader for CSR reporting than the investors and creditors that are the focus of financial reporting, it can be claimed that the various aspects of CSR including environmental, social, and corporate governance performance are relevant to investors and creditors as these items relate to the value creation strategies of business (GRI 2009), potentially making the information needs of investors and creditors congruent with the information needs of the wider stakeholder group for CSR reporting. Indeed, the importance of CSR reporting is related, in part, to the ability of the company to identify and manage the full range of risks and opportunities in the market, and CSR information may be particularly relevant with respect to the strategies that the business uses to be successful (GRI 2009). Mintz (2011) notes that risk management is essential if an organization is to be sustainable, and that the improved use of non-financial metrics is a critical component of improved risk management.

The purpose of CSR reporting is to provide accountability, as well as to communicate the performance of a company relative to its targets (KPMG 2010). Further, the "wider accountability implies that companies have to fulfill the [information] needs of those who provide them with other economic resources such as labour, space, air, or natural resources and those who enter into transactions with the organization, such as customers. Therefore, a company's current performance and future ability to continue operations and achieve business growth needs to be evaluated on the basis of a comprehensive set of factors" (KPMG 2010, 4). Among the internal and external benefits that may be associated with sustainability reporting are: increased transparency, the creation of financial value, enhancing reputation, a framework for management to measure continuous improvement, improved regulatory compliance, and establishing competitive positioning and market differentiation (KPMG 2008). While some claim that integrating financial reporting and CSR reporting would require a de-emphasis of investors and creditors in favor of a broader stakeholder base (e.g., O'Dwyer 2000), the information needs of the broader base of CSR stakeholders may be compatible with the information needs of investors and creditors.

However, the Conceptual Framework notes that even among investors, creditors, and their advisors, users have "different, and possibly conflicting, information needs and desires" (FASB 2010a, OB8), and that general purpose financial reports "do not and cannot provide all of the information that existing and potential investors, lenders, and other creditors need" (FASB 2010a, OB6). The Conceptual Framework also states that the Board will seek to provide the information set "that will meet the needs of the maximum number of primary users" (FASB 2010a, OB8). Because the primary users are defined as investors and creditors, the potentially different and/or evolving needs of a wider stakeholder base are not considered under the existing conceptual framework for financial reporting.

#### 9.3.1.2 Qualitative Characteristics and Characteristics for Ensuring Reporting Quality

The Fédération des Experts Comptables Européens (FEE) has recommended that the same qualitative characteristics that have been established for financial reporting should be modified and applied to CSR reporting (FEE 1999), and the European Federation of Financial Analysts Societies (EFFAS 1994) has suggested that these qualitative characteristics are transferable to CSR reporting. Indeed, there are significant similarities between the qualitative characteristics defined in SFAC No. 8 (FASB 2010a) and the GRI's *Principles for Defining Report Content and Principles for Ensuring Report Quality* (GRI 2011).

SFAC No. 8 (FASB 2010a) details the qualitative characteristics that make information useful. To the extent that the underlying characteristics are similar both for information currently included in the financial reports and information included in CSR reports, it is worthwhile to examine potential overlap between the two reporting frameworks. SFAC No. 8 defines the primary qualitative characteristics of useful financial information as relevance and faithful representation. Information is relevant if it is "capable of making a difference in the decisions made by users" by either having predictive or feedback (confirmatory) value (FASB 2010a, QC6 and QC7). With respect to faithful representation, information should be "complete, natural, and free from error" (FASB 2010a, QC12). The quality of information is enhanced to the extent it allows comparisons between companies, is verifiable, timely, and understandable (FASB 2010a, QC19). Further, information must be "material"; that is, omitting or misreporting the information could impact a user's decisions (FASB 2010a, QC11).

The qualitative characteristics specified in the GRI's reporting framework are consistent with those defined in SFAC No. 8 (FASB 2010a). Relevance is incorporated into the GRI's principle of materiality, which calls for information that "would substantially influence the assessments and decisions of stakeholders" (GRI 2011, 8). Similar to SFAC No. 8 (FASB 2010a) constructs, the GRI's reporting framework calls for completeness, comparability, accuracy, timeliness, clarity, and reliability (GRI 2011). However, the GRI's reporting framework also includes the concepts of stakeholder inclusiveness, which is specifically omitted from SFAC No. 8 (FASB 2010a), and a sustainability context, which calls for a performance report that details the organization's activities in sustainability, which is generally a wider context than that of financial reporting. It would appear that there is a reasonable amount of similarity between the qualitative characteristics that define the usefulness of financial reporting and CSR reporting, but that the broader range of stakeholders and the sustainability context for CSR reports are significant differences.

### 9.3.1.3 Elements, Recognition, and Measurement

Differences in the stakeholder base, the divergent interests of a stakeholder base that goes beyond the investor/creditor defined in SFAC No. 8 (FASB 2010a), and the sustainability context are likely to mean that the range of relevant activities reported also diverges. Kieso et al. (2010, 46) note that recognition on the financial statements should be limited to items that meet the definition of one of the basic elements, which are defined as assets, liabilities, equity, revenue, expenses, gains, and losses. Further, the item must be measurable, relevant, and reliable. Additionally, the elements reported in the financial statements are limited to those that can be measured in terms of a monetary unit (FASB 1984) which may not be appropriate (or possible) for the elements that are expected in CSR reporting.[10]

Indeed, CSR reporting is likely to differ from financial reporting because the elements to be reported are likely to differ. Even to the extent that the underlying construct is the same, the nature of reporting is likely to differ. Solomon (2000) examines the broad base of potential CSR reporting elements and cites as an example the concept of assets. To be recognized as an asset in the financial reports, a company has to legally own or control the asset (FASB 1985), but CSR reporting for assets might be based on constructs such as air, land, water, and sound, which are neither owned nor controlled by the entity, but rather are societal assets (Solomon 2000). For instance, a material issue for Coca Cola is the management of water consumption, which is critical to their product and also a scarce resource and a societal asset (Ioannou and Serafeim 2011). The U.K. Environmental Protection Act of 1990 introduced the concept of integrating pollution control and focused on the need for information about activities impacting air, land, and water, while the Canadian Institute of Chartered Accountants (CICA) (1994) noted that the consumption of resources should be the focus of measurement and reporting, linking natural resources and pollution controls. The United Nations (UNEP 1994, 1996) posits a mixed approach, suggesting a disclosure on products, including consideration of inputs and outputs of the production cycle. EFFAS (1994) identifies elements that relate to environmental problems, including global warming, ozone depletion, smog, acidification, and waste, while the Confederation of British Industry (CBI) (1995) considers the measurement of energy and natural resource use. Solomon (2000) concludes that there is no single approach to the adoption of a uniform set of well-defined elements for CSR disclosure. Indeed, the topics that are identified in an outline of standard disclosures and environmental performance indicators

[10]The FASB/IASB conceptual framework convergence project has not yet finalized the definition of elements of financial reporting or the related measurement concepts, and the timeline for defining the elements of financial statements has not been announced. However, the basic structure of assets, liabilities, equities, revenues, and expenses appears likely. Examination of SFAC No. 5, Recognition and Measurement in Financial Statements of Business Enterprises (FASB 1984) and SFAC No. 6, Elements of Financial Statements (FASB 1985) is therefore the basis of this discussion.

from the GRI reporting framework include measures on the environment, human rights, labor practices, society, product responsibility, and economics (GRI 2011). Examples of information that might be found in CSR reports are presented in the Appendix.

It is hard to categorize these elements within the financial reporting conceptual framework and its definitions of assets, liabilities, equities, revenues, expenses, gains, and losses (FASB 1985). However, even if it were possible to develop a set of reporting elements that meets the needs of the wider stakeholder base for CSR that coincides with the needs of investors and creditors, the issue of measurement remains. A key measurement principle for financial reporting is the monetary unit assumption (FASB 1984), which defines money as the common denominator of economic activity and the appropriate basis for accounting measurement and analysis. As early as 1982 it was suggested that corporate responsibility is largely a matter of externalities, and that while the constructs are economic in nature, they cannot be measured unambiguously, making it difficult to require that these constructs be reported under accounting standards promulgated to be consistent with the conceptual framework of financial reporting, its definition of elements, and its measurement requirements (Benston 1982). While components of CSR may have financial implications for an entity, given the nature of the disclosure topics deemed appropriate for CSR reporting, measuring the full range of elements in terms of monetary units does not appear to be feasible. For example, it is difficult to imagine faithful representations of items such as privacy, customer health and safety, forced and compulsory labor, or compliance defined in terms of a monetary unit. Indeed, it seems unlikely that such items could even be measured in terms of a more basic assumption: that quantitative data are the most appropriate/useful for communicating economic information and are used to make rational economic decisions (Kieso et al. 2010). KPMG (2010, 13) cautions that it is important to "take care to balance the story with the figures; not all information can be captured in figures and quantitative targets—while telling a story may be incomplete without the concrete reports to support it." Given the difficulty in defining the elements of CSR reporting within the structure of financial reporting whereby measurability, company control, and/or company obligations trigger recognition on the financial statements, integration of these concepts with financial reporting framework does not seem feasible.

Further, defining and developing meaningful linkages given the underlying differences in the nature of the items reported and the lack of a common measurement base would be difficult. The IIRC (2011) states that a goal of integrated reporting is to clarify and integrate what are currently disconnected strands of information on strategy, governance, operations, and financial and non-financial performance into a coherent whole. Such a report should combine the material elements of separate reporting on financial performance, management commentary, governance and remuneration, and sustainability into a report that shows the connectivity between the different information streams (IIRC 2011, 6). However, for reporting to recognize meaningful linkages, there needs to be a level of commonality in definition, construct, and measurement. Without this theoretical underpinning, meaningful linkages are problematic at best.

## 9.4 The Need for Assurance Services

Models for valuation, accountability, and decision making emerge in part as a function of availability, so wider availability of comparable information is a function of mandatory reporting. A second issue is credible information, and credibility is enhanced both by mandatory reporting and by assurance, which raises questions about the potential to provide assurance services for CSR disclosures. To date, given the mandatory nature of financial reporting and the largely voluntary and separate nature of CSR reporting, governmental and non-governmental bodies have developed standards for the auditing of company financial reports and non-governmental bodies have developed standards for providing assurance on company CSR disclosures.[11]

The GRI has encouraged assurance services by assigning a rating to company reports based on the extent of information provided and if the information was subject to external assurance. The GRI has identified qualities for the external assurance of reports that include the need for assurance to be systematic, documented, and evidence-based (Mintz 2011). While assurance is possible for CSR reports, the potential for auditing an integrated report that captures both financial information and CSR information would require an integrated audit that examines the linkages between the financial and nonfinancial information. In order to fully integrate financial reports with CSR reports, it would be necessary to provide assurance on (1) the fair presentation and completeness of CSR disclosures and (2) the links between CSR disclosures and financial information. Research to address the appropriateness of risk assessments and audit techniques and on the feasibility of auditing such links between CSR and financial reporting should precede any potential integration of the two reporting paradigms.

Accounting professionals are uniquely suited to expand their expertise in evaluating, attesting to, and communicating information to stakeholders to include application of such expertise to include the auditing of CSR information. Should CSR reporting be mandated but not integrated with financial reporting, inclusion of CSR information in the annual report might still create the impression that the information has been audited. Further, CSR disclosures are expected to be complete, comparable, accurate, timely, clear, and reliable. Confidence that these attributes are present in CSR information can be enhanced by an audit. While assurance of CSR information can be accomplished, assurance of integrated reports that are not well-defined and which lack consistent measurement that can be documented makes the assessed risk of an integrated report and the related potential for assurance unlikely.

## 9.5 Analysis of the Potential for Integration

Based on our analysis, we believe that at the present time, CSR reporting should not be integrated with financial reporting. The purpose, defined stakeholders, framework, elements, and measurement issues across the range of CSR activities are

[11] Such standards include the AA1000 Assurance Standard (AccountAbility 2008) and the International Standard on Assurance Engagements (ISAE) 3000 (IFAC 2003).

more broad-based than the financial reporting model. CSR reporting addresses the needs of a wider stakeholder group, uses a broader definition of reporting elements, and is not limited to reporting items that can be expressed in terms of a monetary unit. To attempt to incorporate CSR reporting into the financial reporting framework given this incompatibility seems likely to detract from the relevance of CSR items, the completeness of disclosures, and the perceived importance of CSR reports. Further, the lack of compatibility between the financial accounting and CSR reporting paradigms make it unlikely that a single body that has been structured to meet the goals and needs of financial reporting, such as the IASB, could effectively and efficiently promulgate standards to address the information needs of the broader range of stakeholders. To the extent that some elements of CSR reports might also meet the definition of financial statement elements and may be measurable in terms of a monetary unit, financial accounting standard setters such as the IASB should evaluate these items for inclusion in financial reports. Nothing precludes some items from appearing in both the financial report and the CSR report of a given corporation. However, the more diverse stakeholder base and information set that supports CSR reporting goes beyond financial reporting.

The difficulty in identifying and quantifying CSR activities for inclusion in the financial records of the corporation raises the potential for alternative disclosure such as supplementary reports, presence in Management's Discussion and Analysis, or footnote presentation. Information presented in one of those formats would not have to be quantifiable, nor would it need to fit the relatively narrow definitions of financial statement elements. Further, such disclosure could be narrative. However, Kieso et al. (2010, 46) note that disclosure is not an appropriate substitute for "proper accounting." Indeed the purpose of alternative disclosure is normally to provide additional information with respect to the items included on the face of the financial statements, and these disclosures are generally considered secondary information. To relegate CSR reporting to alternative disclosure formats within the published financial statements seems to imply that this information is less relevant for decision making.

Accounting practice encompasses the full range of a corporation's business activities; financial reporting is but one aspect of the communication between the corporation and outside parties. Standards, such as those promulgated by the FASB or the IASB, generally define the nature of the financial information reported and the minimum reporting requirements. Financial reporting, therefore, is a subset of all information available. The broader scope of CSR reporting relative to financial reporting raises the possibility that it may be appropriate to integrate financial reports into the more comprehensive CSR report.

While financial reporting limits the construct of performance to financial performance, CSR reporting focuses simultaneously on multiple dimensions of performance, including financial, social, environmental, and governance. A company's financial condition has implications for sustainability, but CSR is a more comprehensive reporting framework than financial reporting, considering the information needs of broad-based stakeholder group, a wider range of a company's activities, and information beyond that which can be expressed in terms of a monetary unit.

Further, CSR reporting supports a broader range of informed decision making and evaluation. To somehow suggest that CSR should be subsumed into financial reporting seems to frame it as somehow smaller than financial reporting when it is actually a broader performance report than financial reporting about the entity. CSR reporting that includes financial reporting as one of several dimensions of performance may therefore facilitate decision making with respect to expectation of long-term corporate performance and the viability of the entity.

Financial accounting standards were historically developed using a "bottom-up" approach as practice emerged through debate and in response to social norms, with the focus shifting to a "top-down" approach whereby regulators determined reporting requirements and were empowered to enforce these standards after the stock market crash of 1929. The tremendous losses suffered by investors and creditors caused a lack of trust in the relevance and reliability of financial reports, and regulation was seen as the appropriate response. The trend toward regulation accelerated after subsequent high-profile market failures and fraudulent reporting. To date, CSR reporting has evolved from a "bottom-up" approach whereby a network of interested parties participate, subject to little regulation, and reporting guidelines are developed by and for stakeholders in response to stakeholder preferences for information. As CSR has evolved into a major business activity and the demand for CSR reporting has grown, calls for a more structured, "top-down" reporting framework have emerged with the focus on the potential integration of CSR reporting and financial reporting a key theme (e.g., Deloitte 2010; Kanzer 2010; Jeffrey and Perkins 2013).

Those calling for the integration of financial reporting and CSR reporting have failed to adequately address the very basic differences in the nature of the information or how, given the different users, elements, and measurement techniques, a single group of financial standard setters could efficiently and effectively develop a coherent and consistent framework for such integration and the subsequent development of disclosure standards. The progress on the converged financial reporting framework being jointly developed by the FASB and the IASB has been slow, extending over a period of years, with no specific time for completion yet defined. Indeed, the initial views on the new framework were published in 2006 (IASB 2006) and as of December 2010 there was still no timeline identified for completing the projects on elements, recognition, and measurement (FASB 2010b). The conceptual framework being jointly developed by the FASB and the IASB does not attempt to address a broader base of users, focusing instead on the information needs of investors and creditors and explicitly noting that financial reporting does not address all of the information that would be relevant even to this narrow set of users. The expertise of the financial accounting standard setters has been developed in a narrow and well-defined domain, and the complexity and challenge of developing and integrated set of reporting guidelines would thus appear to be beyond what the financial accounting boards are willing (or able) to address. Given the diversity of stakeholders, the range of elements, and the correlated range of appropriate measurement techniques required for CSR reporting, the paradigm shift called for at the 2010 GRI Conference (Deloitte 2010) would require a change to the foundation of theory that has developed over more than 30 years in support of financial reporting. While this may be a worthy goal, the potential to achieve it seems limited.

Not only does the call for integration fail to address the differences in the underlying foundations of financial reporting and CSR reporting, the appropriateness of a "top-down" regulatory model for CSR disclosure is seldom addressed. We agree that the overwhelming importance of CSR disclosure to a variety of stakeholders requires an effective and efficient delivery mechanism and a baseline level of comparability. Because of this, we believe that CSR reporting should be mandatory. Further, because a company's annual report is widely distributed and easily accessible, it may be the appropriate mechanism for the disclosure of CSR reports. However, we do not believe that CSR reporting should be defined and limited by standards developed by governmental bodies such as the SEC, FASB, and IASB, or limited to a top-down approach where by a small group is empowered to promulgate disclosure standards. Rather, requirements for mandated CSR reporting should be promulgated by one or more non-governmental bodies such as the Global Reporting Initiative. Participation is inclusive, representing the interests of diverse stakeholders, so the guidelines that evolve in response to the information needs of this broad-based user group represent social norms to which entities should be held accountable. The direct involvement of the stakeholders in this process should allow reporting guidelines to adapt quickly to changing societal norms regarding the importance of different types of CSR information. As Sunder (2009) states, the reliance on societal norms and diverse inputs encourages discovery of and evolution towards better methods of reporting. By allowing one or more non-governmental bodies to develop guidelines, competition among various CSR reporting frameworks could emerge. Sunder (2009) also notes that there is no available measure of the quality of a reporting standard, and one measure of the appropriateness of reporting guidelines promulgated by one or more non-governmental bodies would be determined by market forces, which could lead to the development of stronger reporting frameworks over time. The benefit to society from improved reporting would be an improved information set for stakeholder decision-making, and a more effective and efficient use of scarce resources. Even as society allows an entity to control its assets because of a perceived contribution to society as a whole, the entity should be accountable to society and should be evaluated on how well it conforms to societal norms (Dillard 2008). Reporting systems that emerge in response to societal values allow greater accountability to society.

As Benston (1982, 10) noted: "[A]n accounting standard that requires corporations to disclose the amount of negative externalities it creates should provide relatively unambiguous numbers that measure the social costs of such actions." Future research in CSR reporting should address the financial impact of the current and future social costs of companies' CSR policies. If measurement of such costs is intractable, another line of research might focus on modeling the relationship between CSR information and financial information by examining links between CSR and financial activities, including causal relationships between financial and non-financial metrics. Such research should also consider the potential to incorporate financial reporting into the broader field of CSR reporting.

## 9.6 Conclusion

We believe that CSR reporting should be mandated. The perceived and growing importance of CSR reports and the benefits from disclosure and from comparable disclosure across firms can best be served by mandated reporting. The development of reporting standards should also be facilitated by requiring disclosure. Within each jurisdiction, the appropriate regulatory body (such as the SEC in the United States) must be responsible for establishing the mandate and for enforcement of the mandate. However, establishing a mandate and developing the reporting framework are different constructs, and the regulatory body that establishes the mandate should allow the framework to continue to develop through a participatory process such as the GRI. The combination of mandated disclosure and a "bottom-up" approach to the development of standards in response to the demand for information and evolving norms for performance are expected to lead to timely and high quality reporting. Further, allowing the disclosure framework to emerge from a non-governmental body such as the GRI which encourages broad-based international participation may facilitate global comparability similar to the movement toward global financial reporting standards.

At this time, however, CSR should not be integrated into financial reporting. Not only is the financial reporting conceptual framework narrower on key dimensions when compared with the CSR reporting framework, making the successful integration of CSR information into the financial reports unlikely, the lack of clear links between CSR information and financial information would appear to make the assurance of such "integrated" reports difficult, if not impossible, at this time. Rather, the potential to integrate financial reporting into the broader CSR reporting framework should be evaluated. Financial performance is one aspect of the viability of the entity, and therefore of interest to a broad range of stakeholders that includes, but is not limited to, investors, creditors, and their advisors.

## Appendix

The following are excerpts from BP's sustainability report, *Sustainability Review 2011* (BP 2011)[12]:

<u>Stakeholder Engagement</u>

> Engaging with local communities is a vital element of our work. Talking with local people and other stakeholders helps our business to define what a positive or negative impact on the local community means. It also helps us more fully understand the broader potential environmental and social impacts of our work. The engagement process typically begins long before any physical work has started and continues through the lifespan of a project.

---

[12] The full report can be found at http://www.bp.com/liveassets/bp_internet/globalbp/STAGING/global_assets/e_s_assets/e_s_assets_2010/downloads_pdfs/bp_sustainability_review_2011.pdf.

We welcome, and value, BP's open engagement with the Church Investors Group since the Deepwater Horizon oil spill and, specifically, the initial developments in the area of safety and operational risk over this period. We look forward to continuing our engagement with the company as they approach the challenges that lie ahead.

— Richard Nunn, Chair, Church Investors Group

During our work we interviewed staff responsible for engaging with external stakeholders and received evidence of how information from these dialogues is captured. We have also attended a selection of briefings to investors and two of the roundtable discussions held in 2011 to understand the perspectives on various thought leaders on how BP should evolve its reporting and communications. We noted that stakeholders welcome this dialogue but there remains a desire for more comprehensive reporting on how BP is changing.

— Ernst & Young, external assurance provider

## Risk Management

We have initiated a review of our risk management system and begun enhancing the clarity, simplicity and consistency of the way we manage and report risks. We have standardized our reporting processes so that businesses and functions have a consistent way of reporting risk – from our frontline operations to the board. … We will continue to embed the enhancements to our risk management system through greater alignment of our risk management activities and business processes.

## Environmental

Scientists are studying a range of species to understand how wildlife populations may have been affected by the [Deepwater Horizon] spill. Teams of experts are also studying habitats, such as wetlands and beaches, with the goal of returning them to the condition that they would have been in if the Deepwater Horizon incident had not occurred. … The federal and state trustees have responsibility for the [Natural Resource Damages assessment] process and BP is a participant.

BP refers to studies that have been undertaken to help understand the impact on habitats. Whilst it is clear that a wide range of activities are under way or have been completed, the full analysis of the various studies is pending and BP should provide updates in due course.

— Ernst & Young, external assurance provider

We factor a carbon cost into our investment appraisals and engineering designs for some new projects. We do this by requiring larger projects, and those for which emissions costs would be a material part of the project, to apply a standard carbon cost to the projected GHG emissions over the life of the project. The standard cost is based on our estimate of the carbon price that might realistically be expected in particular parts of the world. In industrialized countries, this standard cost assumption is currently $40 per tonne of CO2 equivalent.

BP sets out an overview of its programme of action on climate change but there is limited explanation of the difference that this is making on its decisions or practices. For example, BP has incorporated carbon pricing into its projects but it is not clear to what extent this process has impacted project plans; or whether BP can explain how targets set for energy efficiency through the local operating management system can be linked to real sustainable reductions reported.

— Ernst & Young, external assurance provider

Our direct GHG emissions were 61.8 million tonnes (Mte) in 2011, compared with 64.9 Mte in 2010. … The net effect of acquisitions and divestments is a decrease of 1 Mte, primarily the result of the sale of assets as part of our disposal programme. Operational changes led to a decrease of 1.8 Mte, principally due to temporary reductions in activity from maintenance work. Adjustments to the way businesses calculate emissions resulted in a decrease of 0.1 Mte. In 2010, we did not report on GHG emissions associated with the Deepwater Horizon incident or response. We have since estimated the gross direct CO2 equivalent emissions from response activities in 2010 to be approximately 481,000 metric tonnes, which includes drilling ships and major vessels deployed, support vessels, flaring of oil and gas, and in situ burning of oil on the sea. This figure does not include emissions associated with the 'vessels of opportunity' programme, the onshore vehicles and equipment, and the incident itself, which are estimated to be minor.

Society

Our Tangguh liquefied natural gas (LNG) plant in the Papua Barat province lies in a remote area where livelihoods depend on fishing and farming. The local ecosystem is both beautiful and fragile, and there is almost no infrastructure or industry. We are working with the government, oil, and gas regulator BPMIGAS and local villagers to manage the sustainability impacts of the operation. This includes employing local people as security personnel, training local businesses and support capacity building of local government officials. We are also supporting education and health programmes.

One of the areas where stakeholders continue to request increased transparency in BP's sustainability reporting is the value that is delivered to society as a whole. Different stakeholder groups take an interest in different elements of the value chain, and economic impacts may either be direct or indirect. This report has attempted to capture these explicitly but BP will need to seek feedback on how it has described the contribution that it is making and consider incorporating additional socio-economic metrics in the future.
— Ernst & Young, external assurance provider

Labor Practices and Decent Work

BP's code of conduct clarifies the ethics and compliance expectations for everyone who works at BP. We updated our code in 2011 to incorporate our refreshed values and to align with new external requirements. The code reflects a values-based approach. Where rules are not stated explicitly, our everyday business decisions are guided by our values. The code includes sections on operating safety, responsibly, and reliably; our people; our business partners; the governments and communities we work with; and our assets and financial integrity. The code takes into account key points from new BP standards related to anti-bribery and corruption, anti-money laundering, competition and anti-trust law, and trade sanctions. The code also takes account of changing external expectations on business and human rights. To help us reflect best practice, we consulted employees and external subject matter experts and benchmarked the code with more than 40 companies.

Self-audit programmes for operations and health, safety, security and environment are a key tool for delivery of good, sustainable performance in operations. Our central [safety and operational risk (S&OR)] audit team conducts independent audits, including the testing of those self-audit programmes. We risk-rank our operations, with the higher hazard facilities audited on a risk-prioritized frequency. By the end of 2011, the S&OR audit team had completed 150 operating management system and process safety management audits. More than 16,000 actions were raised and approximately 12,200 were closed. We have piloted new audit programmes for rig audits and major project audits.

Human Rights

We seek to identify human rights issues before making investments. We have undertaken significant human rights-related impact assessment work in Brazil and have established a grievance process, which includes an ombudsman for receiving and resolving issues raised by workers. Tropical BioEnergia S.A. was certified to the social accountability standard SA8000, which audits labour practices, in December 2011.

During 2011, BP commissioned three human rights experts to carry out a detailed review of our current policies and practices and the expectations in the Guiding Principles [for Business and Human Rights], to help us identify what work will be needed to achieve alignment with the principles. These experts provided a summary of our strengths and gaps, together with a number of recommendations that we are integrating into our plans.

Frameworks and Guidelines

We continue to report against the Global Reporting Initiative's (GRI) G3 sustainability and reporting guidelines to an A + level. We are actively involved in the development of the GRI Oil and Gas Sector Supplement and welcome its introduction. We also report in line with the second edition Oil and Gas Voluntary Guidance on Sustainability Reporting (2010) from the oil and gas industry association IPIECA, the American Petroleum Institute and the International Association of Oil and Gas Producers. In addition, we report against the UN Global Compact's 10 principles.

## References

AccountAbility. 2008. *AA1000 assurance standard*. London: AccountAbility.

Artiach, T., D. Lee, D. Nelson, and J. Walker. 2010. The determinants of corporate sustainability performance. *Accounting and Finance* 50(1): 31–51.

Bebbington, J., J. Brown, B. Frame, and I. Thomson. 2007. Theorizing engagement: The potential of a critical dialogic approach. *Accounting, Auditing & Accountability Journal* 20(3): 356–381.

Benston, G.J. 1982. An analysis of the role of accounting standards for enhancing corporate governance and social responsibility. *Journal of Accounting and Public Policy* 1(1): 5–17.

Biondi, Y., J. Glover, K. Jamal, J.A. Ohlson, S.H. Penman, S. Sunder, and E. Tsujiyama. 2012. Some conceptual tensions in financial reporting. *Accounting, Horizons* 26(1): 125–133.

BP. 2011. *Sustainability review 2011*. London: BP.

Brown, J., and M. Fraser. 2006. Approaches and perspectives in social and environmental accounting: An overview of the conceptual landscape. *Business Strategy and the Environment* 15(2): 103–117.

Brown, H.S., M. de Jong, and T. Lessidrenska. 2009. The rise of the global reporting initiative: A case of institutional entrepreneurship. *Environmental Politics* 18(2): 182–200.

Buhmann, K. 2006. Corporate social responsibility: What role for law? Some aspects of law and CSR. *Corporate Governance* 6(2): 188–202.

Canadian Institute of Chartered Accountants (CICA). 1994. *Reporting on environmental performance*. Toronto: CICA.

Confederation of British Industry (CBI). 1995. *Introducing environmental reporting: Guidelines for business*. London: CBI.

Deloitte. 2010. *Sustainability reporting: The emerging challenge*. New York: Deloitte Touche Tohmatsu.

Dillard, J. 2008. An ethic of accountability. *Research on Professional Responsibility and Ethics in Accounting* 13: 1–18.

Eccles, R.G., and G. Serafeim. 2011. Accelerating the adoption of integrated reporting. In *CSR index 2011*, ed. F. de Leo and M. Vollbracht, 70–92. Zurich: Innovatio Publishing, Ltd.

European Federation of Financial Analysts Societies (EFFAS). 1994. Environmental reporting and disclosures: The financial analysts view. Edinburgh: EFFAS.

Fédération des Experts Comptables Européens (FEE). 1999. FEE discussion paper towards a generally accepted framework for environmental reporting. Brussels: FEE.

Financial Accounting Standards Board (FASB). 1984. Recognition and measurement in financial statements of business enterprises. Statement of financial accounting concepts statement no. 5. Stamford: FASB.

Financial Accounting Standards Board (FASB). 1985. Elements of financial statements. Statement of financial accounting concepts statement no. 6. Stamford: FASB.

Financial Accounting Standards Board (FASB). 2010a. Conceptual framework of financial reporting. Statement of financial accounting concepts statement no. 8. Norwalk: FASB.

Financial Accounting Standards Board (FASB). 2010b. Current technical plan and project updates. http://www.fasb.org/cs/ContentServer?c=Page&pagename=FASB/Page/SectionPage&cid=1218220137074. Accessed on 29 Nov 2010.

Global Reporting Initiative (GRI). 2009. Reaching investors: Communicating value through ESG disclosures (GRI research and development series). Amsterdam: GRI.

Global Reporting Initiative (GRI). 2011. Sustainability reporting guidelines (Version 3.1). Amsterdam: GRI.

Gray, R.H., D.L. Owen, and K.T. Maunders. 1987. *Corporate social reporting: Accounting and accountability*. Hemel Hempstead: Prentice Hall.

Gray, R.H., D. Owen, and C. Adams. 1996. *Accounting and accountability*. Hemel Hempstead: Prentice Hall.

GS Sustain. 2009. Change is coming: A framework for climate change – A defining issue of the 21st century. The Goldman Sachs Group, Inc. (May 21): 1–21. Available at: http://www2.goldmansachs.com/ideas/environment-and-energy/goldman-sachs/gs-sustain/climate-change-research.pdf

Initiative for Responsible Investment (IRI). 2012. *Current corporate social responsibility disclosure efforts by national governments and stock exchanges*. Cambridge, MA: IRI.

International Accounting Standards Board (IASB). 2006. First steps toward a converged conceptual framework. *IASB Insight*, October, 1–3.

International Accounting Standards Board (IASB). 2010. *IFRS practice standard: Management commentary – A framework for presentation*. London: IFRS Foundation.

International Federation of Accountants (IFAC). 2003. International Standard on Assurance Engagements (ISAE) 3000. New York: IFAC.

International Federation of Accountants (IFAC). 2010. A public interest framework for the accountancy profession. IFAC policy position paper no. 4 (exposure draft). New York: IFAC.

International Integrated Reporting Committee (IIRC). 2011. Towards integrated reporting: Communicating value in the 21st century. London: IIRC.

Ioannou, I., and G. Serafeim. 2011. Sustainability and capital markets: How firms can manage the crucial link. *The European Business Review*, March. http://www.europeanbusinessreview.com/?p=3588

Jeffrey, C., and J.D. Perkins. 2013. Social norms and disclosure policy: Implications from a comparison of financial and corporate social responsibility reporting. *Social and Environmental Accountability Journal* 33(1): 5–19.

Jensen, J.C., and N. Berg. 2012. Determinants of traditional sustainability reporting versus integrated reporting: An institutionalist approach. *Business Strategy and the Environment* 21(5): 299–316.

Kanzer, A. 2010. When CSR and financial reporting meet: Integrated reporting. Comments from breakout session at the BSR Conference, November 2–5, 2010. Available at http://bsr.org/ClientFiles/BAS/Conference2010/Materials/BSR_Conf2010_Summary_When_CSR_and_Financial_Reporting_Meet_Integrated_reporting.pdf

Kieso, D.E., J. Weygant, and T.D. Warfield. 2010. *Intermediate accounting*, 13th ed. Hoboken: Wiley Publishers.

Klassen, R.D., and C.P. McLaughlin. 1996. The impact of environmental management on firm performance. *Management Science* 42(8): 1199–1214.

KPMG. 2008. *Sustainability reporting: A guide*. Melbourne: KPMG Australia.
KPMG. 2010. *Integrated reporting: Closing the loop of strategy*. Amstelveen: KPMG Advisory N.V.
KPMG. 2011. *International survey of corporate responsibility reporting 2011*. Amstelveen: KPMG International.
Leonard, H.B. 2008. Foreword. In *Making sustainability work: Best practices in managing and measuring corporate social, environmental, and economic impacts*, ed. M. Epstein. San Francisco: Berrett-Koehler Publishers.
Mintz, S.M. 2011. Triple bottom line reporting for CPAs: Challenges and opportunities in social accounting. *The CPA Journal* (September): 2–8.
Noble, G., and B. Kotevski. 2008. *The sustainability reporting journey: Sustainability reporting practices of S&P/ASX 100 companies*. Melbourne: Responsible Investment Consulting.
O'Dwyer, B. 2000. Evidence and the public interest versus expediency: Critical commentary of "Could Corporate Environmental Reporting Shadow Financial Reporting?" by Aris Solomon. *Accounting Forum* 24(2): 223–230.
Patten, D. 2014. Environmental disclosure as legitimation: Is it in the public interest? In *Accounting for the public interest: Perspectives on accountability, professionalism and role in society*, ed. S. Mintz. 201–215. Heidelberg: Springer.
Slob, B., and G. Oonk. 2007. *Developing the future ISO SR 26000 standard*. ISO Working Group on Social Responsibility Briefing Paper. Amsterdam: Centre for Research on Multinational Corporations. http://www.indianet.nl/pdf/briefing_iso_sr.pdf
Social Investment Forum (SIF). 2009. Letter to Mary L. Schapiro, SEC Chairman, dated July 21, 2009. Available at: http://ussif.org/documents/ESG_Letter_to_SEC.pdf
Solomon, A. 2000. Could corporate environmental reporting shadow financial reporting? *Accounting Forum* 24(1): 30–55.
Stengel, R. 2009. The responsibility revolution. *Time* 174(11): 24–27, September 21.
Sunder, S. 2009. IFRS and the accounting consensus. *Accounting Horizons* 23(1): 101–111.
United Nations Environment Programme, Industry and Environment Office (UNEP). 1994. Company environmental reporting: A measure of the progress of business and industry towards sustainable development. Technical report series 24. London: SustainAbility, Ltd.
United Nations Environment Programme, Industry and Environment Office (UNEP). 1996. Engaging stakeholders: 1. The benchmark survey. Sustainability and the United Nations Environment Programme. London: SustainAbility, Ltd.
United States Securities and Exchange Commission (SEC). 2010. Commission guidance regarding disclosure related to climate change. Release Nos. 33-9106; 34-61469; FR-82. Washington, DC: SEC.

# Chapter 10
# Environmental Disclosure as Legitimation: Is It in the Public Interest?

**Dennis M. Patten**

## 10.1 Introduction

In his 2009 editorial on accounting and the environment, *Accounting, Organizations and Society* Editor Anthony Hopwood acknowledged the great potential for environmental reporting "to give a greater degree of visibility to corporate environmental activities and consequences, casting light on what is often invisible" (Hopwood 2009, 437). Given society's long-term interests in, and concerns about corporate impacts on the world in which we live, such transparency would clearly appear to be within the public interest. However, Hopwood followed his optimistic claim by citing an alternative possibility for corporate use of environmental disclosure. He noted:

> Companies are also interested in the possibilities for environmental reporting to increase their legitimacy in the wider world. Not only that, they can also have an interest in using reporting to facilitate construction of a new and different image of the company. To the extent that such strategies work, it is possible that fewer questions might be asked of the legitimated organization and thereby less might be known of it. It is as if the reporting serves as a corporate veil, simultaneously providing a new face to the outside world while protecting the inner workings of the organization from external view. Done with skill and a fair amount of planning and thought, it is possible for some forms of reporting to thicken that veil such that even less is known of the corporation despite the apparent openness of its reporting (Hopwood 2009, 437).

Unfortunately, a considerable body of research to date suggests it is this latter view that seems to dominate the world of corporate voluntary environmental reporting. In this chapter, I lay out the evidence in support of the argument that companies appear to use voluntary environmental reporting more as a tool for

D.M. Patten (✉)
Department of Accounting, Illinois State University, Normal, IL 61790, USA
e-mail: dmpatte@ilstu.edu

S. Mintz (ed.), *Accounting for the Public Interest: Perspectives on Accountability, Professionalism and Role in Society*, Advances in Business Ethics Research 4,
DOI 10.1007/978-94-007-7082-9_10, © Springer Science+Business Media Dordrecht 2014

corporate legitimation than as a vehicle for transparency and increased accountability making the case that, as it currently exists, corporate environmental reporting is not serving the public interest.[1] I do, however, offer my suggestions for bringing the practice more into alignment with what it would seem society desires. I begin with a brief overview of legitimacy theory as a lens for examining corporate environmental disclosure.

## 10.2 Legitimacy Theory and Environmental Disclosure

As noted by Deegan (2002), legitimacy theory[2] is grounded in the concept of a social contract between business and society. Shocker and Sethi (1974, 67) explain this as:

> Any social institution – and business is no exception – operates in society via a social contract, expressed or implied, whereby its survival and growth are based on: (1) the delivery of some socially desirable ends to society in general, and (2) the distribution of economic, social, or political benefits to groups from which it derives its power. In a dynamic society, neither the sources of institutional power nor the needs for its services are permanent. Therefore, an institution must constantly meet the twin tests of legitimacy and relevance by demonstrating that society requires its services and that the groups benefitting from its rewards have society's approval.

Legitimacy then, as summarized by Suchman (1995, 574), represents the perception "that the actions of an entity are desirable, proper, or appropriate *within* some socially constructed system of norms, values, beliefs, and definitions" (Suchman's emphasis). Patten (1992) argues that while the economic legitimacy of business organizations is monitored through the marketplace, their social legitimacy is addressed through the public policy process. Indeed, he notes that "whenever a relevant public is dissatisfied with the performance of an organization it can apply pressure to the firm to meet expectations or it can use the legal system to require improved performance" (Patten 1992, 472). As such, corporations have an incentive to participate in the public policy process, and, from the legitimacy theory perspective, disclosure can be used as a tool for this participation. For example, Higginson et al. (2006) note prior research indicating that firms facing threats to their perceived legitimacy attempt to demonstrate that their actions are commensurate with stakeholders' norms and values by increasing communication with the public. Patten (1992) more specifically claims that businesses can use disclosure either to address specific social or political concerns or as way of projecting an image of the company

[1]The argument I develop in this chapter relates to the environmental disclosures corporations voluntarily provide, usually as part of their annual reports, through separate stand-alone reports, or on their websites.

[2]For a more detailed discussion of legitimacy theory, including its relation to other political economy-based theories of disclosure (Gray et al. 1995), see Deegan (2002, 2007) or Milne and Patten (2002).

as socially aware. In either case, they are attempting to reduce what Miles (1987) refers to as the 'exposure' to the social and political process.[3]

### *10.2.1 Legitimacy Evidence*

Numerous studies provide evidence that variables assumed to capture differences in social and political exposures are associated with differences in the extent of corporate environmental disclosure. Factors consistently found to be related to this reporting include firm size (e.g., Clarkson et al. 2011; Cormier and Magnan 1999; Magness 2006; Patten 1992, 2002b), industry classification (e.g., Cho and Patten 2007; Deegan and Gordon 1996; Hackston and Milne 1996; Patten 2002b), and media exposure (e.g., Aerts and Cormier 2009; Brown and Deegan 1998; Patten 2002a). More specifically, larger companies, presumably due to visibility issues (Watts and Zimmerman 1986), are assumed to face greater exposure to the public policy process as are firms from industries whose activities can potentially harm the environment.[4] Media exposure, like firm size, is assumed to increase social and political exposure due to the increased visibility regarding poor environmental performance.

Considerable evidence also documents that *changes* in social and political exposures appear to lead to *changes* in environmental disclosure. For example, Patten (1992) shows that the extent of annual report environmental disclosure for petroleum companies other than Exxon increased significantly following the 1989 *Exxon-Valdez* oil spill off the coast of Alaska. Patten also documented that differences in the changes in disclosures were associated with firm-specific social and political cost factors (firm size and part ownership of the Alyeska pipeline), thus supporting the claim that the differences were due to these exposures. Other studies documenting changes in environmental disclosure relative to changes in social and political exposures include Deegan et al. (2000), Patten (2000), and Walden and Schwarz (1997).

## 10.3 The Relation Between Environmental Performance and Environmental Disclosure

While the studies summarized above provide a fairly substantial body of evidence indicating that the level of corporate environmental disclosure appears to be influenced by broad-based measures of exposure to social and political cost, and that

[3] Certainly, firms can also reduce their exposures by changing their socially undesirable behavior. But, as noted by Dowling and Pfeffer (1975) and Lindblom (1994), they can also use disclosure to alter society's perceptions of their legitimacy. It is this latter tactic that is the concern addressed in this chapter.

[4] The chemical, metals, mining, paper, petroleum, and utility industries are those most often classified as being environmentally sensitive.

changes in social and political exposure lead to changes in disclosure, the primary focus of this chapter is on evidence examining the relation between environmental performance and voluntary environmental disclosure. From a normative perspective, it seems logical that users of corporate reports ought to be able to use the information provided to identify, at least to some degree, a company's environmental performance, and at least in the United States, certain mandated disclosures would appear to be targeted at the goal. For example, the Securities and Exchange Commission (SEC) requires through its Regulation S-K that companies identify in their 10-K filings any pending legal proceedings arising from federal, state, or local environmental provisions where registrants believe sanctions will be in excess of $100,000 (Mobus 2005, 503). Similarly, increased authoritative guidance from the SEC, the Financial Accounting Standards Board, and the American Institute of Certified Public Accountants in the early and mid-1990s targeted better disclosure of corporate exposures arising from hazardous waste remediation requirements such as Superfund.[5] These types of mandated disclosures clearly appear to be required to allow users of corporate reports to better assess environmental performance as it relates to potential liabilities,[6] and as pointed out by Jeffrey and Perkins (2014) in the previous chapter of this book, they help to ensure a minimum level of comparable information across companies. But in addition to these mandated disclosures, companies often choose to provide information on other aspects of their environmental relations including, for example, statements on company concerns for the environment, disclosures related to processes and procedures related to pollution abatement or control, and identification of awards received in the environmental arena.

### *10.3.1 Early Evidence*

A number of early studies of the environmental performance/environmental disclosure relation (Ingram and Frazier 1980; Wiseman 1982; Freedman and Wasley 1990; Fekrat et al. 1996) failed to find a significant association between the two. Part of the problem, as noted by Patten (2002b), was that these early investigations suffered from sample selection problems, inadequate measures of environmental performance, and/or failure to control for other factors influencing differences in disclosures (firm size and industry classification). However, they also failed to take into consideration that companies with poorer environmental performance

[5] See Barth et al. (1997) for an overview of this authoritative guidance.

[6] As noted by Blacconiere and Patten (1994), SEC guidelines also, in theory, require companies to disclose the material impacts compliance with environmental regulations has on current or future capital spending and operating costs. However, the actual provision of this information, as documented in numerous prior studies (e.g., Blacconiere and Patten 1994; Gamble et al. 1995; Cho and Patten 2008) is quite limited. Further, Cho, Freedman, and Patten (2012) show that, at least for environmental capital expenditures, disclosed amounts are almost always well below quantitative materiality thresholds suggesting the choice to actual disclose is discretionary.

may have incentives to use disclosure as a tool of legitimation. As explained by Cho and Patten (2007), a poor environmental performance record is assumed also to increase social and political exposures, and thus, according to legitimacy theory arguments, worse performing companies have an incentive to use the voluntary disclosure of positive or mitigating environmental information to reduce these exposures. Two relatively recent legitimacy-based studies (Patten 2002b; Cho and Patten 2007) provide evidence that companies with worse environmental performance exhibit more extensive voluntary environmental disclosure, and each is discussed in more detail below.

## *10.3.2 More Recent Investigations*

### 10.3.2.1 Controlling for Size and Industry

Patten (2002b) specifically attempted to overcome the problems of the prior research into the environmental performance/environmental disclosure relation. His sample of 131 U.S. companies was drawn from the Environmental Protection Agency's listing of the top 500 companies from the 1988 Toxics Release Inventory (TRI).[7] This list was published in 1990. Patten's sample was considerably larger and more diverse in terms of industry make-up than the samples for any of the prior studies. Patten measured each sample firm's environmental performance as its total amount of TRI releases divided by the company's 1988 revenue level. Similar to Wiseman (1982), Patten calculated the extent of annual report environmental disclosure using both a content analysis scheme and a line count.[8] However, although based on Wiseman's (1982) 13 item scale, Patten excluded litigation-related disclosures noting Blacconiere and Patten's (1994) argument that such items were likely not discretionary in nature. Finally, and in contrast to all of the prior studies, Patten controlled for firm size and industry classification.

Patten (2002b) found that both content analysis scores and line counts for the environmental disclosures were significantly related to his environmental performance measure. Firms with higher levels of size-adjusted TRI releases included more extensive discretionary disclosures, thus supporting the legitimacy theory argument. However, Patten also found that poorer performance appeared to influence disclosure more for firms from non-environmentally sensitive industries than for those whose industries were classified as environmentally sensitive.

[7] TRI, created as part of the Superfund Amendments and Reauthorization Act of 1986, requires manufacturing facilities meeting program guidelines to report to the Environmental Protection Agency, on an annual basis, the estimated amount of releases to the land, water, or air for more than 300 different toxic chemicals. The data are made publicly available, although there is about a 2-year gap between reporting and public availability.

[8] Patten compared 1990 disclosures with 1988 performance data because the latter did not become publicly available until 1990.

Patten (2002b) argues that a potential explanation for this difference is that firms from environmentally sensitive industries already faced enough social and political exposure to warrant the use of disclosure as a legitimating tool, whereas companies from non-environmentally sensitive industries did not. For these latter companies, the poorer environmental performance could be expected to trigger disclosure-inducing exposures.

#### 10.3.2.2 Focusing on the Nature of the Information

The second of the legitimacy-based environmental performance/environmental disclosure studies, Cho and Patten (2007), builds on Patten's (2002b) findings by investigating for differences in the types of environmental information provided by better and worse performing companies across industry classification. Cho and Patten argue that, due to potential proprietary costs (see Verrecchia 1983), companies may be more reluctant to disclose monetary environmental information such as capital expenditures or operating costs for pollution abatement and control. However, following Patten's (2002b) reasoning, they argue that firms from environmentally sensitive industries, due to that exposure, already have an incentive to disclose non-monetary environmental information as a way of reducing social and political cost exposures while firms from non-environmentally sensitive industries do not. Cho and Patten therefore hypothesize that worse environmental performers from non-environmentally sensitive industries will use non-monetary environmental disclosures to address their increased exposure while worse performers from environmentally sensitive industries will need to use monetary environmental disclosures to accomplish that goal.

Cho and Patten (2007) partition their sample of 100 U.S. firms into four size-matched groups partitioned on industry membership – environmentally sensitive (ESI) and non-environmentally sensitive (non-ESI) – and environmental performance – worse and better performers. Environmental performance was classified using assessments from the firm KLD Research and Analytics, Inc. (KLD).[9] Cho and Patten label firms identified by KLD as having one or more environmental concerns as the worse performers. The authors use Patten's (2002b) eight item content analysis scheme to code disclosures, although they break down the scores across monetary and non-monetary disclosure areas (four items in each).

Based on comparisons across sample groups, Cho and Patten (2007) find, as expected, non-monetary environmental disclosures are more extensive for non-ESI firms who are worse performers than for non-ESI companies classified as better

[9] KLD assesses strengths and concerns across a variety of social and environmental areas for a broad sample of U.S. companies, and their metrics have been used as a measure of social and/or environmental performance in a wide variety of studies in both the accounting and the management literature. Chatterji et al. (2009) assessed the relative strength of the KLD environmental assessments against other performance measures and determined that only the concern scores appear to be valid measures of corporate environmental performance.

performers, whereas there is no significant difference in non-monetary disclosure across the better and worse performing ESI companies. In contrast, monetary environmental disclosures do vary across the two ESI groups. ESI companies with KLD concerns include more extensive monetary environmental information than their better performing ESI counterparts. They also include more extensive monetary environmental disclosures than non-ESI firms with KLD concerns. Cho and Patten (2007, 646) thus conclude that their results "provide additional evidence that companies do appear to use financial report environmental disclosure as a legitimizing tool."

#### 10.3.2.3 Other Evidence

Evidence of a negative relation between environmental performance and environmental disclosure is not limited to U.S. firms. For example, Deegan and Rankin (1996) examine a sample of Australian companies cited for violations by the Environmental Protection Authority and find that while disclosure of the violations was very limited, almost all of the firms increased their provision of positive environmental information in their annual reports. Further, Brammer and Pavelin (2006) show for their sample of U.K. firms that higher levels of size-adjusted environmental fines (worse performance) are positively and significantly associated with their measure of disclosure extensiveness, a finding consistent with Warsame et al.'s (2002) results for their investigation of the relation between environmental fines and environmental disclosure for a sample of Canadian companies.[10] Also based on a sample of Canadian firms, Cormier and Magnan (1999) report that excess levels of pollution are associated with higher levels of environmental disclosure, although other measures of environmental performance are not. Finally, Aerts and Cormier (2009), examining a sample of both Canadian and U.S. firms, find that worse environmental performance (based on size adjusted levels of TRI releases) is associated with more elaborate environmental disclosures, but only for social-based, as opposed to economic-based information. Importantly, none of these additional investigations report any instances of a significant positive relation between corporate environmental performance and disclosure (companies with better performance disclosing more).

Finally, and from a slightly different perspective, Cho et al. (2010) rely upon legitimacy theory to examine the relation between corporate environmental performance and environmental disclosure, but rather than focusing on the extent of disclosure, they investigate for differences in the use of language and verbal tone in the disclosures across better and worse performing companies. Using the content analysis software DICTION, they evaluate the environmental disclosures in the 10-K reports from 2002 for a sample of 190 Fortune 500 firms with available KLD environmental performance evaluation data. Controlling for firm size, industry

[10] Brammer and Pavelin (2006) also report that their measure of performance is not statistically significant in relation to the choice to disclose.

classification, capital intensity, profitability, and company age, Cho et al. find that environmental performance (measured using KLD concern scores) is negatively related to DICTION's 'certainty' construct and positively associated with 'optimism'. The first of these results suggests that companies that are worse environmental performers use more obfuscating language in their disclosures than do better performers, presumably in an attempt to make the actual performance less transparent. The findings with respect to 'optimism' in the language used indicates that the worse performers tend to focus their disclosures more on good news and tend to attribute any good performance to internal company attributes, whereas attribution for poor performance is blurred. Overall, Cho et al. (2010) argue that their results support prior work in impression management (e.g., Merkl-Davies and Brennan 2007), and indicate that poorer environmental performers use language and verbal tone in their environmental disclosures in an attempt to "present a more favorable depiction of their performance."

In sum, evidence from a substantial number of studies suggests that companies appear to use environmental disclosure as a tool for reducing social and political pressures potentially arising from poor environmental performance.

## 10.4 An Alternative View – Voluntary Disclosure Theory

In spite of the body of articles documenting a negative relation between environmental performance and environmental disclosure, the evidence is not unequivocal. Most notably, Clarkson et al. (2008) rely on financial economics-based voluntary disclosure theory (VDT) arguments to examine for differences in environmental disclosures through standalone environmental reports or on company websites. As noted by Clarkson et al. (2008), VDT assumes that, given information asymmetry between managers and investors, firms with an unobservable superior environmental strategy have an incentive to make disclosures to signal the market, while worse performers would prefer to remain silent and be judged as 'an average type' firm. Further, Clarkson et al. (2008, 309) posit that better environmental performers will focus on "objective, 'hard' measures that cannot be easily mimicked by poor environmental performers."

### *10.4.1 Evidence for VDT*

Clarkson et al. (2008) utilize a broad disclosure metric based on Global Reporting Initiative (GRI) guidelines to measure the extent of disclosure for a sample of 191 U.S. companies from the pulp and paper, chemical, oil and gas, metals and mining, and utilities industries. The disclosure scale allows for measurement across seven major areas, the first four of which are considered 'hard' disclosure items. The major areas (and possible disclosure points) are governance structures and management systems (0–6 points), credibility (0–10 points), environmental performance indicators (0–60 points), environmental spending (0–3 points), vision and strategy claims (0–6 points), environmental profile (0–4 points), and environmental initiatives (0–6). Clarkson et al. use two alternative measures for environmental performance. The first measure used is the ratio of toxic waste that is treated, recycled, or processed over total toxic waste generated. The second performance metric is size-adjusted total TRI releases. For both measures, Clarkson et al. identify performance as the rank (based independently on each performance item) within industry.

Using multiple regression models controlling for firm size, media exposure, and a variety of financial performance and capital asset attributes, Clarkson et al. (2008) find that environmental performance using either of their performance metrics is positively and significantly related to the extensiveness of environmental disclosure. That is, in contrast to the legitimacy-based findings summarized above, Clarkson et al.'s results indicate that better performers include more extensive disclosures. These results hold for disclosure across both the hard and soft disclosure categories. Clarkson et al. (2011) also report a positive relation between environmental performance and environmental disclosure, but this is not unexpected as their study is based on a sub-set of the Clarkson et al. (2008) sample and uses the same disclosure and performance measures.

Another recent study, Al-Tuwaijri et al. (2004), also shows a positive association between environmental performance (measured as the ratio of hazardous wastes recycled to total hazardous wastes generated) and environmental disclosure. However, as noted by Clarkson et al. (2008), Al-Tuwaijri et al.'s disclosure scale focuses on items that are largely non-discretionary (designation as a potentially responsible party under Superfund, toxic wastes, oil and chemical spills, and environmental fines and penalties).

### *10.4.2 Reconciling the Differences*

One possible explanation for the differing relation reported in the Clarkson et al. (2008) study relative to the legitimacy-based investigations noted above is its focus on only firms from environmentally sensitive industries and the use of a broader, more comprehensive disclosure metric. However, Cho, Guidry et al. (2012) use the Clarkson et al. (2008) scale to measure the extent of disclosure for a sample of firms from environmentally sensitive industries included in *Newsweek* magazine's first ever ranking of the greenest companies in America (McGinn 2009) and compare this to the companies' environmental performance using the Trucost environmental impact scores also reported by *Newsweek*. In contrast to Clarkson et al. (2008) and consistent with the legitimacy-based research, Cho et al. report a significant negative relation. Thus, rather than being due to industry focus or disclosure measurement, Cho et al. suggest the positive relations found by Clarkson et al. (2008, 2011) may instead be due to the latter studies' inclusion of numerous smaller firms in their samples, a factor that also applies to Al-Tuwaijri et al. (2004).

Rather than trying to reconcile the differences in results between the legitimacy-based and the VDT-based environmental disclosure research, Cho, Guidry et al. (2012) instead investigate whether the disclosure of one specific item of environmental information – capital spending for pollution abatement and control – appears to be used to signal a superior, but unobservable, corporate environmental strategy. According to Cho et al., if the signaling argument is valid, disclosing firms would be expected to exhibit better future environmental performance than non-disclosing companies. Based on a sample of 119 U.S. firms drawn from the 2006 *Fortune* 500, Cho et al. determine the change in total TRI releases across 1 year, 2 year, and 3 year windows. They report no significant differences in improvement across disclosing and non-disclosing companies, and the results hold in multi-variate analyses controlling for firm size, industry classification, and capital spending intensity. These authors thus conclude that the choice to disclose environmental capital expenditure data does not appear to signal superior future environmental performance, and they thus question the validity of the VDT arguments.

Overall, the preponderance of the evidence makes a fairly strong case that corporate environmental disclosure seems to be more about fostering an image of environmental concern than about providing accountability for environmental actions. Of course, if the attempts at legitimization made no differences, the use of disclosure as a tool of impression management wouldn't really matter. Unfortunately, that doesn't seem to be the case.

## 10.5 Does Disclosure as Legitimation Matter?

Two recent studies attempt to identify whether corporate environmental disclosure appears to reduce exposures to potential social and political exposures. Freedman and Patten (2004), the first of the two, examine the issue relative to investor behavior. More specifically, they investigate the market reaction to the unexpected proposal for changes in the U.S.'s Clean Air Act in 1989 and attempt to determine whether environmental performance information recently available through TRI influenced that reaction across firms. However, they also examine whether prior levels of environmental disclosure serve to mitigate negative market reactions to the announcement. They find, based on an analysis of 112 companies subject to TRI reporting requirements, that companies with higher levels of TRI air releases suffered more negative market adjustments at the time of the proposal but that companies with more extensive prior environmental disclosure suffered less negative reactions. By mitigating market impacts associated with poor performance, voluntary disclosure, as argued by Freedman and Patten, may be reducing the impacts that 'information as regulation' programs such as TRI might have in improving corporate environmental performance.

From a slightly different perspective, Cho, Guidry et al. (2012), in addition to investigating the relation between environmental performance and environmental disclosure, as discussed above, also examine the impacts of performance and disclosure on assessments of companies' environmental reputations.[11] They also test whether a proposed mediating factor, membership in the Dow Jones Sustainability Index (DJSI), is also related to these constructs. Focusing only on firms from environmentally sensitive industries, Cho et al.'s results indicate that more extensive environmental disclosure is positively and significantly associated with membership in the DJSI and environmental reputation measures, while, contrary to normative expectations, environmental performance is negatively related to both. That is, firms with worse environmental performance have better reputation scores than better performing companies, and they are also more likely to be included in the DJSI. Cho et al. (2012) and Cho, Guidry et al. (2012) argue these unexpected relations are due to the mitigating impacts of environmental disclosure, given that, as already noted above, they also find that the extent of the disclosure is negatively related to the environmental performance measure (worse performers have more extensive disclosure). The authors summarize the potential harm these findings suggest by noting "to the extent that this disclosure lessens the potential negative effects of performance … [it] may actually reduce the incentives companies have for bettering their actual environmental performance in the future" (Cho, Guidry et al. 2012, 23).

## 10.6 Conclusion – Moving from Legitimation to Accountability

As it currently exists, environmental reporting appears to be more about 'thickening the veil' that shrouds corporate environmental impacts than providing the transparency with respect to those activities and consequences that would seem to be in the public interest. On the positive side, however, the past decade has seen increasing guidance being provided, particularly from the GRI, on how organizations can better and more fully report on their environmental (as well as their social) impacts. But while this increased guidance is, I believe, a step in the right direction, it alone won't transform environmental disclosure from being an act of legitimation into being a true reflection of accountability. To illustrate, Dingwerth and Eichinger (2010) examined the greenhouse gas emissions disclosures for a sample of ten international auto manufacturers. They note that while all ten claimed to be in conformance with GRI reporting guidelines, the variability in the way the data were aggregated and the emphasis on qualitative as opposed to quantitative targets made comparisons across companies virtually impossible.

Unfortunately, I believe that even if the issues of comparability can be resolved, enhanced reporting guidelines alone are not likely to bring corporate environmental

[11] In a prior study, Toms (2002) provides evidence that perceptions of corporate reputation for a sample of U.K. firms were significantly associated with the extent of the companies' environmental disclosures. However, Toms does not include a measure of actual environmental performance in his analysis.

disclosure into accord with the public interest. The problem, as noted by, for example, Gray and Bebbington (2000), is that as long as the reporting takes place as a voluntary activity, it will reflect only those aspects of performance that organizations are willing to release. As they summarize, it can "only be a legitimation device and not an accountability mechanism" (Gray and Bebbington 2000, 16).

Accordingly, I believe that to transform corporate environmental reporting into a tool of transparency and accountability we need to establish a framework that, like financial reporting, requires organizations to disclose a collective set of information on environmental performance and related issues where the data are defined and measured in a similar way. One mechanism for accomplishing that change is to combine environmental (and social) disclosure into a reporting package that is integrated across environmental, social, and financial dimensions, and in the remaining chapter in this section of the monograph, Jeffrey and Perkins (2014) explore the possibility for movement in this direction. They assess the comparability of the underlying attributes desired of environmental reporting relative to those for financial reporting and also consider whether concerns with assurance on the non-financial information in an integrated report might inhibit movement toward a combined reporting package. Based on their analysis, Jeffrey and Perkins (2014) argue that the key dimensions underlying the financial reporting model are far narrower than those for environmental disclosure, and that without clear links between environmental and financial information, assurance of integrated reports would be difficult. As such, they do not believe that an integrated reporting model is currently feasible, and I concur. However, like me, they also argue that environmental (and social) reporting cannot be a voluntary initiative, it needs to be mandated. I could not agree more with this important claim, but I also feel compelled to note, that requiring mandated environmental disclosure is not a new concept.

More than three decades ago, Medawar (1976), in discussing the problem with the broader, but related concept of social accounting, noted that social accounting and social accountability are not the same thing. Social accountability, according to Medawar (1976, 393), is the "process in which those within corporate bodies, with decision-making powers, propose, explain and justify the use of those powers to those without." He predicated this definition by noting:

> Business behaviour may cause nuisance, damage or loss and may cause real and widespread distress. If this problem has in time diminished in terms of the numbers who are affected by serious loss, the underlying problem remains the same. We have taken for granted too readily and for far too long that the purpose and practice of business owes society little or nothing more than it provides by its very existence. Profit, the business community argues, is in fact wealth for society, but of course this is not necessarily the case. Not only are many of the costs involved in generating corporate wealth borne by society rather than by the corporation, but it is also largely left to the corporation to decide both on the allocation of these costs and on the distribution of the wealth.

"It begs," he argued, "a political solution" (Medawar 1976, 392). Unfortunately, political solutions are difficult to bring about, particularly in a world where large multi-national corporations are major players in the political landscape. Therefore, I believe the burden remains on us, as champions of the public interest, to continue to explore, and to bring to light, the consequences and the potential costs of allowing corporate environmental disclosure to continue as a voluntary regime. My hope is that with enough credible information on the harm that corporate voluntary disclosure allows, even those in the political arena will be compelled to move toward a mandated model. After all, it is only through mandatory reporting that we can make environmental disclosure a tool not of corporate legitimation, but instead a tool of the public interest.

## References

Aerts, W., and D. Cormier. 2009. Media legitimacy and corporate environmental communication. *Accounting, Organizations and Society* 34(1): 1–27.

Al-Tuwaijri, S.A., T.E. Christensen, and K.E. Hughes II. 2004. The relations among environmental disclosures, environmental performance, and economic performance: A simultaneous equations approach. *Accounting, Organizations and Society* 29(5–6): 447–471.

Barth, M.E., M.F. McNichols, and G.P. Wilson. 1997. Factors influencing firms' disclosures about environmental liabilities. *Review of Accounting Studies* 2: 35–64.

Blacconiere, W.G., and D.M. Patten. 1994. Environmental disclosure, regulatory costs, and changes in firm value. *Journal of Accounting and Economics* 18: 357–377.

Brammer, S., and S. Pavelin. 2006. Voluntary environmental disclosures by large UK companies. *Journal of Business, Finance, and Accounting* 33(7–8): 1168–1188.

Brown, N., and C. Deegan. 1998. The public disclosure of environmental performance information – A dual test of media agenda setting theory and legitimacy theory. *Accounting and Business Research* 29(1): 21–42.

Chatterji, A.K., D.I. Levine, and M.W. Toffel. 2009. How well do social ratings actually measure corporate social responsibility? *Journal of Economics and Management Strategy* 18(1): 125–169.

Cho, C.H., and D.M. Patten. 2007. The role of environmental disclosures as tools of legitimacy: A research note. *Accounting, Organizations and Society* 32(7–8): 639–647.

Cho, C.H., and D.M. Patten. 2008. Did the GAO get it right? Another look at corporate environmental disclosure. *Social and Environmental Accounting Journal* 28(1): 21–32.

Cho, C.H., R.W. Roberts, and D.M. Patten. 2010. The language of U.S. environmental disclosure. *Accounting, Organizations and Society* 35(4): 431–443.

Cho, C.H., M. Freedman, and D.M. Patten. 2012. Corporate disclosure of environmental capital expenditures: A test of alternative theories. *Accounting, Auditing and Accountability Journal* 25(3): 486–507.

Cho, C.H., R.P. Guidry, A.M. Hageman, and D.M. Patten. 2012. Do actions speak louder than words? An empirical investigation of corporate environmental reputation. *Accounting, Organizations and Society* 37(1): 14–25.

Clarkson, P.M., Y. Li, G.D. Richardson, and F.P. Vasvari. 2008. Revisiting the relation between environmental performance and environmental disclosure: An empirical analysis. *Accounting, Organizations and Society* 33(4–5): 303–327.

Clarkson, P.M., Y. Li, G.D. Richardson, and F.P. Vasvari. 2011. Does it really pay to be green? Determinants and consequences of proactive environmental strategies. *Journal of Accounting and Public Policy* 30: 122–144.

Cormier, D., and M. Magnan. 1999. Corporate environmental disclosure strategies: Determinants, costs and benefits. *Journal of Accounting, Auditing and Finance* 14(4): 429–451.

Deegan, C. 2002. Introduction: The legitimising effect of social and environmental disclosures – A theoretical foundation. *Accounting, Auditing and Accountability Journal* 15(3): 282–311.

Deegan, C. 2007. Organizational legitimacy as a motive for sustainability reporting. In *Sustainability accounting and accountability*, ed. J. Unerman, J. Bebbington, and B. O'Dwyer, 127–149. London: Routledge.

Deegan, C., and B. Gordon. 1996. A study of environmental disclosure practices of Australian corporations. *Accounting and Business Research* 26(3): 187–199.

Deegan, C., and M. Rankin. 1996. Do Australian companies report environmental news objectively? An analysis of environmental disclosures by firms prosecuted successfully by the environmental protection authority. *Accounting, Auditing and Accountability Journal* 9(2): 50–67.

Deegan, C., M. Rankin, and P. Voght. 2000. Firms' disclosure reactions to major social incidents: Australian evidence. *Accounting Forum* 24(1): 101–130.

Dingwerth, K., and M. Eichinger. 2010. Tamed transparency: How information disclosure under the global reporting initiative fails to empower. *Global Environmental Politics* 10(3): 74–96.

Dowling, J., and J. Pfeffer. 1975. Organization legitimacy: Social values and organizational behavior. *The Pacific Sociological Review* 18(1): 122–136.

Fekrat, M.A., I. Inclan, and D. Petroni. 1996. Corporate environmental disclosures: Competitive disclosure hypothesis using 1991 annual report data. *The International Journal of Accounting* 31(2): 175–195.

Freedman, M., and D.M. Patten. 2004. Evidence on the pernicious effect of financial report environmental disclosure. *Accounting Forum* 28(1): 27–41.

Freedman, M., and C. Wasley. 1990. The association between environmental performance and environmental disclosure in annual reports and 10Ks. *Advances in Public Interest Accounting* 3: 183–193.

Gamble, G.O., K. Hsu, and R. Radke. 1995. Environmental disclosures in annual reports and 10Ks: An examination. *Accounting Horizons* 9(3): 34–54.

Gray, R., and J. Bebbington. 2000. Environmental accounting, managerialism and sustainability. *Advances in Environmental Accounting and Management* 1: 1–44.

Gray, R., R. Kouhy, and D. Lavers. 1995. Corporate social and environmental reporting: A review of the literature and a longitudinal study of UK disclosure. *Accounting, Auditing and Accountability Journal* 8(2): 47–77.

Hackston, D., and M.J. Milne. 1996. Some determinants of social and environmental disclosures in New Zealand companies. *Accounting, Auditing, and Accountability Journal* 9(1): 77–108.

Higginson, N., C. Simmons, and H. Warsame. 2006. Environmental disclosure and legitimation in the annual report – Evidence from the joint solutions project. *Journal of Applied Accounting Research* 8(2): 2–23.

Hopwood, A.G. 2009. Accounting and the environment. *Accounting, Organizations and Society* 34(4–5): 433–439.

Ingram, R.W., and K.B. Frazier. 1980. Environmental performance and corporate disclosure. *Journal of Accounting Research* 18(2): 614–622.

Jeffrey, C., and J.D. Perkins. 2014. Developing corporate reporting in the public interest: Should corporate social responsibility and financial reports be integrated? In *Accounting for the public interest: Perspectives on accountability, professionalism and role in society*, ed. S. Mintz. 177–200. Heidelberg: Springer.

Lindblom, C.K. 1994. The implications of organizational legitimacy for corporate social performance and disclosure. Presented at the critical perspectives on accounting conference, New York.

Magness, V. 2006. Strategic posture, financial performance, and environmental disclosure: An empirical test of legitimacy theory. *Accounting, Auditing and Accountability Journal* 19(4): 540–563.

McGinn, D. 2009. The greenest big companies in America. *Newsweekr*, September 28, 2009, 34–54.

Medawar, C. 1976. The social audit: A political view. *Accounting, Organizations and Society* 1(4): 389–394.

Merkl-Davies, D.M., and N.M. Brennan. 2007. Discretionary disclosure strategies in corporate narratives: Incremental information or impression management? *Journal of Accounting Literature* 26: 116–194.

Miles, R.H. 1987. *Managing the corporate social environment*. Englewood Cliffs: Prentice-Hall.

Milne, M.J., and D.M. Patten. 2002. Securing organizational legitimacy: An experimental decision case examining the impact of environmental disclosures. *Accounting, Auditing and Accountability Journal* 15(3): 372–405.
Mobus, J.L. 2005. Mandatory environmental disclosures in a legitimacy theory context. *Accounting, Auditing and Accountability Journal* 18(4): 492–517.
Patten, D.M. 1992. Intra-industry environmental disclosures in response to the Alaskan oil spill: A note on legitimacy theory. *Accounting, Organizations and Society* 17(5): 471–475.
Patten, D.M. 2000. Changing superfund disclosure and its relation to the provision of other environmental information. *Advances in Environmental Accounting and Management* 1: 101–121.
Patten, D.M. 2002a. Media exposure, public policy pressure, and environmental disclosure: An examination of the impact of TRI data availability. *Accounting Forum* 26(2): 152–171.
Patten, D.M. 2002b. The relation between environmental performance and environmental disclosure: A research note. *Accounting, Organizations and Society* 27(8): 763–773.
Shocker, A.D., and S.P. Sethi. 1974. An approach to incorporating social preferences in developing corporate action strategies. In *The unstable ground: Corporate social policy in a dynamic society*, ed. S.P. Sethi, 67–80. Los Angeles: Melville.
Suchman, M.C. 1995. Managing legitimacy: Strategic and institutional approaches. *Academy of Management Review* 20(3): 571–610.
Toms, J.S. 2002. Firm resources, quality signals and the determinants of corporate environmental reputation: Some UK evidence. *The British Accounting Review* 34(3): 257–282.
Verrecchia, R. 1983. Discretionary disclosure. *Journal of Accounting and Economics* 5: 179–194.
Walden, W.D., and B.N. Schwartz. 1997. Environmental disclosures and public policy pressure. *Journal of Accounting and Public Policy* 16: 125–154.
Warsame, H., D. Neu, and C.V. Simmons. 2002. Responding to 'Discrediting' events: Annual report disclosure responses to environmental fines. *Accounting and the Public Interest* 2: 22–40.
Watts, R., and J. Zimmerman. 1986. *Positive accounting theory*. Englewood Cliffs: Prentice-Hall.
Wiseman, J. 1982. An evaluation of environmental disclosures made in corporate annual reports. *Accounting, Organizations and Society* 7(1): 53–63.

# Part V
# Virtue and Public Interest Considerations of Bribery and Whistle-Blowing

# Chapter 11
# Facilitation Payments in International Business Transactions: Law, Accounting, and the Public Interest

**Cindy Davids**

## 11.1 Introduction

An increase in bribery and corruption has accompanied major growth in global trade and cross-border transactions over the last 50 years to the extent that in some quarters bribery has come to be regarded as a normal (and unavoidable) part of doing business in some jurisdictions (OECD 2007; Transparency International 2008). The public works, defence, minerals and resource exploration, real estate, and telecommunications sectors are particularly vulnerable (Riaño and Hodess 2008). A range of significant social and economic problems are recognised to flow from bribery and corruption, bringing a significant public interest dimension to this issue. As the managing director of Transparency International (TI) stated in a recent report from Big 4 Accounting firm Ernst and Young:

> The demand for people for the accountable use of power and an end to corruption is indeed one of the key social drivers of our time (de Swardt, in Ernst and Young 2012: 3).

Foreign bribery issues and problems arise in many cases through the activities of large multinational corporations and their subsidiaries, agents and intermediaries, often operating in developing world contexts (Riaño and Hodess 2008; OECD 2009; Hardoon and Heinrich 2011). The Ernst and Young (2012) report found that while the risks of bribery and corruption are rising, standards of practice within corporations that operate internationally are not, with an increasing willingness to make payments in order to obtain or retain business.

Illicit payments to foreign public officials bring about a range of harms, many of which are directly related to the manner in which bribery of public officials distorts processes such as public procurement and the awarding of major public sector construction contracts. Significant amongst the concerns are that such payments work

C. Davids (✉)
School of Law, Deakin University, Melbourne, Australia
e-mail: cindy.davids@deakin.edu.au

S. Mintz (ed.), *Accounting for the Public Interest: Perspectives on Accountability, Professionalism and Role in Society*, Advances in Business Ethics Research 4,
DOI 10.1007/978-94-007-7082-9_11, © Springer Science+Business Media Dordrecht 2014

against the appropriate operation of the global market and trading system, and consequences for inappropriate infrastructure development in developing nations (including unneeded, poorly designed, and/or costly projects, poor decisions about infrastructure priorities, and, in general, the awarding of contracts and other commercial advantages on the basis of a payment of bribes rather than on the merits of development proposals) (see Davids and Schubert 2011a). As noted in a recent OECD report:

> The bribery of foreign public officials in international business deals continues to take a major toll on the world economy, on companies that try to compete fairly, and on governments undermined by corruption. (Pieth, in OECD Working Group on Bribery 2012: 5).

In addition to the clear *economic* consequences, TI has characterised some of the many *social* and *human* consequences of bribery and corruption:

> When corruption allows reckless companies to disregard the law, the consequences range from water shortages in Spain, exploitative work conditions in China or illegal logging in Indonesia to unsafe medicines in Nigeria and poorly constructed buildings in Turkey that collapse with deadly consequences. (Zinnbauer et al. 2009: 120).

Whether the source of the bribery is domestic or foreign, bribery of public officials erodes good governance and ethical decision making in the public sector, undermining the clear obligations of public officials to serve the 'public interest'. Bribery also undercuts similar obligations – which may be explicit or implicit – that rest on business entities and agents who interact with the public sector in the context of provision of goods, services and related activities that are undertaken in the name of the public and the pursuit of public good. Perhaps the most pernicious dimension of the problem is the potential concentration of wealth and power in corrupt hands. This corruption undermines the rule of law and the operation of democracy, both through the effect on democratic representation and the contamination of public service standards in areas such as policing, customs, immigration, and related areas (see McFarlane 2001). Efforts to tackle (or at least minimise) bribery and other forms of corruption carry a clear and urgent public interest imperative.

In 1997 the member states of the OECD and several other observer states signed the *Convention on Combating Bribery of Foreign Public Officials in International Business Transactions* (hereafter "the Anti-bribery Convention" or "Convention"). The Convention requires member states to implement domestic legislation that criminalises the bribery of foreign officials. To date (as at the start of 2013), 39 countries have joined this "collective crackdown on corruption" (OECD Working Group on Bribery 2010: 3), and have implemented domestic legislation in accord with Convention requirements.

This chapter outlines the problem of bribery of foreign public officials and examines the practice, even in some of the most active jurisdictions in terms of overall condemnation of bribery of foreign officials, of continuing to allow so-called "facilitation payments" – payments made to "get things done" – as an exception to the legal definition of bribery. The continued legal acceptability of facilitation payments has come to be regarded as something of a loophole in the original Anti-bribery Convention (Zinnbauer et al. 2009: xxv). The chapter focuses on the general provisions of the Anti-bribery Convention and draws on experience and case examples in three prominent member countries: the USA, the UK, and Australia. Legislative and enforcement approaches in these three jurisdictions are compared and contrasted. These three countries have been chosen because (1) they are prominent members of the OECD, and signatories to the Convention; (2) they are comparable in terms of socio-cultural and legal systems; and, in addition, (3) they represent different positions on a spectrum of progress and experience in terms of compliance and enforcement of the Anti-bribery Convention.

The remainder of the chapter is organised as follows. Section 11.2 briefly outlines the key elements of the OECD Anti-Bribery Convention and considers how foreign bribery fits within, and relates to, broader anti-bribery frameworks. This includes an outline of the United States Foreign Corrupt Practices Act and the equivalent key legislative provisions in the UK and Australia. In Sect. 11.3, problems relating to the continued legal acceptability of facilitation payments are examined, considering both the rationale for the current state of play and the growing international disquiet with relation to the status quo in this area. Section 11.4 analyses the significance of accounting provisions within legal regimes designed to combat foreign bribery. Such provisions require that companies have systems for accurate record-keeping and internal control, both for the prevention of bribery and the appropriate treatment of facilitation payments (required in the case of the latter if they are to be afforded legal protection). In the United States significant corruption-related enforcement has been based on violation of accounting provisions. Progress that has been made in implementing the OECD Convention and enforcing anti-bribery laws is considered in Sect. 11.5, including the utilization of books and records provisions. Exemplar cases from each of the three jurisdictions (USA, UK, Australia) are briefly outlined to provide specific illustrations of progress in this arena. Section 11.6 outlines some key compliance issues relating to corporate policy and practice in respect of foreign bribery issues, including the need for adequate accounting. Section 11.7 concludes the chapter with a summary and reiteration of the manner in which law, accounting and public interest intersect in the arena of foreign bribery.

## 11.2 Criminalisation of Bribery of Foreign Officials

### *11.2.1 The Offence of Bribery*

Most countries have domestic (that is, within the borders of a legal jurisdiction) legislative regimes that are broadly aimed at combating corruption and bribery. These domestic legal regimes may be supplemented by a number of key international Conventions, such as the OECD Anti-Bribery Convention.[1] In the domestic

[1] To some extent, domestic legal regimes may be specifically designed for compliance with agreed international Convention obligations.

context, relevant legislation against corruption may take the form of prohibitions against embezzlement and illicit enrichment; misconduct in public office; various types of conspiracy, and similar offences. A problem with such legislative regimes is that, despite the appearance of a comprehensive approach (at least in the domestic arena) there is the potential for a kind of over-criminalisation in the form of multiple and overlapping offences, and inconsistent terminology. As noted by the OECD, following a thorough review of all jurisdictions in the Asia Pacific region (OECD 2011b), this can result in uncertain interpretation and may provide the context for *inertia* on the part of prosecuting and enforcement officials, thus undermining the effect of what may appear to be a rigorous legal regime.

As a form of corrupt conduct, bribery may take many forms in domestic law. Many jurisdictions have both general and specific forms of the offence of bribery and further break it down into active and passive forms. The extent of prohibition varies widely – for example, from the very specific offence of 'receipt or solicitation of secret commissions by an agent', to general and broadly encompassing bribery ordinances or anti-bribery laws. Regardless of the name given to the domestic offence, what most of these regimes have in common is that bribery is defined (in the business context) as involving: the payment or offer, or the receipt or demand, of anything of value, with the purpose of influencing a person to provide an unjust (business or related) advantage.

### *11.2.2 The Foreign Corrupt Practices Act (USA)*

Whilst many countries have a long history 'at law' of actively discouraging bribery of domestic public officials within their own sovereign borders in the manner outlined above, prohibition at an international level of bribery of foreign officials has been a relatively recent phenomenon with its roots in the passage of the United States Foreign Corrupt Practices Act (FCPA) in 1977 (15 USC § 78dd–1 *et seq.*). International action on criminalising foreign bribery was subsequently led by the USA following the introduction of the FCPA, which prohibited the practice in an attempt to close an apparent loophole that had allowed major US corporations to make highly questionable payments to a variety of foreign recipients in the context of various forms of corporate activity (Salbu 1997: 233). The FCPA was a response to the public exposure between 1974 and 1977 of transnational corrupt practices prevalent in the operations of a number of United States corporations, including the Lockheed bribery scandal that involved the payment of millions of dollars in bribes by the Lockheed Aircraft Corporation to secure US contracts with a Japanese airline for the manufacture of aircraft (see Schroth 2002; Koch 2005; Davids and Schubert 2011a). Investigations into the Watergate affair eventually led to dramatic revelations of both domestic and foreign corrupt practices by United States businesses (Santangelo et al. 2007; Osajda 2010: 2). The FCPA response was to introduce offences proscribing foreign bribery into the *United States Criminal Code*. Significant amendments in 1988 and 1998 broadened and tightened the relevant provisions (see Koch 2005; Carrington 2007).

The FCPA prohibits the "offer, payment, promise to pay, or authorization of the payment of any money, or offer, gift, promise to give, or authorization of the giving of anything of value" to a foreign official in order to influence that official in a way that advantages the payer (15USC §§78dd–1(a),2(a),3(a)). There is an explicit exception for "any facilitating or expediting payment" that is made to "expedite or to secure the performance of a routine governmental action" (§§78dd–1(b),2(b),3(b)) (the issue of facilitation payments is further considered later in the chapter).

The reaction of the corporate and commercial sector to the FCPA was, on the whole, negative. The fear was that the requirements imposed by the FCPA placed United States companies operating overseas at a competitive disadvantage (Salbu 1997). As a result, in 1988 the Congress called on the President of the United States "to seek the cooperation of OECD members in adopting FCPA standards" (Salbu 1997: 248), thus establishing an "executive charge" (Salbu 1997: 248) to foster *global* adherence to FCPA principles and policies. It was largely through the subsequent advocacy of the USA that the OECD Convention was developed.

### *11.2.3 International Framework: The OECD Convention*

The OECD *Convention on Combating Bribery of Foreign Public Officials in International Business Transactions* entered into force in 1999. It requires signatories to implement legislation to make bribery of foreign officials a criminal offence and to provide a framework for the prosecution of individuals and companies for engaging in this conduct. The preamble to the Convention clearly outlines international concerns about foreign bribery in the following terms:

> ... bribery is a widespread phenomenon in international business transactions, including trade and investment, which raises serious moral and political concerns, undermines good governance and economic development, and distorts international competitive conditions ... (OECD 2011a)

Article 1 of the Convention outlines the nature of the offence of bribery of a foreign public official in broad terms (see Exhibit A) such that the direct or indirect offer, promise, or provision of any "pecuniary or other advantage" to a foreign public official, with the purpose of influencing a person to act or refrain from acting in a way that assists the offeror to "obtain or retain business or other improper advantage". Inciting, aiding, abetting, or authorising bribery of a foreign public official is also to be criminalised in a manner that is consistent with the domestic laws of the relevant country.

It is evident from the Convention and official Commentaries to the Convention (see OECD 2011a) that the overriding concern regarding foreign bribery lies in the manner in which "public officials" exercise their "public functions", where the former includes:

> ... any person holding a legislative, administrative or judicial office of a foreign country, whether appointed or elected; any person exercising a public function for a foreign country, including for a public agency or public enterprise; and any official or agent of a public international organisation (Anti-Bribery Convention, ¶4).

**Exhibit A** The offence of bribery of foreign public officials

| Article 1 |
| --- |
| The offence of bribery of foreign public officials |
| 1. Each Party shall take such measures as may be necessary to establish that it is a criminal offence under its law for any person intentionally to offer, promise or give any undue pecuniary or other advantage, whether directly or through intermediaries, to a foreign public official, for that official or for a third party, in order that the official act or refrain from acting in relation to the performance of official duties, in order to obtain or retain business or other improper advantage in the conduct of international business |
| 2. Each Party shall take any measures necessary to establish that complicity in, including incitement, aiding and abetting, or authorisation of an act of bribery of a foreign public official shall be a criminal offence. Attempt and conspiracy to bribe a foreign public official shall be criminal offences to the same extent as attempt and conspiracy to bribe a public official of that Party |
| 3. The offences set out in paragraphs 1 and 2 above are hereinafter referred to as "bribery of a foreign public official" |

From the *OECD Convention on Combating Bribery of Foreign Public Officials in International Business Transactions* – OECD (2011a)

The Commentaries note that public function "includes any activity in the public interest, delegated by a foreign country" (OECD 2011a: 15 ¶12 – "Commentaries on the Convention on Combating Bribery of Foreign Public Officials in International Business Transactions", Adopted by the Negotiating Conference on 21 November 1997).

At the time of writing in 2013, a total of 39 countries have implemented legislation in accord with Convention requirements. The significance and reach of the Convention is not merely in the number of countries, but in the specific countries that have joined: the 34 OECD members, plus Argentina, Brazil, Bulgaria, Russia, and South Africa. The 39 State Parties to the Convention account for eighty percent of world exports and ninety percent of foreign direct investment (OECD 2012). The Convention has been described by the Secretary-General of the OECD as one of the "strongest standards the OECD has developed" to further its aim to "safeguard the health of the international economy" (OECD Working Group on Bribery 2010: 2).

The USA and UK were amongst the earliest signatories to the Convention, ratifying in late 1998, while Australia ratified in late 1999 and criminalised foreign bribery through an amendment to the *Commonwealth Criminal Code* (see Davids and Schubert 2011a, b).

## *11.2.4 Overview of Key Legislation and Elements of the Offence*

Jurisdictions enacting the OECD Anti-bribery Convention typically include in their legal provisions the key components of a *physical element* (conduct) and a *fault element* for the offence to be proven (see Davids and Schubert 2011a). The *physical* element can be demonstrated where the offeror, directly or indirectly, offers or provides a benefit to another person (the offeree). The term 'benefit' is usually given a wide meaning as is consistent with the Convention and is not restricted to 'property'. Common examples include money, travel, assets, access to eminent overseas schools and universities for an official's family, but may even extend to such things as career opportunities and the provision of valuable information (as long as the benefit offered or received is identifiable and quantifiable).

The *fault* element relates to an *intention* to influence a foreign public official (who may or may not be the direct recipient). The immediate recipient need not be the foreign official directly. This stipulation provides for situations where intermediaries are used, and their benefits to third parties are caught. However, in all cases, it must be proven that the benefit 'was not legitimately due' to a third party to induce the official to do something that would not ordinarily be required or expected by one's official duties. In this context, claims that the amount was nominal or that the benefit was customary, required, or officially tolerated provide no safe haven.

However there may be variations in the jurisdictional reach proscribed by various countries. Countries may apply different territorial criteria relating to the physical element of the offence – for example, requiring that some (or no) part of the offence was committed within the domestic jurisdiction. They may also apply nationality criteria to the offence – for example, applying the law to all citizens or residents, regardless of the specific location of the act of bribery (Davids and Schubert 2011a).

The key US FCPA provisions were outlined in Sect. 11.2.2. Until 2010, the UK relied on provisions in the *Prevention of Corruption Act 1906*, the common law offence of bribing a person in public office, and some provisions in other legislation as being sufficient to implement the Convention. The OECD Working Group on Bribery in International Business (1999), however, urged the UK to enact specific legislation to deal with the problem of foreign bribery. An initial response from the UK government was to strengthen their anti-bribery regime via the *Anti-Terrorism, Crime and Security Act 2001*, which included an extension to the jurisdiction of UK courts to include bribery committed abroad by UK nationals or incorporated bodies, and a widening of the definition of public bodies to encompass foreign public bodies. Subsequently, the new *Bribery Act 2010* has become the key piece of UK legislation that implements Anti-Bribery Convention requirements (OECD Working Group on Bribery in International Business 2011).

In Australia, the *Criminal Code Amendment (Bribery of Foreign Public Officials) Act 1999* (Cth) criminalised the practice of pursuing commercial advantage through transnational bribery of public officials. This Act was Australia's formal response to the OECD Convention, and was modelled on the US FCPA (see Attorney-General's Department 2011). Exhibit B provides the precise wording of the key legislative provisions in each of these three jurisdictions. Although each jurisdiction has used different structure and wording in their respective laws, the key elements in each provide that a person or corporation must not provide, offer, or cause an offer or promise the provision of a benefit to another person that is not legitimately due to that person, with the intent to influence a foreign public official (who may or may not be the immediate recipient) in the exercise of the official's duties so as to obtain

**Exhibit B** Key legislative provisions – USA, UK and Australia

| | Enacting legislation and key provisions |
|---|---|
| USA | *Foreign Corrupt Practices Act of 1977*<br>15 USC §§78dd–1(a),2(a),3(a)[a]<br>It shall be unlawful … to make use of the mails or any means or instrumentality of interstate commerce corruptly in furtherance of an offer, payment, promise to pay, or authorization of the payment of any money, or offer, gift, promise to give, or authorization of the giving of anything of value to—<br>(1) any foreign official for purposes of—<br>(A)<br>(i) influencing any act or decision of such foreign official in his official capacity,<br>(ii) inducing such foreign official to do or omit to do any act in violation of the lawful duty of such official, or<br>(iii) securing any improper advantage; or<br>(B) inducing such foreign official to use his influence with a foreign government or instrumentality thereof to affect or influence any act or decision of such government or instrumentality,<br>in order to assist such issuer in obtaining or retaining business for or with, or directing business to, any person … |
| UK | *Bribery Act 2010*<br>s 1<br>(1) A person ("P") is guilty of an offence if either of the following cases applies.<br>(2) Case 1 is where—<br>(a) P offers, promises or gives a financial or other advantage to another person, and<br>(b) P intends the advantage—<br>(i) to induce a person to perform improperly a relevant function or activity, or<br>(ii) to reward a person for the improper performance of such a function or activity.<br>s 6<br>(1) A person ("P") who bribes a foreign public official ("F") is guilty of an offence if P's intention is to influence F in F's capacity as a foreign public official.<br>(2) P must also intend to obtain or retain—<br>(a) business, or<br>(b) an advantage in the conduct of business.<br>(3) P bribes F if, and only if—<br>(a) directly or through a third party, P offers, promises or gives any financial or other advantage—<br>(i) to F, or<br>(ii) to another person at F's request or with F's assent or acquiescence, and<br>(b) F is neither permitted nor required by the written law applicable to F to be influenced in F's capacity as a foreign public official by the offer, promise or gift.[b] |

(continued)

**Exhibit B** (continued)

| | Enacting legislation and key provisions |
|---|---|
| Australia | *Criminal Code Amendment (Bribery of Foreign Public Officials) Act 1999*<br>Criminal Code s 70.2(1)<br>(1) A person is guilty of an offence if:<br>(a) the person:<br>(i) provides a benefit to another person; or<br>(ii) causes a benefit to be provided to another person; or<br>(iii) offers to provide, or promises to provide, a benefit to another person; or<br>(iv) causes an offer of the provision of a benefit, or a promise of the provision of a benefit, to be made to another person; and<br>(b) the benefit is not legitimately due to the other person; and<br>(c) the first-mentioned person does so with the intention of influencing a foreign public official (who may be the other person) in the exercise of the official's duties as a foreign public official in order to:<br>(i) obtain or retain business; or<br>(ii) obtain or retain a business advantage that is not legitimately due to the recipient, or intended recipient, of the business advantage (who may be the first-mentioned person) |

[a]The structure of the US law is that §78dd–1(a) applies to "issuer which has a class of securities ...", §78dd–1(b) applies to "any domestic concern, other than an issuer ...", and §78dd–1(c) applies to "any person other than an issuer ... or a domestic concern". Otherwise the wording of each provision is identical, thus the combined effect of the three provisions to cast a wide net
[b]The USA FCPA §§78dd–1(d),2(d),3(d) and the Australian Criminal Code s 70.3 include similar "affirmative defences" in separately numbered provisions of the relevant Acts

or retain business, or to obtain or retain a business advantage, that is not legitimately due to the recipient, where the payment is not permitted under the written law of the relevant (foreign) country.

Although enactment of the provisions of the Anti-bribery Convention requires that the person who is intended to be influenced is in fact a foreign public official, the UK *Bribery Act 2010* also prohibits offering or receiving foreign bribes within the private sector under the provisions of section 3 of the Act, which captures four broad categories of "relevant function or activity" to which the Act applies: "(a) any function of a public nature, (b) any activity connected with a business, (c) any activity performed in the course of a person's employment, (d) any activity performed by or on behalf of a body of persons (whether corporate or unincorporate)" (Bribery Act 2010, s3).

In both the US and Australian models the notion of "recipient" is given a wide definition, thus casting a relatively broad ambit. It includes any office-holder, member of the legislature, executive or judiciary of a foreign country; any person employed by or under contract for or in the service of a foreign government body. The scope of "recipient" extends even further to include any authorised intermediary of an official or even in certain circumstances persons purporting to be so.

## 11.3 Facilitation Payments

### *11.3.1 Acceptability*

Despite the apparent rigour of the action against foreign bribery discussed above, one category of payment to foreign public officials is still permitted in many jurisdictions and may be specifically recognised as a defence to charges of bribery: facilitation payments. These are "payments made to obtain routine services from public officials who provide these services as part of their customary duties" (Zinnbauer et al. 2009: 120) and may also be referred to more colloquially as "speed" or "grease" payments. These payments are generally made on an unofficial basis, and the payer is generally already entitled (legally or administratively) to the relevant action for which payment is made (Director of Public Prosecutions and Serious Fraud Office 2010). Commercial entities can often claim a legitimate tax deduction for facilitation payments.

The UK is one of the few countries that has, to date, prohibited facilitation payments (similar prohibitions are in force in France and Japan). However, both the USA and Australia allow facilitation payments for 'routine governmental action', and neither set a specific cap on the amount of what may be argued to be facilitation payments (Zinnbauer et al. 2009). Such 'grease payments' are regarded as a legitimate exception to the general anti-bribery framework provided that they are limited to the 'non-discretionary' acts of the official and limited to 'ordinarily and commonly-performed' actions in a number of specified circumstances (e.g. s70.4, *Criminal Code*, Australia). The focus is thus on the decision-making power of the recipient public official – for example, if the payment is made to 'speed up' an administrative process where the outcome is already known. Proponents for the legal acceptability of facilitation payments contrast this to a situation where the payment would be made to change the outcome of, for example granting a visa application – this type of payment-for-positive-result would clearly constitute a bribe.

### *11.3.2 Rationale for the Acceptability of Facilitation Payments*

There are several justifications given for this category of exception to generally applied bribery provisions, including arguments that facilitation payments do not involve the exercise of discretion by the official and therefore do not result in the same harms (largely because, it is argued, the benefit obtained is not an *undue* one). A variant on this argument is the idea that because a facilitation fee is one routinely required by the official, there is less moral culpability than in those situations in which larger bribes are paid voluntarily in order to influence the exercise of official discretion in specific cases (Nichols 2009).

In the USA, commentary surrounding the FCPA has often included the claim that it is not practically possible to do business in some countries without making facilitation payments, and that to implement a ban would unduly disadvantage USA companies. Interestingly, the original rationale for the 'facilitation payments' exception in the FCPA, as outlined in the report of the House of Representatives Committee on Interstate and Foreign Commerce, was somewhat more equivocal:

> The language of the bill is deliberately cast in terms which differentiate between [corrupt] payments and facilitating payments, sometimes called "grease payments". In using the word "corruptly", the committee intends to distinguish between payments which cause an official to exercise other than his free will in acting or deciding or influencing an act or decision and those payments which merely move a particular matter toward an eventual act or decision or which do not involve any discretionary action.
>
> … While payments made to assure or to speed the proper performance of a foreign official's duties may be reprehensible in the United States, the committee recognizes that they are not necessarily so viewed elsewhere in the world and that it is not feasible for the United States to attempt unilaterally to eradicate all such payments. As a result, the committee has not attempted to reach such payments. (US Congress 1977)

The FCPA defines "routine governmental action", for which facilitation payments are permitted as "… only an action which is ordinarily and commonly performed by a foreign official" in a number of standard government services such as: obtaining permits, licenses, or other official documents; processing governmental papers; scheduling inspections associated with contract performance; and "actions of a similar nature" (15 USC §§78dd-1(f),2(f),3(f)).

The legal acceptability of facilitation payments in the FCPA was carried into the official OECD Commentaries provided with the original Anti-bribery Convention. Here, the commentary suggested that "small 'facilitation' payments" did not constitute a bribery offence, and the following justification for this position was provided:

> Such payments, which, in some countries, are made to induce public officials to perform their functions, such as issuing licences or permits are generally illegal in the foreign country concerned. Other countries can and should address this corrosive phenomenon by such means as support for programmes of good governance. However criminalization by other countries does not seem a practical or effective complementary action.
>
> (OECD 2011a: 15 ¶9 – from "Commentaries on the Convention on Combating Bribery of Foreign Public Officials in International Business Transactions", Adopted by the Negotiating Conference on 21 November 1997)

During the 1999 Parliamentary debate on the Australian legislation, the Attorney-General argued that although facilitation payments may be illegal in the jurisdiction in which they are paid, foreign enforcement of this illegality was not appropriate due to the smaller size of the payments and their frequency (Commonwealth of Australia 1999). Section 70.4 of the Australian Commonwealth *Criminal Code* limits facilitation payments to situations where the payment is of minor value; is made to secure performance of minor and routine government action; and record-keeping and retention requirements are complied with. Mirroring the FCPA, the Australian provision includes a similar list of routine governmental actions in s70.4(2)(b) of the Code.

The key facilitation provisions discussed above are reproduced in Exhibit C.

**Exhibit C** Facilitation Payment exceptions – USA, UK and Australia

| | Key provisions |
|---|---|
| USA | 15 USC §§78dd–1(b),2(b),3(b)<br>(b) **Exception for routine governmental action**<br>Subsections (a) and (g) of this section shall not apply to any facilitating or expediting payment to a foreign official, political party, or party official the purpose of which is to expedite or to secure the performance of a routine governmental action by a foreign official, political party, or party official<br>15 USC §§78dd–1(f),2(f),3(f)<br>(3)<br>(A) The term "routine governmental action" means only an action which is ordinarily and commonly performed by a foreign official in—<br>(i) obtaining permits, licenses, or other official documents to qualify a person to do business in a foreign country;<br>(ii) processing governmental papers, such as visas and work orders;<br>(iii) providing police protection, mail pick-up and delivery, or scheduling inspections associated with contract performance or inspections related to transit of goods across country;<br>(iv) providing phone service, power and water supply, loading and unloading cargo, or protecting perishable products or commodities from deterioration; or<br>(v) actions of a similar nature<br>(B) The term "routine governmental action" does not include any decision by a foreign official whether, or on what terms, to award new business to or to continue business with a particular party, or any action taken by a foreign official involved in the decisionmaking process to encourage a decision to award new business to or continue business with a particular party |
| UK | *No exception for facilitation payments* |
| Australia | Criminal Code s 70.4<br>(1) A person is not guilty of an offence against section 70.2 if:<br>(a) the value of the benefit was of a minor nature; and<br>(b) the person's conduct was engaged in for the sole or dominant purpose of expediting or securing the performance of a routine government action of a minor nature; and<br>(c) as soon as practicable after the conduct occurred, the person made a record of the conduct that complies with subsection (3) …<br>(2) … *routine government action* is an action of a foreign public official that:<br>(a) is ordinarily and commonly performed by the official; and<br>(b) is covered by any of the following subparagraphs:<br>(i) granting a permit, licence or other official document that qualifies a person to do business in a foreign country or in a part of a foreign country;<br>(ii) processing government papers such as a visa or work permit;<br>(iii) providing police protection or mail collection or delivery;<br>(iv) scheduling inspections associated with contract performance or related to the transit of goods;<br>(v) providing telecommunications services, power or water;<br>(vi) loading and unloading cargo;<br>(vii) protecting perishable products, or commodities, from deterioration;<br>(viii) any other action of a similar nature; and |

(continued)

**Exhibit C** (continued)

| Key provisions |
|---|
| (c) does not involve a decision about: |
| (i) whether to award new business; or |
| (ii) whether to continue existing business with a particular person; or |
| (iii) the terms of new business or existing business; and |
| (d) does not involve encouraging a decision about: |
| (i) whether to award new business; or |
| (ii) whether to continue existing business with a particular person; or |
| (iii) the terms of new business or existing business |

## *11.3.3 Changing OECD Position*

In 2009, the OECD's position notably shifted from one of inaction or 'resigned acceptance' of facilitation payments to one of active dissuasion of their legal acceptability. Exhibit D provides the text of the relevant OECD recommendations. Even small facilitation payments were described as having a "corrosive effect" and it was recommended that countries should takes steps to "effectively combat the phenomenon", including encouraging companies to implement internal controls, ethics and compliance measures to prohibit or discourage their use. It was also noted that all company payments must be accurately accounted for in corporate books and financial records. This shift represents a change of position and a tightening of the anti-bribery regime. Far from the 'harmless' implication that previously attached to such payments, facilitation payments are explicitly now recognised to be "harmful, as

**Exhibit D** OECD Recommendations for Further Combating Bribery of Foreign Public Officials

THE COUNCIL [for Further Combating Bribery of Foreign Public Officials in International Business Transactions]

...

VI. RECOMMENDS in view of the corrosive effect of small facilitation payments, particularly on sustainable economic development and the rule of law, Member countries should:

i) undertake to periodically review their policies and approach on small facilitation payments in order to effectively combat the phenomenon;

ii) encourage companies to prohibit or discourage the use of small facilitation payments in internal company controls, ethics and compliance programmes or measures, recognising that such payments are generally illegal in the countries where they are made, and must in all cases be accurately accounted for in such companies' books and financial records.

VII. URGES all countries to raise awareness of their public officials on their domestic bribery and solicitation laws with a view to stopping the solicitation and acceptance of small facilitation payments.

Source: OECD Working Group on Bribery in International Business Transactions (2009)

they are funnelled up through the system and help nurture and sustain corrupt bureaucracies, political parties and governments" (Zinnbauer et al. 2009: xxv).

Part of the concern over the legal acceptability of facilitation payments is that while the term itself has a specific and narrow legal meaning, it is often used colloquially to describe an array of payments or benefits that have come to be associated with doing business. Many businesspeople think of corporate hospitality and gifts as simply facilitating (or 'greasing') the wheels of business/client relationships. A 2006 survey of UK accountants working in or with small and medium enterprises (SMEs) (ACCA 2007), found a discernible lack of clarity on what constitutes bribery and corruption and a general pessimism about the capacity to make appropriate distinctions between bribery and corruption and related scenarios such as the provision of corporate hospitality, contract-related consultancy fees, facilitation fees, business-related gifts, unsolicited payments, and preferential treatment by regulatory officials.

Action in the USA has focused on raising awareness of the nature of facilitation payments and generally discouraging their use, but there have been no formal moves to change the relevant FCPA provisions. At the time of writing, Australia is formally reviewing the facilitation payments defence to foreign bribery, with an official discussion paper opened for public comment in late 2011 (Attorney-General's Department 2011). In part as a response to the clear imperative from the OECD to "combat" facilitation payments (OECD Working Group on Bribery in International Business Transactions 2009), the Australian Government is considering the removal of the provision in the *Criminal Code* that permits this as a defence to bribery, together with the removal of tax deductibility for facilitation payments. As noted earlier, the UK Bribery Act does not specifically provide for a facilitation payments defence.

The continued legal acceptance of facilitation payments in most jurisdictions has come to be regarded as "one of the most controversial issues in anti-bribery legislation" (Zinnbauer et al. 2009: xxv).

## 11.4 Regulatory Language and Accounting Provisions

### *11.4.1 The Importance of Accounting: Books and Records, Internal Controls*

A requirement on corporations to keep accurate records, including in relation to transactions involving foreign bribery (and facilitation payments), is a key element of the OECD Convention. The Convention requires member states to prohibit accounting practices that conceal foreign bribery, requiring that measures be taken in relation to several key dimensions of the accounting and auditing process that may be implicated in the process of bribing foreign public officials or concealing

**Exhibit E** OECD Convention on Combating Bribery of Foreign Public Officials in International Business Transactions (extract)

| Article 8 |
|---|
| Accounting |
| 1. In order to combat bribery of foreign public officials effectively, each Party shall take such measures as may be necessary, within the framework of its laws and regulations regarding the maintenance of books and records, financial statement disclosures, and accounting and auditing standards, to prohibit the establishment of off-the-books accounts, the making of off-the-books or inadequately identified transactions, the recording of non-existent expenditures, the entry of liabilities with incorrect identification of their object, as well as the use of false documents, by companies subject to those laws and regulations, for the purpose of bribing foreign public officials or of hiding such bribery<br>2. Each Party shall provide effective, proportionate and dissuasive civil, administrative or criminal penalties for such omissions and falsifications in respect of the books, records, accounts and financial statements of such companies |

such bribery. Thus, although there may be an apparent immediate business interest to disguise bribes or other similar payments through ‘creative’ forms of accounting, such action is not deemed to be in the public interest and the force of law is to be used to reinforce this position: the connection between law, accounting, and public interest is quite tight in terms of these requirements.

Member states are to: require the maintenance of adequate accounting books and records, financial statement disclosures, and application of accounting and auditing standards by companies; establish provisions that prohibit the establishment of off-the-books accounts or transactions and the recording of non-existent expenditures or entry of incorrectly described liabilities, and the use of false documents. Countries are required to “provide effective, proportionate and dissuasive civil, administrative or criminal penalties for omissions and falsifications in respect of the books, records, accounts”. Exhibit E provides the text of the relevant article of the Anti-Bribery Convention.

Article 8 of the Anti-Bribery Convention clearly reflects the approach taken earlier in the USA FCPA. The FCPA amended the *Exchange Act 1934* (US) to require issuers of securities registered with the Securities and Exchange Commission (SEC) to “make and keep books, records and accounts, which, in reasonable detail, accurately and fairly reflect the transactions and dispositions of the assets of the issuer” (15USC §78m(b)(2)(A) (2006)). Companies must also establish adequate accounting control systems to provide reasonable assurance that transactions are properly authorised (§78m(b)(2)(B)). These provisions are crucial to companies that seek to rely on a facilitation payments defence to a charge of foreign bribery, since the accounting for any such payments must be in accordance with these requirements.

Whilst the FCPA has been the dominant model in both the formation of the Convention and for specific legal approaches in many other jurisdictions, few (including Australia) have mirrored this key aspect of the US foreign bribery legislation. However, other legislation in these jurisdictions imposes general obligations on corporations to keep sufficient and accurate accounting records – section 386 of the UK Companies Act (s 386); section 286 of the Australian Corporations Act 2001 (Cth). These records are primarily for the purposes of being able to disclose "with reasonable accuracy" the financial position of the company (UK) or to "enable true and fair financial statements to be prepared and audited" (Australia). Corporations in the UK or Australia that conceal foreign bribery through inaccurate or vague financial record keeping will clearly breach these requirements of the Companies Act or Corporations Act, constituting an offence under the Act. Penalties are likely to be much lower than those applied under the FCPA accounting provisions, and there appears to be little enforcement appetite for pursuing these channels for foreign bribery offences in Australia and the U.K. (see Davids and Schubert 2011a). However the recent successful prosecution of a senior executive on a 'false accounting' charge in connection with an ongoing foreign bribery case in Australia may signal a change of tact in relation to prosecutorial enforcement strategies.

Breaches of the accounting requirements of the FCPA are regarded as criminal if they involve the knowing circumvention of, or failure to implement, such controls, or the knowing falsification of a book, record or account; or "wilful blindness", as may, for example, be demonstrated by a deliberate refusal to enquire into such matters (Sebelius 2008: 586; Davids and Schubert 2011a: 109). Claims of ignorance as a defence can often be defeated on the facts of the case – that is, evidence of circumstances that demonstrate that the accused was not ignorant of the matters claimed (OECD Working Group on Bribery 2009).

These provisions do not imply a need for proof of specific act/s of bribery, because evidence of false or inaccurate accounts is sufficient to secure a conviction, thus many evidentiary difficulties related to proving allegations of bribery (which may include the need to prove a long chain of acts and offences that lead to the act of bribery itself – see Davids and Schubert 2011b: 325) are overcome. Significant penalties can be imposed for such knowing breaches: up to US$5 million and 20 years imprisonment (§78ff(a)).

The above accounting provisions can come into play in circumstances where foreign agents are engaged by a company, and sham contracts or inflated commissions, for example, are utilised, but are not accurately recorded in the books of account. Parent entities are still exposed if the foreign agent is "engaged by a subsidiary or affiliate, and even if the improper recording is made in that subsidiary's or affiliate's books and records" (Koehler 2009: 402). As Koehler (*ibid.*) notes:

> The enforcement theory is that the subsidiary's or affiliate's books and records are consolidated with the parent's books and records for financial reporting purposes. A parent company will also face internal controls exposure on the theory that had the parent implemented sufficient internal controls throughout its organization, the improper payment would never had occurred.

**Exhibit F** Typical record-keeping requirements for acceptable facilitation payment

| |
|---|
| Description of the benefit secured and the circumstances; |
| Date of the benefit; |
| Amount/gift/value; |
| Country in which the benefit was secured; |
| Method of payment; |
| Date of benefit to the company; |
| Identity and position of the foreign public official or other person; |
| A signature on the record by the Company's authorizing officer or other identification |

Draws on: Income Tax Assessment Act 1997, Australia, s26–52

The United States SEC has a strong record of corruption-related enforcement based on violation of the books and records provisions, but in many non-US jurisdictions the proof of false or inaccurate accounting or internal controls is, on its own, insufficient to secure a conviction (OECD Working Group on Bribery 2009).

### *11.4.2 Public Interest Considerations*

Accurate record-keeping is a key element in a business being able to claim that a payment was merely for facilitation of routine government action, as a defence to an accusation that the payment was a bribe. Typically, a number of specific pieces of information are required by a country's respective tax regime – for example, requirements under the Australian Income Tax Assessment Act are summarised in Exhibit F. Clearly, failure to keep detailed records such as these would render an amount as non-deductible for tax purposes, but, more broadly, it is likely to invalidate a facilitation payment defence to a charge of foreign bribery.

The situation under the UK *Bribery Act* remains uncertain. Facilitation payments are not distinguished from bribes in the Act (therefore not offering an explicit defence, as in Australia or the USA), but the practice of facilitation payments may not necessarily be *prosecuted*. The Serious Fraud Office (SFO) has issued joint guidance on the matter, along with the Director of Public Prosecutions, and has included an outline of several public interest factors that may tend in favour of or against prosecution in matters involving facilitation payments, as outlined in Exhibit G.

The Guidance makes it clear that there is "no exemption [in the Bribery Act] in respect of facilitation payments" and that "[a] prosecution will usually take place unless the prosecutor is sure that there are public interest factors tending against prosecution which outweigh those tending in favour" (p. 9). The overall emphasis in the new UK anti bribery regime (*Bribery Act* 2010) is on companies proving that they have 'adequate procedures' in place and a genuine cultural commitment to non acceptance of bribery including routine facilitation payments.

**Exhibit G** Public interest factors in prosecution decisions (UK)

| Factors tending in favour of prosecution: | Factors tending against prosecution: |
|---|---|
| Large or repeated payments are more likely to attract a significant sentence (Code 4.16a); | A single small payment likely to result in only a nominal penalty (Code 4.17a); |
| Facilitation payments that are planned for or accepted as part of a standard way of conducting business may indicate the offence was premeditated (Code 4.16e); | The payment(s) came to light as a result of a genuinely proactive approach involving self-reporting and remedial action (additional factor (a) in the Guidance on Corporate Prosecutions); |
| Payments may indicate an element of active corruption of the official in the way the offence was committed (Code 4.16 k); | Where a commercial organisation has a clear and appropriate policy setting out procedures an individual should follow if facilitation payments are requested and these have been correctly followed; |
| Where a commercial organisation has a clear and appropriate policy setting out procedures an individual should follow if facilitation payments are requested and these have not been correctly followed | The payer was in a vulnerable position arising from the circumstances in which the payment was demanded |

Source: Director of Public Prosecutions and Serious Fraud Office (2010: 8–9)

## 11.5 Enforcement

### *11.5.1 Progress in Enforcement*

The OECD has a Working Group that periodically monitors how countries are meeting their obligations under the Anti-Bribery Convention. In 2009, the OECD Working Group on Bribery provided the first publicly available official data on the enforcement efforts undertaken by Parties to the Convention. According to data provided by member countries to the OECD Working Group on Bribery, and reported in the Working Group's Annual Report (2009: 25–26), action in 13 different countries had resulted in 148 individuals and 77 entities (legal persons) being criminally sanctioned by the end of 2009. At least 40 of the sanctioned individuals had been sentenced to prison for foreign bribery, with the largest fine for a company being €1.24 billion (being a combination of several fines). There were approximately 280 ongoing investigations, and criminal charges pending against approximately 180 individuals and 20 entities.

Most of this reported action and the associated outcomes related to prosecutions in the USA, with some 60 individuals and entities sanctioned. Six other countries (notably Italy, Hungary, Germany, and Luxembourg; with a small number of cases in Japan, Sweden, Switzerland and the UK) had also successfully prosecuted and sanctioned individuals and entities.

In the 2010 Annual Report of the OECD Working Group (the latest OECD data available at the time of writing), it was reported that the total number of individuals and entities that had been criminally sanctioned had risen to 199 and 91, respectively, with at least 54 individuals sentenced to terms of imprisonment. Most of the additional criminal action had been in the USA and Germany, with a small number of new successful prosecutions in the UK and Switzerland. It was further reported that there were approximately 260 ongoing investigations in 15 countries, with criminal charges pending against more than 120 individuals and 20 entities in 5 countries.

TI also undertakes regular assessment based on in-country expert review of data regarding the investigation, prosecution, and sanctions record of the relevant countries (this includes, but is not limited to, data from the OECD Working Group on Bribery). Recent TI assessments indicate that most member states continue to score poorly, with very little enforcement activity and only a small number of cases investigated (Heimann and Dell 2010). Some progress in 2010 was described by TI as "very positive", with the number of countries rated as "active" in enforcement increasing from four to seven (Heimann and Dell 2010: 8), but overall progress was still too low to enable the Convention to succeed.

The USA was consistently regarded as "active; the UK was one of the countries that moved from "moderate" – having previously described as a "laggard" – to "active" in 2010; while Australia was one of the 21 countries consistently rated as exhibiting "little or no enforcement". It has been suggested by T.I that "lack of political will is the major cause of lagging enforcement", including both inadequate legislative action (the UK was characterised as being in this situation prior to the passage of the new Bribery Act) and a failure to provide adequate staffing and funding for enforcement authorities and agencies Heimann and Dell 2009: 6). In addition, "active obstruction of investigations and prosecutions" (Heimann and Dell 2010: 8) is a cause of lack of progress in curbing foreign bribery in international business transactions.

Concern was expressed that the Convention "may be losing momentum", again primarily due to a lack of political will (Heimann et al. 2011: 5). The reported data make it clear that, apart from the OECD itself, the key source of current pressure on companies to 'clean up their act' on foreign corruption and bribery is coming from the enforcement activities of activist jurisdictions such as the USA, the UK, and Germany.

### *11.5.2 Utilization of Books and Records Provisions*

The strong record in the USA of corruption-related enforcement efforts, based on violation of accounting "books and records" and "internal control" provisions, demonstrates the determination of the SEC and prosecuting authorities. This enforcement track-record also sends a significant signal to the USA corporate sector (see Davids and Schubert 2011a, b). These provisions are crucial to companies that seek to rely on a 'facilitation payments' defence to a charge of foreign bribery, since the accounting for any such payments must be in accordance with the rules and failure to account correctly provides an avenue for prosecution and enforcement even where it may be more difficult to meet the evidentiary burden to successfully prosecute bribery charges.

### 11.5.3 Exemplar Prosecutions: USA

The USA has the strongest and most consistent prosecution and enforcement record of all OECD Convention member countries, with dozens of companies and individuals having been convicted of foreign bribery offences and dozens more having been held civilly liable and been sanctioned under pre-prosecution agreements.

The SEC's enforcement record includes successful action against General Electric in relation to the UN Oil-for-Food scandal which provides an illustration of a preparedness to use the accounting provisions of the FCPA to full effect. In this case, it was found that the company and its subsidiaries failed to accurately record improper (and very large) kickbacks and surcharges, and failed to maintain adequate internal controls to prevent and detect such payments. The SEC charged GE and two of its subsidiaries alleging that the companies "made illegal kickback payments in the form of cash, computer equipment, medical supplies, and services to the Iraqi Health Ministry or the Iraqi Oil Ministry in order to obtain valuable contracts under the U.N. Oil for Food Program" (Securities and Exchange Commission 2010). The SEC settled these and associated matters for significant penalties, disgorgement (surrender of profits obtained by illegal acts) and interest:

> GE agreed to pay $23.4 million to settle the SEC's charges against the company as well as the two subsidiaries for which GE assumed liability upon acquiring: Ionics Inc. and Amersham plc. The SEC charged GE, Ionics and Amersham with violating the books and records and internal controls provisions of the FCPA. The SEC has now taken 15 FCPA enforcement actions against companies involved in Oil for Food-related kickback schemes with Iraq, recovering more than $204 million (Securities and Exchange Commission 2010; see also Davids and Schubert 2011b).

The case of the large engineering company Siemens provides a further example of the use of books and records provisions. In November 2006, the Munich offices of Siemens were raided following allegations of corrupt payments. The initial German investigation led to parallel investigations in other jurisdictions, including Argentina, Austria, Bangladesh, China, Greece, Hungary, Indonesia, Israel, Nigeria, and the USA. In December 2008, Siemens settled numerous FCPA violations with the US Department of Justice and the SEC commission with a record $800 million in penalties based on guilty pleas to a pervasive pattern of widespread bribery and illicit payments in excess of $1.36 billion in total. Siemens provisioned $4 billion to cover the debacle. Further prosecutions are likely to follow as 16 countries are still exploring allegations against the company (see Heimann and Dell 2009, 2010).

### 11.5.4 Exemplar Prosecutions: UK

In the UK, the SFO is the main law enforcement agency with responsibility for prosecuting foreign bribery offences. A small number of individuals and companies have been convicted of foreign bribery offences; some others have been fined under corporate compliance regulatory arrangements; and a small number have been subject to civil recovery orders (OECD Working Group on Bribery 2012).

The case of BAE Tanzania led to a conviction and sanctions for accounting-related misconduct (failure to keep sufficient accounting records) however specific foreign bribery allegations were not proven. The conviction resulted from a guilty plea rather than a trial. The matter involved the 2002 sale of a UK£25 m military radar system to the Tanzanian government. BAE admitted a failure to keep proper accounting records, relating in particular to a US$12.4 m payment to a Tanzanian middleman for 'marketing' purposes, but in settling the case with the SFO the company avoided any admission of corruption. The plea agreement between the company and the SFO set the financial penalties, including a fine of UK£0.5 m and an ex gratia payment of £29.5 m to the Tanzanian government "for the benefit of the people of Tanzania" (OECD Working Group on Bribery 2012: 73). BAE also agreed around the same time to pay a $400 m fine in the United States, after admitting to allegations relating to the sale of fighter planes to Saudi Arabia and Eastern Europe. UK proceedings in relation to the Saudi matter were controversially halted on the grounds of 'national security' (OECD Working Group on Bribery 2012). The BAE cases illustrate the complex web of accounting, legal, ethical, public interest, and political matters that may be implicated in foreign bribery cases.

### *11.5.5 Exemplar Prosecution: Australia*

Australia has been heavily criticised in the past for its lax enforcement efforts on bribery of foreign officials with the 2011 TI Progress Report still placing Australia in the category of "little or no enforcement" (Heimann et al. 2011). As Davids and Schubert (2011a) point out, the effectiveness of the Australian government's response against foreign bribery still awaits clarification by the courts, although at the time of writing, Australia is part-way through its first legal test of the anti-foreign bribery provisions.

Securency is an Australian joint venture company that manufactures and supplies polymer substrate used in banknotes in Australia and at least 28 other countries (the company was 50 % owned by the Reserve Bank of Australia subsidiary, Note Printing Australia, and 50 % owned by the UK-based Innovia Films, which manufactured the polymer. Allegations in this case are that executives of the company were responsible for millions of dollars in payments over several years (2003–2009) that were made to influence key foreign public officials to award note printing contracts to the company. The business model utilised overseas agents, paid on a commission basis, to secure contracts with foreign governments. A company-commissioned audit by KPMG (2010) revealed that agents were paid very large commissions by Securency ($47.5 million) and were very successful in growing the business globally, in particular through various Asian markets. The audit also revealed irregularities and failure to follow legal advice on payments to agents.

In July 2011 the Australian Federal Police commenced a string of arrests of eight senior executives of the company. It is alleged that they facilitated millions of dollars in payments designed to influence key foreign public officials to award note printing contracts to Securency. Charges are proceeding against the executives and are a result of joint investigations conducted by the Australian Federal Police, the UK's Serious Fraud Office, and Malaysia's Anti-Corruption Commission; there have been raids and searches in all three nations and arrests have also been made in Malaysia and the UK. It remains to be seen whether any of the executives will try to utilise a facilitation payments defence to the bribery charges (however, given the size of the payments overall, this seems unlikely). Prior to the commencement of the trial, allegations emerged that payments took many forms including the paying of English University tuition fees for the son of a senior official of Vietnam's Central Bank. As with the pattern in recent prosecutions by the US, it is possible that practices of facilitation payment may be bundled with bribery allegations.

## 11.6 Compliance Issues

### *11.6.1 Corporate Policy and Practice*

Corporate awareness of foreign bribery and associated accounting provisions such as those discussed above seems to be growing. A recent global anti-bribery and corruption survey (KPMG 2011) finding that around half of the USA and UK executives surveyed (responsible for anti-bribery and corruption matters within their companies) felt their companies were vulnerable to anti-bribery legislation violations in terms of improper recording of facilitation payments (54 % in the USA; 49 % in the UK). The maintenance of documentation to support adequate books and records was reported as a "very challenging" or "somewhat challenging" area by 34 % (USA) and 41 % (UK) of respondents. An Australian study that canvassed similar issues found that three quarters of the top 100 companies on the Australian Stock Exchange report that they are exposed to high risk sectors or countries where bribery is a potential problem (CAER 2011).

The Australian study found that 69 % of the top-100 companies on the ASX prohibit bribery in their corporate Codes of Conduct or in specific anti-bribery policies, compared with 76 and 86 % for top-100 companies in the USA and UK, respectively (CAER 2011). The findings on company policies towards facilitation payments also showed differences between the three jurisdictions. Almost all USA and UK respondents in the KPMG study reported that their company either prohibited facilitation payments outright or prohibited with an exception only for personal safety concerns; only 9 and 13 % of UK and USA respondents, respectively, reported that their company policies allowed for facilitation payments (KPMG 2011: 17). The Australian study found that only 16 % of Australian top-100 companies have policies that explicitly prohibit facilitation payments (CAER 2011: 14). For both the KPMG and the CAER studies the 2011 figures represented progress on the findings from earlier studies (2006 for CAER; since 2008 for KPMG). Of course, the translation of policy into action is the key issue, but these findings do suggest a growing awareness of relevant issues relating to foreign bribery.

Of some concern in the era of multinational corporations and growing international trade is the KPMG finding that corporate policies often do not address the legal regimes in jurisdictions other than their home countries; yet corporations and their employees may find themselves subject to such provisions. In relation to the specific findings referred to above, it should be noted that the anti-bribery laws of the USA, the UK, and Australia are applicable to multinational companies that come within their jurisdictional reach.

The extra-territorial component of domestic legal regimes arising from the OECD Convention is exemplified by the profiles of multinational operations caught through an increasing web of interconnected legal regimes and law enforcement processes and cooperation. Extra-territorial liability is clearly indicated in the high profile example of Siemens, as discussed above – it engaged in widespread foreign bribery practices in more than ten countries, involving several subsidiaries, different lines of business and thousands of payments, many through intermediaries. The current case against Securency under the Australian regime also exhibits the same patterns of multi-jurisdictional exposure.

### *11.6.2 Action and Awareness: Accounting Provisions and Law Enforcement*

High-profile enforcement actions such as the GE, Siemens and Securency cases can contribute to corporate awareness-raising of the legal position. The OECD working group continues to advocate that countries take "concrete and meaningful steps" in relation to:

> ... (v) company and business accounting, external audit, as well as internal control, ethics, and compliance requirements and practices ... (Recommendation III (v))

Addressing the need for "[a]dequate accounting requirements," the OECD specifically recommends that:

> i) Member countries shall ... take such measures as may be necessary, within the framework of their laws and regulations regarding the maintenance of books and records, financial statement disclosures, and accounting and auditing standards, to prohibit the establishment of off-the-books accounts, the making of off-the-books or inadequately identified transactions, the recording of non-existent expenditures, the entry of liabilities with incorrect identification of their object, as well as the use of false documents, by companies subject to those laws and regulations, for the purpose of bribing foreign public officials or of hiding such bribery;
> ii) Member countries should require companies to disclose in their financial statements the full range of material contingent liabilities;
> iii) Member countries shall ... provide effective, proportionate and dissuasive civil, administrative or criminal penalties for such omissions and falsifications in respect of the books, records, accounts and financial statements of such companies. (Recommendation X part A)

These recommendations clearly demonstrate an international recognition of the significance of strong accounting and internal control provisions within an anti-bribery regime. Awareness within companies must include active transmission of issues, rules, and practices to all employees through internal company process, including the dissemination of appropriate corporate cultures.

## 11.7 Conclusions: Foreign Bribery and the Intersection of Law, Accounting, and Public Interest

Bribery in the context of international business transactions, even when involving so-called facilitation payments, is now widely recognised to undermine good governance and ethical decision making by those who should be motivated solely by notions of 'public interest'. Although making payments to foreign officials is often characterized as necessary or justifiable in the name of 'getting things done' and 'doing business' (as in the standard rationalisation for the legal acceptability of facilitation payments), the longer-term corrosive effect on public sector values and the pursuit of the common good cannot be ignored.

Recent recommendations from the OECD Working Group on Bribery have emphasised the importance of tightening both the legal regime in relation to accounting, and the associated provisions relating to the facilitation payments loophole. As was noted in TI's *Global Corruption Report 2009*, business action must also come to match its rhetoric in this area, for "while businesses have declared their opposition to bribing foreign government officials, many nevertheless continue to use loopholes, such as facilitation payments, to suborn foreign officials" (Vogl, in Zinnbauer et al. 2009: 153).

Effectively dealing with facilitation payments would assist in attacking a 'culture of corruption'. It is generally recognised that whilst facilitation payments do not represent a problem of the same scale as bribery, they can be very socially damaging to the extent that they promote a cultural *acceptance* of corruption. This culture can eat away at governance structures and, ultimately, at the rule of law.

The analysis in this chapter demonstrates the significant role played by accounting practices in facilitating foreign bribery, and the possibility for effective legislative and enforcement action with regard to accounting (books and records) and internal control provisions to help combat the problem. Notwithstanding its acceptance of facilitation payments, the broader record of the USA in utilising the FCPA to implement the OECD anti-bribery agenda has exceeded the record of both the UK and Australia, with the use of the books and records provisions enabling considerable success for the SEC in obtaining settlements worth billions of dollars.

The accounting "books and records" and "internal control" provisions of the USA's FCPA have been a significant factor in the effectiveness of the law in combating foreign bribery. The strong record of enforcement efforts to date under these provisions demonstrates the determination of the prosecuting authorities, sending a significant signal to the USA corporate sector (see Davids and Schubert 2011a, b).

These provisions provide a clear route for the gathering of documentary evidence that can support a prosecution. The lower standard of proof required for civil prosecutions in relation to books and record provisions may also be a key factor in the success of these provisions. Jurisdictions beyond the USA could find that enacting similar measures into their domestic legal frameworks is beneficial from an enforcement perspective.

If the "increasing momentum of commitment" (ACCA 2007: 4) towards tackling the problem of foreign bribery is to be maintained, the somewhat artificial existence of facilitations payments in a grey area between bribery and corruption and clearly legitimate business activities must be tackled. The accounting profession has recognised both the general economic importance of the problem of corruption and its significance to the employers and clients of the profession (e.g. ACCA 2007; ICAEW 2010; KPMG 2011). This domain also represents a considerable challenge to the profession as it aims to meet its public interest obligations. There may be a need to broaden the range of accountants' knowledge, skills and expertise, to enable them to deal adequately with this area.

The broader role of accountants in providing advice to clients, employers, and policy-makers magnifies the role played by the profession in this arena. Facilitation payments and foreign bribery more generally is an area where there is a clear intersection between law, accounting, and the public interest.

## References


ACCA – The Association of Chartered Certified Accountants. 2007. *Bribery and corruption: The impact on UK SMEs*. London: ACCA.

Attorney-General's Department. 2011. Divisions 70 and 141 of the Criminal Code Act 1995: Assessing the 'facilitation payments' defence to the Foreign Bribery offence and other measures, Public Consultation Paper, 15 November 2011. http://wwwcrimeprevention.gov.au/Financialcrime/Pages/Briberyofforeignpublicofficials.aspx.

CAER – Corporate Analysis, Enhanced Responsibility. 2011. Anti-Corruption and Bribery Practices in Corporate Australia: A review of exposure to corruption and bribery risk across the S&P/ASX 200. Research Paper, Australian Council of Superannuation Investors, Melbourne.

Carrington, P.D. 2007. Law and transnational corruption: The need for Lincoln's law abroad. *Law and Contemporary Problems* 70(4): 109–138.

Commonwealth of Australia. 1999. Parliamentary debates, House of Representatives, Daryl Williams, Attorney-General, 3 June, 6044–6045.

Davids, C., and G. Schubert. 2011a. Criminalising foreign bribery: Is Australia's bark louder than its bite? *Criminal Law Journal* 35(2): 98–115.

Davids, C., and G. Schubert. 2011b. The global architecture of foreign bribery control: Applying the OECD convention. In *Handbook of global research and practice in corruption*, ed. A. Graycar and R.G. Smith, 319–339. Cheltenham/Northampton: Edward Elgar.

Director of Public Prosecutions and Serious Fraud Office (UK). 2010. Bribery Act 2010: Joint prosecution guidance of the director of the serious fraud office and the director of public prosecutions. London: Serious Fraud Office. http://www.sfo.gov.uk/media/167348/bribery%20act%20joint%20prosecution%20guidance.pdf.

Ernst and Young. 2012. *Growing beyond: A place for integrity. 12th Global Fraud Survey*. London: Ernst and Young.

Hardoon, D., and F. Heinrich. 2011. *Bribe payers index 2011*. Berlin: Transparency International.

Heimann, F., and G. Dell. 2009. Progress report 2009: OECD anti-bribery convention. Berlin: Transparency International.

Heimann, F., and G. Dell. 2010. *Progress report 2010: Enforcement of the OECD anti-bribery convention*. Berlin: Transparency International.

Heimann, F., G. Dell, and K. McCarthy. 2011. Progress report 2011: Enforcement of the OECD anti bribery convention. Berlin: Transparency International.

ICAEW – The Institute of Chartered Accountants in England and Wales. 2010. *Business and economic crime in an international context: A review of international law and practice in relation to crimes committed by or on behalf of business*. London: ICAEW.

Koch, R. 2005. The Foreign Corrupt Practices Act: It's time to cut back the grease and add some guidance. *Boston College International and Comparative Law Review* 28(2): 379–405.

Koehler, M. 2009. The Foreign Corrupt Practices Act in the ultimate year of its decade of resurgence. *Indiana Law Review* 43(2): 389–420.

KPMG. 2010. Assistance with enquiries into matters dealing with agents in overseas territories, 29 March, KPMG, obtained from www.abc.net.au/4corners/special_eds/20100524/money/docs/KPMG_report.pdf.

KPMG. 2011. *Global anti-bribery and corruption survey 2011*. Amsterdam: KPMG Forensic.

McFarlane, J. 2001. Corruption and the financial sector: The strategic impact. *Journal of Financial Crime* 9(1): 8–21.

Nichols, P.N. 2009. Who allows facilitating payments? *Agora without Frontiers* 14(4): 303–323.

OECD – Organisation for Economic Co-Operation and Development. 2007. *Bribery in public procurement: Methods, actors and counter-measures*. Paris: OECD Publications.

OECD – Organisation for Economic Co-Operation and Development. 2009. *OECD bribery awareness handbook for tax examiners*. Paris: OECD Centre for Tax Policy and Administration.

OECD – Organisation for Economic Co-Operation and Development. 2011a. *Convention on combating bribery of foreign public officials in international business transactions and related documents*. Paris: OECD.

OECD – Organisation for Economic Co-Operation and Development. 2011b. *The criminalisation of bribery in Asia and the Pacific*, ADB/OECD anti-corruption initiative for Asia and the Pacific. Paris: OECD.

OECD – Organisation for Economic Co-Operation and Development. 2012. *Foreign bribery factsheet*. Paris: OECD.

OECD Working Group on Bribery. 2009. *Annual report 2009*. Paris: OECD.

OECD Working Group on Bribery. 2010. *Annual report 2010*. Paris: OECD.

OECD Working Group on Bribery. 2012. *Phase 3 report on implementing the OECD anti-bribery convention in the United Kingdom*. Paris: OECD. March.

OECD Working Group on Bribery in International Business. 1999. *United Kingdom: Review of implementation of the convention and 1997 recommendation*. Paris: OECD.

OECD Working Group on Bribery in International Business. 2011. *Steps taken to implement and enforce the OECD convention on combating bribery of foreign public officials in international business transactions*. Paris: OECD.

OECD Working Group on Bribery in International Business Transactions. 2009. *Recommendation of the council for further combating bribery of foreign public officials in international business transactions*. Paris: OECD. 29 November.

Osajda, M. 2010. The FCPA and why it matters, world-check white papers, available at: www.world-check.com/whitepapers/2010. Accessed 30 Nov 2010.

Riaño, J., and R. Hodess. 2008. *2008 bribe payers index*. Berlin: Transparency International.

Salbu, S.R. 1997. Bribery in the global market: A critical analysis of the Foreign Corrupt Practices Act. *Washington and Lee Law Review* 54(1): 229–287.

Santangelo, B., G. Stein, and M. Jacobs. 2007. The Foreign Corrupt Practices Act: Recent cases and enforcement trends. *Journal of Investment Compliance* 8(3): 31–55.

Schroth, P.W. 2002. The United States and the international bribery conventions. *American Journal of Comparative Law* 50(Supplement): 593–622.

Sebelius, N. 2008. 'Foreign Corrupt Practices Act' (2008). *American Criminal Law Review* 45(2): 597–606.

Securities and Exchange Commission [USA]. 2010. SEC charges general electric and two subsidiaries with FCPA violations media release 2010–133, July 27, available at: http://www.sec.gov/news/press/2010/2010-133.htm.

Transparency International. 2008. *Business principles for countering bribery: Small and Medium Enterprise (SME) edition*. Berlin: Transparency International.

US Congress, House of Representatives, Committee on Interstate and Foreign Commerce. 1977. Report on the Unlawful Corporate Payments Act of 1977, 95th Cong., 1st sess., H. Rept. 95-640 (September 28, 1977).

Zinnbauer, D., R. Dobson, and K. Despota (eds.). 2009. *Global corruption report 2009: Corruption and the private sector*. Cambridge: Cambridge University Press (for Transparency International).

## Legislation

*Bribery Act 2010* (UK)
*Corporations Act 2001* (Cth) (Australia)
*Companies Act 2006* (UK)
*Criminal Code Act 1995* (Cth) (Australia)
*Foreign Corrupt Practices Act 1977, 15 USC§§78dd-1–78dd-3* (2006) (USA)
*Income Tax Assessment Act 1997* (Cth) (Australia)
*Proceeds of Crime Act 2002* (Cth) (Australia)
*United States Code*, 15 USC (2006) (http://www.law.cornell.edu/uscode)

# Chapter 12
# Whistle-Blowing in the Classroom: The Influence of Students' Perceptions of Whistleblowers

Richard A. Bernardi, Evan S. Goetjen, and Jennifer M. Brax

## 12.1 Introduction

Longstaff (2012) maintains that blowing the whistle is about protecting society from avoidable harm.[1] For example, one could cite the Enron crisis and Bernie Madoff's Ponzi scheme, which each resulted in $65 billion losses to society. To understand the magnitude of these losses, $65 billion is larger than the gross domestic product of 149 of the world's 215 countries (69.3 %) (Central Intelligence Agency 2012). The question becomes, where were the whistleblowers? Perhaps the well-publicized case of the tobacco industry's whistleblower Jeffrey Wigand served as a negative example of the consequences of blowing the whistle; the consequences of tobacco to society were cancer, heart disease and emphysema (CBSNEWS 2011).

The Ethics Resource Center (ERC 2012, p. 14) reported that the proportion of employees who witnessed and reported wrong doings increased from 53 % in 2005 to 65 % in 2011. This 12 % increase can probably be attributed to the potential incentives (i.e., from 10 to 30 % of the monetary sanction) offered to whistleblowers by the Sarbanes-Oxley Act and the Dodd-Frank Wall Street Reform and Consumer Protection Act (Mintz 2012a, b). However, the ERC (2012, p. 15) also reported that the rate of retaliation against whistleblowers increased from 12 % in 2007 to 22 % in 2011; consequently, the personal cost of blowing the whistle might be too high for many individuals (Ayers and Kaplan 2005) in the future. Bernardi et al. (2011, 2012b) reported that, while 92.8 and 81.9 (9.2 and 12.6) percent (respectively) of students in accounting courses had witnessed another student

[1] Peer reporting can be defined as "lateral control attempts that occur when an in-group member discloses a peer's wrongdoing to higher authorities outside the group" (Trevino and Victor 1992, p. 40).

R.A. Bernardi (✉) • E.S. Goetjen • J.M. Brax
Gabelli School of Business, Roger Williams University, Bristol, RI 02809, USA
e-mail: rbernardi@rwu.edu

S. Mintz (ed.), *Accounting for the Public Interest: Perspectives on Accountability, Professionalism and Role in Society*, Advances in Business Ethics Research 4,
DOI 10.1007/978-94-007-7082-9_12, © Springer Science+Business Media Dordrecht 2014

cheating (would report cheating).[2] While 65 % workers reported wrong doings, it is disturbing that only 11.3 % of students reported wrong doings between 2011 and 2012 (i.e., almost a six-fold difference in the rates).

Smyth and Davis (2003) sampled community college students – the majority of whom go on to 4-year institutions; they reported (p. 5) that, while almost all "respondents believe that cheating is ethically wrong (92 %), a surprising 45 % find cheating to be socially acceptable." Many students do not view academic dishonesty as severely as business dishonesty (Grimes 2004); in fact, about 80 % of the students indicated that they would help a friend to cheat (Davis et al. 1992). The rate of cheating has been steadily increasing from about 50 % in 1960 to about 90 % in 1990 (Sims 1993). This increase is disturbing because research has shown that students' unethical behavior continues into their business careers (Lawson 2004; Lucas and Friedrich 2005; Nitsch et al. 2005). One could posit that, if unethical actions carry forward from college into the business world, the tendency not to blow the whistle should also carry forward from college into the business world. It is important to note the similarity between the corporate and academic setting (Nitsch et al. 2005); competition among peers for jobs after college, which may be dependent on college grades, is similar to competition among peers for promotions and pay raises in the workforce (i.e., could be seen as a zero-sum game).

Students were less likely to cheat than they were to help another student cheat (Whitley and Kost 1999). While Jendrek (1992) reported that only 1 % of students indicated they would report a student who they saw cheating, Bernardi et al. (2011, 2012b) reported that 11.3 % of students indicated they would report cheating if they observed it.[3] Still the question remains: 'why are only 11.3 % of students willing to blow the whistle when they observe another student cheating?' One obvious reason is that it would be hypocritical to blow the whistle when he/she also cheats. Another reason is that whistleblowers are often perceived as traitors (Grant 2002), sneaks and back-stabbers (Rennie and Crosby 2002). Other examples of the negative reinforcement to which students are exposed include the "misuse of … funds, insider trading, and accusations of plagiarism and other forms of dishonesty by national leaders" (Welsh 1993, p. 6).

The goal of this research was to determine whether or not students' perceptions of whistleblowers affected their decision to blow the whistle if they observed another student cheating on an examination. This study surveyed 309 business students (180 men and 129 women) enrolled in introductory accounting and business law classes on various aspects of honesty in academics. Our research indicates that the probability of blowing the whistle in the future increased with having blown the whistle in the past and an increased number of net positive perceptions of whistleblowers.

---

[2] For the purpose of this study, we define blowing the whistle as students reporting having witnessed another student cheating on an examination to the professor or an authority figure (i.e., a dean).

[3] Bernardi et al.'s (2011, 2012b) studies used accounting students as their participants; we will use their weighted average of 86.1 (11.3) percent in the remainder of this research as the proportion of students who have witnessed another student cheating (would report another student who they saw cheating on an examination).

## 12.2 Literature Review

### 12.2.1 Background on Cheating in Accounting Classes

This area is devoted to providing a framework for the frequency of cheating, factors that increase/decrease the probability of whistle-blowing and the rate of whistle-blowing in accounting classrooms. This overview uses as its literature five studies that examined cheating and whistle-blowing whose methodology incorporated students in accounting classes. Salter et al. (2001) and Bernardi and Adamaitis (2007) both studied cheating among accounting students. Salter et al. (2001) found a cheating rate of 55.7 %. Using the same questionnaire, Bernardi and Adamaitis (2007) found the rate of cheating had increased to 62.0 %. While not using the exact questionnaire as these two earlier studies, Bernardi et al. (2012a, b) did use the same questions as these earlier studies. Bernardi et al. (2012a, b) found rates of cheating for their samples to be 64.1 and 53.7 % (respectively).

Factors that influenced cheating in the Bernardi et al. studies included: the intent to cheat in the future, having observed another student cheating and/or knowing a student who regularly cheated, gender, the classroom environment, the expected punishment for getting caught cheating, the student's level of cynicism about cheating and social desirability response bias. The factors that increased the probability of cheating included: the intent to cheat in the future, having observed another student cheating and/or knowing a student who regularly cheated, gender (males were more likely to report having cheated), the classroom environment and the student's level of cynicism about cheating. The factors that decreased the probability of cheating included: gender (females were less likely to report having cheated), the expected punishment for getting caught cheating and social desirability response bias.

With respect to whistle-blowing, Bernardi et al. (2011, 2012b) both used the same questions about cheating as did the previous studies, and added questions on whistle-blowing. Bernardi et al. (2012b), which was a follow-on study to Bernardi et al. (2011), added an additional question on reasons not to whistle-blow. Bernardi et al. (2011) found that a student's intent to whistle-blow in the future was influenced by: his/her past cheating behavior (i.e., it would be hypocritical to whistle-blow on another student for doing what he/she had done), believing that more should be done about cheating, having whistle-blown in the past, gender and social desirability response bias. While a student's past cheating behavior and being a male student decreased the probability of whistle-blowing in the future, the other factors increased the probability of whistle-blowing in the future. Bernardi et al.'s (2011) model had an adjusted $R^2$ of .188.

Bernardi et al. (2012b) found that a student's intent to whistle-blow in the future was influenced by: having whistle-blown in the past, the number of reasons he/she provided about not whistle-blowing, knowing another student who regularly cheated and social desirability response bias. While the number of reasons a student provided about not whistle-blowing and knowing another student who regularly cheated decreased the probability of whistle-blowing in the future, the other factors increased the probability of whistle-blowing in the future. Consequently, by adding a question asking students to provide the reasons for not whistle-blowing, Bernardi et al. (2012b) increased the $R^2$ of the model for blowing the whistle in the future from .188 in Bernardi et al. (2012a, b) to .400 – over a two-fold increase.

### 12.2.2 Cheating in College

Premeaux (2005, p. 416) noted that "cheating [in college] appears to be fairly ingrained in the culture of learning in business." This could be the result of growing up in a society where the distinctions between right and wrong have been blurred and where unethical behavior has become more prevalent (Bruce 2003). For example, the percent of students who believe cheating is dishonest or unethical has been decreasing rapidly in the past few years. For example, while Smyth and Davis (2003) reported that 92 % of their sample reported that cheating was not ethical, Bernardi and Adamaitis (2007) reported that about 84 % of their sample thought cheating was wrong, dishonest. Recently, Bernardi et al. (2012a) reported that only 64 % of the students believed cheating was wrong, dishonest or unethical.

McCabe et al. (2001, p. 219) note that "students' perceptions of peers' behavior, are the most powerful influence" on students' cheating behavior. Students who believed that they would cheat in a similar situation were more understanding about another student's cheating (Alicke 1993). Students were also more supportive of cheaters who were their friends compared to cheaters who were strangers (Jendrek 1992); in fact, about 80 % of the students indicated that they would help a friend to cheat (Davis et al. 1992). These beliefs may arise from students' perceptions that the cheaters' accomplices will probably receive a less severe punishment than the cheater (Whitley and Kost 1999). Students were less likely to adopt questionable behavior when their role models were clergy, youth leaders (i.e., boy-scout leaders), and college advisors (Perry and Nixon 2005).[4]

Consequently, students who perceive cheating as being a socially acceptable behavior, who are more supportive and/or sympathetic towards classmates' cheating behavior, or who have cheated in the past would probably perceive a classmate who blows the whistle as breaching their unwritten societal code of conduct (i.e., cheating is acceptable way of competing). Additionally, if the increasing rate of retaliation against whistleblowers in the corporate environment (ERC 2012, p. 15) can be extrapolated to the college environment, the problems associated with being a whistleblower are exacerbated.

McCabe et al.'s (2001) finding that the most powerful influence on cheating behavior is a student's perception of his/her peers' cheating behavior suggests an implication for students' perceptions of whistleblowers. Peers' behavior has the potential to set the ethical standards for behavior in a student's society. Consequently, if a student perceives cheating as an acceptable behavior (i.e., an attribute of his/her society), he/she should perceive blowing the whistle on a fellow student who has

[4]Role model: A person whose behavior in a particular role is imitated by others (Webster's New American Dictionary 1995, p. 454).

cheated as being unacceptable behavior. Given prior research, we propose the following as our first set of hypotheses:

**H1a**: *Students who have cheated in the past will provide fewer positive perceptions of whistleblowers and be less likely to blow the whistle.*

**H1b**: *Students who have seen other students cheat and/or know students who regularly cheat will have fewer positive perceptions of whistleblowers and will be less likely to blow the whistle.*

### *12.2.3 Perceptions of Whistleblowers*

We use Falk's (1995) model for ethical behavior because it has been frequently cited in prior accounting research. Falk (1995, p. 203) suggests that virtue ethics includes four attributes: accepted virtues, moral judgment, active nurturing community and moral exemplars Some of the characteristics of ethical role models include honesty, trustworthiness, integrity, humility, holding oneself to high ethical standards, and being consistently ethical in public and private life. Other characteristics include: being self-sacrificing, accepting responsibility for and being open about his/her ethical failing(s) (Weaver et al. 2005, p. 316). These characteristics could be classified as 'accepted virtues' (i.e., Falk's first attribute). While these virtues are easily listed, it takes moral judgment to exercise these virtues (Dobson and Armstrong 1995) (i.e., Falk's second attribute). Courage is essential and individuals "have to be prepared to take whatever self-endangering risks are demanded" (MacIntyre 1984, p. 191). The foundations of ethical organizations culminate in an environment that nurtures ethical behavior (Arnold et al. 1997) (i.e., Falk's third attribute). Having an ethical climate was a significant predictor of an individual's willingness to blow the whistle (Rothschild and Meithe 1999). Personal values are a reflection of the individuals a person admires and/or considers a hero (Apostolou and Apostolou 1997) (i.e., Falk's fourth attribute).[5] Badaracco and Webb (1995, p. 25) note the importance of these final two attributes:

> Aristotle's emphasis on the role of character and the influence of community on the shaping of one's values and virtues may be a powerful starting point.

Virtues such as courage, fortitude, and perseverance only become part of our being after practice and repetition; these virtues are enhanced when one's environment nurtures them (Armstrong et al. 2003, p. 10). Students believe that blowing the whistle is also a learned social behavior that is introduced and reinforced over time (Rennie and Crosby 2002; Perry and Nixon 2005). However, just nurturing virtue is not enough; an organization must also eliminate vice (DeMarco 1996, 13–14). For example, students who have cheated typically rationalized their cheating behavior in the belief that everyone has cheated (Ameen et al. 1996; Salter et al. 2001). These authors found that students with a higher level of cynicism are more likely to cheat.

---

[5] Hero/heroine: A man/woman admired for his/her achievements and qualities (Webster's New American Dictionary 1995, p. 243).

Indeed, it is possible that cheating in college has become a socially acceptable behavior (Zerbe and Paulhus 1987). For example, research indicates a steady decrease in the proportion of students who believe cheating is unethical: 92 % (Smyth and Davis 2003), 83.9 % (Bernardi and Adamaitis 2007) and 64.1 % (Bernardi et al. 2012a). To combat this cynicism, teachers could help students identify their hero(es) because students model their behavior after the behavior of those who impress them (Collins 1985).

However, if students admire individuals of questionable behavior (i.e., cheaters, liars, insider traders or entertainment industry stars with questionable values), the goal for instructors becomes to help these students see that this type of individual is not a positive influence on society and the potential penalties for these activities. For example, the 55-year old insider trader Raj Rajaratnam was sentenced to 11 years in prison and fined a civil penalty of $92.8 million (Rothfield 2012), and the 71-year old Bernie Madoff received a sentence of 150 years (Frank and Efrati 2009) for his $65 billion Ponzi scheme.

While the pressures for better grades from parents, the need to get a job, and the desire to excel (McCabe et al. 1999) motivate students to cheat, rationalizing this behavior may enable students to mentally remove the negative stigma attached to cheating (Ameen et al. 1996; Salter et al. 2001). Similarly, if students "cannot justify cheating, they cheat anyway because dishonesty does not need to be justified if it is the norm" (Diekhoff et al. 1996, p. 500); consequently, cheating in college is becoming a socially acceptable behavior. Consequently, one should not be surprised that only 11.3 % would report another student who they saw cheating (Bernardi et al. 2011, 2012b). This may be the result of students' perceptions of whistleblowers as traitors (Grant 2002), sneaks and back-stabbers (Rennie and Crosby 2002). Bernardi et al. (2012b) reported that individuals who have blown the whistle in the past provided fewer reasons not to blow the whistle in the future.

Falk's (1995) model implies that the virtuous student is honest and trustworthy, has a well-developed value system that includes integrity, holds himself/herself to high ethical standards, and is consistently ethical in public and private life. However, as most students are more likely to accept other students' cheating behavior and are less likely to view whistleblowers in a positive manner, we propose our second set of hypotheses:

**H2a:** *Students who have blown the whistle in the past will provide more positive perceptions of whistleblowers.*

**H2b:** *A student's intention to blown the whistle in the future will increase as positive perceptions of whistleblowers increase.*

### *12.2.4 Grade Level*

As a student progresses through college from freshman-through-senior years, he/she makes new acquaintances and has new experiences. As such, he/she must continually make judgments about individuals and their behavior. In general, prior studies have found associations among grade level and various behaviors. For example, medical students' willingness to report a student who had cheated was negatively associated with the student's time in the program – his/her grade level (Rennie and Crosby 2002). First-year medical students indicated that they were more likely to report cheating to faculty; the students least likely to report cheating were those in the fourth-and-fifth years of medical school (i.e., established friendships and/or lack of time to report the cheating). Established friendships could result in accepting a classmate's excuse(s) that could justify unethical acts (Pfarrer et al. 2008; Rothwell and Baldwin 2007; Jendrek 1992; Davis et al. 1992).

Longstaff (2012) argues that there is an inherent contradiction between expected loyalty and honesty. While one may feel an obligation to one's friends and fellow employees, "loyalty cannot afford to bind any more than people can afford to remail silent in the face of wrongdoing" (Longstaff 2012, p. 7). Should loyalty result in an individual remaining silent after witnessing a wrongdoing, Finn (1995) would suggest that the individual has started to accept unethical behavior as acceptable. When this occurs, the person's sensitivity to ethical dilemmas begins to erode (Baack et al. 2000). If the erosion continues, then the individual may begin to accept even larger ethical deviations as acceptable.

Students could also base responsibility for unethical acts on their interpretations of the wrongdoer's motives (Fragale et al. 2009). For example, if a student believes that the unethical act does not reflect the classmate's character (Bolino et al. 2008), the student would likely judge the classmate's behavior more leniently. The lack of time to devote to studying, while at the same time they are searching for employment, could also be a function of grade level as those approaching graduation are experiencing some of their most difficult courses and do not have time to devote to the possibility of a protracted investigation on cheating. If this is the case, then freshmen should be more independent (i.e., more self-oriented than group oriented). As they progress through college, students become more accepting of their group and social norms, which are influenced by familiarity and friendships with their classmates – over half of whom are probably cheaters given the percentages we previously indicated. Consequently, we believe that upperclassmen will have a more negative impression of whistleblowers than underclassmen and leads to our third set of hypotheses:

**H3a:** *Positive perceptions of whistleblowers will decrease as grade level increases.*
**H3b:** *One's propensity to blow the whistle will decrease as grade level increases.*

### 12.2.5 Gender and Whistle-Blowing

Miceli and Near (1984) suggest that, because blowing the whistle is risky, men are more likely to report unethical acts. For example, the whistleblower in the 1986 space shuttle Challenger disaster believed that he "couldn't live with any self-respect if I tailored my actions based upon the personal consequences" (Boisjoly et al. 1989, p. 229). However, later studies report that women are more critical of wrong-doers.

Wise (1995) found that women had significantly higher intentions to blow the whistle. Davis et al. (1992) noted that female students judged cheaters less favorably and the whistleblowers more favorably than did male students. Rothschild and Miethe (1999) suggest that these gender differences may result from women's greater feelings of public responsibility. Similarly, women were more critical of unethical executives and judged whistleblowers more favorably than their male counterparts (Decker and Calo 2007). Kaplan et al. (2009) found that, while women had higher intentions to blow the whistle in an anonymous channel, the intention to blow the whistle was mitigated by considerations of personal costs, which also differed by gender. However, while there appears to be a gender difference between intention to blow the whistle and actually blowing the whistle, one could also suggest that feelings of public responsibility could trump personal costs. We suggest that the results lead to our final set of hypotheses:

**H4a:** *Women will provide more positive perceptions of* whistleblowers *than men.*
**H4b:** *Women are more likely to indicate that they would blow the whistle than men.*

## 12.3 Methodology

### *12.3.1 Participants*

The data for this research are from the responses of 309 business students (180 men and 129 women – Panel A of Table 12.1) enrolled in accounting classes at a private university located in the Northeastern area of the United States. Panel B indicates that the sample composition by class level was: 199 (64.4 %) sophomores, 82 (26.5 %) juniors, and 28 (9.1 %) seniors. The data in Panel C indicate that 48.9 % of male students and 42.6 % of female students indicated they had never cheated. While female students indicated that they had cheated at a 12.5 % higher rate on minor examinations, male students indicated that they had cheated at a 5.3 % higher rate in the minor-and-major examinations category.

### *12.3.2 Survey Questionnaires*

All but one of our survey questions came from published research. Our survey included a three-part questionnaire: background questionnaire (i.e., information on age, gender, major, graduation year and home country); five questions from Ameen et al. (1996), Salter et al.'s (2001), and Bernardi and Adamaitis's (2007) questionnaires on cheating (Appendix A: questions 1–5); two questions from Bernardi et al.'s (2011) research about past behavior and future intentions to blow the whistle (Appendix A: questions 6–7); and, Paulhus' (1991) Impression Management

**Table 12.1** Sample demographics

| | Men | Women | Total |
|---|---|---|---|
| Panel A: Sample demographics | | | |
| Gender | 180 | 129 | 309 |
| Age | 19.7 | 19.6 | 19.7 |
| College level | 2.5 | 2.5 | 2.5 |
| SDRB | 4.3 | 4.6 | 4.4 |
| Panel B: Sample composition by level and gender | | | |
| Sophomore | 119 | 80 | 199 |
| Junior | 45 | 37 | 82 |
| Senior | 16 | 12 | 28 |
| Panel C: Sample composition by cheating activity on examinations | | | |
| Never | 88 (48.9) | 55 (42.6) | 143 (46.3) |
| Minor only | 57 (31.7) | 57 (44.2) | 114 (36.9) |
| Major only | 3 (01.7) | 1 (00.8) | 4 (01.3) |
| Minor and major | 32 (17.7) | 16 (12.4) | 48 (15.5) |
| College level | Students in this research were Sophomores (2), Juniors (3), or Seniors (4) | | |
| SDRB | Social Desirability Response Bias Score | | |
| Panel C | XX (YY) refers to the number of students (percent of sample) | | |

Subscale (Appendix B).[6] All seven of the survey questions were yes/no questions; additionally, we added one open-ended question concerning the participant's perceptions of whistleblowers (Appendix A: question 8). Given the nature of the questions on the survey, we asked the instructors not to be present in their classrooms while their students were filling out our survey. For consistency purposes, the students who passed out the survey used scripted instructions and told the participants that the researchers would only be provided with an Excel file that contained the survey data (i.e., all students' anonymity would be preserved).

### 12.3.3 *Variables*

Our first dependent variable was the net number of positive perceptions each student reported about whistleblowers; this variable took on values from minus four (i.e., all negative perceptions) to plus four (i.e., all positive perceptions). Our second dependent variable was each student's response to our survey question number seven (Appendix A): "Would you report someone else that you witnessed cheating?"

[6] While the Ameen et al.'s (1996), Salter et al.'s (2001), and Bernardi and Adamaitis's (2007) studies examined student cheating, the Bernardi et al.'s (2011) study examined students' propensity to blow the whistle when they observed another student cheating.

This variable was coded as 1 (0) for students who would (not) report witnessing someone else cheating in the future.

We used each student's self-reported behavior from our survey for our independent variables: being personally aware of other student(s) cheating on tests (Questions 1 and 2); having cheated on a minor and/or major examination (Questions 3 and 4); intending to cheat in the future (Question 5); and, having blown the whistle in the past (Question 6). These variables were all coded as 1 for students who were personally aware of other student(s) cheating on tests; had cheated on a minor and/or major examination; intended to cheat in the future; and, having blown the whistle in the past (coded 0 whenever "no" was circled on the survey). For our indicator variable gender, we coded male students as 1 and female students as 0. We controlled for socially desirable responding using Paulhus's Impression Management Subscale that has a range of 0 (responds honestly) to 20 (responds in a totally socially desirable manner).

### 12.3.4 Social Desirability Response Bias

Social Desirability Response Bias (SDRB) can be directly controlled for by using one of several tests (i.e., for example, the Marlow-Crowe scale (Crowe and Marlow 1960) or the Balanced Inventory of Desirable Responding (BIDR) (Paulhus 1991). While each test has its supporters, they significantly increase the length of the research questionnaire, which may explain why they are not usually included in research (Randall and Gibson 1990). We used Paulhus's (1991) Impression Management Subscale (IMS: see Appendix B) to directly control for social desirability response bias for four reasons. First, the IMS portion of the BIDR is a highly correlated to other social desirability measures reported by Fernandes and Randall (1992). Second, scores on the IMS had a .88 correlation with scores on the full BIDR (Fernandes and Randall, p. 811); for the current sample, the IMS had an internal consistency of .80. Third, we used the 1991 version of the test because most accounting research that controls for socially desirable response bias uses this version (i.e., comparability among studies). Finally, we used the 1991 version rather than the later version (Paulhus 1998) because Lanyon and Carle (2007) reported that the IMS of both tests were reasonably equivalent and that the earlier version had a stronger support for general social desirability in a wider population base.

The Impression Management Subscale provides participants with 20 statements that participants respond to on a seven-point Likert scale that uses one (Not True) and seven (Very True) with every other statement reverse coded. For example, the first two questions on Paulhus's IMS are: '(1) *Sometimes I tell lies if I have to*' and '(2) *I never cover up my mistakes*'. On the first statement, responding in a socially desirable manner is on the 'Not True' side of the Likert scale – telling a lie is not a socially desirable behavior. On the second statement, responding in a socially desirable manner is on the 'Very True' side of the Likert scale – covering up mistakes is not socially desirable behavior. The Table 12.1 data show that, while female students were more likely to answer in a socially desirable manner than male students (4.3 compared to 4.6 on a scale from zero to 20), a test of the difference indicates it was not significant.

## 12.4 Analysis

### *12.4.1 Overview*

Our analysis has three sections. The first section tests our research hypotheses concerning the number and category of perceptions that students provided about whistleblowers. The second section tests our research hypotheses concerning their past whistle-blowing and their intentions to blow the whistle in the future. The final section examines the influence that the actual categories of perceptions of whistle-blowers on blowing the whistle in the future. In our analysis, we used multiple regression, stepwise regression and logistic regression. In the initial stage of the analysis, we used stepwise regression because we wanted to determine the order and the explanatory power (partial $R^2$) for each of our variables. Our reason for using logistic regression was that our dependent variables were dichotomous variables (i.e., an individual intention to blow the whistle).

### *12.4.2 Perceptions of Whistleblowers*

In this section, we analyze individuals' perceptions of whistleblowers. The final question in our survey (Appendix A: Question 8) asked students to provide up to four comments regarding their perceptions of whistleblowers. After entering the data, the authors categorized the data into groups that contained similar and/or identical responses. Each of the authors and two other individuals categorized the data about perceptions of whistleblowers into groups. Once each individual completed his/her individual categorizations, the authors then combined their data into one file and compared their categories. While the individuals referred to their categories with different names, the contents of the groups were nearly identical. Any differences in the categories were resolved among the five individuals participating in the grouping of the data. We highlighted responses in different colors in our spread-sheet; for example, students' remarks indicating that whistleblowers were 'snitches' were highlighted in red. The 'no perception given' category contains those students who either wrote in 'no comment' or left this area of the questionnaire blank; we do not believe there was a distinction between these two groups. We coded these two variations of 'no comment' as zero (i.e., neutral) and used group this as our control group in the analysis.

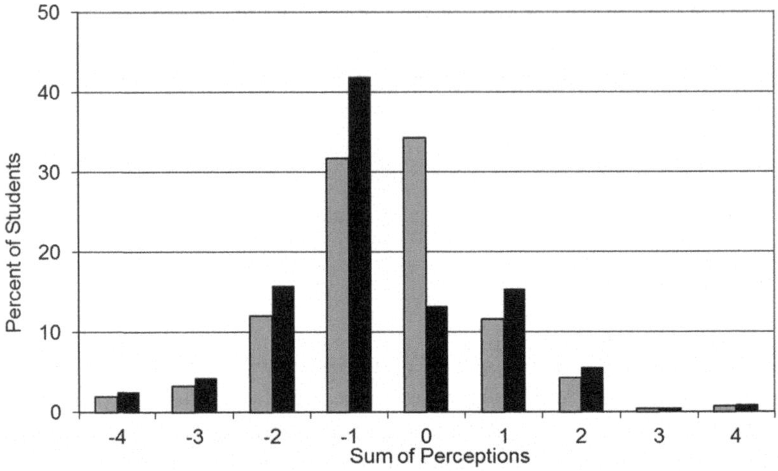


Where: Negative (positive) values indicate negative (positive) perceptions of whistle - blowers.
Grey columns – data including those students who did not provide any perceptions (n = 309).
Black columns – data excluding those students who did not provide any perceptions (n = 234).

**Fig. 12.1** Perceptions of whistleblowers as a percent of the sample

Our final collated grouping of the students' comments included six categories: (1) they are snitches; (2) they should mind their own business; (3) they are honest and/or ethical; (4) they are brave; (5) depends on situation; and, (6) the student did not provide any comments. We considered the first two categories as negative comments, the next two categories as positive comments and the last two categories as neutral comments. We used the sum of each student's positive and negative comments in our analysis. For example, if the student listed three positive comments and one negative comment, their sum would be two positive comments.

Figure 12.1 shows the proportion of sums of each student's comments. The data indicate that 48.9 % of the students had negative perceptions of whistleblowers (i.e., their net sums were negative). Students with neutral perceptions of whistleblowers made up 34.3 % of our sample; these students provided comments that were all neutral or the net sum of their comments was zero (i.e., two positive and two negative comments). Finally, only 16.8 % had net positive perceptions of whistleblowers, which is about one third (one half) the proportion of negative (neutral) comments.

Panel A of Table 12.2 provides the model for the number of positive perceptions subjects gave about whistleblowers. The three significant variables in the model were the student's having cheated on a major examination, having blown the whistle in the past and social desirability response bias. While students who had cheated on a major examination provided fewer positive comments about whistleblowers, students who had blown the whistle in the past provided more positive comments about whistleblowers. As a student's propensity to respond in a socially desirable

**Table 12.2** Perceptions of whistleblowers

**Panel A**: Model for the number of reasons

| Model | Adj R2 | F Stat | Prob F |
|---|---|---|---|
| Regression | 0.084 | 10.37 | <0.000 |
| Term | Coeff | T Stat | Prob T |
| PastW/B | 0.65 | 4.18 | <0.000 |
| Major | −0.26 | 2.72 | 0.007 |
| SDRB | 0.06 | 2.59 | 0.010 |

**Panel B**: Breakdown of the number of perceptions

| | | Self-reported cheating behavior | | | |
|---|---|---|---|---|---|
| [Sample size] or (Number of comments) | | Never cheated | Minor or major | Minor & major | Chi-sq P(Chi-sq) |
| Sample breakdown [309] | n | 143 | 118 | 48 | |
| | % | 46.3 | 38.2 | 15.5 | |
| Perceptions breakdown (485) | (n) | 216 | 193 | 76 | 0.13 |
| | % | 44.5 | 39.8 | 15.7 | NS |
| Perceptions | | | | | |
| They are snitches (147) | n | 60 | 61 | 26 | 1.23 |
| | % | 40.8 | 41.5 | 17.7 | NS |
| Mind own business (128) | n | 47 | 56 | 25 | 3.81 |
| | % | 36.7 | 43.8 | 19.5 | <0.100 |
| Honest and/or ethical (43) | n | 19 | 20 | 4 | 4.41 |
| | % | 44.2 | 46.5 | 9.3 | 0.050 |
| They are brave (69) | n | 36 | 28 | 5 | 5.32 |
| | % | 52.2 | 40.6 | 7.2 | 0.025 |
| No perceptions given (75) | n | 41 | 19 | 15 | 7.13 |
| | % | 54.7 | 25.3 | 20.0 | 0.001 |
| Depends on situation (23) | n | 13 | 9 | 1 | 10.35 |
| | % | 56.5 | 39.1 | 4.3 | <0.000 |

| | |
|---|---|
| Major | Student reported having cheated on a major examination |
| Minor | Student reported having cheated on a minor examination |
| SDRB | Social Desirability Response Bias Score |
| PastW/B | Coded as one (zero) if student reported having (not) whistle-blown in the past |

manner increased, the student was more likely to provide positive comments about whistleblowers. Our hypotheses concerning a student's grade level and gender influencing perceptions of whistleblowers were not supported by the data.

Panel B of Table 12.2 presents a breakdown of the 485 comments individuals made about whistleblowers organized by category of self-reported cheating behavior and the level of significance of the differences among categories.[7] The data suggest that,

[7] While 114 students reported cheating only on a minor examination(s), there were only four students who reported having only cheated on major examinations (Table 12.1, Panel C). Consequently, we collapsed these two categories in Panel B of Table 12.2; however, for analysis purposes, these categories were not collapsed.

on average, each student provided about 1.6 comments about whistleblowers (485 comments/309 participants). The data also indicate that the percent of comments by the self-reported cheating category approximates the proportion of the sample. For the 'Sample Breakdown' and 'Perceptions Breakdown' of the overall data, the 143 students (46.3 %) who reported not cheating provided 216 comments (44.5 %).

The most significant difference among the three cheating categories was in the 'Depends on the situation' category; as one would anticipate, only one of the 48 students who had cheated on both minor and major examinations provided this comment. Students who reported never having cheated (having cheated on a minor or major examination) provided no comments about whistleblowers at a higher (lower) than expected rate. Students who reported never having cheated (having cheated on both minor and major examinations) provided a higher (lower) than expected rate of comments about whistleblowers being "Brave". Students who reported having cheated on a minor or major examination (having cheated on both minor and major examinations) provided a higher (lower) than expected rate of comments about whistleblowers being "Honest and/or Ethical". Finally, students who reported never having cheated (having cheated on a minor or major examination or having cheated on both minor and major examinations) provided a lower (higher) than expected rate of comments about believing whistleblowers should "mind their own business".

### *12.4.3 Probability of Blowing the Whistle*

In this part of our analysis, we use the sum of each student's perceptions of whistleblowers as one of our independent variables. Our initial model (Panel A of Table 12.3) examines students' history of blowing the whistle (i.e., our dependent variable). The data indicate that our model explains 27.0 % of the variation (i.e., estimated $R^2$).[8] The net sum of the number of comments about whistleblowers a student provided and having personally cheated on a major examination were our two most significant variables. Having observed another student cheating and a student's gender were also significant. Students who provided a higher number of positive perceptions about whistleblowers, students who had personally cheated on a major examination (i.e., a counter-intuitive finding) and female students were more likely to have blown the whistle in the past. Finally, witnessing another student cheating on an examination reduced the probability that the student was more likely to have blown the whistle in the past.

Our second model (Panel B of Table 12.3) examines the probability of blowing the whistle in the future (i.e., our dependent variable) considering a student's prior

[8] Our dependent variables in Tables 12.3 and 12.4 are indicator variables about whether the student had blown the whistle in the past or would blow the whistle in the future. Because of this, we used a logistic regression model that does not provide $R^2$ or adjusted $R^2$; rather, the logistic regression model only provides 'estimated $R^2$'.

**Table 12.3** Models for whistle-blowing using the sum of the comments

| | | | | |
|---|---|---|---|---|
| **Panel A**: Model for having whistle-blown in the past | | | | |
| Model | Est R2 | ChiSquare | Prob ≥ ChiSq | |
| Regression | 0.270 | 34.01 | <0.000 | |
| Term | Coeff | ChiSquare | Prob ≥ ChiSq | Partial Est R2 |
| SumCom | 0.83 | 12.58 | <0.000 | 0.105 |
| Major | 1.26 | 14.41 | <0.000 | 0.088 |
| Observed | −0.71 | 5.19 | 0.021 | 0.039 |
| Gender | −0.66 | 4.44 | 0.035 | 0.038 |
| **Panel B**: Model for intent to whistle-blow in the future considering past whistle-blowing | | | | |
| Model | Est R2 | ChiSquare | Prob ≥ ChiSq | |
| Regression | 0.258 | 60.40 | <0.000 | |
| Term | Coeff | ChiSquare | Prob ≥ ChiSq | Partial Est R2 |
| PastW/B | 1.80 | 24.65 | <0.000 | 0.154 |
| Know | −0.52 | 4.34 | 0.037 | 0.039 |
| SumCom | 0.41 | 5.75 | 0.017 | 0.036 |
| SDRB | 0.11 | 2.95 | 0.086 | 0.016 |
| Minor | −0.38 | 2.95 | 0.086 | 0.013 |
| **Panel C**: Model for intent to whistle-blow in the future not considering past whistle-blowing | | | | |
| Model | Est R2 | ChiSquare | Prob ≥ ChiSq | |
| Regression | 0.166 | 38.78 | <0.000 | |
| Term | Coeff | ChiSquare | Prob ≥ ChiSq | Partial Est R2 |
| SumCom | 0.64 | 15.98 | <0.000 | 0.075 |
| Observed | −0.35 | 2.73 | 0.099 | 0.039 |
| Major | 0.83 | 8.10 | 0.004 | 0.011 |
| Minor | −0.53 | 4.77 | 0.029 | 0.026 |
| Know | −0.44 | 3.35 | 0.067 | 0.015 |
| Gender | Coded one (zero) for male (female) students | | | |
| Know | Coded one (zero) if the student (does not) knows a student who routinely cheats | | | |
| Major | Coded one (zero) if student had (not) cheated on a major examination | | | |
| Minor | Coded one (zero) if student had (not) cheated on a minor examination | | | |
| Observed | Coded one (zero) if the student had (not) observed another student cheating | | | |
| PastW/B | Coded as one (zero) if student had (not) whistle-blown in the past | | | |
| SDRB | Social Desirability Response Bias Score | | | |
| SumCom | Sum of the positive and negative comments | | | |

blowing-the-whistle behavior. The data indicate that our model explains 25.8 % of the variation. Having blown the whistle in the past and the net sum of the number of comments about whistleblowers a student provided were our two most significant variables. While knowing a student who regularly cheats was significant ($p = 0.037$), having cheated on a minor examination and social desirability response bias were marginally significant (both at $p = 0.086$). Students who had blown the whistle in the past and students who perceived whistleblowers more positively were more likely to indicate that they would blow the whistle in the future; however, if the sum comments variable was negative (Fig. 12.1), this variable would reduce the probability of blowing the whistle. Knowing another student who regularly cheats on examinations and having personally cheated on a minor examination reduced the probability of a student indicating he/she would blow the whistle. Students who had a higher propensity to respond in a socially desirable manner also were more likely to indicate that they would blow the whistle.

Our third model (Panel C of Table 12.3) examines the probability of blowing the whistle in the future (i.e., our dependent variable) but does not include a student's prior whistle-blowing behavior in the modeling process. The data indicate that our model explains 16.6 % of the variation. The net sum of the number of comments about whistleblowers a student provided and having personally cheated on a major examination were our two most significant variables. While having personally cheated on a major examination was also significant, observing another student cheating and/or knowing a student who regularly cheats were only marginally significant. Students who perceived whistleblowers more positively and students who had personally cheated on a major examination (i.e., a counter-intuitive finding) were more likely to indicate that they would blow the whistle in the future. Knowing another student who regularly cheats on examinations, observing another student cheating on an examination and having personally cheated on a minor examination reduced the probability of that student indicating he/she would blow the whistle in the future.

### *12.4.4 Additional Analysis*

In this part of our analysis, we substituted the six categories of perceptions (Panel B of Table 12.2) for the sum of each student's perceptions of whistleblowers as independent variables in our modeling process. We did this because our initial model disclosed that the probability of blowing the whistle decreases as the net sum of a student's positive perceptions decreases. With respect to this part of the analysis, it is important to remember that only 16.8 % of our participants provided positive perceptions of whistleblowers, while 48.9 % provided negative comments (Fig. 12.1).

Our first model (Panel A of Table 12.4) examines the probability of blowing the whistle considering a student's prior whistle-blowing behavior. The data indicate that our model explains 27.5 % of the variation. Having blown the whistle in the past and perceiving whistleblowers as honorable and/or ethical were our two most significant variables. While a student's having cheated on a minor examination and knowing a student who regularly cheats were also significant, social desirability response bias was only marginally significant. Students who had blown the whistle in the past and students who perceived whistleblowers as honorable and/or ethical were more likely to indicate that they would blow the whistle in the future. Students who had a higher propensity to respond in a socially desirable manner were also

**Table 12.4** Models for whistle-blowing using the comments categories

| | | | | |
|---|---|---|---|---|
| **Panel A**: Model for intent to whistle-blow in the future considering past whistle-blowing | | | | |
| Model | Est R2 | ChiSquare | Prob ≥ ChiSq | |
| Regression | 0.275 | 64.41 | <0.000 | |
| Term | Coeff | ChiSquare | Prob ≥ ChiSq | Partial Est R2 |
| PastW/B | 1.57 | 27.35 | <0.000 | 0.154 |
| Hon/Eth | 1.30 | 10.14 | 0.002 | 0.045 |
| Minor | −0.49 | 4.65 | 0.031 | 0.043 |
| SDRB | −0.13 | 3.81 | 0.051 | 0.020 |
| Know | −0.43 | 2.84 | 0.092 | 0.013 |
| **Panel B**: Model for intent to whistle-blow in the future not considering past whistle-blowing | | | | |
| Model | Est R2 | ChiSquare | Prob ≥ ChiSq | |
| Regression | 0.187 | 43.70 | <0.000 | |
| Term | Coeff | ChiSquare | Prob ≥ ChiSq | Partial Est R2 |
| Hon/Eth | 1.34 | 13.10 | <0.000 | 0.067 |
| Observed | −0.36 | 2.83 | 0.092 | 0.040 |
| Snitch | −0.77 | 3.65 | 0.056 | 0.022 |
| Minor | −0.65 | 6.80 | 0.009 | 0.018 |
| Major | 0.76 | 7.13 | 0.008 | 0.028 |
| SDRB | −0.11 | 2.85 | 0.091 | 0.012 |
| Hon/Eth | Student perceived whistleblowers as honorable and/or ethical | | | |
| Know | Coded one (zero) if the student (does not) knows a student who routinely cheats | | | |
| Major | Coded one (zero) if student had (not) cheated on a major examination | | | |
| Minor | Coded one (zero) if student had (not) cheated on a minor examination | | | |
| Observed | Coded one (zero) if the student had (not) observed another student cheating | | | |
| PastW/B | Coded as one (zero) if student had (not) whistle-blown in the past | | | |
| SDRB | Social Desirability Response Bias Score | | | |
| Snitch | Student perceived whistleblowers as snitches | | | |

more likely to indicate that they would blow the whistle. Knowing another student who regularly cheats on examinations and having personally cheated on a minor examination reduced the probability of a student indicating he/she would blow the whistle. Our hypotheses concerning a student's grade level and gender influencing the probability of blowing the whistle were not supported.

Our second model (Panel B of Table 12.4) examines the probability of blowing the whistle but does not include a student's prior behavior with respect to blowing the whistle in the modeling process. The data indicate that our model explains 18.7 % of the variation. Students who perceived whistleblowers as honorable and/or ethical, having personally cheated on a major examination, and personally having cheated on a minor examination were the three most significant variables. Having observed another student cheating on an examination and social desirability response bias were marginally significant. Students who perceived whistleblowers as honorable and/or ethical and students who had personally cheated on a major examination (i.e., a counter intuitive finding) were more likely to indicate that they would blow the whistle in the future. Students who had a higher propensity to respond in a socially desirable manner also were more likely to indicate that they would blow the whistle in the future. Students who had observed other students cheating on an examination and having personally cheated on a minor examination reduced the probability of a student indicating he/she would blow the whistle. Our hypotheses concerning a student's grade level and gender influencing the probability of blowing the whistle were not supported.

## 12.5 Conclusions

The major contribution of the current research is the finding that students' perceptions of whistleblowers influence their intentions to blow the whistle if they witness another student cheating. The data indicate that students who had never cheated (had cheated on both minor and major examinations) were more (less) likely to perceive whistleblowers as being 'brave' and to believe that the decision to blow the whistle 'depended on the situation' (Panel B of Table 12.2). Students who had never cheated (had cheated on either or both minor and major examinations) were less (more) likely to perceive whistleblowers as 'not minding their own business'. Students who had only cheated on minor examinations (had cheated on both minor and major examinations) were more (less) likely to perceive whistleblowers as being 'honest and/or ethical'.

The implications of our findings can be highlighted by employing Rest et al.'s (1986, pp. 3–16) Four-Component Model for morality to form a framework for students' behavior. Rest's model has four stages: recognizing an ethical dilemma exists and identifying the available alternatives; making a judgment about what action is morally necessary to resolve the dilemma; committing to one alternative; and, taking action. From the prior research, it is apparent that students do not recognize cheating as being unethical (i.e., the first step in the process is contaminated for many students). For example, while 92 % of their sample reported that cheating was not ethical (Smyth and Davis 2003), Bernardi and Adamaitis (2007) (Bernardi et al. 2012b) reported that about 84 (64) percent of their sample thought cheating was unethical, wrong, or dishonest. One could suggest that, as cheating is perceived as being ethical by 36 % students, cheating and studying for the exam are both available ethical alternatives for these students. This suggests that approximately 18 % (54–36 %) of the students in Bernardi et al.'s (2012b) study perceived cheating as unethical, wrong, or dishonest and then made the decision to cheat (i.e., one third (18/54) acted contrary to their ethical evaluation).

More disturbingly are the data indicating that, while 46 % (100–54 %) of students indicated they had never cheated and 86.1 % of students had observed another student cheating (Bernardi et al. 2011, 2012b), only 11.3 % of students would blow the whistle if they saw another student cheating. If this behavior (i.e., remaining silent in the face of unethical behavior) continues into their business careers as does dishonesty (Lawson 2004; Lucas and Friedrich 2005; Nitsch et al. 2005), then the increases reported by the ERC (2012) may only be temporary as a new generation of students that views cheating as acceptable behavior and whistle-blowing as "snitching" enters the workforce.

Using the sum of students' perceptions of whistleblowers, our first set of models (Table 12.3) found that the net sum of the positive and negative perceptions (Fig. 12.1 and Table 12.2) influenced both their past behavior with respect to blowing the whistle and their intentions to blowing the whistle in the future. As the sum of the comments decreased, the probability of blowing the whistle decreased. The data from Fig. 12.1 (n = 234) indicate that approximately two-thirds of our sample had negative perceptions of whistle-blowers. This should not be surprising as there has been a decrease in students' belief that cheating is wrong or unethical from 92 % (Smyth and Davis 2003) to 64 % (Bernardi et al. 2012a). This decrease and the data from Fig. 12.1 indicate that, as dishonesty has become the norm (Diekhoff et al. 1996, p. 500), students who blow the whistle are violating the norm.

Using the actual categories of students' perceptions of whistleblowers, our second set of models (Table 12.4) found that positive (negative) perceptions of whistle-blowers being either 'honorable and/or ethical' ('snitches') is also significant to this area of research. Our research using students supports Weaver et al.'s (2005, p. 316) finding that values such as honesty, trustworthiness and integrity are important in the decision making process. However, our research also found students' perceptions of whistleblowers being 'snitches' reduced the probability of students' intention to blow the whistle in the future. Consequently, our research also supports prior research that found whistleblowers are often perceived as 'traitors' (Grant 2002) and/or 'back-stabbers' (Rennie and Crosby 2002).

Our most disturbing finding is that there were no significant differences among our three groups of students (i.e., not cheated, cheated on minor or major examination and having cheated on both) with respect to perceptions about whistleblowers being 'snitches' (Table 12.2 Panel B; Chi-squared statistic = 1.23, not significant). However, a careful examination of this section of Table 12.2 Panel B shows that students who had never cheated had a lower rate, while students who had only cheated on a minor or major examination had a correspondingly higher rate. While students are exposed to the consequences of dishonesty in the corporate world by our news media, the same media does not highlight the positive effects of whistle blowing. This seems to suggest the need to highlight the need to blow the whistle and the positive results of blowing the whistle to our students.

The final models in both Tables 12.3 and 12.4 of our analysis had counter-intuitive findings; students who had cheated on major examinations reported a higher intention to blow the whistle in the future. While the overall rate of intention to blow the whistle in the future was 12.6 %, the rates for each group of students varied: 18.2 % for students who had not cheated; 5.1 % for students who had cheated on either a minor or major examination; and, 14.6 % for students who had cheated on both a minor and major examinations. One explanation of this counter-intuitive finding is that students who had cheated on major examinations do not intend to allow other students to level the playing field by also cheating (McCabe et al. 2001).

Prior research indicates that women are more critical of ethical deviations (Davis et al. 1992; Decker and Calo 2007), have a higher sense of public responsibility (Rothschild and Miethe 1999), and have higher intentions to blow the whistle (Wise 1995). Our data indicate that, while females had a higher rate of blowing the whistle in the past (Panel A of Table 12.3), gender was not a significant variable in any of the other models in Tables 12.3 and 12.4. Miceli and Near (1984) suggested that because blowing the whistle is risky men may be more willing to blowing the whistle; Kaplan et al.'s (2009) found that women's intentions to blow the whistle were negatively influenced by considerations of personal costs. Our data (Table 12.3 Panel A) may support Kaplan et al.'s finding; it could be that having experienced the personal costs of blowing the whistle in the past, female students may think twice about blowing the whistle in the future. While this premise cannot be proven by the current data, it offers an opportunity for future research.

Finally, Badaracco and Webb (1995) use Aristotle's emphasis on the importance of character and the influence of community on the shaping of one's values and virtues. Virtues such as courage, fortitude, and perseverance are enhanced when one's environment nurtures them (Armstrong et al. 2003, p. 10) by reinforcing these virtues over time (Rennie and Crosby 2002; Perry and Nixon 2005). However, Demarco (1996) maintains that nurturing virtue is not enough; an organization must also eliminate vice (i.e., enable continuous ethical improvement (Arnold et al. 1997)). As college advisors and teachers, we have a responsibility to be ethical and nurture ethical behavior because students are less likely to adopt questionable behavior when their role models were their college advisors (Perry and Nixon 2005). Finally, while we can help students identify their hero(es) to model their behavior (Collins 1985), we must also work at reducing the environment that accepts cheating as our academic society's norm.

Our research has two apparent limitations both of which speak to the overall generalizability of our results. First, our sample was only 309 students and was a convenience sample. Second, our sample came from the Northeastern area of the United States. These limitations provide potential opportunities for future research. One could extend our analysis to include other geographic areas both within the United States and internationally. Should one decide to use an international sample, countries should be selected with consideration given to Hofstede's (2001) cultural constructs as well as Transparency International's Corruption Perceptions Index (2011).

**Acknowledgment** The authors wish to thank Marc Julien and Jeffrey Mullany for their assistance in an earlier version of this research.

# Appendices

## *Appendix A: Questionnaire*

**Gender (please circle): Male female**
**Age:** ___________
**Home country:** ______________________
**Year in college:** ______________________
**Major:** ______________________________
**Circle yes or no for the following:**

1. Have you ever observed another student cheating on an exam?
   Yes No
2. Do you know anyone who routinely cheats on exams?
   Yes No
3. Have you ever cheated on a major exam (20 % or more of the final grade) in college?
   Yes No
4. Have you ever cheated on a minor exam (less than 20 % of the final grade) in college?
   Yes No
5. Do you think you will cheat in the future?
   Yes No
6. Have you ever witnessed someone else cheating and reported it?
   Yes No
7. Would you report someone else who you witnessed cheating?
   Yes No
8. If you indicated that you would NOT report someone else who you witnessed cheating, please list the possible reasons you would not report this violation
   1.
   2.
   3.
   4.

## *Appendix B: Paulhus's Impression Management Subscale*

**Using the scale below as a guide, write a number beside each statement to indicate how much you agree with it**

| **1** | **2** | **3** | **4** | **5** | **6** | **7** |
|---|---|---|---|---|---|---|
| **Not True** | | | **Somewhat True** | | | **Very True** |

1. Sometimes I tell lies if I have to
2. I never cover up my mistakes
3. There have been occasions when I have taken advantage of someone
4. I never swear
5. I sometimes try to get even rather than forgive and forget
6. I always obey laws, even if I am unlikely to get caught

(continued)

(continued)

| | |
|---|---|
| 7. | I have said something bad about a friend behind his/her back |
| 8. | When I hear people talking privately, I avoid listening |
| 9. | I have received too much change from a salesperson without telling him or her |
| 10. | I always declare everything at customs |
| 11. | When I was young, I sometimes stole things |
| 12. | I have never dropped litter on the street |
| 13. | I sometimes drive faster than the speed limit |
| 14. | I never read sexy books or magazines |
| 15. | I have done things that I don't tell other people about |
| 16. | I never take things that don't belong to me |
| 17. | I have taken sick leave from work or school even though I wasn't really sick |
| 18. | I have never damaged a library book or store merchandise without reporting it |
| 19. | I have some pretty awful habits |
| 20. | I don't gossip about other people's business |

## References


Alicke, M.D. 1993. Egocentric standards of conduct evaluation. *Basic and Applied Social Psychology* 14(2): 171–192.

Ameen, E., D.M. Guffey, and J.J. McMillan. 1996. Accounting students perceptions of questionable academic practices and factors affecting their propensity to cheat. *Accounting Education* 5(3): 191–205.

Apostolou, B., and N. Apostolou. 1997. Heroes as a context for teaching ethics. *The Journal of Education for Business* 73(2): 121–125.

Armstrong, M.B., J.E. Ketz, and D. Owsen. 2003. Ethics education in accounting: Moving toward ethical motivation and ethical behavior. *Journal of Accounting Education* 21(1): 1–16.

Arnold, V., J.C. Lampe, and S.G. Sutton. 1997. Understanding the factors underlying ethical organizations: Enabling continuous improvement. *Journal of Applied Business Research* 15(3): 1–18.

Ayers, S., and S.E. Kaplan. 2005. Wrongdoing by consultants: An examination of employees' reporting intentions. *Journal of Business Ethics* 57(2): 121–137.

Baack, D., C. Fogliasso, and J. Harris. 2000. The personal impact of ethical decisions: A social penetration theory. *Journal of Business Ethics* 24(1): 39–49.

Badaracco Jr., J.L., and A.P. Webb. 1995. Business ethics: A view from the trenches. *California Management Review* 37(2): 8–28.

Bernardi, R.A., and K.L. Adamaitis. 2007. Data contamination by social desirability response bias: An international study of students' cheating behavior. *Research on Professional Responsibility and Ethics in Accounting* 11: 157–184.

Bernardi, R.A., C.A. Banzhoff, A.M. Martino, and K.J. Savasta. 2011. Cheating and whistle blowing in the classroom. *Research on Professional Responsibility and Ethics in Accounting* 15: 165–191.

Bernardi, R.A., C.A. Banzhoff, A.M. Martino, and K.J. Savasta. 2012a. Challenges to academic integrity: Identifying the factors associated with the cheating chain. *Accounting Education: An International Journal* 21(3): 247–263.

Bernardi, R.A., M.B. Larkin, L.A. LaBontee, R.A. Lapierre, and N.C. Morse. 2012b. Classroom cheating: Reasons not to whistle-blow and the probability of whistle-blowing. *Research on Professional Responsibility and Ethics in Accounting* 16: 203–233.

Boisjoly, R.P., E.F. Curtis, and E. Mellican. 1989. Roger Boisjoly and the challenger disaster: The ethical dimensions. *Journal of Business Ethics* 8(4): 217–230.

Bolino, M.C., M.K. Kacmar, W.H. Turnley, and J.B. Gilstrap. 2008. A multi-level review of impression management motives and behaviors. *Journal of Management* 34(6): 1080–1109.

Bruce, T. 2003. *The death of right and wrong: Exposing the left's assault on our culture and values.* New York: Three Rivers Press.

CBSNEWS. 2011. Wigand: 60 minutes' most famous whistleblower. http://www.cbsnews.com/8301-504803_162-20094836-10391709.html. August 21.

Central Intelligence Agency. 2012. Gross domestic product – Official exchange rate. https://www.cia.gov/library/publications/the-world-factbook/fields/2195.html

Collins, S.M. 1985. Today's kids and hero worship: Who can they look up to? *English Journal* 74(5): 21.

Crowne, D.P., and D. Marlowe. 1960. A new scale of social desirability independent of psychology. *Journal of Consulting Psychology* 24(4): 349–354.

Davis, S.F., C.A. Grover, A.H. Becker, and L.N. McGregor. 1992. Academic dishonesty: Prevalence, determinants, techniques, and punishments. *Teaching of Psychology* 19(1): 16–20.

Decker, W.H., and T.J. Calo. 2007. *The heart of virtue: Lessons from life and literature illustrating the beauty and value of moral character.* San Francisco: Ignatius Press.

DeMarco, D. 1996. Observers' impressions of unethical persons and whistleblowers. *Journal of Business Ethics* 76(3): 309–318.

Diekhoff, G.M., E.E. LaBeff, R.E. Clark, L.E. Williams, B. Francis, and V.J. Haines. 1996. College cheating: Ten years later. *Research in Higher Education* 37(4): 487–502.

Dobson, J., and M.B. Armstrong. 1995. Application of virtue ethics theory. *Research on Accounting Ethics* 1: 187–202.

Ethics Resource Center. 2012. 2011 national business ethics survey: Workplace ethics in transition. http://www.ethics.org/nbes/files/FinalNBES-web.pdf

Falk, H. 1995. Professional services and ethical behavior. *Research on Accounting Ethics* 1: 203–212.

Fernandes, M.F., and D.M. Randall. 1992. The nature of social desirability bias in ethics research. *Business Ethics Quarterly* 2(2): 183–205.

Finn, D.W. 1995. Ethical decision making in organizations: A management employee-organization whistle-blowing model. *Research on Accounting Ethics* 1: 291–313.

Fragale, A.R., B. Rosen, C. Xu, and I. Merideth. 2009. The higher they are, the harder they fall: The effects of wrongdoer status on observer punishment recommendations and intentionality attributions. *Organizational Behavior and Human Decision Process* 108(1): 53–65.

Frank, R., and A. Efrati. 2009. Evil Madoff gets 150 years in epic fraud. *The Wall Street Journal.* http://online.wsj.com/article/SB124604151653862301.html. June 30.

Grant, C. 2002. Whistle-blowers: Saints of secular culture. *Journal of Business Ethics* 39(4): 391–399.

Grimes, P.W. 2004. Dishonesty in academics and business: A cross-cultural evaluation of student attitudes. *Journal of Business Ethics* 49(3): 273–290.

Hofstede, G. 2001. *Culture's consequences*, 2nd ed. Beverly Hills: Sage Publications.

Jendrek, M.P. 1992. Students' reactions to academic dishonesty. *Journal of College Student Development* 33(3): 260–273.

Kaplan, S., K. Pany, J. Samuels, and J. Zhang. 2009. An examination of the association between gender and reporting intentions for fraudulent financial reporting. *Journal of Business Ethics* 87(1): 15–30.

Lanyon, R.I., and A.C. Carle. 2007. Internal and external validity of scores on the balanced inventory of desirable responding and the Paulhus deception scales. *Education and Psychological Measurement* 67(5): 859–876.

Lawson, R.A. 2004. Is classroom cheating related to business students' propensity to cheat in the 'Real World'? *Journal of Business Ethics* 49(2): 189–199.

Longstaff, S. 2012. Public interest whistleblowing. In *Think piece*, 2–9. Sydney: St. James Ethics Centre.

Lucas, G.M., and J. Friedrich. 2005. Individual differences in workplace deviance and integrity as predictors of academic dishonesty. *Ethics & Behavior* 15(1): 15–35.
MacIntyre, A. 1984. *After virtue*. Notre Dame: University of Notre Dame Press.
McCabe, D.L., L.K. Trevino, and K.D. Butterfield. 1999. Academic integrity in honor-code and non honor-code environments: A qualitative investigation. *Journal of Higher Education* 70(2): 211–234.
McCabe, D.L., L.K. Trevino, and K.D. Butterfield. 2001. Dishonesty in academic environments: The influence of peer reporting requirements. *Journal of Higher Education* 72(1): 29–45.
Miceli, M.P., and J.P. Near. 1984. The relationships among beliefs, organizational position, and whistle-blowing status: A discriminant analysis. *Academy of Management Journal* 27: 687–705.
Mintz, S. 2012a. Public interest whistleblowing. In *Think piece*, 2–9. Sydney: St. James Ethics Centre.
Mintz, S. 2012b. Retaliation against whistleblowers in the workplace on the rise. In *Think piece*, 1. Sydney: St. James Ethics Centre.
Nitsch, D., M. Baetz, and J.C. Hughes. 2005. Why code of conduct violations go unreported: A conceptual framework to guide intervention and future research. *Journal of Business Ethics* 57(4): 327–341.
Paulhus, D.L. 1991. Balanced Inventory of Desirable Responding (BIDR). In *Measures of personality and psychological attitudes*, vol. 1, ed. J.P. Robinson, P.R. Shaver, and L.S. Wrightsman, 37–41. New York: Academic.
Paulhus, D.L. 1998. *Paulhus Deception Scales (PDS): The balanced inventory of desirable responding – 7*. North Tonawanda: Multi Health Systems.
Perry, G.M., and C.J. Nixon. 2005. The influence of role models on negotiation ethics of college students. *Journal of Business Ethics* 62(1): 25–40.
Pfarrer, M.D., K.A. Decelles, K.G. Smith, and M.S. Taylor. 2008. After the fall: Reintegrating the corrupt organization. *The Academy of Management Review* 33(3): 730–749.
Premeaux, S.R. 2005. Undergraduate student perceptions regarding cheating: Tier 1 versus tier 2 AACSB accredited business schools. *Journal of Business Ethics* 62(4): 407–418.
Randall, D.M., and A.M. Gibson. 1990. Methodology in business ethics research: A review and critical assessment. *Journal of Business Ethics* 9(6): 457–472.
Rennie, S.C., and J.R. Crosby. 2002. Students' perceptions of whistle blowing: Implications for self-regulation. A questionnaire and focus group survey. *Medical Education* 36(2): 173–179.
Rest, J., M. Bebeau, and J. Volker. 1986. Chapter 1: An overview of the psychology of morality. In *Moral development: Advances in research and theory*. New York: Praeger.
Rothfield, M. 2012. In Gupta sentencing, a judgment call. *The Wall Street Journal*. http://online.wsj.com/article/SB10000872396390443294904578046893155693624.html
Rothschild, J., and T.D. Miethe. 1999. Whistle-blower disclosures and management retaliation: The battle to control information about organizational corruption. *Work and Occupations* 26(1): 107–128.
Rothwell, G.R., and J.N. Baldwin. 2007. Ethical climate theory, whistle-blowing, and the code of silence in police agencies in the state of Georgia. *Journal of Business Ethics* 70(4): 341–361.
Salter, S.B., D.M. Guffey, and J.J. McMillan. 2001. Truth, consequences and culture: A comparative examination of cheating and attitudes about cheating among U.S. And U.K. students. *Journal of Business Ethics* 31(1): 37–50.
Sims, R. 1993. The relationship between academic dishonesty and unethical business practices. *The Journal of Education for Business* 68(4): 207–211.
Smyth, M.L., and J.R. Davis. 2003. An examination of student cheating in the two-year college. *Community College Review* 31(1): 17–33.
Transparency International. 2011. 2011 corruption perceptions index. http://cpi.transparency.org/cpi2011/results/
Trevino, L.K., and B. Victor. 1992. Peer reporting of unethical behavior: A social context perspective. *Academy of Management Journal* 35(1): 38–64.

Weaver, G.R., L.K. Trevino, and B. Agle. 2005. Ethical role models in organizations. *Organizational Dynamics* 34(4): 313–330.
Webster's New American Dictionary. 1995. New York: Smithmark Publishers.
Welsh, J.F. 1993. Student academic dishonesty in higher education: Social context and institutional response. Unpublished Report, Kansas Board of Regents, Topeka.
Whitley, B.E., and C.R. Kost. 1999. College students' perceptions of peers who cheat. *Journal of Applied Social Psychology* 29(8): 1732–1760.
Wise, T.D. 1995. An analysis of factors proposed to affect the decision to blow the whistle on unethical acts. Unpublished doctoral dissertation, Louisiana Tech University.
Zerbe, W.J., and D.L. Paulhus. 1987. Socially desirable responding in organizational behavior: A reconception. *Academy of Management Journal* 12(2): 250–264.

# Index



S. Mintz (ed.), *Accounting for the Public Interest: Perspectives on Accountability, Professionalism and Role in Society*, Advances in Business Ethics Research 4,
DOI 10.1007/978-94-007-7082-9, © Springer Science+Business Media Dordrecht 2014

The manufacturer's authorised representative in the EU is Springer Nature Customer Service Centre GmbH, Europaplatz 3, 69115 Heidelberg, Germany. If you have any concerns regarding our products, please contact ProductSafety@springernature.com

Printed and bound by CPI Group (UK) Ltd, Croydon, CR0 4YY
25/09/2026
02222898-0010